this book is dedicated to
FRANK WILLS
Who, as an ordinary citizen of the United States,
possessing neither high office nor great wealth,
made a single call that will echo through the republic
as long as it stands.

International Standard Book Number: 0-8256-3902-6
Library of Congress Catalog Card Number: 73-84001
Distributed by:
Quick Fox, Inc., 33 West 60th Street, New York 10023
Quick Fox Ltd., 40 Nugget Avenue, Agincourt, Ontario, Canada
Quick Fox/ATP, Ltd., Box 10-292, 194 Sydney Street West, Wellington
Flash Books, 78 Newman Street, London W1E 4JZ

ACKNOWLEDGMENTS

*Thanks to Candy Roncone, Eric Turkington, Sherry Graham, Martin Smith, Diane
Perkins, Lee Buschel, Jeff Feinberg, Jack Weiner, Mimi Barton, Paul Labess, Fran Katz,
Eric Levine, Al Abramson, Carol Snapperman, Andy Fischer, Fred Linge, Tina Stronach,
Louis Leaff, Leah Elijah, Joan Horvath, Margarite D'Oxylion, Ann Kirby, Linda DiAgos-
tino, Janet Gladen, Maria Van Dessel, Gary Moses, Jimmy Whitaker, Jimmy Coulter
Timothy Claxton, Ielyne, and Brian Zahn.*

*Thanks also to Bernard Ford of the University of Pennsylvania Library, and to Peter
Eglick, Norman Kaner, Lonnie Moseley, Mae Brussel, Paul Krassner and Carl Oglesby.*

*And a special thanks to Rod Nordland, the long distance editor, who must have broken
every existing endurance record while editing for the most consecutive hours, days, and
nights with neither sleep nor sugar in his coffee.*

PRINTED IN THE UNITED STATES OF AMERICA

THE WATERGATE FILE

Buschel · Robbins · Vitka

edited by Rod Nordland

NEW YORK

Flash Books

LONDON

The Watergate File/Contents

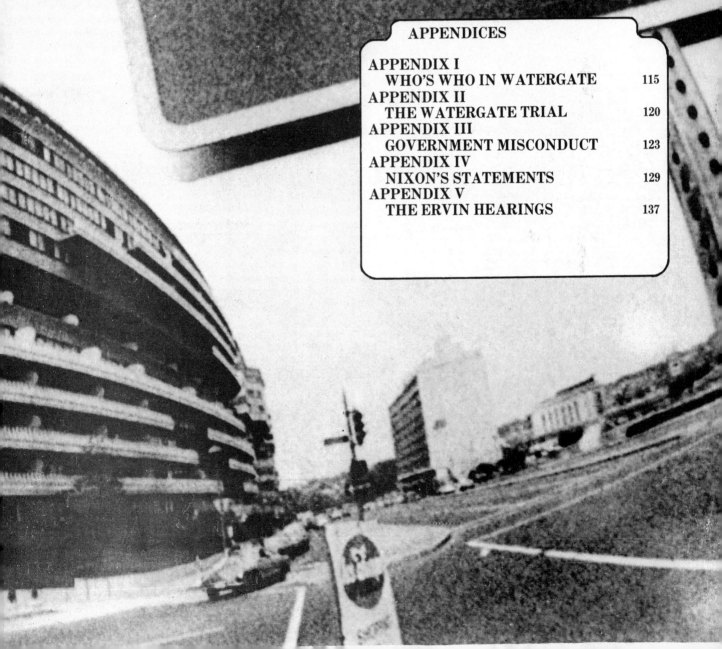

Introduction

The Watergate break-in of June 17, 1972 spawned a crisis in government and public faith that has been headline news for over a year. Yet, for the vast majority of the American people, Watergate is a complex and often incomprehensible issue. To some the matter is limited to possible presidential involvement in a crime. To others Watergate represents something far more serious: an incident which signalled the wholesale deterioration of American politics and government. To others still, who find it difficult to agree with Senator Sam Ervin when he calls Watergate the greatest tragedy in American history, it is merely a series of pecadillos committed by minor bureaucrats to be dealt with quickly and quietly in the courts and then forgotten.

The difficulties in understanding Watergate are very real. Faces and testimony become blurred beneath the hot television lights in the Senate Caucus Room. Anyone interested in getting at the roots of the crisis is forced to grapple with complex bureaucratic chains of command, a plethora of dates, numerous tangential issues and incidents, and a web of contradictory testimony. What began as a hapless burglary has mushroomed into a scandal of titanic dimensions. That single act has uncovered a network of circumstance which has, in turn, raised serious questions about the balance of power and, indeed, the entire structure of American government as it was originally conceived and as it has evolved.

There is a compelling need on the part of the public to know the truth about Watergate. We are told that this is the greatest crisis of presidential leadership since the Civil War. We learn that a Senate committee and a government prosecutor have taken the nearly unprecedented and certainly dire step of subpoenaing the President of the United States. We watch amazed and horrified as political careers and private lives are exposed and destroyed. Our minds are boggled by tales of wiretapping, master spies, secret memorandums, paper shredding parties, and government sanctioned burglary. Our wildest fantasies are exceeded by reports of inter-agency sabotage, high-level influence peddling, and international money chains. We are shown a landscape peopled by presidents, senators, congressmen, wealthy executives, foreign dictators, former CIA operatives, and ex-New York Cops. We wonder what really happened. We wonder how they expected to get away with it. We wonder how deep the current of corruption runs. But perhaps most of all, we wonder how we as the public could have been so innocently unaware of what was going on.

Perhaps the greatest irony of the whole affair lies in the disclaimer offered by many former Nixon officials before the Ervin Committee. Men such as John Mitchell and Jeb Stuart Magruder pointed to the demonstrations and random acts of violence and lawlessness that swept America in the sixties as justification for their own lawless actions. Yet these men, entrusted with protecting the American system, may have accomplished more in terms of bringing about political reform than decades of demonstrations could possibly have achieved. We stand today on the brink of great change in our system of government. But if this country is to emerge on the other side with a vital and viable future, the time is now for the people to involve themselves, at least insofar as a thorough knowledge of the facts of the Watergate affair will allow.

It is for this reason, aside from simple curiosity, that the facts revealed thus far must be laid out in coherent form. That is the purpose of this book.

To bring the facts into focus, we have organized the material to read as a passage through a revolving door. Alternating chapters in the book deal with the chronological development of the Watergate affair in the minds and the media of the nation, beginning with the break-in of the Democratic National Headquarters and ending with the Ervin hearings. Each chapter of chronology is complemented by a chapter which provides background to the major issues raised in the narrative. In addition, appendixes have been provided which include a schematic chronology of events, a Watergate Who's Who for easy identification of the players in the drama, and transcripts from the trials of the Watergate burglars, testimony before the Senate Select Committee, and all of President Nixon's statements on Watergate to date.

In this way we have attempted to outline the vast empire of information which has been produced and to explain how Watergate evolved and what encouraged its growth. Watergate was not an isolated event but a culmination of several different forces which exploded suddenly like a stick of dynamite. Above all, it is a story about power and what men will do to get and keep power.

Al Robbins
Bill Vitka
September 1973

Chapter I

Break-In: "Third Rate Burglary"

Frank Wills, an asthmatic $80-a-week employee of General Security Services, Inc., was on the first round of night patrol in the prestigious Watergate Hotel and office complex in Washington, D.C. It was a Friday and Wills worked the lonely midnight-to-dawn shift. His only weapon was a can of mace.

On other nights lately the security guard had found the Watergate bustling with activity. The headquarters of the Democratic National Committee occupied the entire sixth floor of the building, and party workers often labored into the morning hours in anticipation of the Democratic Convention less than one month away. But on that night, the Watergate was unusually quiet.

Wills made his way to the ground floor level. There he noticed masking tape covering the latches and disengaging the locks of two doors connecting the office complex with the underground garage. Obviously, someone moving furniture or equipment earlier in the day had taped the latches and forgotten to remove the tape when they left. The guard removed the tape, shut the door, and went across the street for a bite to eat. Nothing was amiss at the Watergate.

When Wills returned to the job half an hour later, he quickly found that assumption wrong. Tape once again covered the latches of the two doors. Wills rushed to the telephone in the lobby of Watergate and notified the offi-

cer on duty at Washington's Second Precinct Police Headquarters that he suspected someone had made an illegal entry into the Watergate.

The alarm was logged at 1:52 A.M. on the morning of Saturday, June 17, 1972. Soon the entire world would know of Frank Wills' discovery.

Upstairs, on the sixth floor, five men were setting about to do their night's work. One of them, who would later identify himself to police as Frank Carter, was in walkie-talkie communication with someone stationed at the Howard Johnson's Motel across the street. The others were equipped with 35mm cameras, forty rolls of unexposed film, and equipment less identifiable to the layman, equipment designed to be anonymous, almost invisible: electronic surveillance devices.

The five men were well dressed, either in suits or sports jackets, and all wore neckties. One other mode of dress distinguished them. They all wore blue surgical gloves to guard against fingerprints. They were meticulous men, well trained to accomplish the mission they had undertaken. As they went about their job, the offices of the Democratic National Committee began to resemble the assembly area of an electronics factory.

Earlier, the men had picked the lock on the basement door of the Watergate and taped the latch so that it would not lock behind them. They had then made their way up the rear stairwell of the building to the sixth floor and jimmied the door to the Democratic National Committee headquarters. It was a simple operation for these men who were no strangers to the Watergate.

At least three of the men had participated in a similar operation on the night of May 26, according to testimony given later. They had entered the Watergate complex clandestinely, stolen into the sixth floor, and installed a wiretapping device in the phone of Spencer Oliver, a Democratic National Committee worker. The earlier raid had been led by a man who would be apprehended that night, a man who would later tell police his name was Edward Martin.

All of the men except Martin had flown to Washington from Miami earlier that day, aboard Eastern Airlines flight 190. They had registered at the Watergate Hotel under fictitious names in rooms 214 and 314. Later, it had been a simple task to leave the hotel, enter the underground garage that connected the hotel with the office complex, and make their entry.

When Police Sergeant Paul Leper first heard the report of a possible illegal entry at the Watergate, he did not think much of it. The call had been made for a regular patrol car with police markings and uniformed officers.

Then a second dispatch had come over police radio asking if there were a tactical squad available to investigate the Watergate report. The regular patrol car was low on gas.

Leper and his two companions that night, officers John Barret and Carl Shollfer, were part of the tactical squad of the Washington Metropolitan Police. Their uniforms were long hair, beards, golf caps, and anything else that would make them seem inconspicuous. They traveled in an unmarked car and patrolled the streets of the Second Precinct from 4 P.M. to midnight. It was almost 2 A.M. but overtime was overtime, and crime knew no hours. Leper called in saying that his unit was at 30th and K Streets, N.W. They would be at the Watergate in two minutes.

Washington Police cruiser 727 arrived and parked about fifty feet from the main entrance. The three men were met in the lobby by Frank Wills, who told them what he had discovered, and they began a systematic search of the building. Another man, stationed across the street on one of the balconies of Howard Johnson's, also saw their arrival. He had a walkie-talkie, and it was his job to warn the five men then inside the offices of the Democratic National Committee if police showed up. But three men in casual dress did not seem suspicious.

The officers proceeded up the stairwell with flashlights and pistols drawn. On the eighth floor, they discovered that the door to the offices of the Federal Reserve Board had also been taped. However, the guard on duty inside the eighth floor offices assured the officers that nothing suspicious had occurred there that evening. The police fanned out. Barret went up to check the ninth floor while Leper and Shollfer descended to the seventh. Again, nothing was amiss.

On the sixth floor, though, Barret and Shollfer noticed that the office doors of the Democratic National Committee had been taped and that some lights were on inside. Sgt. Leper called upstairs for Barret to come down, and he and Shollfer entered the office.

They proceeded slowly, turning on lights as they entered darkened rooms. At one point, two of them went out on the balcony of the sixth floor, searching almost frantically for whomever had entered the offices. On the balcony, officer Shollfer noticed the man standing on one of the balconies of the Howard Johnson's across the street. He pointed the man out to Leper and asked jestingly, "You don't think he'll call the police, do you?"

The thought never even crossed the mind of the man on the balcony. He picked up his walkie-talkie and asked

one of his five cohorts in Democratic National Committee Headquarters if their men were wearing suits or if they were casually dressed.

"What?" came the nervous reply.

He repeated the question from across the street.

"Our people are dressed in suits," a voice said.

"Well, we've got problems," the man said, according to an account later published in the Los Angeles *Times*. "We've got some people dressed casually and they've got guns. They're looking around the balcony and everywhere, but they haven't come across our people."

As the man spoke over his walkie-talkie, officer John Barret was pausing at a glass partition inside the sixth floor offices. He had seen a raised arm dart down beneath a desk top. He proceeded with utmost caution.

Leper and Shollfer joined him at the glass partition. Together, they ordered the man from behind the desk. But instead of one man, the police officers suddenly discovered five of the most impeccably dressed burglars they had ever encountered.

Leper ordered the men up against the nearby wall. "Raise your arms and spread your feet," he commanded. Officer Barret systematically searched each man. He informed tham that they were under arrest for suspicion of burglary. It was 2:30 A.M.

The five men were captured in the office of Stanley Greigg, Deputy Chairman of the Democratic National Committee. Two file drawers stood open near where they had been apprehended, and the cameras they had with them were positioned to photograph documents. Police also reported that two ceiling panels in the office of Dorothy V. Bush, Secretary of the Democratic National Committee, had been removed.

The five men would not say what they were doing in the offices. Nevertheless, they were very polite and very cooperative, and Sgt. Leper was later to testify that they "were five of the easiest lock-ups I ever had."

Leper knew that he had more than an ordinary burglary on his hands. While he called the Washington Police mobile crime unit for an investigation of the scene of the crime, three of the men were taken to the Second Precinct in a paddywagon. Police transported the other two separately. At headquarters, the men gave their names as Edward Hamilton, Frank Carter, Edward Martin, Jean Valdez, and Raul Godoyn. All of the names were false. Police confiscated the men's belongings, including $2300 in consecutively numbered $100 bills.

The waiting began. The five suspects were repeatedly asked if they wished to use the phone to call an attorney. They declined each request. But, later that morning, an attorney for the five mysteriously appeared. He simply stated that he represented the five men who had been locked up and gave his name as Douglas Caddy.

Caddy was a corporate lawyer who one year earlier had met the man who called himself Frank Carter. A member of the Washington law firm of Gall, Lane, Powell and Kilcullen, Caddy had been the first executive director of Young Americans for Freedom, an ultra-conservative, libertarian youth group which arose on college campuses in the early sixties. He had also been one of the leaders of Youth for Goldwater in 1964. According to Caddy, Carter's wife had called him at 3:00 that morning. She had been instructed to call the lawyer if she had not heard from her husband by then, he said. The cover-up had begun.

At nine o'clock in the morning, another lawyer arrived at the Second Precinct. His name was Joseph A. Rafferty Jr. Rafferty was a criminal lawyer who had been summoned by Caddy to speak for the five men at their arraignment later in the day since Caddy was not accustomed to criminal procedure. The attorneys were informed that their clients were being charged with attempted burglary and attempted interception of telephone and other communications.

At 2:30 in the afternoon, a warrant was obtained to search rooms 214 and 314 of the Watergate Hotel. The names that the five suspects had given the police appeared on the register for those rooms under the date of June 16. Sgt. Paul Leper accompanied two other police officers and a Special Agent of the Federal Bureau of Investigation in searching room 214. They found six suitcases full of electronic surveillance equipment and burglary tools, $4200 in $100 bills whose serial numbers fitted the sequence of those found on the five suspects the night before, an address book containing a host of Miami addresses along with the cryptic notation *E. Hunt-W.H.*, and a $6 check from E. Howard Hunt to the Rockville (Maryland) Country Club with a bill for that amount attached. The first connection—one of many—had been made.

Through the search of the two rooms, police and the FBI also began to ascertain the real names of the five men, although they were unsure at first which name belonged to whom. They knew that Edward Hamilton was also known as Frank Sturgis; that Frank Carter was aka Bernard L. Barker; that Jean Valdez was aka Eugenio R. Martinez; that Raul Godoyn was aka Virgilio R. Gonzales. And they knew that Edward Martin had an alias of James W. McCord Jr.

By that time police had also ascertained that four of the five men had come to Washington from Miami, but Martin-McCord was from the Washington area and had connections in the nation's capital.

The five men were arraigned at four o'clock in the afternoon on June 17, before Superior Court Judge James A Belson. Assistant U.S. Attorney Earl Silbert argued that the men be held without bond because they were known to travel extensively and there was no assurance they would return to Washington for the trial. This was an unusual request for a mere attempted burglary.

Rafferty countered that minimum bond should be ordered on the grounds that the five men were unarmed and there was no evidence they had planned to remove anything from the premises. He further argued that the men had offered no resistance to the police when apprehended and, in fact, had been most cooperative.

Judge Belson was unmoved. He set bond at $50,000 dollars each for Barker, Sturgis, Martinez, and Gonzales, and ordered them to report to his court in person every day thereafter to assure their presence in Washington. For McCord, Belson set bond at $30,000 and ordered that he report in person to the court once a week.

McCord's relaxed bail requirements might have puzzled some of those in the courtroom—although not a young Washington *Post* reporter who had heard McCord whisper to the judge that he was a former employee of the Central Intelligence Agency.

Who was his current employer? And who, exactly, was James W. McCord Jr.?

The Men Who Almost Stole America

"The President's ability to govern is at stake. Another Teapot Dome scandal is possible, and the government may fall. Everybody is on the track but you. You are not following the game plan."

anonymous message received by McCord in a phone booth on January 8, 1973.

He was a loner. He had a reputation for acting independently. He was a wild card in a deck of company bureaucrats.

When James Walter McCord Jr. started working for the Committee to Re-elect the President (affectionately known as CREEP to its friends and its enemies), it wasn't even a full-time job. Not yet anyway.

McCord had originally been approached to work for the Republican National Committee. Later he was interviewed by a hard-assed former New York detective named Jack Caulfield. Caulfield was a White House staff assistant who worked in John Ehrlichman's Domestic Affairs Office, ostensibly as a liaison with law enforcement agencies.

Caulfield had wanted somebody with experience who could advise him on certain security matters. He needed an operative tested by fire and McCord, a one-time FBI agent with nineteen years in the CIA, seemed to be made of a tempered steel which could stand the heat of any furnace.

McCord was approved by Caulfield and then passed upon by the counsel to the President himself, John Dean. In his testimony before the Senate Select Committee on Presidential Campaign Activities, McCord said the Good White Housekeeping Seal of Approval had come when Caulfield arranged a meeting between McCord and Dean.

One of McCord's first duties as CREEP's chief of security was to throw a security net around Martha Mitchell, the loquacious wife of Attorney General John Mitchell. McCord visited the Mitchell's apartment several times, making sure the telephones were clean of bugs, and even x-raying the furniture for possible taps or bombs.

This was child's play for McCord, a man used to tinkering with history, who had already left his mark on the futures of entire countries. L. Fletcher Prouty, a retired Air Force colonel who remembered McCord, said he had been "the Number one man," in charge of security for the CIA. Prouty, ex-director of the CIA's military operations and author of *The Secret Team*, said that when he was introduced to McCord by Allen Dulles, the former CIA Director, Dulles said, "Here is my top man." The meeting took place following the downing of a U.S. Air Force C-118 over the Soviet Union in 1959. Prouty said McCord was such a good interrogator that, after questioning the crew when they returned, he was able to identify the Soviet agent who questioned the downed airmen by finding a photograph of the agent in the CIA's office files.

When McCord was hired by CREEP, he did not think of himself as a thief or a political spy. More likely, he believed he was basically a good family man, selflessly serving his country and his Christian god; or so it appears. McCord went to his church pastor, Reverend Walter C. Smith of the Rockville Methodist Church in suburban Maryland, and volunteered to work half a day each week for the church. Reverend Smith said McCord and his family attended Sunday services faithfully. He even arranged a monthly social program for older members of the parish.

In bugging telephones, collecting blackmail material,

and recruiting political agents, McCord said he believed he was not breaking the law but fulfilling it. The break-in was an act on behalf of national security, like the invasion of Cuba. McCord had gotten it on good authority, from the man who can make and break all the laws: Attorney General Mitchell. In testimony before Senator Sam Ervin's select committee, McCord said, "This man, the Attorney General, had approved it in his offices over a series of meetings in which he had obviously given careful consideration to it, while he was the top legal officer of the U.S. government [and] I was advised that it was within the Attorney General's purview and authority to authorize such operations if it were in the national interest to do so."

McCord had every reason to believe Mitchell was authorizing and directing CREEP's espionage activities. In 1971 and early 1972, the nation was still suffering the pain and unrest left over from a turbulent decade. Threats against the AG and his wife were common; an assassin almost succeeded in killing presidential candidate George Wallace; and dozens of radical groups were promising to disrupt the Republican National Convention in Miami.

McCord understood what was meant by "national security." As a lieutenant colonel in the Air Force Reserve, he was one of a fifteen-member military unit in charge of cataloguing radicals and devising plans for censoring the U.S. Mail and the news media.

CREEP hired other operatives for their security network. One who was to figure prominently in the Watergate affair was G. Gordon Liddy.

Liddy was the mustachioed counsel to CREEP and later to its finance committee. Liddy sometimes worked alongside McCord and was also hired by John Dean. But the similarities ended there. McCord was scrupulously quiet and precise; Liddy was loud and flamboyant. McCord enjoyed going home to his wife and children; Liddy wore a shoulder holster and propositioned CREEP secretaries. McCord might have been a loyalist, but Liddy was prepared to genuflect before the king.

Like many of the hard-working, nose-to-the-grindstone CREEP employees, Liddy came to Washington to learn how to be a politician. He had already unsuccessfully campaigned for a New York congressional seat against Hamilton Fish in 1968.

Liddy had Marshalled a stock law-and-order challenge in that campaign, but was narrowly defeated by liberal Republicanism. He campaigned against drugs, using Timothy Leary's Millbrook bust as grapeshot, and circulated a poster of himself waving down a crowd of unruly blacks. The photograph, appropriately, was faked.

Political defeat did not hamper Liddy's promotion of himself as a self-made Wyatt Earp who would rescue American civilization from Washington-marching, blue-jeaned, long-haired degenerates.

Once, as assistant district attorney in Duchess County, New York, Liddy found himself prosecuting a man accused of hitting his client with a two-by-four. To drive his point home, Liddy smashed the court railing with his own two-by-four. He was ordered to pay for the broken rail.

Liddy once held his hand over a candle flame, scarring the flesh and burning the nerve endings, to prove to a girl just how tough he was. On another occasion, Liddy fearlessly dispersed a group of neighborhood children. Thinking the kids were making too much noise one night, Liddy climbed on to his garage roof and leaped off, Batman-like, chasing the kids through the yard. When disturbed parents went to Liddy's home to complain, he wasn't in but they found Liddy's gun collection displayed on the dining room table.

On yet another occasion, while prosecuting a defendant charged with armed robbery, Liddy reached into his coat, pulled out a revolver and fired it into the ceiling of the courtroom.

Liddy's affection for guns is documented two more times in his career. Liddy was fired from his first Washington job at the Treasury Department because of an overzealous and unauthorized speech against gun control he made to the National Rifle Association. Liddy had also urged McCord, four Cubans and another former CIA agent to carry guns in an earlier, milk-run raid on the Watergate.

The other former CIA agent employed by CREEP was Everrette Howard Hunt, a Navy officer who served in the OSS during World War II. Like McCord, Hunt was involved in the Bay of Pigs fiasco, but unlike McCord, he wrote a book about it. Called *Give Us This Day*, the book is scheduled for 1973 publication. Hunt had an alter ego which nicely corresponded to his clandestine military life. A *Life* magazine correspondent and winner of a Guggenheim fellowship in creative writing, Hunt was the prolific author of some forty-six science fiction, mystery and spy novels. He even sold Hollywood a movie script *(Bimini Run)* for $35,000.

So it was appropriate that it was Hunt who produced a written master plan which intricately detailed a step-by-step design for invading Democratic National Headquarters. Ironically, he rejected the plan as unfeasible—but was later ordered to follow it. Hunt's literary ego emerged again when McCord gave Washington police the name of Edward Martin—the same name used by two characters in Hunt's spy novels. In *Stranger in Town*, a woman named Valdes reminds the hero of another woman named Jean. Thus Watergate burglar Eugenio Martinez gave arresting officers the alias Jean Valdes. One of the characters in *Bimini Run*, a novel set in the Miami-Cuba area, is Hank Sturgis. Frank Sturgis, a resident of Miami, who fought with Castro, was another of McCord's fellow burglars. In his own way, Hunt has added to the debate over whether art imitates life.

One of Hunt's more notorious forays in creative writing took place in 1971. Following several conversations with White House aide Chuck Colson (who brought Hunt to CREEP from Robert Mullen's Washington advertising agency where he worked in public relations), Hunt set out to forge a series of State Department cables suggesting that President John F. Kennedy ordered the assassination of South Vietnamese President Diem. The CIA has been named as the instigator of the coup which deposed Diem in order to protect American interests in Southeast Asia.

This was not the first time Hunt was connected with talk of assassination. As one of the planners of the Bay of Pigs, Hunt recommended to his superiors that Fidel Castro be assassinated as part of the invasion of Cuba, or so he says in *Give Us This Day*.

As a result of his involvement with the attempt to overthrow Castro, Hunt won the lasting faith of several members of the Cuban underground, not the least of whom was Watergate burglar Bernard Barker. Members of the Cuban exile community affectionately called Barker "Macho," meaning strong man. When Hunt, who they called "Eduardo," needed agents to execute intelligence gathering operations, he usually called on Barker who in turn recruited other rightwing Cubans.

Hunt drafted other political spies, including a college student named Thomas Gregory. Hunt had asked him to infiltrate the presidential campaign of Democratic Senator Edmund Muskie. When Muskie was forced out of the race after an embarrassing series of political "accidents," Gregory moved over to McGovern's campaign. In both cases, Gregory reported daily to Hunt. West Coast playboy and political spy Donald Segretti was another agent with whom Hunt worked.

Liddy, Hunt, and McCord were all seasoned professionals. During his twenty years with the CIA, Hunt worked for the Operations Department which, among other things, arranged to overthrow the Arbenz Regime in Guatemala in 1954.

In 1971, both Hunt and Liddy were tapped by the White House to plug internal security leaks following disclosures concerning the SALT talks, Indo-Pakistani relations, and the controversial publication of the *Pentagon Papers*. They were called the Plumbers, and received the title, "Consultants to the White House."

Both Hunt and Liddy were patriots who found little conflict between duty and conscience. McCord, however, was different. Testifying before Senator Ervin's committee investigating illegal activities connected with the 1972 presidential campaign, McCord said he believed that, "I was different from the others, that I was going to fight the fixed case and had no intention of either pleading guilty, taking executive clemency, or agreeing to remain silent."

McCord was caught in limbo somewhere between consience and country. Confronted with a massive prison sentence, McCord decided to try to save himself. Ironically, it was the proud, silent McCord, not the novel-writing Hunt or the fast-talking Liddy, who would speak with such moment that the whole world would stop and listen.

June 17 to July 1/Martha's Mouth

The announcement wasn't a bombshell, but it was something more than a mere surprise. John Newton Mitchell—President Nixon's former law partner, close friend, 1968 campaign director, and choice as attorney general in his first cabinet—was resigning as director of the President's re-election campaign.

Four months earlier, Mitchell had resigned as attorney general to direct the 1972 campaign. Now that direction would come from Clark MacGregor, formerly President Nixon's assistant for congressional liaison.

In Mitchell's formal letter of resignation to Nixon, he cited family problems as his reason for leaving the campaign. Mitchell claimed his problem was a wife named Martha.

On June 22, 1972, Mrs. Mitchell was registered as a guest at the Newport Inn in Newport Beach, California. She had accompanied her husband there to attend several campaign fundraising functions during the week of the Watergate. While there, she learned that James W. McCord Jr., her former bodyguard and personal friend, was under arrest for attempting to bug the offices of the Democratic National Committee, located in the same Watergate Hotel and office complex where the Mitchells maintained their Washington residence.

Martha was upset. On the twenty-second she waited until her bodyguard, Steve King, fell asleep and placed a phone call to Helen Thomas, a reporter for United Press International. Mrs. Mitchell described herself to the reporter as a "political prisoner." She also told Ms. Thomas that "they don't want me to talk." Then someone whom Mrs. Mitchell later identified as a security agent for the Republican National Committee came into her room and "pulled the telephone out of the wall." The man was actually an FBI agent.

The report of the phone call, carried in probably every newspaper in the United States, seemed bizarre even for the likes of Martha Mitchell—the most outspoken and colorful character in Nixon's first administration. But many strange events had made those summer days unprecedented in the annals of American politics, and a convoluted web of charges and counter-charges had slowly begun to close around Martha's dear John.

In the wake of the Watergate arrests, a steady stream of detail which was pouring forth in the nation's press pointed an accusing finger at the Committee to Re-elect the President and even at the White House. It was immediately reported that three of the five men apprehended were former CIA operatives and that another was a Miami locksmith. The background of Edward Martin, alias James W. McCord Jr., was less clear.

On June 18, however, it was revealed that McCord was security coordinator for the Committee to Re-elect the President, and that his security firm, McCord Associates, held a contract to provide security for the Republican national convention.

Democratic National Committee Chairman Lawrence O'Brien blasted the attempt to bug his office and said it "raised the ugliest questions about the integrity of the political process that I have encountered in a quarter of a century." The angry party executive added: "No mere statement of innocence by Mr. Nixon's campaign manager will dispel these questions."

But there *were* statements of innocence and they were forceful disclaimers. Mitchell, speaking in Los Angeles, said the five men arrested in the Watergate "were not operating either in our behalf or with our consent." The Republican national chairman, Senator Robert Dole of Kansas, also denied any party involvement: "We deplore action of this kind in or out of politics."

By the time Larry O'Brien and the Democratic Party had filed a law suit for $1 million damages against the Committee to Re-elect the President, Mitchell was thoroughly on the defensive. While Mitchell was calling the lawsuit "another example of sheer demagoguery on the part of Mr. O'Brien," the Democratic leader was charging that there was "a developing clear line to the White House."

At least some sort of connection had been made. The notations *E. Hunt—W.H.* and *E.H.—W. House* in the address books of two of the men captured in the Watergate had led investigators directly to the $100-a-day White House consultant. Hunt refused to answer questions put to him by FBI agents and, shortly thereafter, dropped out of sight. Hunt's White House supervisor, Chuck Colson, reportedly told federal agents that Hunt had assured him he had not been anywhere near the Watergate on the day of the break-in.

Hunt was a mystery man, but details of his past activity started surfacing like dead fish in a stagnant sea. It was revealed that he had been employed by the Central Intelligence Agency for twenty-one years and his operations under the code name "Eduardo," during the Bay of Pigs invasion also came to light. Hunt's strong ties with numerous Bay of Pigs veterans—including those apprehended in the Watergate, supplied another link.

Oddly enough, Mr. Hunt shared an office at Robert Mullen Associates with Douglas Caddy, the attorney who appeared on the day of the break-in to represent the five burglars. The advertising agency was later named as a front for collecting over $10 million in Nixon campaign contributions prior to the April 7 public disclosure deadline.

It took less than a week to discover these first links to the White House—links which would eventually become a chain ensnaring the presidency. At first they were only tenuous associations, but they indicated that something very wrong had been going on. A series of secret meetings that took place during the week of Watergate compounded that wrong.

On the afternoon of June 23, Richard Helms, director of the CIA, and Deputy Director Lt. General Vernon Walters were summoned to the White House to meet with Mr. Nixon's closest aides, H.R. Haldeman and John D. Ehrlichman. Nixon's advisers told Helms and Walters that "it had been decided" that the CIA should intervene in the Watergate case. The men from CIA were requested to see L. Patrick Gray, acting director of the FBI, and inform him that his bureau's investigation into funds being routed through Mexican banks interfered with CIA operations there. The two intelligence officials were told that the Watergate break-in was "being capitalized on by the opposition."

Helms and Walters refused to go along. They couldn't understand what a break-in at Democratic Headquarters had to do with Mexico. The cover-up was on in earnest.

Later in the week, the CIA officials were asked by Counsel to the President John Dean to have their agency pay the bail and salaries of the five men arrested in the bugging attempt. Again, the CIA refused.

At about the same time, counsel Dean went through the contents of E. Howard Hunt's White House safe and removed "classified documents" before the material could be turned over to agents of the FBI. Among those documents were forged State Department cables implicating President Kennedy in the 1963 assassination of Diem. Dean gave the secret papers to Gray, calling them "political dynamite," with instructions that they should "never see the light of day." They didn't. Gray burned them six months later.

If CIA officials were still wondering what Mexico had to do with the Watergate, they had only to look to the June 23 bail hearing for the five Watergate burglars. Assistant U.S. Attorney Earl Silbert disclosed that $89,000 which Bernard Barker had withdrawn from a Miami bank in May had been traced to four checks drawn on Banco Internacional S.A., of Mexico City.

Meanwhile, Martha Mitchell continued to be a political prisoner. On June 25, Mrs. Mitchell again phoned UPI reporter Helen Thomas and said that she couldn't stand the life she had been leading since her husband left his cabinet post. "I have been through so much," Mrs. Mitchell complained. "Martha isn't going to stand for it." Martha said she was leaving her husband until, and unless, he would leave his job as Nixon's campaign director. The explosive Martha claimed she could no longer stand "all those dirty things that go on."

Another distasteful duty confronted Mitchell on June 28 as Democratic charges against the committee mounted. The former Attorney General was forced to dismiss G. Gordon Liddy, the counsel to the finance committee, for refusing to answer FBI questions about the Watergate break-in.

Old skeletons were popping out of new closets, the re-elect apparatus became more tainted with every edition of the newspapers, and to top it all, John Mitchell's marriage was collapsing. So, on July 1, he retired from politics for the good of his family. Presumably, Martha was a happy housewife once again.

In a letter to Mitchell accepting his resignation, President Nixon said that during twenty-six years of political life, he had "often noted that the greater share of sacrifice is usually the wife's, since she must share not only the disappointments and the brickbats, but must accept the frequent absence of a husband and father."

Nixon continued, "I am well aware that this has been particularly true of the Mitchell family, and I am most appreciative of the sacrifice Martha and you have both made in the service of the nation."

It was a fond farewell, the first of many to come.

Mr. Law and Order Comes to Justice

John N. Mitchell started out as Mr. Law and Order and ended up indicted by a grand jury for conspiring to defraud the United States, obstructing justice, and committing perjury. His fall from the graces of justice was nearly as swift as his rise from corporate lawyer to Attorney General. The bumpy road from citizen to top cop to suspected criminal is a remarkable trail that could be traveled only by a dear friend of the President.

The John Mitchell story really begins the day he met Richard Nixon, when their respective Wall Street law firms merged in 1967. The merger spawned the firm of Nixon, Mudge, Rose, Guthrie, Alexander and Mitchell. Mitchell was reportedly making $200,000 a year, while Nixon earned $150,000. The firm's largest clients were Pepsi Cola, Continental Baking—a subsidiary of ITT, General Cigar Company, Warner-Lambert Pharmaceuticals Company, El Paso Natural Gas Company, and Eversharp-Shick Inc.

Instant rapport between the two lawyers quickly blossomed from a mutual respect into a genuine friendship. That was highly unusual since both Mitchell and Nixon are very private people to whom new friendships do not easily come.

Mitchell enjoyed a quiet, almost sedate personal life as a corporate lawyer for thirty-two years. After graduating from Fordham College and Law School, he began to practice corporate law, purposely avoiding the courtroom rigors of trial law. Even at that early stage, he yearned for a proper, dignified lifestyle. His pipe, which became a Mitchell trademark, was more than a prop. It symbolized his desire for a relaxed, frictionless existence, both professionally and socially.

If it seemed an outright contradiction when he married outspoken, fun-loving, irrepressible Martha, close friends thought they complemented one another exquisitely. Mitchell strove to establish the perfect balance. John and Martha were married in 1957, both veterans of broken marriages. John's parting was called "amicable," while

"Clear it with the AG" was already a CREEP cliche.

Martha's was anything but. She had accused her first husband of eleven years, Clyde Jennings Jr., with beating her and running around with other women. Martha retained custody of their only child, Jay.

After their marriage, while John was building a high-rent clientele as a corporate lawyer, the Mitchells lived in a respectable New York City suburb of Westchester County. The have one daughter, Marty, now twelve.

After knowing Mitchell for less than a year, Richard Nixon asked him to commandeer his 1968 presidential campaign. Their political beliefs were similar, and Nixon was no doubt taken with Mitchell's discipline and dedication, not to mention his toughness. Even though the closest Mitchell had been to big-time Republican politics was as a public finance consultant for New York Governor Nelson Rockefeller, Nixon was confident Mitchell could pull off the job.

Law and order was the promise of the low-keyed, no-nonsense campaign, with Mitchell, an ex-PT boat Captain, at the helm. Fear of riots, demonstrations, and rising crime engulfed the Silent Majority. Nixon's political bloodhounds picked up the scent and followed the fear right into the White House. Mitchell ran a tight, efficient operation and it was no surprise when Presidential nominee Nixon offered him the post of attorney general.

It was a surprise, though, when Mitchell accepted. If Mitchell had any passion, it was for his privacy; he had resisted the temptation of public life for many years. Even during the campaign, when rumors of his nomination as attorney general were circulating freely, he unequivocally denied them. "I am vulnerable," he said convincingly. "I will never accept a cabinet post."

He changed his mind. His admiration for and empathy with Nixon grew steadily during the arduous months of campaigning and insiders were saying that Mitchell's experience with high-level politics had left him with a certain social consciousness. Mitchell was now a man with a mission. In addition, the Justice Department seemed like a place where Mitchell could continue his stoic legal life with as little public exposure as possible.

John and Martha and daughter Marty moved to Washington and settled in the Watergate. It was only the first of a chain of ironic events.

John Newton Mitchell became the Attorney General of the United States in 1969. Promoting himself as Mr. Law and Order, he told the stunned senators at his confirmation hearings that he intended to use electronic eavesdropping devices to fight organized crime. He said wiretapping "should be used, carefully and effectively, not only in national security cases but against organized crime and *other major crimes*" (emphasis added). It was the first time in U.S. history that an attorney general had publicly announced plans to use electronic surveillance for domestic reasons.

Wiretapping, meanwhile, shifted into high gear. A report to Congress stated that from 1969 to 1970, federal court-approved taps and bugs had increased more than six-fold; from 30 bugs to 180. These 180 federal bugs netted the government a total of forty-eight arrests, at a cost to the taxpayer of $2,163,781, or $45,079 per conviction.

On July 11, 1971, before the Virginia Bar Association, Mitchell delivered the Justice Department's legal case for eavesdropping on domestic subversives.

". . . it is our position that compelling considerations exist when the President, acting through the Attorney General, has determined that a particular surveillance is necessary to protect the national security and that under those circumstances the warrant requirement does not apply . . . there is no dividing line between hostile foreign forces seeking to undermine our internal security and hostile domestic groups' seeking the overthrow of our government by any means . . . I would say that history has shown the greater danger from the domestic variety."

This new interpretation of presidential power in connection with electronic surveillance inspired the loud and long congressional outcries. Rep. Emanuel Cellar, Democrat of New York and chairman of the House Judiciary Committee, thought Mitchell's remarks pointed toward a "police state." Former Attorney General Ramsey Clark called it "an utterly lawless philosophy. The Constitution applies to the President of the United States," said Clark, "just as it does to the rest of us."

President Nixon answered the blistering charges by calling them "hysteria" and "political demagoguery." At a press conference on May 5, he tried to explain away the widespread fear and apprehension by saying the eavesdrops were limited to fifty at a time. "This is not a police state," he said. "We will wiretap," he assured the public, "only when a wiretap is necessary."

However, on April 6, 1971, the Sixth Circuit Court of Appeals held that the government had no right to eavesdrop on alleged subversives without warrants. The Justice Department swiftly appealed to the Supreme Court. The Supreme Court voted unanimously to uphold the lower court, thus making it illegal for even the President and the Attorney General to bug at will.

But bug they did. On July 13, the New York *Times* started printing excerpts from the *Pentagon Papers*. It hit Capitol Hill like an earthquake. The government's own exposé of wrongdoing in Vietnam—classified for alleged national security reasons—was now being splashed on front pages across the country.

In a bureaucratic mass society, secret information is power—but not if it's disseminated to 200 million people. Daniel Ellsberg had become precisely the domestic subversive that Nixon and Mitchell had warned against. There was no time to waste.

Three days after the original excerpts appeared in the New York *Times*, the Justice Department, under the auspices of John Mitchell, obtained a temporary restraining order against further publication from the Federal Court in New York. It was the first time the government ever halted American presses.

Almost simultaneously, Attorney General Mitchell authorized the wiretapping of the telephones of two *Times* reporters and ten White House aides. Nixon wanted the leaks to the press stopped. To carry out the bugging, the President established the special investigations unit in the White House known as the Plumbers (their official mission: to plug the leaks). The five members of the Plumbers were National Security Council official

David Young, White House aide Egil Krogh, and CIA agents Hunt, McCord, and Liddy. Their future activities, to understate the case, would include much more than the plugging of news leaks.

The Plumbers were to be the beginning of the end for Mitchell, who was up to his neck in their illegal shenanigans. In fact, McCord later testified, it was Mitchell who provided the impetus for the Watergate break-in itself.

A year before that, Mitchell had been busy doing favors he would later regret. Harry L. Sears, a New Jersey GOP pol with a pedigree as long as the Garden State Parkway, needed Mitchell's help. Sears was also a lawyer, and one of his clients, Robert L. Vesco, was sitting in a Swiss jail. Vesco was no ordinary client—he owned a mammoth mutual fund complex called Investors Overseas Services, based in Geneva, and a New Jersey electronics corporation, International Control Inc. Vesco was also a business associate of Richard Nixon's little brother Edward C., and employer of Nixon's nephew Donald. And, if those were not enough credentials to warrant a favor, Vesco had contributed $180,000 to the President's 1968 campaign. It was contribution time 1971 and Sears went straight to John Mitchell. Mitchell in turn went straight to a telephone and placed a call to the embassy in Geneva, Switzerland. The next day, Robert Vesco was out on bail. Thus began a crucial, if long-distance, triangle: Vesco to Sears to Mitchell. It may replace Tinkers to Evers to Chance in the annals of American game plans.

CREEP had put a 100-member staff to work by February 1972, and although Mitchell was still Attorney General, nothing could be done in the campaign without his approval. "Clear it with the AG" was already a CREEP cliché, but the constant trips between the White House and CREEP headquarters down the block were causing some problems, perhaps only least among them an illegal conflict of interest.

The conflict emanated from the White House. Nixon did not want Mitchell to leave his post as AG to become

campaign manager. Mitchell had become Nixon's most trusted political adviser and best Washington friend. He was the only member of the cabinet invited to buy a house in the Nixon compound on Key Biscayne, Florida. Nixon liked having Mitchell around. And even though Mitchell had recommended nine Supreme Court candidates, five of whom either dropped out under fire or were rejected by the Senate, the President's faith in him remained unswerving. He suggested that Deputy AG Richard Kleindienst run the campaign.

Another dissenter to Mitchell leaving the Justice Department was Martha. "I think it's a bad move . . . He said the President needed him. I feel Mr. Nixon doesn't need anyone. He will be reelected on his own . . . I feel very sad. It breaks my heart." Martha Mitchell knew she was being sentimental. She didn't know she was being prophetic.

Four months later the Republicans were left to cast about for a new head for the re-election effort. It was not the best spot to be in as the Democrats prepared to gather in Florida and choose thier candidate.

July 2 to July 14/"Come Home America"

Miami Beach is an aberration that could exist only in America. Once the exclusive haven for the nation's elite, the economic equalizing effects of the Second World War made Miami Beach every developer's fantasyland. Pristine coastline succumbed to gaudy resort hostelry, retirement villages, and random edifices of glowing neon. Miami rapidly became the pot of gold at the end of the rainbow for Middle America.

Miami Beach has a geography that separates it literally as well as figuratively from the rest of America. Connected to the mainland only by four causeways or bridges, the beach reigns over the southernmost tip of the United States like an invader's castle separated from the surrounding populace by moat. The city is self-contained and aloof, its looming hotels bastions of the good life. It was considered the perfect site for both the 1972 Democratic and Republican conventions.

The Democrats needed a safe site after the debacle they suffered in Chicago in 1968. Thousands of young protestors had staged a series of demonstrations that fell prey to what the Walker report, a government study of

the event, termed "a police riot." Violence had even broken out on the floor of the convention itself while party leaders lik Senator Abraham Ribicoff of Connecticut denounced ' police state tactics on the streets of Chicago."

The incident served to polarize America, and it was largely credited for Hubert Humphrey's narrow defeat at the polls in 1968. It was an occurrence that the Democrats could ill afford four years later, but it had prompted broad reforms in the Democratic Party itself. Those reforms were personified in the man who chaired the reform commission of the Democratic Party and approached Miami in July 1972, as the most likely candidate to receive the nomination for President, Senator George McGovern of South Dakota.

As Democratic Convention delegates converged on Miami for the July 10 opening session, it quickly became apparent that the Democratic Party was a changed party dedicated to a changing America. Only a credentials challenge on the seating of the California delegation stood in the way of McGovern, who by June 20 had captured 10 out of 23 state primaries.

At this time, in early July, Watergate disclosures had

begun piling up rapidly like so much dirty stuffing dragged shred by shred from an expensive, overstuffed chair. In U.S. District Court, Judge John Sirica, the jurist assigned to oversee the grand jury investigation of the Watergate break-in, ordered Douglas Caddy, defense attorney for the five bugging suspects, to testify about his own possible involvement with the CIA and his personal relationship with suspect E. Howard Hunt. Twice Caddy refused, citing his attorney-client privilege with Hunt as grounds for silence.

Sirica, who has a reputation as a hard-nosed Republican judge, was unmoved. He briefly held Caddy in contempt of the grand jury for refusing to testify.

Sirica wanted to break the case open quickly. His eagerness may have been founded upon recent disclosures. A diagram of Senator George McGovern's Miami Beach campaign headquarters had been found among the be-

August. The activities of the men apprehended in the Watergate had evidently been going on for some time, in places outside Washington, D.C.

Meanwhile, the mysterious Mr. Hunt was still on the lam. The remaining contents of his White House office had been turned over to federal investigators and two items in particular seemed extremely significant: a .25 caliber automatic Colt revolver and a walkie-talkie of the same make and model as those found on the men who broke into the Watergate. A box marked "Top Secret," and containing documents relating to an investigation Hunt made in 1971 of Daniel Ellsberg and the Pentagon Papers affair, was also given to the FBI agents. It was further revealed that Hunt had been working on an investigation into the death of Mary Jo Kopechne in Senator Edward Kennedy's car at Chappaquiddick.

Hunt, for the moment, was reported to be a fugitive in Europe, probably in Spain. His wife Dorothy, who had recently worked as a translator in the Spanish embassy in Washington, steadfastly maintained that her husband had not fled the country. Hunt became the object of an intensive search. He clearly had ties with the men apprehended in the Watergate, as evidenced by the $6 check and address book notations. On July 7 the hunt for Hunt ended. Mystery man number one informed Judge Sirica, through an attorney, that he would appear and testify before the grand jury.

As the Watergate case escalated, the Democrats became more insistent that something further be done to clear the air. Lawrence O'Brien requested that President Nixon appoint a special prosecutor to get to the bottom of the whole affair. When they learned that Nixon had referred the matter to the Committee to Re-elect the President, Democratic Party leaders became furious. Nixon was forced to take a step to alleviate their anxieties. He said he would impose tighter White House control over his own campaign, giving top assistants John Ehrlichman and H.R. Haldeman more say in the running of CREEP.

One day later, Acting FBI Director L. Patrick Gray reported to the President that his investigation of the Watergate "caper" would likely lead to very high places in the White House. Gray told the President, "people on your own staff are trying to mortally wound you by using the FBI and CIA." Nixon seemingly ignored the warning signal.

Instead, on July 10, the very same day that the turmoil of a major political convention was beginning in Miami Beach, attorneys for the Committee to Re-elect the President asked a U.S. District Court Judge in Washington to postpone the Democrat's $1 million civil suit until after the November 7 election. The lawyers argued that the suit would cause "incalculable" damage to Nixon's re-election campaign. In their brief, the re-election committee maintained that any hearing on the lawsuit would discourage campaign workers, result in fewer campaign contributions, and force disclosure of confidential campaign contributions already made. Unexpectedly, the Republicans themselves made the Watergate affair into something more than an object of John Mitchell's disdain. They showed they really had something to hide.

In Miami, the Democratic Convention began on a level calmer and more serious than anyone had expected. Hordes of demonstrators did show up for the affair, as in 1968, but their presence in Flamingo Park was more to support the candidacy of George McGovern than to create any disturbance. Celebrated activists like Abbie Hoffman and Jerry Rubin quietly urged the nomination and election of George McGovern, the only candidate deemed capable of both winning the election and unqualifiedly ending the long war in Vietnam.

Inside the convention hall, many old party pros expressed admiration for the new delegates participating in

longings in the buggers' Watergate hotel rooms. Also, a Miami Beach architect said that Bernard L. Barker had tried to obtain blueprints of the air conditioning ducts in the city's convention hall in 1971. In still another development, Sirica learned that suspects Frank Sturgis and Eugenio Martinez had attempted to arrange housing for thousands of Young Republicans at the University of Miami to attend the Republican National Convention in the nominee selection process for the first time through the democratization of the party. Rather than bucking the system, the delegates worked diligently within it to bring about the nomination of their candidate.

The party platform officially adopted by the convention contained the declaration: "The new Democratic administration should bring an end to the pattern of political persecution and investigation . . . The epidemic of wiretapping and electronic surveillance engaged in by the Nixon Administration must be ended. The rule of law and the supremacy of the constitution as these concepts have been traditionally understood, must be restored."

On the final day of the convention, McGovern announced his choice for Vice-presidential candidate, Senator Thomas Eagleton of Missouri. In part, Eagleton was a concession to the old line party bosses. After widening party rifts to secure his nomination, McGovern was quick to attempt to heal those wounds to ensure his election. Eagleton came from a border state, he was a moderate who enjoyed strong labor support—something McGovern lacked—and he was a Catholic. Eagleton quickly accepted the nomination.

"Come home America, from secrecy and deception in high places," McGovern said. "Come home America, from a conflict in Indochina which maims our ideals as well as our soldiers. Come home America, to the conviction that we can move our country forward. Come home to the belief that we can seek a newer world. . . . "

Months later Americans were to discover exactly what they had come home to.

The Sabotaging of Ed Muskie

Edmund Muskie, the Senator from Maine, was to discover it a lot sooner. The odd events which toppled him from front-runner in 1971 to has-been in 1972 must at least have given him pause, if not actual cause to suspect what was in fact going on.

The campaign to re-elect the President had shifted into high gear in the early months of 1971, more than a year before campaigns traditionally get underway. President Nixon had returned from his historic trips to Peking and his image had been spit-shined to a high gloss. But the boys in the back room were worried—Muskie remained ahead in many national popularity polls. Muskie's star had been rising steadily, and looked as if it could reach zenith at election time. So sometime in those early days the Nixon team actually decided to assure that George McGovern would be the Democratic nominee. If he were not the weakest of all possible candidates, he certainly was the most vulnerable, the easiest to discredit. So in a wry twist of fate, a coterie of conservative Republicans were among arch-liberal McGovern's earliest and most avid boosters.

The Republican espionage campaign for the 1972 election had its origin even farther back than 1971. Nixon's first inaugural address was still echoing in the wind when Ehrlichman, Haldeman, and Dean, along with Mitchell, Robert Mardian, and Colson, gathered together and drew up plans for the future operations. The assignment for Chuck Colson, special counsel to Mr. Nixon, and superaide Haldeman, was to assemble at least thirty "attack groups" across the country to sabotage the Democratic cause.

To carry out the plans, Haldeman turned to his aide Dwight Chapin and White House staff aide Gordon C. Strachan. Both could be counted on to follow any orders. Chapin, who was appointments secretary for the President, showed "absolute devotion to Richard Nixon," according to Daniel Moynihan. The warm and generally well-liked thirty-one-year-old was once called by a reporter covering the White House "the most obedient man I ever met."

As he had done for ten years at the J. Walter Thompson advertising agency in Los Angeles, Dwight Chapin was again working for Haldeman. Anyone less than completely obedient could not last that long with the Prussian, as Haldeman was known on Capitol Hill.

One of Chapin's old friends from the University of Southern California, and a close associate in the White House, was Gordon Strachan. Strachan's devotion to Nixon emerged during the years he worked with Nixon and Mitchell in their New York law firm.

When Chapin and Strachan were given orders to assemble an espionage network to sabotage the Democratic primaries in February 1971, they called a mutual friend, Donald Segretti. Segretti had also gone to Southern Cal, where he, Chapin, and Ron Ziegler, now Mr. Nixon's press secretary, were members of a political club called the Trojan Knights. Some dubious activities of the Trojan Knights included ripping down posters of student government candidates that the Knights disapproved of, stealing the opposition's leaflets, stuffing ballot boxes, and guarding the campus statue, Tommy Trojan, from university rivals. Southern Cal was a good training camp for political sabotage, and Donald Segretti was its prize product.

After graduating in 1963, Segretti went to England for a year and then returned to earn a law degree at Berkeley, where he met Strachan. Segretti worked as a lawyer for the Treasury Department until he was drafted into the army in 1968. He returned to California from Vietnam with the rank of captain.

Captain Segretti rented a posh apartment in a Marina del Rey complex known as "a single swinger's paradise." The tape deck in Segretti's Mustang played one song constantly—Cat Stevens' "It's a Wild World." He fancied himself the playboy bachelor and played it to the hilt. After all, he had recently returned from Nam and it was time to live a little.

When Chapin contacted him to do some spy work for Nixon, Segretti jumped at the chance. His friends at Marina del Ray told reporters he really was not a fanatical conservative, but the excitement and adventure of spydom apparently turned Segretti on. Of course, he was a lawyer without any clients and a job well done for his old friends in Washington would assure him a good position when Nixon was re-elected.

Segretti adopted the alias of Dan Simmons and traded in his Mustang for a white Mercedes Benz 280SL. Dan Simmons was ready for action.

His work had begun in earnest during the summer of 1971. He crisscrossed the country like a jet-set spider weaving a web of espionage. He contacted people in Portland, Manchester, Tampa, New York, Knoxville, Albuquerque, Washington, and Chicago. He stayed at the best hotels and dined in the best restaurants. Money was no object—CREEP was a wealthy employer.

CREEP had three separate slush funds overflowing with unreported campaign contributions. Maurice Stans, CREEP finance director, was in charge of one; Haldeman had another; and Herbert T. Kalmbach, assistant chairman of CREEP and Nixon's private attorney, watched over the third. Kalmbach's West Coast slush fund coffers had over $500,000 for disbursement to CREEP operatives, and Kalmbach later said he paid Donald Segretti between $30,000 and $40,000 for his efforts. Indeed, money was no object to saboteur extraordinaire Segretti, though not all of it was for his personal bank account.

Segretti traveled around the country, asking people if they wanted to spy for President Nixon—he made no bones about his assignment coming from the very top. He promised his operatives all the money they needed and a fine job after the re-election. One person Segretti contacted, Alex Shipley, an old Army buddy, asked him, "How in hell are we going to be taken care of if no one knows what we're doing?" To which Segretti replied, "Nixon knows that something's being done, It's a typical deal—don't-tell-me-anything-and-I-won't-know."

When Segretti first approached Shipley in June 1971, he listed the kinds of operations the White House wanted performed. They included stealing important documents from Democratic candidates' headquarters, forging campaign literature, contriving phony press releases, disrupting fund-raising dinners by sending out hundreds of extra invitations, harassing campaign workers, posing as gay activists and starting fights at Democratic rallies, shadowing and compiling dossiers on Democratic candidates' families, infiltrating Democratic National headquarters, and other similar activities.

Shipley couldn't believe his ears. He told Segretti he'd have to think about it because it seemed like dangerous work. Segretti emphasized the fun, the excitement, the free travel, the limitless expense accounts, and the James Bond aura of the assignment. Shipley still said he would think about it some more. He was not convinced it would be only fun and games.

Taking a cue from Glenn Turner's pyramid sales technique, Segretti told each of his hundreds of operatives to sign up at least five more trustworthy people. This they did. And like an ever-growing chain letter, Segretti's spy network spread across the nation.

He was in daily communication with either Chapin or Strachan in the White House. The massive effort started to show results during the first primary in New Hampshire. In a January poll, Muskie was leading George McGovern by a 65% to 18% margin. It looked as though Muskie's momentum might bring the final vote in March even higher. Then, on February 24, the Manchester *Union Leader*, a conservative paper that had called Muskie "a phony," "dangerous," and "Moscow Muskie" in previous weeks, printed a letter which read in part:

"We went to Ft. Lauderdale to meet Sen. Muskie...one of the men asked him what he knew about blacks and the problem with them—We didn't have any in Maine, a man with the senator said. No blacks, but we have Cannocks (sic). What did he mean? We ask—Mr. Muskie laughed, and said come to New England and see . . ." The letter was signed "Paul Morrison, Deerfield Beach, Florida, 33064."

The day the letter appeared, the *Union Leader* printed an editorial on the front page with the headline: "Muskie Insults Franco-Americans." The editorial said, "We have always known that Senator Muskie was a hypocrite. . . . "

It may not be known to most of the country, but the term "Canuck" is an offensive and inflammatory slur against Americans of French-Canadian descent. Since

Franco-Americans comprise the largest single bloc of voters in New Hampshire and 60% of the Democrats in the state read the Manchester *Union Leader*, the letter did irrevocable damage. His only recourse, thought the Senator, was to publicly denounce the letter and the editorial.

On February 26, Muskie stood on a platform in the midst of a snowstorm and called *Union Leader* publisher, William Loeb, a "gutless coward" and a "liar." Defending his wife, Jane, who was also slurred by the editorial for using unsavory language, Muskie broke into tears before a national television audience. The "Canuck" letter hurt, but the subsequent "crying speech" depicted Muskie to voters as weak, unstable, and unfit for high office. The New Hampshire polls at the end of February showed a drop from 65% to 42%. It was the beginning of the end for the candidate that Jimmy "the Greek" Snyder had given 2-5 odds to win the Democratic nomination.

The "Canuck" letter was a phony. Paul Morrison of Deerfield Beach, Florida, was never found. But Ken Clawson was. Clawson was an ex-reporter who was then communications director for CREEP and had formerly been deputy director of White House communications. "I wrote the letter," he admitted to Washington *Post* newswoman Marilyn Berger. Since Clawson had previously been employed by the *Post*, he thought he was speaking off the record. The *Post* printed the story.

After that, B.J. McQuaid, the *Union Leader* editor-in-chief, admitted that Clawson had been "helpful during the primaries" and that they had lunched together at an editors' party. "Helpful" may have been one of the understatements of that year.

If New Hampshire was a measure of the potency of the GOP dirty tricks machine, Florida was a measure of its pervasiveness and temerity. George Wallace was a shoo-in in this first Southern primary, but the runner-up was important.

Since Muskie had tied Nixon in a national Harris poll

"We're out to destroy all candidates," Segretti said, "except McGovern."

that January, Muskie was by far the biggest threat to defeat Nixon in the election. Early in the year the Segretti boys began to focus on undermining Muskie's campaign. An open-to-the-public reception to meet Senator Muskie had been planned at the Manger Motel. A news release was sent out the preceding day on Muskie stationery stating that the informal rally had been transformed into a $1,000-per-person fundraising dinner and that 10,000 invitations had already been mailed out. If you didn't have $1,000 lying around and didn't receive an invitation, you weren't entitled to meet Muskie. Not many people greeted Senator Muskie on his first visit to Florida in January. And no one appreciated his elitist attitude. This was to be the year of the common folk. Naturally, the news release was phony.

The undermining did not stop there. In February, another falsified news release was sent out on Senator Henry "Scoop" Jackson's letterhead accusing Muskie of kidnapping congressional typewriters and other office equipment and bringing them to Florida for his campaign workers. The release listed the serial numbers of the equipment. The numbers were, in fact, correct. But the location of the equipment was not—they were still in Washington, where they belonged. The release, in addition to bruising Muskie's integrity even more, showed that the phony letter-writers had access to congressional purchasing records or to congressional inventories. Or else they were skillful burglars. At any rate, they were not the breed of kook usually found along political campaign trails.

By March, Muskie was fed up. He asked for an investigation by the U.S. Attorney General. Donald Segretti, aka Dan Simmons, was undaunted by the request and was already off to the next stop on the primary trail, playing a pernicious advance man. There seemed to be a limitless river of funds flowing to Kalmbach from CREEP, and there were primary battles yet to be fought. In Illinois, Indiana, and Wisconsin—crucial primaries for Muskie—college students were organized to hand out thousands of posters saying: A VOTE FOR MUSKIE IS A VOTE FOR BUSING." The issue of busing was probably the most sensitive in the Midwest.

Three days before the March 14 Florida primary, thousands of letters were mailed from St. Petersburg on Muskie stationery, topped with the Senator's picture. After describing his most winning attributes, the letter went on to say that Senator Henry Jackson had sired an illegitimate daughter in 1929 while still a high school student in Everett, Wisconsin, and was arrested as a homosexual in Washington, D.C. in 1955 and 1957. (The apparent change in Sen. Jackson's alleged sexual preferences went unexplained.)

The letter also said that primary contender Humphrey had "similar skeletons in his closet." He was arrested, said the letter, for drunken driving in Washington, D.C. in 1967. And if that were not enough to dissuade a prospective voter, the letter placed a call girl in the car at the time of the arrest. Their high Government posts kept these "revelations" out of the press, the letter explained dutifully.

The letter was phony, but it was effective. Thousands of people received the letter and by primary day almost everyone else eligible to vote in Florida had heard of its contents. If they thought Muskie, the alleged sender, was stooping to new lows in bad taste and poor judgement, then he would be hurt. If they thought his accusations were true, Jackson and Humphrey would be hurt. And if someone believed both, as some skeptics might, then all three candidates were smeared. That left Lindsay, Wallace, and McGovern to chose from and the attack squad had plans for the former two.

Flyers were handed out and posted on bulletin boards throughout the state, reading: "IF YOU LIKE HITLER, YOU'LL LOVE GEORGE WALLACE." (Florida has a large Jewish population.) All the flyers had an official John Lindsay seal on them. A reader either believed and hated Wallace—or disbelieved and scorned Lindsay. It is safe to say that neither gained any votes from the ploy.

Only McGovern went untouched by the political hatchet work. "We're out to destroy all candidates," Segretti told an Indiana worker, "except McGovern." Shortly thereafter, Charles Snider was contacted and offered a great job in Washington if he abandoned George Wallace. Snider was Wallace's campaign director. Snider said no thank you. The attempts to nominate McGovern continued.

"He recruited, coached, supplied, and paid $2,000," said one of Segretti's associates, referring to the organization of counter-demonstrators at Wallace, Muskie, and Humphrey rallies. The more troublesome, even violent, a rally, the more fearful the populace would be of a candidate who motivated such outbreaks. There were no outbreaks yet at Nixon events. Throughout his term there had been relative calm, especially for his public appearances. (The murder of four Kent State students, the assassination of Black Panther Fred Hampton, and the bombing slaughter in Indochina were not directly attributable to Nixon in most people's minds.)

That calm exterior would soon begin to crack. Shortly after the Watergate break-in, Segretti's name was brought up in the Justice Department's investigation of the Watergate raid, in connection with numerous long distance phone calls he received from Waterbugger Hunt. But the chief prosecutor, Deputy Attorney General Henry Petersen, saw no reason to probe into the Segretti connection. He said that an FBI investigation came to the same conclusion. L. Patrick Gray declared, "On the basis of information available... we need not go into the area of the Segretti sabotage operations." But for the moment, all was well with the Republic and the Republicans, and the senior Senator from South Dakota was heading for certain victory.

July 14 to July 30/1000%

McGovern. The name fell heavily upon the ears of the traditional Democratic party leadership, promising to further splinter a party already wounded by a long, bitter primary campaign. It was plain to millions that party reconciliation would take a great deal more than presidential candidate McGovern standing on the podium at the Miami convention, hand in hand with his former rivals and arms raised in anticipation of November victory.

It was almost as if the Democrats saw 1972 as no more than a catharsis after the climactic turmoil of 1968. Let the radicals have their reforms; let the blacks, the students, and the women have their say. For now, let the party champion the causes for which people have marched in the streets and then be done with it. From the start, it seemed as though the Democratic organization was conceding defeat in 1972.

In place of the old system of party support, McGovern could promise only the vote of something he called the "new constituency for change," a vaguely defined conglomerate of disaffected people, McGovern's version of "the silent majority." It never materialized. The night of McGovern's nomination, Senator Henry Jackson spoke with foreboding about the disaster engulfing his party. "Who ever heard of organized labor on the eve of a possible nomination by the Democratic party being in very strong opposition to the probable nominee? This never happened before."

On July 12, a new suspect identified only as Mr. X was mentioned in connection with the grand jury investigation taking place in Washington. The suspect, thought to have been a denizen of the White House, evidently had close ties with the mysterious E. Howard Hunt, who was still on the lam. Suddenly there were two Watergate mystery men, but not for long.

Hunt made a liar of his wife and turned up in Europe, agreeing to testify before Judge Sirica's grand jury, which he did on July 19. A court of appeals ordered lawyer Douglas Caddy to testify before the investigating grand jury or face up to eighteen months in jail. Caddy began answering Judge Sirica's questions about Hunt, his wife, and Mr. X. The heat was on.

July 22 newspaper reports revealed that G. Gordon Liddy, financial counsel to CREEP, had been fired by Mitchell a month earlier for refusing to answer FBI agents' questions about the Watergate break-in. Devan Shumway, public affairs director for CREEP, said that Liddy's firing was based on a committee policy under which any employee who did not cooperate with authorities was automatically let go. Liddy had good reason not to cooperate: He was Mr. X.

The connection to Liddy was made through Bell Telephone company records which showed that he had been in contact with Bernard L. Barker, one of the five Waterbuggers. Barker had made nine calls to an unlisted number in the finance office of CREEP. When questioned about those calls, Glenn J. Sedam, an attorney with whom Liddy shared the office, claimed no knowledge of them. FBI records showed that Barker made the calls to Liddy up to June 16, the day before the break-in. It was one of the lesser ironies of the Watergate case that the noose around master bugger Liddy's neck turned out to be a

telephone wire.

The grand jury gave Liddy eleven questions to answer on the bugging incident. He refused on the same grounds that Douglas Caddy had cited earlier in the month, attorney-client privilege. In this case, Liddy's client was the Committee to Re-elect the President, and his refusal to answer questions about campaign financing and about whether the clandestine Watergate operations were financed by CREEP cast a shadow of suspicion on Mr. Nixon's re-elect machine.

For the third time, Larry O'Brien asked President Nixon to appoint a special Watergate prosecutor. "John Mitchell's resignation had nothing to do with the alleged distress of his wife," O'Brien charged, "but everything to do with the fact that his operatives had been caught red-handed while attempting to spy on the Democratic party."

No one could accuse Larry O'Brien of missing the political opportunity the Watergate disclosures offered the Democrats, who were as badly in need of miracles as they were of money.

While McGovern professed unconcern at his poor showing in the polls, he could hardly sluff off the action of the AFL-CIO Committee for Political Education, which voted 27-3 not to endorse any presidential candidate for 1972. It was the first time the AFL-CIO, the nation's largest labor organization, took a "neutral" stand. Even so, there was some hope that AFL-CIO president George Meany's hatred of McGovern could be cured through the intercession of such old party regulars as Humphrey, Kennedy, and Muskie. It was a temporary disaster; the permanent disaster took place five days later.

Senator Eagleton, McGovern's last-minute choice as Democratic Vice-presidential candidate, revealed on July 25 that he had been hospitalized three times during the 1960s for nervous exhaustion and depression. The Senator went through a program of repeated electric shock therapy and tranquilizers for the illnesses, he confessed. Earlier that day, Eagleton informed George McGovern of his past medical history, and the candidate—true to his promise of an open campaign—asked Eagleton to hold a press conference to inform the country. Eagleton had made no mention of his medical history when he conferred with

McGovern on July 13 before his selection as the Vice-presidential nominee. He disclosed it only after the story was published by the Knight newspaper chain.

Knight's Washington bureau reporters, Robert S. Boyd and Clark Hoyt had dug out the facts after receiving an anonymous tip detailing Eagleton's past history of mental illness. Who the tipster was may never be known, but Eagleton was a public official at the time he was treated, so the matter would have been kept in the strictest confidence. Of the few who knew, most of them were at this time in McGovern's camp—although word did not apparently reach McGovern. Another man who knew was not in the McGovern camp. He was John Ehrlichman, President Nixon's chief domestic adviser. Ehrlichman had received an FBI file containing the candidate's medical history at least three weeks before the tipster got on the phone with Knight newspapers.

Initially, McGovern felt that Eagleton's past would make no difference to his candidacy. He told a press conference he was behind his runningmate "1000 percent." Controversy changes men's minds, and Eagleton became increasingly determined to remain on the ticket while McGovern backed away from his pledge of support. Party leaders around the country called for Eagleton's resignation from the ticket and serious doubts were cast on McGovern's powers of judgement. How could a man with a history of problems even be considered for a post "a heartbeat away from the presidency?"

The test came on Sunday, July 30, when Eagleton appeared on the television news program "Face the Nation." The Democratic party had offered to buy him half an hour of prime TV time to explain himself, much as the Republicans had bought Vice-presidential candidate Richard Nixon prime time in 1952 to explain away some dubious campaign financing practices that had almost resulted in his being dropped as President Eisenhower's running mate. Eagleton preferred the question and answer format.

It was a bad choice. One member of the panel of eminent journalists was syndicated columnist Jack Anderson, who earlier that week had accused Eagleton of being arrested for drunken driving in Missouri in 1966. Anderson publicly apologized to Eagleton on the air, but the barrage of attacks had already done its damage.

Half an hour later, Democratic National Chairwoman Jean Westwood went on "Meet the Press" recommending that Senator Eagleton be dropped from the Democratic ticket.

The next day, explaining that he had no desire to "divide the Democratic Party, which already has too many divisions," Eagleton announced his withdrawal from the Democratic ticket. McGovern, while claiming that he had no doubts at all about Eagleton's health and suitability for public office, accepted his running mate's withdrawal because "public debate over Senator Eagleton's past medical history continues to divert attention away from the great national issues that need to be discussed." No one believed Eagleton's resignation was voluntary and McGovern's see-sawing self-contradiction in the affair robbed him of public confidence which he would never recover.

On August 1, newspapers around the country blared Eagleton's announcement in banner front-page headlines. In the Washington *Post*, beneath the fold on the same page, a story appeared that a $25,000 check given to Republican finance chairman Maurice Stans by Kenneth Dahlberg, the Republican's Midwest finance chairman, had mysteriously ended up in Watergate suspect Bernard Barker's Miami bank account. It was the first direct link between the Committee to Re-elect the President and the funding of the Watergate break-in. The story was a bit upstaged that day, but would soon be pushing its way into lead slot on page one, along with countless other campaign financing tales.

The Mexican Connection

An interesting thing about Republicans and Democrats who contributed to Richard Nixon's presidential campaigns is that they often didn't want anybody to know who they were. One heavyweight who wanted to preserve his anonymity was Greek shipping magnate Aristotle Onassis, who contributed $100,000 to Nixon's 1968 treasury. The donation was made in the name of "Mr. and Mrs. Aristotle Onassis." There is no reason to think Jacqueline Kennedy Onassis knew about the contribution.

Onassis wasn't alone in trying to conceal his political persuasions. In 1968, other Nixon donors were invited to make out their checks to Barnes Champ Advertising, a dummy agency which compliantly listed the contributions as payment for "service rendered." Besides protecting the anonymity, this provided the wealthy with a handy tax dodge.

A similar front was engineered for New Jersey Republican Governor William T. Cahill's successful 1968 campaign. As a result of later investigations, prominent New Jersey Republicans Nelson Gross and Joseph McCrane were indicted for illegally writing off political contributions as business expenses.

Indictments were more the exception than the rule in California, where United States Attorney Harry Steward, a political appointee, quashed a similar investigation into Nixon re-election campaign spending.

Rules governing campaign contributions changed even more radically in 1972 when Congress enacted the new Fair Campaign Practices Act, effective April 7, 1972. Lauded as the first comprehensive revision of campaign finance legislation in forty six years, the new law was intended to be a major improvement over the loophole-ridden Corrupt Practices Act of 1925. Congress designed the new bill to provide the public with a complete accounting of campaign finances and to eliminate at least the most blatant political payoffs.

In November 1971, Congress decided that the practice of the government of dishing out favors to large contributors, especially big business and big labor, had exceeded the bounds of mere "politics as usual." A Democratic-sponsored amendment to a tax bill would allow each taxpayer to indicate on his income tax return whether he wanted the government to channel one dollar of his tax payment into a nonpartisan campaign fund. Money from the fund would be used to pay campaign expenses of both major party presidential nominees up to the limit of $20.4 million, and expenses of a third party nominee up to $6.3 million. Republicans called this unfair, and pushed a compromise accepted by the Democrats in which the $1 could be designated for a specific party. But Clark MacGregor, chief White House lobbyist at the time, told a press conference that Nixon "would necessarily have to consider the possibility of a veto" because the President considered the proposal "unwise and irresponsible." No further explanation was offered and the amendment was killed by President Nixon (although later the Congress enacted it anyway).

Congress then initiated the Fair Campaign Practices Act, which would ostensibly take the privacy out of the cozy contributor-candidate relationship. The bill required all contributions of more than $100 to be publicly listed, giving each contributor's name, address, and business affiliation.

The new law was a bomb dropped in wealthy backyards across America, and it was devilment for fundraisers in both parties. The boys at CREEP reacted to the new law by sending cadres of open-handed Republicans out into the countryside exhorting donors to beat the April 7 effective date of the law. This fundraising blitz violated not only the spirit of the new law, in some cases the letter of the old law. And even with advance warning, many wealthy Republicans were just not able to move fast enough.

One foot-dragging Republican was Richard Nixon. The President has ten days to sign a piece of legislation after he receives it from Congress.

Though Nixon publicly urged swift enactment of the campaign practices act, his nonactions belied his words. The bill stated that a new disclosure provision would go into effect two months after being signed by the President. It was sent to him on Jan. 28, 1972. While he spoke of the necessity and righteousness of the bill, Nixon did not get around to actually signing it until the last possible day, Feb. 7, assigning the cut-off date as April 7. Nixon's stall allowed his fund-raisers an important ten extra days to gobble up donations whose donors could remain anonymous. If the source of a contribution were not known to the public then no relationship could be proven between a particular executive action and the contributor-beneficiary. The Mexican Connection was but one example of how far contributors would go to remain anonymous.

The virginity of Republican privacy was to be even more crudely raped after the June 17 arrests of McCord and four Cuban-born Americans by Washington police. When authorities emptied the pockets and hotel rooms of the burglars, they discovered fifty three crisp, consecutively numbered $100 bills. To Washington police, this was a bit unusual. U.S. Treasury Records traced the money to the Republic National Bank of Miami and the account of Bernard Barker's real estate firm.

April bank records showed that Barker had deposited a series of checks totalling $114,000. There was, however, no explaining the source of the mysterious checks. Barker's attorney lamely claimed the money was part of a real estate transaction which reverted to him when the deal fell through. But the U.S. Attorney wasn't buying it.

There was only one clue. A bank vice-president remembered balking at accepting a $250,000 check because he couldn't verify the endorsement. Barker resourcefully, but illegally, had used his power as notary to validate the check and deposited it in the Barker Associates account.

The signature on the check was that of Kenneth Dahlberg. The name meant nothing until Washington Post reporter Bob Woodward tracked it down in the Post's morgue. Woodward dusted off a five-year-old photograph of a Kenneth Dahlberg standing with Hubert Humphrey and several long distance phone calls later, Woodward found Dahlberg, a millionaire hearing-aid manufacturer. The Post disclosure prompted the General Accounting Office to conduct an audit of CREEP's activity and it

spurred House Banking and Currency Committee Chairman Wright Patman to initiate open hearings on the matter. Those two probes were to be thwarted but the tide of suspicion was rising.

Dahlberg admitted the $250,000 check was his—a campaign contribution he had personally handed to Maurice Stans. For the first time there was evidence that the Watergate burglary had been financed with money collected for the re-election of Richard Nixon.

Dahlberg said he came by the money on a Florida golf course, where it had been handed to him by Minnesota millionaire and soybean king Dwayne Andreas. If Andreas had wanted anonymity, his cover was blown. Andreas was chief executive officer of Archer Daniels Midland, one of the largest—and least known—American corporations. He was also a close friend of Hubert Humphrey, Thomas Dewey, and other politicians. In fact, Andreas was always careful to make friends with people in high government positions. One way to stay in business, for Andreas, was to stay close to people in power. As one of the country's ten largest grain exporters, he is in a business which is one of the most closely regulated by the federal government. It pays to have friends in Washington on both sides of the aisle and it doesn't pay to have campaign contributions disclosed.

In 1964 Andreas contributed to Lyndon Johnson's presidential campaign. After the election was over, Andreas won approval of a charter for his National City Bank. But money knows no political boundaries. 1972 was shaping up as the year of the elephant, so on April 5, two days before the campaign contribution law took effect, Andreas got on the tube to Dahlberg and offered the Republicans $25,000 which he would leave in a safe deposit box at the Sea View Hotel in Bal Harbour, Florida. Dahlberg claimed he tried to pick the money up on April 7 in compliance with the new law, but he did not arrive at the hotel until after hours. So, he said, he made another appointment for April 9. Even though all political donations over $100 then had to be declared, CREEP refused to betray Andreas' anonymity on the grounds that the contribution *pledge* had been made before April 7.

When the House Banking and Currency Committee staff found out about the check, it also discovered that Andreas was granted a very fishy Federal Reserve Bank charter less than three months after the $25,000 contribution had been made. The Committee report commented that the charter was approved in record time, especially "considering the fact that the shopping center in which the bank is to be located has not been constructed and apparently the bank would not be ready until 1974-75."

Barker had more than $25,000 to spend on espionage. He had $114,000. The other $89,000 was traced to four checks drawn on the Banco Internacional S.A. in Mexico City by a wealthy lawyer named Manuel Ogarrio Daguerre. Ogarrio's law firm, Creel and Ogarrio, until recently operated out of a suite of offices in the same building as the Banco Internacional branch from which the checks originated. Ogarrio represented a number of U.S. corporations, not the least of which was the Gulf Resources and Chemical of Houston, president of which is Robert Allen, who was Texas finance chairman for CREEP.

Allen was part of the Republican monopoly game which benefitted from CREEP's money laundering operations. By sending contributions into Mexico, the money was cleansed of the donor's identity. Allen said he "felt that under the law I had every right to expect and enjoy the right of privacy and full anonymity. It was for this reason, as well as convenience, that I arranged to have the contribution delivered from Mexico."

Allen donated a total of $100,000. Along with other Texas donations, it was collected by William Liedke, President of the Pennzoil United oil and gas empire, and Ray Winchester, Pennzoil's vice-president for public relations. Liedke just happened to be the Southwestern U.S. finance chairman of CREEP.

Liedke and Winchester would send the money to Ogarrio in Mexico City. There identical sums were withdrawn in the form of U.S. dollar drafts and made out to Ogarrio. Once "laundered," Liedke and Winchester would bring the money back across the border into Houston. An estimated $750,000 in political contributions were washed in this way.

When Finance Committee to Re-elect the President Chairman Maurice Stans was originally asked about the border running, he denied it was taking place. Stans, always ready to give himself the benefit of the doubt, said he believed the wetback greenbacks were actually Mexican contributions. Stans did not seem concerned with the fact that foreign contributions are illegal, disclosed or undisclosed. The check writing was on the wall for yet another associate of the President.

When $89,000 of Allen's money reached CREEP, it was added to $600,000 in Texas contributions that had already come to Washington through Pennzoil's good graces. When it left courier Ray Winchester's suitcase, it was dumped into Maurice Stans' safe. Stans said he did not know what was in that safe. From the safe, the $89,000 went to Liddy, one of the CIA musketeers who supervised the Watergate burglary.

But what connection did Robert Allen and Gulf Chemical have in all this? All Allen said he wanted was a nice quiet arrangement—no fireworks, no espionage, no publicity. What he got was an investigation by the Internal Revenue Service which was interested in finding out whether the federal law against corporation contributions was violated (Allen says it was his own money). A Houston grand jury wanted to investigate him, and the Justice Department subpoenaed his bank records.

After suffering these twentieth century trials of Job, Allen finally asked for his $100,000 back for "personal reasons." With regret, Allen said he never would have donated the money if he knew how CREEP would use it. The Republicans gave it back. They could afford to.

Money had been coming into CREEP at a rate of $100,000 a day during the summer, more in the autumn. By convention time CREEP reported $45 million had been contributed. That's what they reported. A month before, the Democrats were displaying their campaign poverty level on a network television fund-raising marathon. They enlisted everyone from Sally Struthers to the Supremes to beg Americans to pledge any amount of money at all to "preserve the two-party system."

The final tally showed the Democrats with $14 million and the Republicans with at least a record $58 million.

Six months after the re-election, those members of CREEP who had not quit, been fired or been indicted were still wondering what to do with $4.7 million remaining in their bottomless treasury. Small wonder they opposed Congress' attempt to limit the spending of a candidate to $20 million.

The Mexico connection—Andreas-Dahlberg-Allen-Liedke-Ogarrio-Winchester-Stans-Waterbugger Barker—accounts for $750,000 in Republican funds. Of the total the Republicans raised $58 million in 1972 an estimated $15 million was obtained before April 7. How much of that went to finance blackmail, espionage, and burglary? How much can it cost to re-elect the President?

Aug. 1 to Aug. 23/Moon Over Miami

Strange events attended this business of re-electing Richard Nixon. $25,000 in soybean money traveled 10,000 miles and slipped into the Miami bank account of a real estate broker arrested inside Democratic National Committee Headquarters with bugs in his pockets. One at least would have expected responsible Nixon campaign officials to set such curiosities straight with a press conference or two.

That was not the case. After the travelogue of Kenneth Dahlberg's check became public, finance chairman Stans was reportedly "angered and frustrated." When finally questioned about the check by federal investigators, the former cabinet member took the honorable course of action—he admitted he had received the check from Dahlberg, but maintained that was the last he saw of it.

Stans told the investigators that upon accepting the check he gave it to Nixon campaign treasurer Hugh Sloan. Sloan, apparently, then gave the well-traveled check to financial counsel G. Gordon Liddy. According to Stans, Liddy exchanged the check for cash with some unidentified individual for some unknown reason, and cash was deposited in the Nixon committee's treasury.

Stans, the man responsible for President Nixon's campaign financing, couldn't explain to federal investigators how those transactions were managed. One might call that bouncing the check, or passing the buck.

(Instead, the onus of explanation fell upon newly appointed campaign director Clark MacGregor, who hadn't worked for the committee when the questionable check was received or while Liddy was financial counsel. Nevertheless, he had an answer. In an interview with reporters, MacGregor claimed that Liddy spent the money to investigate how radicals planned to disrupt the Republican National Convention. "Some campaign funds were used on the initiative of Liddy for the purpose of determining what to do if the crazies made an attack on the President at the convention," MacGregor claimed. "Liddy decided to spend money to determine what the crazies planned."

As Republicans prepared to attend their August convention to nominate Richard Nixon for certain victory in November, the Watergate affair would not go away. It was a blackhead marring the cosmetic veneer of the campaign for the biggest landslide in American history.

There were other reversals in the regent's game plan. The long-awaited trial of Daniel Ellsberg and Anthony Russo, the two men accused of releasing the Pentagon Papers to the public, was postponed by order of Supreme Court Justice William O. Douglas. The trial, in which the government hoped to demonstrate that men couldn't release secret papers without paying a penalty, was delayed when the Justice Department admitted it had monitored the telephone of a defense attorney in the course of what it said was an unrelated "foreign intelligence" wiretap. The government was not about to release the transcript of the conversation. It was the first time in judicial history that a trial was blocked by a Supreme Court Justice after a jury had been sworn in. It would be many months before the government could renew the prosecution.

Meanwhile the Democrats had selected R. Sargent Shriver to succeed Eagleton. Shriver was a good choice as McGovern's running mate. Related to the Kennedys by marriage, first director of the Peace Corps, former commander of the war on poverty, he was a seasoned liberal. But he had been fifth on McGovern's list of substitute Vice-presidential candidates. McGovern's inability to find someone suitable who would agree to run with him was laughable.

And it hurt. While the McGovern campaign deteriorated, Nixon ardently courted the labor support McGovern had failed to attract, exploiting George Meany's anti-McGovern fervor. The Watergate was the only hope for the Democrats.

(Early in August, the Democrats attempted to take depositions (statements in place of testimony) for their $1 million law suit from White House staffers, CREEP campaign officials, and the five Waterbuggers. They also vigorously protested before presiding U.S. District Court Judge Charles Richey when former White House legal counsel Colson attempted to have himself represented by Justice Department lawyers. The Democrats charged conflict of interest. Richey agreed and overruled Colson's request.

The same week, the Committee to Re-elect the President filed its mandatory report with the General Accounting Office listing the contributions it had received since April 7. CREEP had hoped the report would clear the air about its finances, but the only disclosure of real significance was that Stans expected to raise about $35 million dollars overall, making the Nixon re-election effort the most affluent in history. By contrast, Senator McGovern expected to raise only $2.7 million dollars.

But the Democrats soon seemed to have won a decisive victory in their pursuit of the Watergate. Judge Richey denied a petition by CREEP attorneys to delay the $1 million civil suit until after the November election. Edward Bennett Williams, the attorney for the Democrats, said he would question Stans and Mitchell, among others. Those statements, every reporter in the country knew, would leak like a sieve. A few days later, an elated Larry O'Brien added at least thirteen more Republicans to the list of those from whom he wanted depositions.

A *Time* article released only days after Richey's ruling in the civil suit revealed that Democratic headquarters in the Watergate were bugged for almost a month before the June 17 break-in. According to *Time*, the men apprehended in the Watergate were removing the bugging devices, not installing them. The article maintained that phone calls from Democratic central were monitored from a room in the Howard Johnson's Motor Lodge across the street from the Watergate.

The operation was supposedly organized by the re-election committee's "security intelligence squad," itself a relative of the White House Plumbers. They were now doing a lot more than plugging leaks to the media. The article named Hunt, Liddy, Mr. X, and Robert Mardian, former assistant attorney general in charge of the internal security division and now working for CREEP. In response, Mardian said, "Anyone who says that Bob Mardian was investigating or knew about the bugging is full of it." At least that's the way family newspapers printed his quote.

Against this background, a carefully orchestrated and well-rehearsed Republican National Convention came to order attended by an obedient group of theater-goers who knew how the play would end.

Obedience was the only word for it. The Republican Party and the Committee to Re-elect the President programmed the entire event. They even went so far as to write scripts for the Convention. Conscious of free national TV time, the party leadership had decided that all the boring procedural business should be handled during the daylight sessions. Evening prime time could then be devoted to cinematic adulations and verbal plaudits of Nixon. It was the Four More Years Show, a three-day gala media event. The Democrats, who squandered prime time with floor fights, had played it dumb.

The Republican convention was so well choreographed, there was little or nothing to discuss. The only issue that created controversy was the formulation of rules for selecting delegates to the 1976 convention. Richard M. Nixon was officially pronounced the Republican candidate for President of the United States on August 22. All but one of the 1,348 votes at the convention went to Nixon. One lone dissenting vote was cast for California Representative Paul McCloskey, who had dared to challenge both the President's domestic and foreign policies (and who would suffer for such a display of independence). The nomination was planned to end just before airtime for the late evening news. It did.

The only blemish on the Convention was the demonstrators who had come to Miami in angry protest of everything the Nixon Administration stood for. Unlike the Democratic Convention the previous month, where would-be protestors were dubbed non-delegates and allowed to make themselves heard within the convention hall itself, the August demonstrators were perceived as radicals, subversives, and hippies who sought to overthrow the government of the United States through violence. "Crazies," to use MacGregor's word. On the night of Nixon's nomination, 200 youths, many wearing death masks in protest of the Vietnam war, were arrested for blocking the entrance to the convention. The next and last night, Miami police arrested over 1,000 protestors, using bilious masses of tear gas within sniff and choke of many delegates. The incidents which provoked the use of gas were few, sparked by small splinter groups. In all, the affair did not live up to the prognostication of MacGregor and company.

The real story of the Convention's final night was not out in the streets, but inside the convention where candidate Nixon was being feted in full Republican regalia. After numerous congratulatory demonstrations of loyalty by delegates and notables, the President made his acceptance speech, setting forth his vision of an America unchanged by time. "It has become fashionable in recent years to point up what is wrong with our American system," Nixon said. "The critics contend it is so unfair, so corrupt, so unjust, that we should tear it down and substitute a new system in its place. I totally disagree. I believe in the American system." It was a great moment.

To Be The President

When Richard Nixon finally captured the star of his life's work, he wanted to leave behind the petty meanness that dirties the hands of lesser politicians. Nixon had already conquered the Republican Party by winning their presidential nomination three times. He had already conquered the Democrats by defeating Hubert Humphrey in 1968. The only thing left for Nixon to conquer was America.

Nixon wanted to transform the country and stamp it with his own lasting impression. He wanted to triumph again, but in no ordinary way. Nixon wanted and promised to bring a nation divided by racism, poverty, and war together. As a politician, Nixon had outlasted the opposition; now as a statesman, he wanted to survive the litmus test of history. Nixon understood that time itself would be the umpire in this final inning of his public life. Like all the games he played in before, Nixon wanted to win this one too. But in some ways, perhaps, he wanted to win too hard.

Nixon had tasted surprise defeat in the 1960 Presidential campaign and in the 1962 California gubernatorial race and he didn't like it. His political future had appeared finished, when only a moment before it had appeared long.

But that turnaround is precisely what made Nixon's political resurrection such an extraordinary triumph. Nixon was able to win over not only his enemies, but over himself as well.

Using his New York law practice as a base, Nixon traveled the country extensively after his abortive California race, making speeches along the way. In 1964, he campaigned for Barry Goldwater, who ended up in the same political graveyard where many people thought Dick Nixon was buried.

But Nixon never really abandoned the political arena. During his self-announced exile, Nixon finagled, jockeyed, and built up a bank account of favors which he would cash in at the right time in 1968. Nixon also knew there would be debts that other people would want to collect when he became President.

Nixon wanted to leave his past behind! He wanted to forget the image of a loser, the picture of a red-baiting freshman congressman, and Herblock's cartoon of a seedy, long-chinned Dick Tracy who needed a complete overhaul in the barber shop. But Nixon wasn't able to completely escape the scourge of his past, anymore than he could escape himself.

In 1968, Nixon cashed in on the favors and a GOP suffering from a vacuum of leadership. Republican liberals could not arrive at a consensus candidate for President. The conservatives in the party had been so thoroughly defeated in 1964 that they were presented no meaningful competition. Besides, the long-suffering Nixon had earned the right to be President.

What Nixon offered the Republican Party and the country was experience and efficiency. Nixon presented himself as a world statesman who would heal the nation's wounds and bring peace in Vietnam. In domestic affairs, Nixon called for a New Majority that would end or substantially reduce the friction that split the country into two worlds. Kevin Philips, author of Nixon's victory strategy, said that hawkish attitudes combined with less emphasis on integration could permanently steal the South from the Democrats and Wallace. Philips believed that disenchanted blue collar workers and Western GOP stalwarts could be bonded together to form the cornerstone of a permanent coalition in American politics. Nixon could become the Republican FDR.

The brain trust was only one element in Nixon's campaign team. He also recruited a crew of sophisticated technicians from Southern California who would specialize in public relations. Since the famous 1960 Kennedy television debates, Nixon felt uneasy with the mass media. This ghost of his past caused him to hire H.R. Haldeman and John Ehrlichman to improve his relationship with the press. In this technical category, Nixon needed fidelity and hard work and both Haldeman and Ehrlichman were the very acme of parochial devotion. Politically inexperienced, they were masters at manipulating the television image. Ironically, it was Nixon, the man who promoted himself as the great exponent of American fundamentalism built on self-reliance, who triumphed so resoundingly in the 1968 and 1972 elections as the master of the electronic media.

There was a third factor in Nixon's strategy, but it involved debts which Nixon would have to pay off as President. Nixon recognized that he had to neutralize the GOP conservative wing. It had been humbled in 1964, but not permanently handicapped. John Mitchell and Maurice Stans were characteristic of the Conservatives' bruised feelings. They believed the country was in serious danger from the Left. They were suspicious of militant blacks, hippies, Great Society programs, antiwar critics, and very often the Washington *Post* and the New York *Times*. If Nixon thought he left Helen Gahagan Douglas and Alger Hiss behinbehind, Mitchell's Wall Street cronies would persuade him he was wrong.

But even if Nixon wanted to abandon red-baiting, there were other, almost permanent ties with the past that he could never cut. One of those was Nixon's business partner and best friend Bebe Rebozo. In almost every way, the Nixon-Rebozo relationship was an example of how little Richard Nixon had changed. Cuban-born Rebozo was a child of relative poverty. At the start of World War II, he was a gas station attendant, but with a wartime tire shortage, he went into the recapping business and started his financial empire. It is interesting to note that Rebozo started his tire business with a loan from a friend who happened to be on the local Office of Price Administration tire board, a clear conflict of interest according to OPA regulations at the time.

Nixon and Rebozo first met in 1951. They became close friends probably because both are quiet and withdrawn, yet successful and ambitious. In 1960, Rebozo established the Key Biscayne Bank and is still president of it. Richard Nixon opened the first savings account. In 1968 the bank became a haven for stolen stocks channeled there by organized crime. According to *Newsday*, even Rebozo believed there was something suspicious about the stocks because he told an FBI agent that he had called Nixon's brother Donald to establish their validity. Subsequently, Rebozo sold them for cash.

About the same time in 1968, Rebozo, who has amassed a fortune through Florida real estate dealing, applied for and received a loan from the federal Small Business Administration to build a shopping center. The chief Miami officer of the SBA was a close friend of Rebozo and a stock-

holder in the Key Biscayne Bank. This led *Newsday* to denounce the SBA for "wheeling and dealing . . . on Rebozo's behalf." Rebozo leased his shopping center to members of the rightwing Cuban exile community. Rebozo also had business dealings with "Big Al" Polizzi, a convicted black marketeer named by the Federal Bureau of Narcotics as "one of the most influential members of the underworld in the United States."

As testimony of Nixon's inability to leave his past behind, Rebozo invested his good friend's money in a Florida real estate transaction called Fisher's Island Inc. According to public record, Nixon invested $185,891 in 1962 which returned him $371,782 in 1969. Nixon doubled his money but none of the other stockholders did—Fisher's Island stock did not go up a single penny. But President Nixon signed a bill paving the way for a $7 million Federal project for improvements to the port of Miami, where Fisher Island is located.

According to Jack Anderson, Rebozo's real estate confederates ranged from the President to small fry like Watergate burglar Bernard Barker. Rebozo, like Nixon, represented the new money interests which emerged so powerfully following World War II. While they were self-made men, they were also self-serving.

During his Administration, Nixon introduced the White House to his own brand of Orange County conservative chic. Pablo Casals, Leonard Bernstein, Beaujolais Fraise, and the Washington *Post* were not exactly what Nixon wanted in his living room. Nixon was applauded for wholesomeness when he cultivated Johnny Cash, Fred Waring and the Pennsylvanians, *Readers Digest*, and Cadillacs. Billy Graham began making regular White House calls and Sunday non-denominational prayer meetings became an institution. The emphasis was on the nuclear family. Two daughters, for example, equal two White House weddings equal two respectable Marine-crewcut boys equal two prompt (though cozy) military tours of duty. The all-American President, of course, needed an all-American Family. Nixon wanted to be the grandfather the country had sought since Eisenhower died.

Nixon's accomplished media technicians had successfully managed to popularize the new image of a statesman above reproach and beyond political shenanigans. Watergate was a blot on that image. It was all the more shocking to those who bought what Haldeman and Ehrlichman had merchandised. Nixon had wanted to project himself as being above partisan politics to win history's final prize. But Watergate sucked at his heels like mud, even as he accepted the Republican nomination for 1972.

Chapter II

Aug. 24 to Aug. 28/Hardnosing Through

The lights became dim and then dark. The podium stood empty behind the clear bullet-proof shield. A few hours before thousands of ecstatic people thronged the convention hall floor, now only masses of crumpled paper, the remains of popped balloons, and upright placards identifying vanished state delegations were left amidst the disarray of folding chairs. They were the only evidence that something momentous had happened there. Outside, as the Atlantic Ocean gave birth to the sun, the last traces of tear gas drifted over the beach, out to sea.

The Republican Convention was over.

The end of the convention marked the beginning of something else. The flood of campaign news unrelated to the Miami conventions was free to flow onto the front pages. The flood had now entered the vernacular as Watergate, to the delight of headline scribes. Watergate opened a reservoir of bitterness in the man who a few hours before had stood at the high-water mark of a long political career. A new series of Watergate disclosures began on the final day of the convention. A little-known, recently adopted U.S. District Court rule required criminal trials involving "protracted, difficult, or widely publicized cases" to begin within sixty days after an indictment was handed down. Watergate was such a case, but, to the relief of the Republicans, it seemed less than likely that indictments controlled by Justice Department officials

would be returned before September 6. The trial of the men accused in the bugging conspiracy would probably not take place until after the November elections.

Meanwhile, back at Credibility Gap, campaign finance chairman Stans was accused of blocking the release of a General Accounting Office audit of Republican campaign finances. The audit, which the GAO, a Congressional watchdog agency, originally scheduled for release on August 22, proved to be an embarrassment to Stans and the R publicans.Stans reportedly made a telephone call one hour before the audit was to be released to Phillip S. Hughes, director of the GAO elections unit, asking him not to release anything politically sensitive while the Republican Convention was taking place. The GAO complied and rescheduled the document's release.

But even before the convention delegates left Miami Beach, Kenneth Dahlberg was called from a high-level campaign meeting in Nixon's Miami hotel headquarters to testify about the mysterious $25,000 dollar check he gave Stans. While confirming Stans' account of the transfer of funds to the satisfaction of investigators for the Florida State Attorney, he made one admission indicating that Bernard Barker, the ultimate recipient of the check, forged a notary seal on it to cash it.

The controversy of Watergate caught up with the President as he conferred with campaign advisers in

Miami. Could Nixon possibly escape the issue as he embarked on an initial campaign tour of Illinois, Michigan and California?

Efforts to expose the truth about what was going on inside the Nixon campaign gained momentum. A public interest lawsuit filed against CREEP by consumer advocate Ralph Nader charged that large campaign contributions given by various milk lobbies in 1971 were responsible for the rise in federal milk price supports. And, adding an insult to the injury, Nixon appointed Stans to chairman of the Republican Party finance committee, in addition to his CREEP post, despite the attacks on his credibility. Stans announced that he hoped to up the election ante, spending $45 million on Nixon's re-election effort. The $1 million lawsuit brought by the Democrats against CREEP had reached its pretrial hearings. Judge Richey, announcing that he hoped to begin the suit before the November elections, suggested that facts were being withheld in the case. "I think there is a suggestion implicit in all this that if something is not done by this court to bring this matter to a head one way or the other, the integrity of the courts may become subject to question. The integrity of the entire governmental process may become subject to question," Richey stated.

Some problematic questions were beginning to be asked. Why, for example, did Dwayne Andreas receive a federal bank charter for the Ridgedale National Bank in the Minnetonka shopping center near Minneapolis only ninety days after he gave $25,000 earmarked for the Nixon campaign to Kenneth Dahlberg? How did Dahlberg, who coincidentally held a financial interest in Andreas' bank, explain why the charter was granted so quickly, when it normally takes at least six months?

In response to the perplexing questions, only denials were forthcoming from the man in charge of Nixon's campaign financing. Maurice Stans went so far as to swear under oath that he had no knowledge of how $114,000 in CREEP campaign contributions were routed into Bernard Barker's bank account.

At least one government agency, the General Accounting Office, was willing to talk about Stans' activity. When the GAO released its overdue audit on August 26, the words were there in black and white. "Apparent and possible violations" of the Federal Election Campaign Act, involving around $350,000, had been committed by the Finance Committee to Re-elect the President.

The GAO cited the finance committee's failure to keep an accounting of Dahlberg's $25,000 check and failing to report the contribution given four days after the election law took effect. The audit also cited the lack of accounting for $89,000 in campaign funds that somehow went through a Mexican bank, straight to Barker in Miami. Mentioned too, was the balance of some $350,000 in cash deposited on May 25 in the bank account of the Media Committee to Re-elect the President.

True to the game plan apparent throughout the campaign, Stans didn't react to the GAO charge by offering an explanation. Rather, livid with anger, the former commerce secretary counter-attacked, charging the GAO with gross inaccuracies and suggesting they do some investigating of Democratic financing. In a statement released to the press, Stans charged that "the report reaches false and unwarranted conclusions. It is incomplete and inaccurate and it disregards evidence documenting the Finance Committee's compliance with the law." Stans refused further comment on what that evidence might be, however.

Instead, the finance director maintained that any possible violations of the Election Campaign Act were either minor or technical. He welcomed the opportunity to convey to the Justice Department the data that GAO had ignored, he said.

Attorney General Richard Kleindienst said in an August 28 interview with the Washington *Post*, that the Justice Department's investigation of the Watergate affair would be "the most extensive, thorough, and comprehensive investigation since the assassination of President Kennedy." The attorney general promised that when the investigation was completed "no credible, fair-minded person is going to be able to say that we whitewashed or dragged our feet on it."

It was significant that someone in authority in the Nixon administration was beginning to talk somewhat candidly about Watergate. But Senator McGovern's political coordinator Frank Mankiewicz, angry that a special prosecutor wasn't appointed by Nixon for the case, said simply that Kleindienst's probe was like sending "a fox to find out what goes on in the chicken coup."

Richard Kleindienst's integrity had never been in question. Everything else about him had.

"At first, I couldn't figure out whether he was a clown, or really brilliant," is how one congressional aide sized him up. Most people had the same problem even after they got to know Kleindienst well. Just when they thought they knew which way he was headed, he would turn around and run full speed in the opposite direction.

While Richard Nixon surrounded himself with former ad men and polished corporate slickers whose principal qualifications for office were an ability to see what Richard Nixon saw and do what Richard Nixon did, Kleindienst was an exception. He was a militant Goldwaterite and had directed Senator Barry Goldwater's unsuccessful bid for President in 1964. That same year, Kleindienst ran for governor of Arizona and lost. Obviously he was not a Nixonian and he was a tough, seasoned politician.

After growing up in Winslow, Arizona, where he coalesced blacks and chicanos to elect him high school president, he went to Harvard University on a full scholarship and headed up the Conversative Club. After graduating Harvard Law School, he returned to Democratic Arizona and won a seat in the State House of Representatives as a staunch Republican conservative. After gaining the not unwelcome image as a leader of Arizona conservatism, in 1950 he joined the National Urban League, a highly liberal group that was fighting for integration in those pre-civil rights days. Kleindienst's career seemed full of contradictions.

Despite his reputation as a strong civil libertarian, he was once quoted as saying that law-breaking demonstrators should be "rounded up and put in detention camps." He later denied the statement and substituted, "I believe that not only is the First Amendment right of free speech the most important right we have, but I also believe it important that the government, to the extent it can, should create and maintain an atmosphere where people feel free to exercise that right."

The speaker of those eloquent words stood at the helm of the illegal incarceration of approximately 10,000 demonstrators and assorted citizens and journalists at the May Day protest celebration in Washington, D.C. in 1971. The corralling of thousands of persons whom officials knew had broken no law whatsoever was subsequently declared unconstitutional. Then a deputy attorney general, Kleindienst rationalized the action by saying that he and Attorney General John Mitchell feared that "mob rule" would prevail. He also approved whole-heartedly of Mitchell's illegal wiretapping of "domestic subversives" without court orders.

Within weeks of his appointment as deputy attorney general in 1968, Kleindienst ordered everyone in the Justice Department to fill out daily time sheets—and that meant everyone. It came as a shock to the habitually lax Justice Department lawyers, who had heard that the new deputy attorney general was "an easy-going guy."

His relationship with boss John Mitchell was also rife

with apparent contradictions. While working with Mitchell on Nixon's 1968 campaign, Kliendienst made a deep impression; he became the number two man in the Justice Department immediately after Mitchell was appointed attorney general. But their styles differed drastically. As austere, methodical, and private as Mitchell was, Kleindienst was equally informal, impulsive, and gregarious. "Candid" was another adjective frequently attached to Kleindienst, and not always in a complimentary sense.

At a press conference after the May Day celebration, when Mitchell refused to estimate the size of the crowd, Kleindienst, standing to his right, blurted out, "Six or eight thousand."

"Damn it, Kleindienst," Mitchell snarled, "why don't you shut up!"

But the personal bonds between the two men ran deeper than any conflicts of personality. John and Martha Mitchell spent many Christmas holidays with Richard and Marnie Kleindienst. And when it became apparent that Mitchell would step down March 1 from his attorney general post to command the Nixon 1972 re-election effort, he hand-picked "Kleen-dish," as he called him, to take his place. Mr. Nixon needed no further recommendation. The stocky, forty-nine-year-old lawyer from Winslow, Arizona would be the next AG.

The Senate Judiciary Committee approved Kleindienst's nomination without a whisper of dissent. Regardless of his political views, the man's integrity was impeccable. Full Senate confirmation should have been a mere formality; it might have even been unanimous. Then it happened. A bomb was dropped on Richard Kleindienst's nomination in the form of a leaked memo. The bombardier was Dita Beard.

On February 28, 1972, syndicated columnist Jack Anderson published a memorandum from ITT lobbyist Dita Beard to W.R. Merriam, vice president of the International Telephone and Telegraph.

". . . If it gets too much publicity, you can believe our negotiations with Justice will wind up shot down. Mitchell is definitely helping us but cannot let it be known. Please destroy this, Huh?"

Dita Beard was one of many high-pressure ITT lobbyists. Like all corporations concerned with legislation, ITT had a corps of wheeling-dealing advocates stationed in Washington.

Once he disclosed the memo, and supplied details in subsequent columns, Jack Anderson outlined how ITT had pledged $400,000 to the GOP for their convention in San Diego in exchange for a favorable decision by the Justice Department concerning ITT's acquisition of Hartford Fire Insurance. ITT's assets were set at $7 billion; Hartford's, $2 billion.

Anderson accused Mitchell of overseeing the payoff. To top off the charges, Anderson claimed he had caught Richard Kleindienst in "an outright lie," a grave charge against a man whose honesty had been unimpeachable. And the timing could not have been worse; his Senate confirmation was at stake.

San Diego was Richard Nixon's personal choice for the 1972 GOP convention. Not only did he call it his "lucky city," but the San Clemente White House was only a helicopter ride away. Besides, Nixon badly wanted to sweep the state which had burned him in two past elections. San Diego, however, offered no bid for the convention. Its hotel accommodations were less than required for a national convention, its city fathers were fearful of violent demonstrations, and the San Diego treasury was parched. Miami had already offered $1.5 million, while San Diego had neither the money nor the inclination to raise it.

White House wrenches started twisting for the President. The biggest crunches were put on California Lt. Gov. Ed Reinecke and San Diego Congressman Bob Wilson. The choices were exquisite. On May 12, 1971, Congressman Wilson dined with ITT President Harold Geneen and Howard James, President of Sheraton Corporation, an ITT subsidiary. Wilson had persuaded Geneen to start manufacturing aluminum cable in San Diego in order to challenge another aluminum plant for a share of the Navy's $20 million antisubmarine detection project. Wilson made it perfectly clear that the San Diego port authority had land for lease and that a couple of Sheraton hotels would enhance the harbor skyline immensely.

The ITT Scandal

Before the dessert of cherries jubilee had been consumed, Geneen casually promised to underwrite $400,000 for the convention, about half the necessary capital. With that kind of incentive, the rest of the cash was easily raised, and San Diego submitted a bid of $800,000 to the Republican National Committee. On July 23, 1971, San Diego was deemed the official city of the convention. The two new Sheraton hotels being built on the harbor would provide just enough hotel space.

The bid, incidentally, was delivered after the deadline, but the Republican National Committee extended the bidding period an extra month to accommodate the "lucky city."

Democratic National Chairman Larry O'Brien wrote to the Justice Department questioning the propriety of Sheraton's support of the convention. Besides a possible violation of the Corrupt Practices Act, the Justice Department was at that time deciding on three antitrust suits against ITT. Attorney General Mitchell had disqualified

himself from the case because his former law firm (and Nixon's) represented Continental Baking, another ITT holding. Mitchell gave the case to Kleindienst. The antitrust suits—worth billions to ITT—could revoke the conglomerate's merger with Hartford.

ITT proposed its acquisition of Hartford late in 1968. It was a time when conglomerates enjoyed unrestrained growth, but Attorney General Mitchell had warned that 200 corporations now controlled 60 percent of the nation's industrial assets. "This leaves us," Mitchell declared, "with the unacceptable probability that manufacturing and financial assets will be concentrated in the hands of fewer and fewer people—the very evil that the Sherman Act, Clayton Act, and Cellar-Kefauver Act were designed to combat."

In January 1969, Richard McLaren, Assistant Attorney General, became the Administration's top trust-buster. On July 31, 1969, six months after the ITT-Hartford proposal

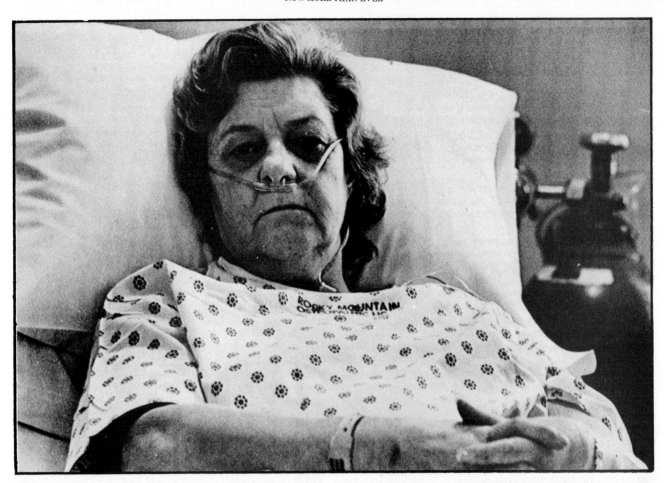

had been submitted, McLaren initiated the three landmark antitrust actions against ITT. McLaren wanted to stop huge conglomerates from sucking up smaller companies. In the past, antitrust suits were used to break up monopolies and ensure competition. McLaren's new suits were based only on the issue of size, and the long-term effects of giantism.

ITT had gobbled its way to the position of eighth-largest industrial complex in America. In ten years, it bought out nearly 100 firms in this country alone. ITT also owned companies in ninety-three other nations. Its assets were more than the gross national products of all but a handful of countries. In "The Sovereign State of ITT," author Anthony Sampson described ITT President Harold Geneen as a man with "strong conservative views and a deep distrust of all governments, who runs (ITT) not as a battleship or an ocean liner, but as a pirate ketch." With 331 subsidiaries, and 708 subsidiaries of subsidiaries, 218,000 share holders and 428,000 employees, ITT was not likely to sink without Hartford Fire, itself a conglomerate. But Hartford was to be the flagship in Geneen's pirate fleet, and its $1 billion a year cash flow was vital to ITT's expansionary vision.

McLaren was not merely out to halt ITT's maraudings. The ITT-Hartford merger was a perfect test case which McLaren could see clear through to the Supreme Court, and use to reverse a dangerous trend in American business. McLaren pursued the case with unbridled zeal, at least until Mitchell and Kleindienst reined him in.

McLaren was one of those occasional Republican oddities. In his first two years in the Justice Department, he initiated more antitrust suits than his predecessors had in eight years. He was highly regarded as an antitrust crusader. He gained a reputation of going after only what he could get. The Nixon Administration loved having him around to parade before the critics—until he stepped over the line. "I think without question we'd have won in the

courts," he later said. But the case never made it to court.

The Justice Department announced on July 31, 1971, that it would allow Hartford and ITT to merge provided ITT sold off some other smaller holdings, including Canteen Corporation, Avis Rent-a-Car, ITT Levitt and Sons, Hamilton Life, and one division of Grinnell Corporation. The total earnings of these six concerns was less than $41 million a year. Hartford Fire, meanwhile, earned $105 million a year. The settlement was strangely identical to a 1970 proposal made by ITT itself. In a rare moment of antitrust history, the case was settled out of court. Why?

"Mr. Geneen was evangelical about his feeling that Mr. McLaren was out to destroy the company, the economy, and the country," said ITT director Felix Rohatyn. "He made his case as forcefully as he could to every government official he could talk to."

Letters from Geneen and other ITT executives, released by the House Commerce Investigation Committee well after the settlement, showed that ITT had been in constant contact with at least nine members of the Nixon Administration during the antitrust case. Names mentioned in the memos were Nixon, Agnew, Mitchell, Kleindienst, Ehrlichman, Colson, Stans, and Connally. In one memo, addressed to "Ted" Agnew and stamped "personal and confidential," ITT Vice-president Edward Gerrity quoted Mitchell as telling Geneen that President Nixon "was not enforcing a business-bad policy and that the President had instructed the Justice Department along these lines." To this memo was stapled a brief letter saying, "I deeply appreciate your assistance concerning the attached memo. Our problem is to get to John Mitchell the facts concerning McLaren's attitude because, as my memo indicates, McLaren seems to be running all by himself . . . After you read this, I would appreciate your reaction on how we should proceed."A reaction was forthcoming, all right.

Jack Anderson said the ITT-Sheraton promise of $400,000 in the early summer was the key. Richard Kleindienst met with ITT's Felix Rohatyn five times during the settlement stages of the antitrust case. He also arranged a rendezvous between Rohatyn and Justice Department experts handling the case, in particular Richard McLaren, Anderson charged.

Kleindienst had denied any role at all in the ITT settlement. Anderson called him a liar. Shortly thereafter, Kleindienst remembered all the meetings, but refuted Anderson's charges that he had tampered with the outcome of the ITT-Hartford question.

For the next few days, Anderson's columns went on to explain how Dita Beard had met with Attorney General John Mitchell on May 1, 1971—two months before the surprising out-of-court settlement—at a party thrown by Kentucky's Republican Governor Louis Nunn, after the Kentucky Derby. Dita Beard told Anderson she spent an hour explaining to Mitchell what ITT wanted. She later told Anderson that Mitchell had agreed, and voluntarily added that he was under pressure from President Nixon to "lay off ITT."

Mitchell admitted speaking to Dita Beard that day, but strenuously denied her account of the conversation. Kleindienst, now accused of carrying out the plan of settlement, was outraged. He requested that the Senate Judiciary Committee reopen hearings on his confirmation so he could take office without "a cloud over my head, so to speak."

His request may have been a bit impulsive—the whole shaky deal would be brought before the public in an election year. The cloud he wanted removed would be raining on his head for some time.

When the new hearings began, Dita Beard could not be found. An FBI search ensued. In his first day on the stand, Kleindienst admitted meeting Rohatyn, but explained that Rohatyn merely told him that a loss for ITT would be a loss for the U.S., severely damaging the sensitive balance-of-payments situation. So Kleindienst arranged for Rohatyn to prove it to McLaren and other Justice Department experts on April 29, 1971. Eleven days later, Rohatyn told Kleindienst that McLaren was rethinking his position.

After weeks of grueling testimony, the pieces were in place. McLaren had asked White House aide and big business liaison Peter Flanigan to recommend an expert to make a report. McLaren must have known what he would get. Flanigan had been called the "most evil man in Washington" by consumer advocate Ralph Nader. Flanigan's shady deals were legion. In 1970, he was accused of exerting White House pressure on the Treasury Department to allow an oil tanker to engage in coastal shipping trade, a previously illegal practice. The value of the tanker increased $5 million. It was discovered that Flanigan had owned a share of the ship which he sold to a former employer for a handsome profit.

Flanigan's expert, Richard Ramsden, turned out to be a Wall Street investment consultant. Ramsden spent a total of two days analyzing the masses of material on the ITT-Hartford deal, and issued a report favoring ITT. A mere $224 was the fee he charged for a consultation on one of the most important antitrust cases ever before the Justice Department.

Ramsden's Wall Street firm, incidentally, managed some 200,000 shares of ITT stock. When McLaren was asked if he thought a negative report by Ramsden would have lowered ITT stock values, McLaren said, eloquently, "I have no comment."

But McLaren insisted that his final judgment to drop the suit was made from his own antitrust experience and after consultations with the Treasury Department. He admitted later that his Treasury Department consultations consisted of a single phone call.

The fulcrum of the hearings was the Dita Beard memo. She had disappeared after telling Jack Anderson that ITT security men had put her files through the paper shredder. She turned up at the Rocky Mountain Osteopathic Hospital in Denver, Colorado, where, her doctor said, she was suffering from severe chest pains, diagnosed as acute angina pectoris. Although she was on the list of witnesses to testify later in the week, the Judiciary Committee could not wait. They called several witnesses who testified in the hearings, collaborating in a scathing indictment of Dita Beard's character in an attempt to dismiss her as a lunatic.

Her personal physician, Dr. Victor Vizka, said she was "emotional, very disturbed," and that her behavior was "distorted and irrational." He also claimed that her diet included much alcohol and many pills.

Dr. Vizka's testimony seemed a blatant violation of physician-patient confidentiality. The judiciary committee later learned that Dr. Vizka himself had been investigated for federal Medicare abuses, and his wife, Dr. Katherine Greene, was still under investigation for similar charges. Dr. Vizka made several visits to the Justice Department just prior to the ITT hearings. His testimony was worthless—but it pointed up the extreme steps taken to discredit Dita Beard. Gov. Louis Nunn testified that he had heard the Beard-Mitchell conversations at his May 1 party. Nunn said when Beard started talking about ITT, Mitchell insisted that he "was sick and tired of hearing babout this." The statement could have meant many things. Dita Beard, Nunn continued, was later laid out on the floor either from "a light heart attack" or "drinking too much." He did not know which.

Dita Beard, meanwhile, was in the Denver hospital with her recurring heart problem. She was doing fine, hospital authorities said, until she heard about the testimony of Dr. Vizka and Gov. Nunn. She promptly had a relapse. Shortly thereafter, her lawyer said she "categorically denies the allegations that there was ever an arrangement between ITT and the administration. . . ." Why the sudden change of heart?

During her stay in the hospital, a stranger in sunglasses and a scruffy red wig paid her a visit. It was E. Howard Hunt, then employed by special counsel to the President Chuck Colson, in a CIA disguise. What transpired at that meeting is not known. Sources said that Hunt wanted to know if the memo were a forgery, and went in red wig to find out—or to convince Dita that it was.

The FBI tried to prove the same thing, but ended up proving only that the memo had been typed on a typewriter in Dita Beard's office around June 25, 1971—the date on the leaked memo. Meanwhile, the White House drafted a speech for Senator Marlow Cook of Kentucky to read before the Senate Judiciary Committee, calling the memo a forgery. William Merriam, the ITT vice-president to whom the memo was addressed, denied ever seeing it.

On March 20, 1972, three weeks after the initial Anderson disclosure, Dita Beard made it unanimous with a hospital bed statement that the memo was a "forgery and a hoax." Then she had another heart attack and hasn't been heard from since.

Richard McLaren received a federal judgeship in Chicago. ITT gobbled up Hartford. The protagonists were all cleared of any criminal charges. No definite cause and effect relationship could be drawn between ITT's $400,000 pledge and the mysterious out-of-court antitrust settlement. Everyone involved vehemently denied any outright hanky panky. The real fascination of the entire affair was peeking behind the closed doors of a giant international conglomerate and seeing how it exerted power in a suspect, if perhaps legal, manner.

The infinite threads between big business and the Nixon Administration were so subtle and crisscrossed that legal action was impossible. But people knew. It was written on Dita Beard's sickly face. Sen. Philip Hart of Michigan probably summed it up best when he said that the ITT scandal would be "one more chapter in the long history of why people lack faith in the System."

On June 8, 1972—four months after his nomination— Richard Kleindienst was confirmed by the Senate, 64-19. But the cloud he so desperately wanted removed still hovered above his head, darker than ever.

Aug. 29 to Sept.15/"A Most Bizarre Incident"

Richard Nixon walked to a microphone facing the horde of reporters assembled in his San Clemente White House. The occasion was a Presidential press conference, a rare phenomenon in the Nixon Administration. For the first time during his tenure, the President found himself talking about things other than international and domestic policy. Lead-off questions at the press conference sought answers to what Nixon referred to as "political matters," charges of financial corruption and political espionage connected with his re-election campaign. A giant question mark called Watergate was finally drawn out in front of the President.

Nixon began characteristically by admitting that indeed some of the charges were true. Technical violations of the new campaign spending act had occurred, but violations were committed by both Democrats and Republicans. The apparent violations were minor, anyway, and President Nixon assured the press that Maurice Stans, whom he described as an honest and meticulous man, would correct any Republican errors.

Then, after acknowledging a particle of dirty truth, the President proceeded to deny any soiling complicity on the part of the White House or CREEP. He cited five investigations then under way by the FBI, the Justice Department, the GAO, the Senate Banking and Currency Committee, and CREEP itself.

"In addition to that," Nixon asserted, "within our own staff, under my direction, counsel to the President Mr. Dean has conducted a complete investigation of all leads which might involve any present members of the White House staff or anybody in the Government. I can say categorically that his investigation indicates that no one in the White House staff, no one in this administration, presently employed, was involved in this very bizarre incident.

"What really hurts in matters of this sort," Nixon continued, "is not the fact that they occur, because overzealous people in campaigns do things that are wrong. What really hurts is if you try to cover it up."

The offensive was on in defense of the Re-election Committee and the White House. But White House Counsel John Dean was flabbergasted when he heard a report of the President's remarks over the radio. What investigation, he wondered. No one at the White House had requested him to make an investigation; no such investigation had taken place as far as he knew—or so he claimed later.

Nixon's San Clemente statement on August 29 spearheaded a Republican counterassault on the embarrassing Watergate accusations of the Democrats. The very next day, after Nixon's press conference, in a letter to the GAO Federal Elections Office, Republican National Chairman Robert Dole accused the Democrats of "a purposeful intent to be less than totally honest in revealing the true identity of contributors." Dole went on to cite seven specific charges of Democratic campaign spending violations which the GAO said it was looking into.

Meanwhile, Attorney General Richard Kleindienst, speaking at a Nixon campaign rally in Wisconsin, promised that indictments in the Watergate case would be handed down "prior to the election and possibly as early as September." Kleindienst knew, however, that there was no chance of a trial beginning before November 7.

The McGovern for President campaign wanted in the worst way to expose the seaminess underlying Watergate. A widespread scandal was probably the only chance for winning the election and the McGovern campaign apparatus began to zero in on this Republican achilles heel. But as McGovern and his campaign director Larry O'Brien hammered away, Nixon's people responded with new and inventive denial techniques.

John Mitchell, former director of CREEP, pulled a surprise move by refusing to give more than "name, rank, and serial number" in his deposition for the Democrats' $1

"What really hurts," Nixon said, "is if you try to cover them up."

million civil suit. Mitchell's silence was based on a motion to dismiss the civil suit filed by attorneys for the five men caught inside Democratic National Headquarters. The lawyers contended that publicity engendered by the controversy prevented the Waterbuggers from receiving a fair trial. Mitchell, nevertheless, swore to reporters that he had no advance knowledge of the break-in.

Judge Charles Richey nullified Mitchell's contention, ruling that any depositions given in the case would remain secret. "There has been more suspicion generated in this case than any other in my lifetime," Richey told William O. Bittman, Hunt's lawyer who had asked him to dismiss the civil suit. "If you don't believe it," Richey continued, "why did the President make a statement in San Clemente? Why would the Attorney General make a statement?" The civil suit continued, although it did not provide the public exposure of Watergate for which the Democrats had prayed. Nor did it answer any Republican prayers.

A Miami photographic processor named Michael Richardson told the Florida State Attorney that Bernard Barker and Frank Sturgis, two of the Watergate five, had given him two rolls of 35mm film to develop on June 10, a week before the break-in. Richardson said that he developed thirty-eight prints depicting Democratic National Committee memorandums, letters, and documents held for photographing by hands wearing rubber gloves.

In Washington, Common Cause, a citizens' action group, filed suit against the Finance Committee to Reelect the President. John Gardner, head of Common Cause, charged that the committee violated the 1925 Corrupt Practices Act superseded by the new campaign spending law on April 7, by failing to disclose its sources of revenue for 1971 and early 1972. "The way to dispel the aura of mystery and suspicion is to bring all the facts out in the open," Gardner told a news conference. Leonard Garment, special assistant to the President, argued for the dismissal of the Common Cause suit.

Enough pieces of the Watergate puzzle had now accumulated to give the public a glimpse of the cover-up. On September 9 the Washington *Post* quoted sources in the Justice Department as saying that the most thorough investigation since the assassination of President Kennedy had already ended—less than three months after it began. Acting under guidelines established by Richard Kleindienst and FBI Director L. Patrick Gray, the investigators had confined themselves to the narrowest possible probe, looking into only the break-in itself and ignoring the apparent channeling of funds for the operation. And the White House was reportedly receiving daily reports on the investigation from the Justice Department.

Stories also began circulating about another participant in the June 17 bugging who had talked to Democratic party investigators. The man claimed to have monitored wiretaps on phones inside Democratic National Headquarters from a room in the Howard Johnson's Motor Lodge across the street from the Watergate. He also claimed to have been in walkie-talkie communication with the five burglars on the night of the break-in, playing the role of look-out. Later, the mysterious new bugger would be identified as Alfred C. Baldwin III, an ex-FBI agent.

Baldwin gave a detailed description of how telephone conversations were monitored and reported. Rather than identifying the source of the wiretap transcripts, the illegally obtained information would always be written up as a memorandum beginning with the phrase "confidential informant says . . ." CREEP officials who read the "memorandums" could then deny ever seeing wiretap information. Baldwin said his boss was James McCord.

On September 11, in an interview with the New York *Times*, Watergate suspect Bernard L. Barker admitted there was more to the plot than met the eye, but that he would not be a stool pigeon. Preferring to go to prison rather than talk, Barker said, "Just because I get in trouble, I don't want nobody else to get in trouble." Barker described co-conspirator E. Howard Hunt as the most patriotic individual he had ever met.

Also on September 11, supposedly based on information received from Baldwin, the Democratic Party filed an amended complaint in its civil suit against the Republicans. The Democrats charged the Republicans with conspiring to commit political espionage, and specifically charged Maurice Stans with knowingly supplying $114,000 for the illegal activity. Hunt, Liddy, and Hugh Sloan were added to the list of defendants in the suit. The Democrats also upped the cost of damages from $1 million to $3.2 million. Nixon campaign director Clark MacGregor immediately labeled the action a "prostitution of the judicial process," announcing the Republicans would file a countersuit.

As the Watergate exploded into the civil courtroom similar bombardments were taking place in the House Banking and Currency Committee which was conducting its own investigation into Republican campaign slush funds. Maurice Stans, CREEP finance chairman, refused to appear as a witness before the House committee. Commenting on Stans' decision, committee chairman Rep. Wright Patman of Texas said, "a high level decision has obviously been made to continue a massive cover-up and to do everything possible to hinder a full-scale public airing of the Watergate case."

When the House Banking and Currency Committee's fifty-eight page preliminary report on Watergate was made public on September 12, accusing Stans of approving the clandestine transfer of campaign funds through Mexican banks, the finance chairman freaked. Labeling the Congressional report "rubbish," Stans filed a $5 million libel suit against Larry O'Brien. Stans charged the Democratic chieftain with falsely and maliciously attempting to name him as a conspirator in the Watergate bugging plot.

The same day, CREEP filed its threatened countersuit, charging O'Brien with using the Federal courts as "an instrument for creating political headlines." Ironically, while the Republicans were filing their suit, a bugging device was discovered inside the Watergate headquarters of the Democratic National Committee and turned over to the FBI. The headlines the next day spoke for themselves.

The courts had become the Republicans' last resort in their attempt to quash the incipient Watergate furor. Daily front-page stories on the sordid episode were beginning to hurt President Nixon's credibility. The enormous publicity given the story had to be stopped, or ameliorated, and countersuit seemed the only way. Someone else had an edge on the truth.

On September 15 a federal grand jury returned an eight-count indictment against seven men for conspiring to steal documents and eavesdrop on Democratic headquarters from May 1 through June 17, 1972. The indictment charged that Hunt and Liddy had actually entered the Watergate on June 17, although they were not caught. Also named in the indictment were the five men who were caught in the Watergate—McCord, Barker, Gonzales, Martinez, and Sturgis.

The timing of the indictment fit the Republican game plan well enough under the circumstances. With the prosecution represented by Justice Department lawyers and the defense represented by lawyers friendly to the White House, and with sixty days permitted by law before the trial would have to start, there appeared little likelihood of a pre-election trial. But the presentation of the charges prior to the election conveyed to the public the impression that Mr. Nixon had speedily apprehended the guilty and would bring them to justice. No mention was made in the indictment of what motivated the break-in, who ordered it, and who financed it. As conspiracy indictments go, that one was not heavy on dirty details.

Referring to the Watergate break-in at his August 29 press conference, President Nixon said, "This kind of activity has no place whatever in our political process. We want the air cleared. We want it cleared as soon as possible." As soon as possible turned out to be not soon enough.

Spooks for the CIA

Question: Who did you think you were working for?
Answer: Sir, I was not there to think. I was there to follow orders, not to think.
Bernard Barker testifying before the Senate Select Committee on Presidential Campaign Activities, May 24, 1973

As early as 1960, Nixon had committed himself to a major reorganization of the American intelligence community. Writing in *Six Crises*, Nixon said, "As far as the CIA was concerned, I felt that its assignment was presently too broad. It should continue to have primary responsibility for gathering and evaluating intelligence, in which it is doing a good job. But I said it had been my plan, had I been elected, to set up a new and independent organization carrying out covert para-military operations."

The White House's first assignment for the Plumbers, who called themselves "Room 16," after their White House office number, was to assemble an in-depth profile of Daniel Ellsberg. In federal grand jury testimony, Hunt testified that the Administration was particularly concerned about the publication of the Pentagon Papers and did not want to be embarrassed at a subsequent trial. A decision was made to burglarize the office of Ellsberg's psychiatrist to see, according to Hunt's testimony, "if some way could be found whereby a judgement could be made on Ellsberg in regard to his prosecutability." Since the FBI had stopped training its agents for entry operations, and since the White House did not have sufficient confidence in the Secret Service, the Plumbers were nominated by default.

According to CIA memorandums released by the Justice Department, superaide John Ehrlichman asked CIA deputy director Robert Cushman in July 1971 to give Hunt technical help for an undisclosed mission. Cushman, who had long known Ehrlichman and who had served as a personal aide to Vice-president Nixon, agreed to assist Hunt and on July 22, a meeting between the two men was arranged. The following day, Hunt met with the CIA's "technical personnel" in a Washington "safe house" to pick up false identification and disguises. On August 20, Hunt was provided with additional materials, including business cards, a recording device, a voice-altering machine, and an experimental camera that was concealed in a tobacco pouch.

Hunt and Liddy flew to Los Angeles on August 25 to case the offices of Lewis Fielding, Ellsberg's psychiatrist. Hunt took several photographs of Liddy posing in front of the building in order to prepare a "vulnerability study" which was eventually presented to the White House. Hunt returned to Washington on August 26. He asked the CIA to meet him at the airport to pick up and develop the film that the two Plumbers had taken in Los Angeles.

Since it was chartered by Congress in 1947, the CIA has groomed agents to execute sensitive intelligence operations. However, the CIA charter prohibits the agency from exercising "police, subpoena, law enforcement powers, or internal security functions" within the boundaries of the United States. This had little apparent influence on Hunt who unabashedly demanded that the CIA transfer a

former secretary assigned to the Paris office and attach her to his secret operation. General Cushman was put off by Hunt's aggressive manner and finally informed Ehrlichman that he was cutting the link to Hunt because it "might possibly be construed as involving the agency in improper activities."

But it was a determined Hunt who went to Miami to recruit former CIA operative Bernard Barker. Hunt left a phone message at the home of Barker, a fifty-five-year-old native of Cuba who immigrated here in 1959 to escape Castro's revolution.

When Barker arrived home from his Miami real estate agency, he read a message saying, "If you are the same man I remember ten years ago, get in touch with me—Eduardo." The monied son of a Cuban mother and an American father, Barker admired Hunt for the simple reason that he conspired to overthrow Castro. As the CIA paymaster for the Bay of Pigs, Barker was all the more loyal because Eduardo once recommended that the only proper way to liberate Cuba was to assassinate Castro. This was a sentiment Barker was quick to embrace.

In Cuba, Barker's family enjoyed a comfortable and profitable relationship with Batista's government. Barker even served as a government employee for a brief period in 1947 or 1948—as a member of Batista's secret police. Castro, of course, usurped Barker's wealth and special privileges and there is every reason to believe Barker hated the Cuban guerrilla with a passion. In Miami, Barker became a leader of the Cuban Revolutionary Council which was one of 100 exile organizations promoting a second invasion.

In 1959, over 30,000 Cubans, disenchanted with Castro's new government, emigrated to Miami. Some had even fought with Castro's guerrillas in the mountains, but became alienated from the socialist state. The Cuban Revolutionary Council and its sister organizations attempted to organize this unrest by circulating anti-Castro newspapers, broadcasting propaganda and funneling guns to the Cuban underground.

Since the American government was not disinterested in the Castro government, it began to secretly subsidize several of the Cuban exile organizations. The Cuban Revolutionary Council, in fact, was a CIA-funded and supervised operation to recruit volunteers specifically for the Bay of Pigs. According to Manuel Panaboz, who was hired in the summer of 1960, "I was told there would be an invasion of Cuba fairly early in 1961 backed and supported by the United States."

The original American decision to finance Cuban exile groups was apparently made in the Eisenhower Administration. After a three-hour conference with Fidel Castro in April 1959, Vice-president Richard Nixon wrote several memos to the CIA, the State Department and the White House arguing that he was personally convinced that Castro was "incredibly naive about communism or under communist discipline" and that the U.S. would have to deal with him accordingly. Very early in 1960, Nixon's recommendations were implemented by the CIA, which began providing arms, ammunition, and training for exiled Cubans with the intention of equipping an army that would overthrow the Castro government. More recently, Howard Hunt has maintained in his book about the Bay of Pigs, *Give Us This Day*, that Richard Nixon was the invasion's "action officer" within the White House during the last days of the Eisenhower Administration.

In the summer of 1960, the CIA began airlifting volunteers to training camps at Trax Base and Retalhuleu in Guatemala. The same year, Hunt was assigned as the CIA's representative to the Cuban Revolutionary Council. It was during one of several inspection tours of the invasion brigade that Hunt first met Barker. Testifying before the Ervin Committee, Barker said, "Eduardo represents the liberation of Cuba, the anticommunist symbol. It represents the Government of the United States in one form, its covert form." Despite the inevitable failure of the Cuban counter-revolution, Barker's image of Eduardo never tarnished.

When Hunt went to Miami in the summer of 1971 to recruit agents for the "bag job" at Ellsberg's psychiatrist, Barker was not the only CIA, Bay of Pigs veteran that he drafted. Barker tapped Eugenio Martinez, a friend of fifteen years who, like Barker, had smuggled refugees out of Castro's Cuba for the CIA. Martinez was a forty-nine-year-old Miami real estate broker sometimes employed by Barker's firm. Both Barker and Martinez were reported to have had business dealings with another Cuban-born American—Richard Nixon's closest friend and sometime business associate Bebe Rebozo.

After hiring a third Cuban exile and former CIA agent named Felipe deDiego, Hunt armed his burglary team with false papers, disguises, and CIA equipment and flew to Los Angeles. On September 3, 1971, Hunt's squad of Cubans, along with Gordon Liddy, registered at the Beverly Hills Hotel using various aliases, and reconnoitered Fielding's office building. In his testimony before the federal grand jury, Hunt said, "we wanted a pretested entry, a fact that was obtained by equipping two of the men from Miami with delivery men's clothes and a large green suitcase which actually carried the camera equipment inside. The suitcase itself was adorned with air express invoices and stickers, 'Rush Immediately' to Doctor Fielding." On the night of the break-in, a janitor reported that he had found two men who spoke Cuban-style Spanish, dressed as mailmen, in Fielding's waiting room. They explained they were leaving a suitcase for Fielding; then they left, but not before punching the unlocking button on the inside of the door.

At about 11 P.M. that same night, while Hunt kept watch on Fielding's home, and Liddy patrolled Beverly Hills in a car, Barker and Martinez went back to the office building. It was a Labor Day weekend, however, and the cleaning lady had left early and locked the doors. Undaunted, Barker and Martinez forced their way in. However, according to Hunt, they could not find a single thing about Ellsberg in the files (Fielding has filed an affidavit charging that the files were in his cabinet and *were* tampered with).

The team reported back to Krogh by telephone and later returned to Washington. Having failed to produce Ellsberg's psychiatric profile, Hunt asked David Young of the National Security Council to contact Doctor Bernard Melloy, who headed a CIA unit which specialized in providing "second-hand profiles of persons of interest to the United States Government." Testifying before the Senate's Armed Services Committee, former CIA Director Richard Helms said he reluctantly went along with the request even though he "didn't think it was quite proper by reason of the source." Helms' successor, James Schlesinger, later described these missions as "ill-advised."

This was not, however, the last time that former CIA operatives, Cuban exiles, and the Plumbers collaborated. Their next known target was an antiwar rally scheduled to take place on May 4, 1972 outside the Capitol building in Washington. FBI Director J. Edgar Hoover had died on May 1 and his body was lying in state inside the Capitol rotunda as protestors converged on Washington. According to the *Post*, Charles Colson or his administrative aide W. Richard Howard requested Jeb Stuart Magruder to arrange a counter-demonstration to disrupt the May 4th antiwar rally. Magruder, CREEP's Deputy Campaign Director, was number 2 man on the re-elect team, and the man directly in charge of approving funding for many clandestine CREEP activities. It was Magruder who passed the request along to Liddy and Hunt who in turn contacted Bernard Barker in Miami.

Barker solicited the help of Frank Sturgis, a forty-nine-year-old U.S. Marine turned soldier of fortune who once smuggled guns for Castro's rebel army, then turned against Castro and trained Cuban exiles for the CIA. In 1960, Sturgis lost his U.S. citizenship for serving in a foreign military force (Castro's army), but he regained it with the aid of Florida Senator George Smathers. Smathers was one of Richard Nixon's early political allies and advisers. He was also a member of the Small Business Administration Committee and interceded for Bebe Rebozo when Rebozo sought to obtain that loan from the SBA in the early 1960s.

For the counter-rally, Barker also re-enlisted the aid of Martinez from the Ellsberg mission and Vergilio Gonzales, a forty-five-year-old locksmith working at the Missing Link Key Shop in Miami. Barker, Sturgis, Martinez, and Gonzales were the four Cubans arrested along with McCord in the ill-fated Watergate burglary on June 17, 1972.

Barker also drafted Reinaldo Pico and Felipe deDiego for the antiwar counter-demonstration. Both were Miami area anti-Castro Cubans who worked on and off for the CIA since the Bay of Pigs operation. In an interveiw with the Miami *Herald*, Pico said, "I've worked for the CIA all my life. I always worked for them through Macho. I assumed if Macho asked it must be official. Before we went to Washington, Macho told me 'la gente' wanted people to take care of the demonstrators at the Hoover funeral. When we talked about 'la gente' it was always the CIA."

Barker and his team of nine Cuban vigilantes flew to Washington on May 4, 1972. Each of the counter-demonstrators had his air fare, hotel bills, and other expenses paid by Barker in addition to being given $100 in cash. Barker told the men that "there are hippies and men who are traitors to this country and democracy who are going to perpetrate an outrage to Hoover." One of the men Barker was referring to was Daniel Ellsberg who was scheduled to make an appearance on the Capitol steps at about 6 P.M. that day.

Barker and his confederates then left the hotel and went to the Capitol. Barker immediately engaged one long-haired young man in fierce debate. Pico stepped up and knocked the protestor down. Frank Sturgis also slugged one of the antiwar demonstrators and was immediately arrested along with Pico by Capital policemen. As they were being led down the steps, Pico said, a third member of the vigilante squad explained to a police lieutenant that the two men in custody were "anticommunists" and "good men." They were then freed with a warning and left. Barker, meanwhile, ordered the rest of the Miami Cubans to "get" Ellsberg and radical lawyer

William Kunstler who were both addressing the rally. Felipe deDiego told the Miami *Herald* later that "we saw Ellsberg, that traitor, having a victory demonstration during the Hoover funeral and it incensed me. Hoover was a hero and here was this traitor gloating over his death. We started calling them traitors and finally we broke up the Ellsberg thing."

Two weeks after the Hoover funeral, Barker called the group together and flew the Cuban vigilante team to Washington where they registered at the Hamilton Hotel. Pico said, "I was told they were expecting more antigovernment demonstrations at the White House and we were to break them up. If we saw a Viet Cong flag go up we were to pull it down. I was looking forward to bringing one of those flags with me as a souvenir." DeDiego, who was captured in the Bay of Pigs fiasco and served in U.S. Army Intelligence for four years after his release, said no reason was provided for their second Washington trip. After several days of inactivity, the group was shuttled over to the Watergate Hotel.

It was during this period that the original break-in at Democratic National Headquarters occurred. Pico and deDiego, however, were not recruited for the first Watergate burglary. According to the Miami *Herald*, both insisted that the only conspiracy they participated in was to buy identical pairs of pajamas in a Washington shop.

Pico and deDiego both said they were following standard CIA operating procedure in not asking any unnecessary questions about their mission. Pico said, "When I worked for the CIA, if they told me to go out to the bay and blow up a ship I would do it." DeDiego said their primary concern was to liberate Cuba and fight against communism. "We have been waiting for fourteen years to do something against Castro and against communism. We take any chance we can get. It is like a fever that takes hold of you. We had worked for the CIA and people knew we would work against communism anywhere."

Barker's anticommunist squad surfaced in several other sabotaging efforts. Pablo Fernandez, who accompanied Barker when the Cuban team attacked Ellsberg and Kunstler on the Capitol steps, said Martinez offered him $700 a week to disrupt the McGovern headquarters in Miami Beach during the summer of 1972. According to the Washington *Post*, Fernandez was encouraged to recruit hippies to throw rocks, break windows, and defecate and urinate in public in order to "give the voters a bad impression of the people supporting McGovern." Fernandez said he turned down Martinez's offer because he was already working for the FBI and the Miami police.

Gradually it became apparent that Barker's vigilante squad was not a simple extension of the usual dirty tricks to be found in American political campaigns. The attempts to apply international espionage techniques to national politics represented a form of political warfare which struck at the very foundations of a democratic society.

Ironically, Bernard Barker testified before the Ervin Committee that he believed he was preserving America's institutions. "I cannot deny my services," Barker said, "in the way that it was proposed to me on a matter of national security." Howard Hunt echoed a similar theme in one of his many novels about espionage, *Hazardous Duty*. After a carnage is set in motion by the government's efforts to capture a Soviet defector, secret agent Peter Ward waxes philosophical and says, "We become lawless in a struggle for the rule of law—semi-outlaws who risk their lives to put down the savagery of others."

On June 16, 1972, Hunt contacted Barker in Miami and asked him to re-enlist his former CIA confederates to put down some Democratic Party "savagery" in the Watergate Hotel. It was the last time they ever worked together.

Sept. 16 to Oct. 10/Charge and Countercharge

The message from the White House to campaign headquarters was all systems go. George McGovern seemed the most beatable presidential candidate since the origin of the species. Concern over the Watergate was being co-opted in the courts and out of them. If the Democrats condemned White House cover-ups, the Republicans countered by condemning Democratic smear tactics. If the Democrats screamed for answers, the Nixon Administration's lawyers reminded them of the prohibitions against discussing pending criminal prosecutions. It was perfect.

Or almost. One thorn remained in the Republican side—the national press. Nixon had had trouble with news leaks in the past, and now Watergate was springing them even in such closed-mouth bastions as the Federal Bureau of Investigation. Despite the Plumbers, despite the Administration's efforts at harassment to the point of jailing journalists for not revealing confidential sources, the leaks persisted, drip by drip.

To see what the Administration had to fear, one need only look at the disastrous effects of newspaper revelations in the Eagleton affair. As Napoleon Bonaparte once said, "Four hostile newspapers are more to be feared than a thousand bayonets." Already, numerous newspapers, led by the *Post* and the *Times*—both of which had news-sharing arrangements with hundreds of others—were running the accounts of "confidential," "informed," "well-placed," and "unimpeachable" sources close to their front-page flags.

It was in such a position—front-page upper right-hand corner—that the Washington *Post* threw its flying block against the Nixon team's broken field run for victory. *Post* staff writers Carl Bernstein and Bob Woodward, who had covered Watergate for months, pieced together a story that received the most careful editing since Thomas Jefferson wrote the Declaration of Independence. Washingtonians awoke on October 10 to an incredible tale that began:

"FBI agents have established that the Watergate bugging incident stemmed from a massive campaign of political spying and sabotage conducted on behalf of President Nixon's re-election and directed by officials of the White House and the Committee for the Re-election of the President.

"The activities, according to information in FBI and Department of Justice files, were aimed at all the major Democratic presidential contenders and—since 1971—represented a basic strategy of the Nixon re-election effort."

The Post Company, already an object of Nixon Administration scorn and possible antitrust investigations, had placed its life on the line. It was the biggest step yet in uncovering a cover-up whose proportions had become increased greatly in the previous few weeks.

Predictably, the first charges of whitewash had come from the lips of the man with the most to gain. Referring to the Watergate indictments, McGovern said, "I suggest that this blatant miscarriage of justice was ordered by the White House to spare them from embarrassment in an election year." McGovern called attention to a long list of unanswered questions. "Who ordered this net of political espionage?" the candidate asked. "Who paid for it? Who received the memoranda of the tapped telephone conversations at Democratic headquarters?"

Smear, the Republicans responded; or, in the words of

Assistant Attorney General Henry Petersen, the man who supervised the Justice Department's investigation, "a grievous attack on the integrity of twenty-three good citizens of the District of Columbia who served on the Watergate grand jury faithfully and well."

Petersen went on to call the Watergate investigation "among the most exhaustive and far-reaching in my twenty-five years in the Justice Department." Less than two weeks later, on September 29, Petersen sent a letter to each member of the House Banking and Currency Committee urging the Congressmen not to subpoena witnesses in their investigation of the Watergate case. In a rare display of Justice Department concern, Petersen claimed that such action would jeopardize the civil rights of the Watergate defendants.

Deny and delay were administration passwords as headlines screamed that the secret floating fund in Stans' safe—the one he said he did not know about—actually totalled $350,000, and was used for other espionage efforts beyond the Watergate. "Absolutely untrue," said Jeb Stuart Magruder when he and CREEP scheduling director Herbert Porter were linked to Stans' secret fund. The spy money was supposed to be so secret that all record of its sources had been destroyed months before by CREEP personnel director Robert Odle, under the direction of committee political coordinator Robert Mardian and committee special assistant Frederick LaRue.

Not surprisingly, all seven defendants in the bugging trial pleaded not guilty, before Judge Sirica on September 19. Bail for each was set at $10,000. At the same time, Stans submitted a list of forty-two depositions he required for his countersuit against the Democrats. Topping the list were Katherine Graham, publisher of the *Post* and *Newsweek*, *Post* managing editor Howard Simons, *Post* reporters Woodward and Bernstein, and reporters from the Washington *Evening Star* and the New York *Times*. It was the Nixon offensive defense, not without an element of danger for the President—and certainly a measure of how scared the Administration had become. Also, there was the matter of those unplugged leaks.

With all the furor, no one had yet explained the motivation behind the June 17 break-in of Democratic headquarters. But Vice-president Spiro Agnew, at a news conference in Minneapolis, offered a novel theory of Watergate as a *Democratic* conspiracy. Agnew contended that one of the Watergate defendants had set up the others for arrest so the issue could then be used by the likes of Larry O'Brien against the Republicans. Agnew did not base such an assertion on fact, however, saying he was "engaging in the same sort of wild fancy in which Mr. O'Brien is." Four days later, Henry Petersen told a national conference of federal prosecutors that the American people may never learn the motivation of the Waterbuggers. Judging from the success of the Justice Department's investigation, Petersen's prediction seemed likely to come true.

U.S. District Court Judge Richey announced on Sept. 21, in reference to the suits and countersuits, that "it has become patently obvious to the court today that the court's wish to have these cases brought to trial before the election is impossible." Richey also stayed the taking of all deposi-

tions until the completion of the criminal action against the Watergate seven. In the Watergate criminal action, U.S. District Court Judge Sirica granted a defense-requested stay effectively delaying the trial until after November. Lawyers for the Finance Committee to Re-elect the President asked U.S. District Court Judge Joseph C. Waddy to dismiss the suit brought by Common Cause against the Committee. Waddy refused, and the attorneys filed an immediate appeal, thereby delaying that action until after the election. The skeletons in Watergate's closets would not rattle all the way out until at least late in November.

Meanwhile, another article in an escalating series of Woodward and Bernstein articles in the *Post* charged former Attorney General John Mitchell with control over the secret Republican campaign fund in Stans' safe. Informed beforehand of the *Post* story, Mitchell responded, "All that crap, you're putting in the paper? It's all been denied. Jesus. Katie Graham is gonna get caught in a big, fat wringer if that's published. Good Christ. That's the most sickening thing I've ever heard."

The charges leveled at the Nixon Administration were indeed difficult for administration members to believe. In comments to a UPI editors' convention, Acting FBI Director L. Patrick Gray probably summed up Administration feeling:

"It strains the credulity," said Gray, "that the President of the United States—if he had a mind to—could have done a con job on the whole American people. Look at Watergate. If the President of the United States were so-minded, he would have had to give an order to the attorney general, who would have had to order the assistant attorney general for the Criminal Division and the acting director of the FBI, who would have had to order 1200 agents. He would have to control the United States attorney for the District of Columbia and the men and women of the grand jury.

"Even if some of us are crooked, there aren't that many of us. I don't believe everyone is a Sir Gallahad, but there's not been one single bit of pressure put on me or any

of my special agents."

Given the apparent absurdity of the charges made against President Nixon, then, it came as no surprise when the House Banking and Currency Committee voted 20-15 on October 3 not to hold public inquiries into the Watergate affair. Committee Chairman Wright Patman was somewhat perturbed, however. Six Democrats voted along with the Republican minority on the committee, ensuring the defeat of the investigation and probably of the Democratic candidates. Patman accused the White House of engineering the outcome. "I predict," said Patman, "that the facts will come out and when they do, I am convinced they will reveal why the White House was so anxious to kill the committee's investigation. The public will fully understand why this pressure was mounted."

With the House Banking and Currency Committee vote, every possible investigation into Watergate prior to the November election had been canceled, stifled, or unavoidably delayed.

The press, however, continued chipping away. In an exclusive interview with Jack Nelson of the Los Angeles *Times*, Alfred Baldwin III, the lookout and monitor of wiretaps in Democratic headquarters, disclosed details of his activity. Baldwin revealed that memoranda summarizing the telephone transcripts were addressed to William Timmons, Robert Odle, and Glenn Sedam, all CREEP officials. The Committee to Re-elect the President promptly denied the allegations.

But Baldwin's detailed disclosures were enough for Judge Sirica to order anyone involved with the case then under adjudication not to comment publicly on it. Sirica was immediately accused of trying to muzzle Congress, McGovern, and the press. The judge clarified his order several days later, saying he intended it only for people directly involved in the case. Alfred Baldwin was the prosecution's star witness.

President Nixon gave a surprise press conference on

October 6, his first since the San Clemente appearance of August 29. Responding to questions about Democratic charges of corruption in his administration, Nixon said he wouldn't dignify those attacks by commenting on them. The President also refused comment on the Watergate case, recalling the criticism he received after speaking about Charles Manson, the California mass-murder cultist, while Manson's trial was in progress (Nixon's remark labeled Manson guilty before proven guilty, and was a breach of legal ethics which Manson's defense attorney used in an unsuccessful attempt to get a mistrial declared. It would have been a different matter if Nixon were Manson protesting his innocence—there are no prohibitions against that. And Mr. Nixon was now being accused of being the Charlie Manson of the Watergate). Nixon did say that his own effort in the 1949 Alger Hiss investigation was "basically a Sunday school exercise compared to the amount of effort" channeled into the Watergate affair. One way or another, he was right.

It was the same day that the Washington *Post* reported that the $89,000 in Republican campaign money laundered in Mexico and channeled into Bernard Barker's bank account had been traced to a $100,000 donation made by the Gulf Resources and Chemical Corporation of Houston, whose president was the Nixon campaign's Texas fund raiser, Robert Allen. Allen apparently had forgotten that donations from corporations are illegal.

Investigative reporters had come by default to the roles belonging to government investigators, and their efforts began to exact a toll. Response to embarrassing charges leveled by prestigious newspapers was not in the Nixon game plan. The explosive Bernstein and Woodward article of Oct. 10 crossed the tolerability threshold for the men in the government. Something had to be done.

They couldn't do what Senator Sam Ervin wanted them to. On Oct. 7, Ervin, chairman of the Senate Subcommittee on Constitutional Rights, had demanded an immediate trial for the Waterbuggers. "Anybody who can't prepare the case in fifteen minutes," Ervin wrote to Attorney General Richard Kleindienst, "ought to have his law license taken away. The obvious way to ensure a prompt, fair and impartial trial and avoid any possible encroachment on the rights of those indicted would be to adhere to the Constitution's Sixth Amendment speedy trial provision. Any lawyer who is qualified to try cases before a justice of the peace ought to be able to try five men caught red-handed in a burglary within ten days."

Ervin promised a full post-election Congressional investigation of the Watergate affair, including a probe of why the Justice Department delayed prosecuting the case. But the Administration did not listen to Ervin. It read the newspapers, and grew angry.

The Sabotaging of George McGovern

"I would remind all concerned that the way we got into Vietnam in the first place was through overthrowing Diem, and the complicity in the murder of Diem."

**Richard Nixon,
Sept. 16, 1971**

"I will do anything Richard Nixon asks me to do—period."

Chuck Colson

E. Howard Hunt's first assignment as a $100-a-day White House consultant, aka Plumber, was to investigate the Pentagon Papers leak but he performed some other duties as well. Hunt has testified before a federal grand jury that he obtained classified cable traffic between Washington and Saigon for the period of April 1 to November 30, 1963. The 140 top-secret cables came from the State Department on request from White House staff aide and leader of the Plumbers, David Young.

While going over the cables, Hunt testified, Colson asked him, "What kind of material have you dug up on the files that would indicate a Kennedy complicity" in the assassination of President Diem of South Vietnam?

Hunt said he had found nothing to prove it, but he thought that Kennedy "had pretty close pulled the trigger against Premier Diem's head. . . ."

"Well, this isn't good enough," snapped Colson. "Do you think you could improve on them?"

"Yes, I probably could," Hunt replied. "After all, I had been given some training in my past CIA career to do just this sort of thing and had done it successfully on numerous occasions, floating forged newspaper accounts, telegrams, that sort of thing."

"Well, we won't be able to give you any technical help," warned Colson. "This is too hot. See what you can do on your own."

With Xerox machine, razor blade, typewriter, and the 140 classified cables, Hunt sat down and forged a cable that proved Kennedy *complicity* in the murder of Diem. And in so doing, on orders from Colson, he blamed John F. Kennedy and the Democrats for the murder of Diem and in a sense for the entire Vietnam war. It was part of the plot to re-elect Richard Nixon.

Nixon knew whom he took on when he hired Chuck Colson. Colson was a superpatriot who hated the Kennedys and everything for which they stood. Years before, Harvard University had offered Colson a full scholarship. He declined, saying that he "was turned off by Harvard Square. They already had their bomb throwers." That was during the safe and secure 1950s.

Since becoming part of the White House elite in 1968, Colson's loyalty was never doubted. His father called him "viciously loyal." The ex-Marine prided himself on following orders to the letter. His nicknames on Capitol Hill demonstrated both his subservience and his duties: "Hatchet Man," "Chief of Dirty Tricks," "The Power Mechanic," "The Cold Bastard," "Super Loyalist," "King of the Hard Hats." Colson himself defined his role as "chief ass kicker around the White House."

While some men take their jobs home with them at night, Chuck Colson took the entire iconography of Republicanism with him. His house looks like a GOP jungle—ceramic and wicker elephants stampede through the dining and living rooms. His ties are decorated with elephants. On a bar Colson built himself is inscribed the Green Beret motto: *"When you've got 'em by the balls, their hearts and minds will soon follow."*

When the Colsons entertain guests, and his wife asks Charles to play some music, he invariably puts on "Marine

Battle Hymn," not as a joke, but because he loves the music. His wife said she was attracted to Charles because he is "so commanding. He says hop and you hop."

The intense dedication of the forty-one-year-old, paunchy Colson caught up with him last year when he was forced to see a doctor for severe stomach problems. The doctor ordered him to cut out the three packs of cigarettes a day and to try to curtail the fifteen-hour workdays. The cigarette habit was easy to kick—the workload was something else. He was too valuable to the President of the United States, he said, to start shirking his duties now.

After all, it was Colson who architected the New Republican Coalition of Labor-Ethnic-Catholic-Wallaceites which ensconced Nixon in the presidency. It was Chuck Colson who suggested that the President commute Teamster leader Jimmy Hoffa's sentence, which he did. And it was Chuck Colson who was engaging in so much sabotage, spying, and dirty tricks that he himself concluded at one point—and reiterated the statement when critics expressed astonishment—that "I would walk over my grandmother if necessary." As special counsel to the President during the re-election campaign, he came damn close to doing that. He commandeered at least thirty "attack groups" that perpetrated nearly every imaginable campaign sin.

Colson had a sabotage dress rehearsal in 1970. About three months before the November U.S. Senate election in Maryland, Colson voluntarily helped a reporter dig up some charges against Democratic Senator Joseph Tydings, who was up for re-election. Colson arranged meetings between *Life* magazine reporter William Lambert and important sources who would allegedly "prove" that Senator Tydings had acted illegally in dealings of Charter Company, a Florida real estate firm in which Tydings had a financial interest.

In 1964, a Charter Company request for a loan of $7 million from the Agency for International Development (AID) was awaiting approval just after Tydings' election victory that year. The following May, Charter Company received the loan.

A *Life* story by Lambert, accusing Sen. Tydings of improprieties, appeared two months before the senator came up for re-election. Tydings was defeated by Republican J. Glenn Beall. A week after the election, a government investigator who had conducted an extensive probe into the Charter Company loan, confirmed there was no conflict of interest on the part of Senator Tydings or any other party. Although the reputation of the former senator was cleared, his political life was finished. His interest in democracy was not. In May 1973 Tydings accused Colson of using the 1970 Senatorial scheme as a "dry run" for the widespread campaign sabotage of 1972.

The Tydings caper a success, Colson began his dirty work for Nixon's re-election. He chose a national AFL-CIO convention as his first proving ground. George Meany, AFL-CIO president, accused Colson of sending forty operatives to the convention in November 1971 to "contrive a confrontation between the President and the AFL-CIO." Meany then characterized the Nixon Administration as "steeped in scandal and twisted by privilege." The AFL-CIO received a lot of flack after newspaper accounts said the convention had booed and ridiculed Mr. Nixon during his remarks.

Meany brought up Colson's name again when discussing a bogus invitation he received to meet with Sen. McGovern. The invitation came by telephone from a person who said he was Gary Hart, McGovern's national campaign manager. Meany said the caller arrogantly demanded that Meany be at a certain place at a certain time. No one showed. The labor leader described the call as an attempt by the White House to widen the already existing breach be-

tween the Democratic Party and the mammoth AFL-CIO. When asked by reporters who he thought made the call, Meany smiled and asked wryly, "You don't think Chuck Colson made that call, do you?"

The reporters smiled back. They knew the answer because they knew Chuck Colson. It was Colson who dispatched Hunt to the Denver hospital bedside of ITT lobbyist Dita Beard. When Colson heard the theory that her infamous memo might have been forged, he shouted, "Hot damn!" After making sure Hunt had his red wig and a plane ticket to Denver, Colson sent word of the purported forgery to Senate Minority Leader Hugh Scott, who subsequently released the unsubstantiated theory to the press.

Colson had his greasy tentacles in everything and it started to irk even the strongest Nixon supporters. "He wants control of everything," said one White House aide, "and I mean everything." Colson was the main strategist for many of the 1970 GOP congressional candidates. His frequent attacks on the press and Democratic opponents were so vitriolic that they may have, in effect, hurt the Republicans. Eleven congressional seats were lost in a year when Nixon was riding high and Republicans expected to gain, not lose. The pols wanted no part of Colson's relentless vindictiveness.

Another example of GOP powerbrokers' discontent with Colson's viciousness occurred during the hearings on the nomination of Kleindienst for attorney general. Sen. Edward Kennedy, an old and dear target of Colson's, was one of the senators trying to stall Kleindienst's nomination until the truth was known in the ITT antitrust scandal.

As was the usual practice, White House aides and speech writers sent Republican senators helpful statistics supporting Kleindienst. The material Colson sent them was "so extreme, no one would use it," said one aide. Colson wrote complete speeches condemning Senator Kennedy's character and morals. He harped on the Chappaquiddick incident, alleged that Kennedy cheated in college, and included a host of other unfounded allegations. No honorable senator would touch the stuff—it would be a breach of ethics. This sense of propriety eluded Chuck Colson; that no one would read his speeches incensed him. The schism between the White House and the Congress grew ever wider and Colson made more and more trips to the inkwell with his poison pen.

Since his venom was unappreciated in formal Washington circles, the White House figured it could be used to better advantage on the campaign trail. Colson was put in charge of the attack groups mobilized to devastate the McGovern campaign. There were meetings every morning at 9:15 in Colson's office, where a huge Marine poster hung behind his desk. The White House generals gave Colson permission to declare war on Senator McGovern. Directly or indirectly, Colson was behind every para-military maneuver launched against the Democrats. Captain Colson was back in business.

0140

On May 8, 1972 President Nixon ordered the mining of Haiphong harbor, the sea entrance to North Vietnam. It was perhaps the riskiest international action he took in the Vietnam war. The placing of mines in Haiphong was a blatant challenge to Russia's merchant marine, which used the harbor to deliver materiel to North Vietnam. The President's order came just two weeks prior to his scheduled visit to Moscow and was viewed by many as an extremely dangerous move at a highly sensitive time. Criticisms of the President's judgement came pouring in from all over the world—from hawks and doves, from the Right and the Left. It was a period of great tension. "We felt the Haiphong decision could make or break the President," said one White House official in retrospect.

It may have been with this in mind that CREEP began one of the largest campaigns of deception known in American politics. On May 10, Press Secretary Ziegler reported that telegrams, letters and telephone calls were running 5 or 6 to 1 in support of the President's action. Although the statement was true, Ziegler didn't say that an overwhelming percentage of the communications came from CREEP.

"The entire staff was in overdrive for two weeks . . . the work included petition drives, organizing calls to the White House, getting voters to call their congressman," explained a former CREEP staffer.

At least $84,000 in $100 bills of unreported campaign funds was spent in tricking the world. The expenditures were authorized by deputy campaign director Magruder, with the approval of chairman Mitchell. The $84,000 was not reported to the GAO, which was a violation of the law. When the GAO found out, it forwarded its findings to the Justice Department. The Justice Department filed them under "So What." No court action was taken.

A full-page ad ran in the *New York Times* on May 17. It read, in part:

"THE PEOPLE VS. THE NEW YORK TIMES . . . a *New York Times* editorial, critical of President Nixon's closing of North Vietnam land and sea routes, argued that the President's action ran 'counter to the will and conscience of a large segment of the American people.' . . . WHO CAN YOU BELIEVE—THE NEW YORK TIMES OR THE AMERICAN PEOPLE?"

The ad had ten signatures, including, "Ms. Patricia O'Leary, Coordinator, Scenic Drive." There was no such person. The ad was placed by the November Group, an ad agency which handled $6 million of Nixon's campaign advertising. This particular ad was paid for with forty-four hundred-dollar bills. Chuck Colson wrote it. The ad was a violation of campaign law.

If Americans would not believe Americans, Colson figured, a letter from Europe might help. He drafted a mass-mailed letter postmarked London and signed Walter Annenberg, Ambassador to England Annenberg's appointment followed a $250,000 contribution to Nixon's 1968 campaign.). The letter praised Mr. Nixon's "strong but quiet leadership" and "solid achievement." Enclosed were two reprints from British newspapers critical of "trendies," "left-wingers" and the Kennedy Adminis-

tration. Chuck Colson was the man who thought up, printed, and distributed the letter on official State Department stationery. That's also against the law.

According to a CREEP officer, "We were totally mobilized for the biggest piece of deception—we never do anything honestly. Imagine, the President sending himself telegrams patting himself on the back."

He also marched for himself. Two convicted Watergate conspirators, Barker and Sturgis, on orders from Colson, showed up uninvited at a Cuban exile meeting in May and converted the reunion into a pro-Nixon parade. Marching for Nixon through the Cuban section of Miami, the Cubans were told, would help rid Cuba of Castro. Sturgis admitted, or boasted, that he drove the lead truck in what looked like a convoy. There was some talk that the man Cubans call Eduardo and look upon as their "friend in the White House"—E. Howard Hunt—was also there. Apparently, he donned one of his many disguises and went incognito.

By the Autumn of 1972, Frank Mankiewicz, director of the sabotaged and fading McGovern campaign, was making charges against Colson and company—and he had facts to back them up.

Someone had called CBS anchor man Walter Cronkite in the waning weeks of the campaign and identified himself as Frank Mankiewicz. The voice told Cronkite that the deal Cronkite had made with Mankiewicz to give 80% of the news coverage to McGovern and only 20% to Nixon was getting out of hand. "Everybody's getting suspicious," said the voice, "better give more to Nixon." Veteran newsman Cronkite knew Mankiewicz's voice and swore the caller was an imposter. He added quickly that the caller was "definitely not just a crank."

Someone claiming to be Oliver Tyrez, McGovern's television expert, called CBS officials and said that McGovern had canceled his scheduled speech on network television outlining his plan to end the war. It was a lie.

On numerous occasions the press was notified that McGovern was going to arrive in a certain city four or five hours later than planned. Because delays were common on a whirlwind national tour, reporters were inclined to believe the phony calls.

Hundreds of Colson operatives were allegedly hired to disrupt McGovern rallies across the country. For the Democratic convention in Miami, home of many Cuban exiles, forces were marshalled to start fights and damage property. Eugenio Martinez, a convicted Waterbugger, testified that he was paid to create riots. He said his orders also instructed him to "urinate and defecate in public."

The well-oiled McGovern machine that swept so smoothly through the primaries to the amazement of political pundits, seemed to fall apart during the campaign for the presidency. Finally there was proof that the machine did not collapse all on its own but was disassembled, nut by nut, bolt by bolt, by a vast corps of saboteurs working for the re-election of the President.

The primary sabotage had been good—this general election sabotage was great. Chuck Colson, once again, had proved his loyalty to Richard Nixon.

Oct. 11 to Oct. 25/Hearsay and Innuendo

The shocking Washington *Post* allegations of widescale political spying and sabotage by the Nixon re-election team was the torpedo that almost sunk the Republican ship of state. As damaging as the Oct. 10 charges appeared, though, they were soon reduced to mere campaign flack. With less than a month remaining in the presidential campaign, time was on Nixon's side.

The tactics employed in the Republican response to the sabotage and spy charges were noteworthy only for their heightened intensity. What had been denials became forceful and often dramatic repudiations. What were previously gentlemanly counterattacks were transformed into blistering old Nixon assaults.

But after the Oct. 10 stories, Nixon's three batteries of rhetorical cannon—the White House, the Committee to Re-elect the President, the Republican National Committee—remained silent for five days as their opponents grew hoarse screaming foul. Then on Oct. 16 the Republicans, ears smarting from the despoilment of that week, opened fire. White House Press Secretary Ziegler lambasted the *Post* in particular and the American press in general. Addressing the daily morning press briefing, Ziegler whined indignantly "I will not dignify with comment, stories based on hearsay, character assassination, innuendo, or guilt by association." Ziegler put the power of the office behind his harsh attack by later adding, "That is the White House position; that is my position."

Nixon's new campaign director, Clark MacGregor, read a similar statement at a 5 P.M. press conference about "the unusual developments of the past few days." Declining to answer reporters' questions, MacGregor commented only about the damaging stories in the *Post*, recalling that same newspaper's role in releasing the secret Pentagon Papers in 1971. "While the Post itself openly and actively collaborated in the publication of stolen top secret documents of the Government of the United States sixteen months ago—today, it is faking shock and outrage at some obvious volunteers who allegedly were spying on Larry O'Brien," he said.

"While each crime is reprehensible," MacGregor continued, "which is the more serious? Stealing top secret documents of the government of the United States; or allegedly stealing Larry O'Brien's political papers?"

Later that evening, addressing an audience of black Republicans, Chairman Dole called the *Post* spy-sabotage saga a piece of "garbage." Dole joked that the abhorrent journalistic standards of the *Post* would cause massive resignations at the *Quicksilver Times*, a Washington underground newspaper.

The Republicans slung the mud to unprecedented lengths, scoring the *Post* thrice in a single day. Nixon's first law of political gravity, to deny with equal force every dangerous allegation or attack, guided his instruments of recrimination.

Predictably, the very day Bernstein and Woodward's incredible exposé hit the newsstands, the McGovern campaign condemned the acts of Republican espionage in the strongest possible terms. At last, the true dynamics behind Nixon's re-election campaign were revealed in greater graphic detail than the Democrats had hoped for in their wildest fantasies.

Wright Patman saw the *Post* allegations as justification to reconsider his Banking and Currency Committee's vote against hearings on Republican finance practices. The controversial story was beginning to reopen cracks in the Watergate that a few days earlier the Republicans thought forever sealed.

It was not surprising when four Republican officials—John Mitchell, Clark MacGregor, Maurice Stans, and John Dean—declined to testify before Patman's committee two days later. White House Counsel Dean informed the committee chairman immediately prior to the meeting that the doctrine of executive privilege protected presidential assistants and barred his own appearance. Patman failed to take issue with Dean on his unprecedented assertion, however, because the Banking and Currency Committee, through lack of a quorum, once again voted against the necessary subpoena power.

While Democratic leaders across the nation echoed the Bernstein and Woodward sabotage story's informal charges against CREEP, newly opened avenues of investigation in the Watergate tangle penetrated Republican ranks. Federal Judge Joseph Waddy set Oct. 31 as trial date for the Common Cause civil suit against the Finance Committee to Re-elect the President. This development threatened the Republicans with the potential disaster of disclosure of anonymous campaign contributors before the Nov. 7 election. Oct. 25 was set as the deadline for all sworn statements in Common Cause's suit.

In Florida, meanwhile, Watergate bugger Bernard Barker was standing trial for misusing his notary seal in cashing Kenneth Dahlberg's $25,000 check. On Oct. 13, the same day as Waddy's ruling in the Common Cause suit, Dade County Criminal Court Judge Paul L. Baker signed extradition orders for Republican finance chairman Maurice Stans, former CREEP treasurer Hugh Sloan, and Dahlberg himself. The three men were ordered to appear as material witnesses in the Barker case on October 26.

The Republicans, overconfident of avoiding embarrassing judicial actions before the November election, suddenly had two more court fights scheduled. In addition, the silencing of Patman's House Committee was counterbalanced by Senator Ted Kennedy who announced that he had ordered a "preliminary inquiry" into the Watergate bugging to be held before election day by his Senate judiciary subcommittee.

Exactly why the Nixon camp was silent until Oct. 16 about the damaging *Post* article is unclear. Did the Nixon team think Bernstein and Woodward were just guessing, or did they spend those precious days in damning silence attempting to locate their sources? Whatever the reason, it became unimportant when a series of Bernstein and Woodward articles elaborating on the initial Oct. 10 expose began to appear on Oct. 15.

High past and present Nixon officials were being accused daily of committing crimes in connection with the sabotage and spying plot. The *Post* disclosed that Dwight Chapin, Nixon's appointments secretary, and Hunt both served as White House contacts for the elaborate campaign spy network. In another story, the *Post* revealed that Herbert W. Kalmbach, President Nixon's personal counsel, was one of five people authorized to disburse money from the Nixon secret campaign espionage fund in Stans' safe, and he had made payoffs to *agent provocateur* Donald Segretti. It identified the four other officials with the combination to Stans' safe as Mitchell, Magruder, an undisclosed high White House official, and Stans himself, who claimed not to know the safe's contents. The *Post* implied that the President of the United States knew of the plot to violate the law on his behalf.

The Republican counterattack of Oct. 16 brought bedlam to the campaign. The remainder of the contest was reduced to a grandiose shouting match in a case which had already grown too large for most Americans to even fathom, let alone regard as a bonafide campaign issue. The Republicans and Democrats played a new intramural game called Watergate while most of the American public yawned and President Nixon's support barely slipped.

Only two elements of the Watergate episode remained stable as the presidential campaign deteriorated from issues to tissues to dirty laundry. The *Post*, unmoved by veiled threats from the Nixon election machine, continued to publish startling exposés of clandestine and illegal intrigue by the re-elect apparatus working in conjunction with the White House. Less dramatically, the groundwork was being laid in the courts for discovering the truth about Watergate.

On October 17, after heated arguments from both defense and prosecuion for a delay, Judge John J. Sirica set Nov. 15 as the date for the trial of the Watergate burglars. If it were impossible for the American people to ascertain the facts about Watergate prior to the election, it at least would be their due to have the unsettling question disposed of shortly thereafter.

The Watergate affair became what appeared to be a politician's issue in a presidential election touted as the first clear choice in many years. A Harris survey published on Oct. 19 showed that fully 62 percent of the American electorate dismissed Watergate as a mere political issue. McGovern confessed his confusion and dismay at the voters' apathy concerning Watergate.

Perhaps McGovern failed to see that the average American made no connection between Watergate and his daily life. A job, a family and a home, the economy, the question of the war—these were the issues which elevated candidates to office. Richard Nixon, while maintaining a low profile in the campaign, realized basic political reality when he sent his national security adviser, Henry Kissenger, to Paris in October to meet with Le Duc Tho and representatives of North Vietnam. Nixon recognized what would impress the ordinary citizen, too, when he went before Congress on August 9 and declared his 90-day wage and price controls. It was no coincidence that wage-price controls were almost coterminous with the presidential campaign.

McGovern must have understood that dirty politics was neither new nor shocking to a cynical American electorate. Since McGovern saw Watergate as his only hope for cutting President Nixon's re-election edge, then the onus for American lack of outrage and revulsion over the sordid conspiracy fell upon the Democrats.

It was up to McGovern to hammer home that Watergate was the first instance in American electoral dirty dealings when the White House—in the person of an overwhelming number of White House staff, even at the top—was involved.

Another electrifying Bernstein and Woodward story on the top right front-page of the Oct. 25 *Post* traced the re-election conspiracy to the White House's top echelons. H. R. Haldeman, White House chief of staff, was the undisclosed fifth man empowered to disburse payments from Stans' safe. With this disclosure, Watergate involvement was laid at the very top of the White House ladder. The President stood only one rung higher.

Supercabinet

"Every President needs his S.O.B. and I'm Nixon's."
H.R. Haldeman quoted in the New York Times Magazine May 6, 1973

In *The Twilight of the Presidency*, George Reedy, former press secretary to the late President Lyndon B. Johnson wrote: "The White House is a court . . . This raises the greatest of all barriers which will plague the White House so long as the President is a reigning monarch rather than an elected administrator."

When the problems of war and national security have isolated a President from the people, then he is left at the mercy of a small group of privileged messengers and White House appointees. They, in turn, are at the mercy of the President, who serves as the only yardstick for measuring their course of action.

Like his predecessors, Richard Nixon found the duties of the office so great, he had to delegate huge parcels of responsibility to advisers and friends. He selected men whose political philosophies were often carbon copies of his own. They were always men who had already demonstrated their unerring loyalty. Nixon sought men who

"There is no policy that Haldeman is responsible for, yet there is no policy that he doesn't have a hand in somehow..."

were willing to be anonymous wheels in the engine of the Presidency—wheels not politically ambitious for themselves, but willing to turn on behalf of Richard Nixon. No glory, no amount of money, not even the country itself mattered as much to the chosen few as did the President.

This virtue of unswerving loyalty was carried into such excess, however, that the zealots became myopic. Nixon became a symbol for them. He was too important to be flawed, too great to be in error. In vindication of their own selflessness, Nixon swelled out of all proportion. Finally they confused the man with his image and marshaled their resources to protect and aggrandize Nixon's public record—his radio voice, newspaper smile, his television ego. They came to worship an idol. As disciples, they became their own worst enemies. They became pharisees.

Just as the Lord banished Adam and Eve from the Garden of Eden, Nixon would expel his loyal servants from the circle of White House power.

In *Nixon Agonistes*, Garry Wills described the development of the White House staff as one of "ever greater refinement, reduction, purification of what gets to him through his 'final filter.' "

Nixon radically reorganized the executive branch to invest one man with final accountability in each of a few compartments. In foreign affairs, it was Kissinger; in economics, it was George Shultz; in domestic policy, it was John Ehrlichman; in legal matters, it was John Dean; in White House management, it was H.R. Haldeman.

Essentially, there was a triumvirate of power in the White House composed of three men: Haldeman, Ehrlichman, and Dean. They had special access to the President, participated in high-level policy decisions, and generally were Nixon's final filter. All three figured prominently in the Watergate affair.

The man Nixon picked to run the White House as chief of staff was Harry Robbins Haldeman, the earliest and most devoted convert Nixon attracted. Next to the President, he was the most powerful, if most invisible, man in Washington.

Mitchell wanted Erlichman fired. "He'll go before I do," Erlichman replied.

Nixon placed what had been a somewhat independent Cabinet under White House control. Where as Congress formerly had some power to review the actions of departments of the government, under Nixon it had none. That power had its greatest concentration in the person of Bob Haldeman, the unchallenged boss of the 6,000 civil servants who worked for the President—everyone from White House janitors to Kissinger. Haldeman was responsible for mapping out the President's itinerary and he was the gatekeeper of the Oval Office. He directed the speech writers, the press secretaries, and the liaisons who navigated legislation through Congress. He signed their checks and supervised their budgets.

Haldeman also controlled, according to the *Times* and the *Post*, a secret $350,000 slush fund which was illegally used to finance Nixon's re-election campaign. Haldeman appointed Jeb Stuart Magruder second-in-command at the Committee to Re-elect the President. Magruder made large sums of money, at least $235,000, available to G. Gordon Liddy for his investigation of national security leaks following publication of the Pentagon Papers. Liddy was hired on July 19, 1971 and operated out of John Erhlichman's domestic affairs office. Liddy, along with White House consultant Hunt, reported all their plumbing activities to Haldeman. When Liddy and Hunt were tied to the Watergate burglary it fell to Haldeman to conceal the sensitive existence of the Plumbers internal security team.

David Young, co-director of the Plumbers, and former National Security Council aide, has testified before Judge Sirica that Haldeman attempted to cover up Watergate to ensure that Hunt and Liddy would remain silent about their espionage roles during the campaign.

Republican Senator Lowell Weicker believes this indicates that Haldeman probably knew about the massive campaign of political sabotage against Democratic primary candidates of which Watergate was just the tip of the iceberg. Haldeman must have known an internal security operation was underway. He certainly believed there was a need for plugging White House leaks and as always the Prussian's primary concern was to ensure the loyalty of the President's staff.

This was not forty-six-year-old Haldeman's first experience with tricky dicking. Ten years earlier, during the 1962 California gubernatorial contest, Dick Nixon and Bob Haldeman were directly involved in an effort to disrupt the campaign of Nixon's Democratic opponent Edmund G. Brown. According to a California judge's ruling, Nixon and campaign manager Haldeman personally authorized attempts to sabotage Brown's credibility among his constituency. Using a phony voters poll, a dummy organization called the "Committee for the Preservation of the Democratic Party in California" contacted registered Democrats, telling them Brown was an extremist and asking them to donate their money to bring the party back to the middle of the road. While neither Nixon nor Haldeman was a defendant in the suit brought against the dummy committee, Judge Byron Arnold of San Francisco Superior Court later ruled that the poll "was reviewed, amended and finally approved by Mr. Nixon personally." The judge noted that the company hired to conduct the survey sent the contributions it received directly to Haldeman. Nixon lost the election but the suit was filed so long after the campaign that it had no impact on voter returns.

Haldeman first met Nixon when he introduced himself to the freshman Senator from California in 1951, just after Nixon's successful prosecution of the Alger Hiss case. Anticommunism was the glue of their early relationship. Haldeman's family had been politically active against the alleged red menace. His grandfather was one of the pillars of the Better America Foundation, an ardently anticommunist organization founded in 1922.

Haldeman's political consciousness apparently began with communism. While a student at the University of California, Haldeman said, he became "fascinated by the communist front organizations, what they were trying to do."

Between working as an advance man for Nixon's 1956 vice-presidential and 1960 presidential campaigns, Haldeman returned to the prestigious J. Walter Thompson advertising agency, where he merchandised Black Flag bug killer, Seven Up, Sani-Flush, and Griffin shoe polish. Thompson's advertising agency also proved to be a kind of farm club for Haldeman's future White House staff. Two key Presidential appointees, press secretary Ziegler and appointments secretary Chapin, were Walter Thompson veterans. Ziegler, as White House reporters are bemusedly aware, handled Disneyland's account.

When Nixon lost in California in 1962, Haldeman was one of the few who still believed in Nixon's political future. So great was Haldeman's fidelity that he would not join the chorus of campaign aides who were critical of Nixon's last press conference in which he roasted the press for bias and proclaimed, 'You won't have Richard Nixon to kick around anymore.'

In return, Nixon relied almost exclusively on Haldeman to coordinate his 1968 Presidential campaign. Haldeman's earlier experience promoting bug killer and the Uncola appeared in the character and direction of Nixon's 1968 effort. You don't sell bug killer by kissing babies or visiting shopping centers. You do it on television.

Haldeman's own politics were unabashedly conservative. On a scale of zero to 100, where zero represents radical and 100 represents reactionary, Haldeman says he would score a 75. In a rare television appearance on the NBC Today Show Feb. 1, 1972 (Haldeman has allowed only six interviews in four years), Haldeman described antiwar critics as "consciously aiding and abetting" the communists. The President's critics, he said, were asserting "partisanship above peace." Haldeman's comments came shortly after an anti-war speech made not by George McGovern but by Edmund Muskie. Since the "aiding and abetting" phrase parroted the constitutional definition of a traitor, the White House immediately issued a statement saying that Haldeman spoke for himself only.

Haldeman's nickname, the Prussian, is appropriate not only because of his national origin. He does not smoke or drink and assumes a manner of dress and speech which is emblematic of streamlined efficiency, straight up to his regulation marine-length haircut.

Haldeman also earned the nickname "Chief Frog Man," a term coined by Communications Director Herb Klein during the old advance man days. Frog derived from Haldeman's hopping and jumping from city to city in Nixon's campaign. Since then, a former campaign aide said, the Haldemans have amassed an enormous collection of frogs from around the country.

Haldeman's private life seemed to be a function of his public one. He rarely entertained guests and amused himself by spending evenings at home showing movies of the Boss. Haldeman is said to own the most comprehensive private film library of Richard Nixon owned by anyone outside the President's immediate family.

While Nixon's influence on Haldeman obviously was great, it is difficult to measure Haldeman's influence on Nixon. Administration publicist Ken Clawson said, "there is no policy that Haldeman is responsible for, yet there is no policy that he doesn't have a hand in somehow." In an interview with Allen Drury, Haldeman described his own duties by saying, "Ehrlichman, Kissinger, and I do our best to make sure that all points of view are placed before the President. We act as a screen because there is a real danger of some advocate of an idea rushing in to the President or some other decision-maker, if the person is allowed to do so, and actually managing to convince them in a burst of emotion or argument. We try to make sure all arguments are presented calmly across-the-board."

It was Haldeman who was a major factor in firing Secretary of the Interior Walter Hickel, Secretary of Commerce Peter Peterson, and CIA director Richard Helms for their various transgressions against a President who began his first term in office saying he wanted no yes men.

The *Post* said Haldeman's influence was so great that he was responsible for keeping Vice-president Agnew on the hook over whether he would be Nixon's running mate in 1972.

Few challenged that influence. In 1972, during a campaign rally at Providence, R.I., Haldeman ordered Secret Service agent Robert Taylor to permit an airport crowd to pass over the restraining ropes and meet candidate Nixon. Haldeman wanted to take full advantage of a nearby group of television cameras. Taylor, the Secret Service chief of White House guard, refused because the swarming crowds might jeopardize Nixon's safety. Haldeman threatened to have Taylor arrested. Taylor held his ground then, but later found himself transferred to a minor, insignificant post.

Superaide John Ehrlichman served Nixon with vigor and loyalty equal to Haldeman's. Often working in Haldeman's shadow, the chief counselor on domestic affairs had the job of filtering through the mountains of paper which arrived for the President, extracting the most important material, and presenting Nixon with a list of viable options. Whatever the domestic issue—budget messages, government reorganization, school desegregation, the energy crisis—Ehrlichman played probably the most crucial role in formulating the President's final strategy.

Haldeman drafted Ehrlichman into Nixon's service during the 1960 campaign. He worked briefly in the 1962 California gubernatorial failure, and in 1968 served as campaign tour director. His reputation for punctuality became legend. In order to stay on schedule, Ehrlichman once ordered the campaign plane to take off, abandoning two Nixon speech writers to finish their work in telephone booths in Lansing, Michigan.

As the chief of domestic affairs, Ehrlichman was also the chief of domestic espionage in the White House. It

was Ehrlichman who authorized former Transportation Undersecretary and head Plumber Egil Krogh and White House staff member and Plumbers co-director David Young to investigate Daniel Ellsberg. Ehrlichman also asked Gen. Robert Cushman, then the deputy director of the CIA, to equip White House secret agents Liddy and Hunt with fake identification, disguises, and electronic devices. The result of this was the burglary of Ellsberg's psychiatrist Lewis Fielding, which Ehrlichman learned about but failed to report as required by law. Ehrlichman also encouraged Nixon to offer the empty FBI directorship to Pentagon Papers Judge Matt Byrne, perhaps to influence the verdict, one of several factors resulting in the declaration of a mistrial in the case.

Ehrlichman supervised other phases of the Administration's "national security" internal espionage. He hired former New York cop Jack Caulfield in March 1969 to serve ostensibly as liaison between the White House and state and local law enforcement agencies. But Ehrlichman wanted him for certain discreet investigations of a delicate and sometimes illegal nature. For example, Caulfield and his staff probed possible financial links between Maine Senator Edmund Muskie and corporations with significant pollution problems. According to *Time* magazine, they investigated rumors that the brother of a potential Democratic candidate was involved in a homosexual affair. Another investigation by Caulfield that would take on great significance later, when McGovern was pleading for pre-election congressional hearings, concerned Senator Kennedy's involvement with Mary Jo Kopechne who drowned when the Senator's car went off a bridge at Chappaquiddick. In each instance Caulfield's investigations were undertaken at Ehrlichman's request.

The Washington *Post* reported that Ehrlichman possessed copies of Senator Eagleton's confidential health records several weeks before the story—based on an anonymous tip—broke that Eagleton had undergone shock therapy for mental depression.

The FBI's Gray said Ehrlichman ordered him to destroy "potentially sensitive" documents removed from the safe of Watergate spy Howard Hunt. Gray obeyed.

Like Haldeman, Ehrlichman neither smokes nor drinks. At forty-eight his private life is as anonymous as Haldeman's. They were frequent tennis partners whose friendship evolved while they were roommates at the University of California. Ehrlichman graduated from Stanford Law School in 1951 and practiced in Seattle. Washington was his native state.

Haldeman and Ehrlichman were Nixon's arms and legs. Neither had ever worked for another politician. Their zealous devotion was not, however, a subject of universal admiration, even among members of Nixon's own party. To Republican Minority Leader Senator Hugh Scott they were "overzealous amateurs," uninformed about the political process. Former GOP Chairman Robert Dole said, "They say we can bring you two Nixon pens but otherwise we can't help you." Haldeman and Ehrlichman were often charged with being responsible for Nixon's deteriorating relationship with Congress. They were accused of arrogantly isolating the President from his country and from his own administration. Senator Lowell Weicker said they acted "like children politically." They were called the "Berlin Wall," and "Hans and Fritz." Republican Iowa Representative William Scherle called them "the Katzenjammer Kids." Republican Senator William Saxbe of Ohio once called them "Nazis."

No love was lost on the "Berlin Wall," even by those who had passage through it. According to conservative columnist Joseph Alsop, Attorney General Mitchell detested Ehrlichman because he was "much too far to the left." Mitchell emphatically threatened to see Ehrlichman excised after the election. Ehrlichman calmly replied that "he'll go before I do." History was to prove him right.

Even in a Nixon team which could mastermind a ripple-free convention, there were deep divisions. Haldeman and Ehrlichman represented one faction buttressed by a series of their own appointments: Ziegler as press secretary, Jeb Magruder as deputy director of CREEP, Dwight Chapin as appointments secretary, Hugh Sloan as CREEP's treasurer, and Gordon Strachan as CREEP–White House liaison. Mitchell and Dean represented another faction, strengthened by the campaign appointments of special White House assistant Fred LaRue, Harry Fleming, and Assistant Attorney General Robert Mardian.

It would be many months before the American public would get more than small glimpses of the factional strife which separated these men. In fact, in 1972 few had even heard of presidential counsel John Dean.

At thirty-four the cherubic Dean became counsel to the president only eight years after graduating from Georgetown Law School with only brief service in private practice. He was as ambitious as he was intelligent. An A and B student in college, Dean taught himself self-hypnosis to improve his powers of concentration. After graduating in 1966, Dean's first job was with the Washington law firm of Welsh and Morgan. According to Jack Anderson, Dean was effectively fired from his first position due to unethical conduct. While his law firm was filing an application for a television station license, Dean was industriously working on a rival application. His law partners

were not pleased and it was "mutually decided" that Dean should resign.

Dean's first political appointment was to the House Judiciary Committee. After two years he became associate director of the National Commission on Reform of Criminal Laws, advising both the President and Congress. His commission proposed to eliminate mandatory prison sentences and abolish the death penalty. Ironically both positions were never highly regarded by his future boss, Richard Nixon.

By 1969 Dean's reputation as a friend of the Administration had earned him a job as legislative liaison in the Justice Department. He was responsible for lobbying in behalf of Supreme Court nominees Clement Haynsworth and G. Harold Carswell, both of whom were recommended by Mitchell and both of whom were rejected by the Senate. At the Justice Department Dean was the government's chief negotiator with antiwar groups, which probably explains his alleged role in the Administration's efforts to crack down on radicals. When Dean was promoted to the White House, Richard Kleindienst said, "I cried when he left here." Dean was reputed to be the White House resident expert on executive privilege, that unwritten doctrine under which presidents and their aides decline to testify and provide information before Congress. Nixon was to invoke that privilege to deny congressional investigating committees access to Dean's Watergate file. Dean also developed Nixon's legal basis for the impoundment of funds and encouraged his broad use of the pocket veto.

Unlike Haldeman and Ehrlichman, Dean has led an active social life. Often described as outgoing, Dean enjoys both tennis and sailing. He and his wife once took Berlitz classes together to learn French. In his spare time Dean builds small furniture for his fashionable townhouse in the Washington suburb of Alexandria, Virginia. Handsome and athletic in appearance, Dean drives a Porsche 911 sports car and generally does not conform to the dull technician or anonymous bureaucrat image of many Nixon staff members.

However, as Dean's complicity in the Watergate affair emerged, the characteristic pattern of secret involvement and official evasion made him look very much like Haldeman and Ehrlichman. Mitchell went through much the same transformation. While no one was aware of it at the time, a chapter was closing in presidential politics. The hunters would become the hunted.

Oct. 26 to Nov. 7/Peace is at Hand

Often in the chronicles of nations cryptic aphorisms abound. Watergate has spawned more than its share. One day, after the *Post* fingered Haldeman, the President's national security adviser made a statement which was as arcane as it was welcome.

"We believe peace is at hand," Dr. Henry Kissinger told a press conference in Washington Oct. 26. Kissinger, just back from secret peace talks in Paris, announced that the United States and North Vietnam had reached tentative agreement on a nine-point peace plan including withdrawal of all American forces from South Vietnam and the return of all U.S. prisoners of war. But, unlike his

North Vietnamese counterpart who announced a peace agreement would be signed on Oct. 31, Kissinger maintained that one more conference session, lasting three or four days, was needed to work out minor details.

American jubilation at the announced end to the longest, ugliest, and least understood of all U.S. armed conflicts was clouded by a nagging suspicion. Richard Nixon had promised, as a candidate in 1968, to bring peace to Vietnam. During his first term of office, Nixon drastically reduced American troop strength in Indochina, but at the same time he stepped up the air war there. The brutalities and horrors once experienced by American Ma-

rines and infantrymen, went unnoticed by B-52 crews high in the atmosphere. Yet American bombs, weapons, and money devastated the landscape of Indochina. One of the McGovern camp's favorite quotations was of Mr. Nixon's 1968 remark that a President who had tried for four years to produce peace and failed should not be given another chance. But, ten days before the election, Mr. Nixon appeared to be making good on his promise.

McGovern campaign workers were at their wit's end. Richard Nixon, they felt, had engineered unprecedented manipulations of U.S. domestic and foreign policy merely to ensure himself a second term, and he got away with it— just as it appeared that, for now, his surrogates would get away with Watergate.

If the Democrats fell prey to the Nixon re-election campaign, new Republican abuses of governmental procedure showed they were not unique. John Ehrlichman, Nixon's chief adviser for domestic affairs, reportedly asked the FBI to gather helpful data about local constituents' feeling on criminal justice. The FBI directive, ordered by Acting Director L. Patrick Gray III and sent to twenty-one field offices in fourteen states, asked agents to gather information "to give the President maximum support during campaign trips." Ehrlichman, responding to the charge, said he requested the information from the Justice Department.

Aside from hints about Ehrlichman and Haldeman, Watergate was cooling off. Two impending court actions were delayed and once again the GOP had slipped out of the jaws of justice. Judge Sirica postponed the Watergate criminal trial from Nov. 15 to Jan. 8 for personal health reasons—was recuperating from a pinched nerve. At the same time, Common Cause made a deal with Maurice Stans. In return for disclosing the sources and amounts of campaign contributions made to the Finance Committee to Re-elect the President before March 10, Common Cause leader John Gardner agreed to halt further legal action until after the presidential election. Donations received between March 10 and April 7, when the campaign disclosure act took effect, would remain secret prior to election day. It was a good deal for Stans. He was not required to reveal how the campaign contributions were spent. Financial information released piecemeal as election day approached

identified most unnamed contributors as representative of the nation's wealthy business community. Chicago insurance tycoon, W. Clement Stone, gave the Republicans $1 million. Arthur K. Watson, an IBM executive named ambassador to France by Nixon in 1968, contributed $300,000. Richard N. Scaife, heir to the Mellon banking fortune, gave Nixon $800,000. It was easy to see how the 1972 Nixon campaign came to be the best financed in history.

More difficult to explain was Henry Kissinger's "peace is at hand" statement after Oct. 31 passed and no Vietnam accord had been signed. The question of peace suddenly became a fumbled pass in the Nixon game plan. For the first time in his re-election campaign, the President addressed the nation on TV to explain why the prospect of peace arose so suddenly and vanished just as abruptly. It was five days before the election.

Nixon told the nation that he expected a ceasefire in Indochina soon. In a proper and presidential above-it-all tone, Nixon said he would not permit "an election deadline or any other kind of a deadline to force us into an agreement which would be only a temporary truce and not a lasting peace. We are going to sign the agreement when the agreement is right, not one day before; and when the agreement is right, we are going to sign it without one day's delay." The President's speech on the Vietnam situation was a political broadcast paid for by CREEP to clear the air about peace.

Whose hand was peace at? George McGovern assured the electorate that he was the peace candidate in the 1972 election, appearing on his own coast-to-coast broadcast the night following Nixon's Vietnam disclosures. A "cruel political deception" McGovern called Kissinger's peace announcement. "We see now that when the President's most important adviser announced that peace had come, it was actually a deception designed to raise our hopes before we went to vote on Tuesday. This is blunt language and a strong accusation. I am sorry to say it, but I believe it to be true."

61.3 percent of the American voters on November 7 did not believe it. In the biggest presidential landslide ever, Mr. Nixon received everything he hoped for—a new majority, a mandate for change, support for the pursuit of peace as he saw fit. Even the Watergate seemed shut by the tidal wave of Nixon's victory.

Chapter III

Nov. 7 to Jan. 10/The Watergate Seven

President Re-elect Richard Nixon spent the months between his unprecedented November victory and January inauguration mostly at Camp David, the presidential retreat tucked neatly away in the Maryland woods. The President, as was his habit, worked many lonely hours deciding the direction his second administration would take. Talk of the past election's unanswered charges of sabotage and spying was non-existent at Camp David. Nixon pondered what to do with what he considered to be his personal mandate to rule for four more years.

Characteristically, as the President wrought great changes in American government, he spoke to the press only once, refusing to answer questions. Speaking at Camp David on November 27, the President announced, in a preliminary way, what was to be expected from his second term of office. In a prepared statement, he pointed out that presidential administrations often "run out of steam after the first four years," while the chief executive becomes victimized by the bureaucracy surrounding him. "The only way that historical pattern can be changed is to change not only some of the players, but some of the plays," said Nixon. "The American people want change . . . change that works, not radical change, not destructive change, but change that builds rather than destroys."

What the President announced in bits and pieces during the weeks that followed was no less than the complete reorganization of the executive branch of government. Nixon consolidated executive power in the White House, imparting even more force to presidential decisions and insulating himself from congressional disapproval.

Hints of the impending change in executive power structure came only two days after the November election. Press Secretary Ziegler announced that Mr. Nixon had requested the resignations of some 2,000 government appointees. The resignations themselves were a tradition following a presidential election. What was unusual was that Ziegler publicly announced them. Something was afoot.

While Nixon strengthened his presidential hand in decision-making, he was provoking a bitter confrontation with the new Congress. The 93rd Congress came together on Jan. 3, 1973 in a defiant mood, determined to halt what it saw as executive encroachment on legislative powers. The Congress had many grounds for complaint.

On Dec. 13, the unfinished Paris peace talks ended abruptly with no peace at hand. Five days later, without the President informing Congress beforehand, American B-52's began 12 days of bombing the North Vietnamese cities of Hanoi and Haiphong with a violence unparalleled in the long history of the war in Indochina. A nation promised peace found itself the Christmas witness to new savagery. Even after the termination of the bombing on Dec. 30, Nixon remained silent to Congress about the bombing decision until just before the resumption of the Paris peace talks on Jan. 8, when he spoke only to Congressional leaders.

The Democratic Congress was also incensed over the issue of presidential impoundment of funds. Nixon had begun, in his first administration, to refuse to spend funds which Congress appropriated for various domestic programs which conflicted with Nixon policy—despite the fact that the Constitution vests the power of the purse in Congress alone. Congress began to consider methods of overcoming presidential impoundments. It also expressed hostility to Nixon's dictate of a $250 billion dollar federal spending ceiling.

Another serious question under the scrutiny of Congressional inquiry was the Watergate affair. Charges and counter-charges of electoral misconduct had blackened the 1972 election campaign. With proper non-partisan, post-election detachment, Congress had the opportunity to examine not only the source and use of Republicans' campaign funds, but the roles of the men who put those funds to use.

On Nov. 16, consumer advocate Ralph Nader brought suit against Treasury Secretary George Shultz to recover the salaries of several White House staff members, accusing the men of spending all their time working on Nixon's re-election campaign. The suit named Charles Colson, Robert Finch, and Herbert Klein. "Never before," Nader said, "has there been such an open, flagrant, and large conversion of taxpayer's revenues and government facilities for a re-election campaign."

Pressure to investigate Nixon campaign activity was building. On Nov. 18, Donald Segretti returned to his Los Angeles home. His whereabouts had been unknown since allegations charging him with campaign spying and sabotage appeared in papers across the country. Segretti refused to comment about the matter even after he was subpoenaed to testify before the Senate Judiciary Subcommittee on Administrative Practice and Procedure.

It was a premature subpoena, however. Senator Edward Kennedy, chairman of the Judiciary Subcommittee, was reluctant to handle so political a controversy. On November 17, Senate Majority Leader Mike Mansfield wrote a letter to Senator Sam Ervin asking him to make a thorough investigation of the Watergate bugging and "other insidious campaign practices." Mansfield said in the letter that "the question is not political, it is constitutional. At stake is the continued vitality of the electoral process in the governmental structure of the nation." Mansfield reflected the cautious view of the Congress in his letter to Ervin, who was chairman of both the Senate Government Operations Committee and the Judiciary Subcommittee on Constitutional Rights. The majority leader promised to supply "whatever you may agree is necessary in the way of funds, staff and subpoena powers to pursue a complete and impartial investigation which will lay bare all the facts on the Watergate affair and other insidious campaign practices. With the election behind us, it seems to me we can proceed to an inquiry into these matters in a dispassionate fashion."

The mystery enveloping the whole Watergate affair took on a new aspect when a United Airlines plane crashed into four houses as it approached Midway airport in Chicago on Dec. 8. Dead in the crash was Dorothy Hunt, wife of Watergate conspirator E. Howard Hunt, and forty-four other persons. Mrs. Hunt was carrying $10,000 in $100 dollar bills which her husband claimed she was carrying to invest in a Chicago motel. It seemed more than coincidence that

Mrs. Hunt chose to carry money in much the same way the Watergate conspirators had. It seemed even more strange that she died just as suspicions were being raised as to her role in the conspiracy. Later, it was learned that Dorothy Hunt acted as a courier, carrying funds to the people implicated in Watergate to buy their silence.

Meanwhile, the Watergate affair was being opened up on other fronts. On Dec. 4, Judge John J. Sirica announced that he wanted the trial of the seven men indicted in the Watergate break-in to be much broader than had been previously expected. "The jury is going to want to know," Sirica told lawyers at a pretrial hearing, "what did these men go into that headquarters for? Was their sole purpose political espionage? Were they paid? Was there financial gain? Who hired them? Who started this?"

Judge Sirica wanted to get to the bottom of the Watergate even if it meant encroaching upon the freedom of a press which had been so diligent in uncovering the massive scandal. At the request of the defense, Sirica subpoenaed five hours of tape recordings made by Los Angeles *Times* reporters Jack Nelson and Ronald Ostrow in their October interview with Watergate participant Alfred C. Baldwin III. The journalists refused, and a battle of wills ensued wherein John Lawrence, Washington bureau chief for the *Los Angeles Times*, was briefly jailed for contempt of court. On Dec. 22, the *Times* turned the tapes over to Sirica.

Sirica's apparent hard-nosed attitude toward the Watergate trial struck fear in the hearts of White House staff. What if one or more of the defendants talked and the scope of what began as a mere burglary became known? For John Caulfield, a White House aide experienced in security, that fear became a reality in late December. Caulfield received an anonymous letter which simply said, *"Dear Jack—I am sorry to tell you this, but the White House is bent on having the CIA take the blame for the Watergate. If they continue to pursue this course, every tree in the forest will fall and it will be a scorched earth. Jack, even you will be hurt in the fallout."* The letter was postmarked Rockville, Maryland. Caulfield knew who the letter was from—James W. McCord Jr. John Dean, counsel to the President, was immediately informed about the letter and Caulfield's fears about McCord. The cover-up began to take on a more sinister tone.

On Jan. 9, the long-awaited trial of the seven men indicted in connection with the Watergate break-in began in U.S. District Court in Washington D.C. The same day, the Senate Democratic Policy Committee agreed unanimously that there should be a Senate investigation of the Watergate incident and that Senator Sam Ervin should head it. The forces of Congress and the Courts began to close in.

The jury in the Watergate trial was selected after only two days, over the protests of defense attorneys. Sirica was anxious to begin testimony in the case, and prosecutor Earl J. Silbert's list of sixty witnesses included many persons whom the judge was anxious to see questioned.

On Jan. 10, the first full day of the Watergate trial, there came a surprise clue to the direction the litigation would take. E. Howard Hunt pleaded guilty to three counts of conspiracy, burglary, and illegal wiretapping. The guilty plea precluded any testimony, at least insofar as Hunt's case was concerned. Outside the courtroom, Hunt—the former White House aide, novelist, and CIA official—told newsmen "anything I may have done I did for what I believed to be in the best interest of my country." And that included keeping a lid on the Watergate garbage pail.

Contributions

"We are certainly not rich—we need money"
CREEP chairman John Mitchell,
March 3, 1972

Money meant votes and the Democrats were in such deepening financial straits that many White House strategists figured Nixon could simply buy his re-election. That job had fallen to Maurice Stans, the fund-raiser's fund-raiser. He had moved easily from Secretary of Commerce, where he had had intimate contact with the fat cats of big business during Nixon's first four years, to chairman of the Finance Committee to Re-elect the President.

He had earned the position. Ten years after joining Alexander Grant and Co. as an office boy in 1928, Stans had risen to an executive partnership. By 1955, under the economic wizardry of Stans, the once small company had become one of the largest in its field. Stans, having amassed a personal fortune, went into government under Dwight Eisenhower. After serving as financial consultant to the postmaster general from 1953 to 1955 and then as deputy postmaster general until 1957, Stans was appointed director of the budget in 1958. During those years Stans and Vice-president Nixon became acquaintances, if not actually friends.

When John Kennedy displaced the Republicans in 1960, Stans moved into the presidency of Western Bancorporation of Los Angeles and then into vice-chairmanship of United California Bank. Shortly thereafter Richard Nixon asked him to head up a finance committee for his abortive run at the California governorship. With Stans' help, Nixon had more than enough money, although not nearly enough popularity. With Nixon's political fate apparently sealed, Stans went back to banking until 1968 when Nixon again needed his services. Stans delivered a whopping $20 million for the Nixon campaign and was promptly appointed commerce secretary after Nixon squeaked by Hubert Humphrey. And when Nixon needed a finance chairman in 1972, Stans was the man.

His favors and friendships were anticipated to bring in bountiful contributions. Stans predicted CREEP would reach the $35 million mark. There were two essential problems: collecting the contributions before April 7, assuring donor anonymity; and setting up a system whereby those contributing more than $3,000 could avoid paying the required gift tax. Stans knew all the angles and all the loopholes. Reportedly he personally raised $20 million before April 7, and half of that in the ten-day grace period provided by Nixon's stalling.

During that extension Stans wined and dined corporate executives in high style. Lunches at the Grammercy Inn in Washington, D.C. came to $1,300. The tab for three visits to New York, including the bill from the Waldorf Astoria Hotel, was $2,985. Among those entertained while Stans was in New York were the president and vice-president of Montgomery Ward.

Since contributions from corporations are illegal, a solicitation scheme was devised to circumvent the law. It was disclosed that Stans sent a letter to Montgomery Ward addressed to "management and key employees." A Montgomery Ward vice-president, Richard Abbott, then sent letters to each employee (addressed "personal and confidential") asking them to make out a check to CREEP and send it to company president Edward Donnell. In this way, Montgomery Ward would know if an employee did not respond—to no one's surprise, few did not respond. The employees' checks were sent to Stans along with large personal donations from Abbott and Donnell. Ward was only a medium-sized corporation; how many others fell victim to this fund-raising method can only be guessed.

Since any single contribution exceeding $3,000 was subject to the IRS's gift tax, CREEP set up over 550 dummy committees to break down contributions. If, for instance, an individual donated $30,000, the donations would come in ten separate checks of $3,000 and be distributed to ten different dummy committees.

The dummy committees were not difficult to establish. An IRS ruling of June 1971 amended the gift tax laws to provide that political committees within the same party would be considered separate and autocratic if one-third of the officers on each committee were different than officers on all other committees. Example: In November 1971, Hugh Sloan, the finance committee treasurer, sent National Savings and Trust Company vice-president Donald Scott charters for the establishment of fourteen separate CREEP accounts with names like Volunteers for Effective Government, Active Friends of a Balanced Society, United Friends of Good Government, and so forth. Scott testified that he was instructed to "provide a treasurer for each of the organizations." Scott went around the bank and told fourteen employees that they were now treasurers of finance committees to re-elect the President. Stans and Sloan were listed as president and vice-president of each one; but now, with a new treasurer on each committee, one-third of the officers were unique and the law was technically inviolate. In this example alone, over $1 million passed through the fourteen bogus committee accounts.

The establishment of dummy committees was not the only technique the Republicans used to flout the spirit, if not the letter, of the law. Advertising agencies and public relations firms often were used as conduits for illegal or tax-free contributions. The way it would work is a corporate contributor would give the agency a sum, and the agency would supply the contributor with an invoice for services rendered. No services would be rendered, and the money would be funneled into the campaign.

One of the many public relations firms which figure prominently in the Watergate affair is Robert R. Mullen & Co., of Washington, D.C., where E. Howard Hunt was employed as a writer at the time of the break-in. Hunt's office-mate Douglas Caddy, served as liaison between Mullen's and General Foods, a major client and incidentally a major source of Republican contributions.

Mullen's president was Robert F. Bennett, son of a conservative Republican senator. Bennett himself established at least seventy-five dummy committees which raised funds for the Nixon campaign. Some of them had names such as Supporters of the American Dream.

During the week before the April 7 deadline, CREEP offices were "a madhouse," according to Sally Harmony, secretary for the counsel to the finance committee, G. Gordon Liddy. An estimated $10 million flooded CREEP during that last week. When April 7 did arrive, all principal Democratic candidates opened their ledgers to the public and disclosed details of every contribution. CREEP did not. John Gardner, head of Common Cause, remarked, "Refusal of the President of the United States to reveal where $10 million has come from can only lead people to conclude that the office of the Presidency has been sold to the highest bidder."

Common Cause, estimating later that CREEP had a flow of approximately $22 million before April 7, demanded a public statement. It was too late. There were no records to make public. Stans had ordered Sloan and Herbert Kalmbach, of CREEP-West, to destroy all records of incoming and outgoing monies contributed before April 7. When Sloan was asked why the records had been destroyed, he answered, ironically, "We were obvious targets for political espionage—what have you."

In spite of this alleged paranoia, CREEP had been caught breaking several laws. The campaign act provided that records of contributions had to be retained—regardless of when they were made. Furthermore, the destruction of the files made it impossible for the IRS to determine whether any donors owed gift taxes.

If CREEP reported $10 million and Common Cause reported $22 million, what happened to the extra $12 million? No one knows for sure, but according to testimony later, there were at least three secret slush funds in which clandestine contributions were stashed. Stans had approximately $1.3 million in his office safe; H. R. Haldeman had $350,000; and Kalmbach presided over $500,000. The money was used to pay spies, saboteurs, and spooks working for CREEP—in addition to financing such stunts as the phony ad in the *New York Times*.

So what does all this have to do with the price of milk? Plenty. A suit filed by Ralph Nader's Public Citizens Inc. charged that the dairy co-op secretly contributed $422,500 in cash to CREEP in exchange for the lifting of the milk price support level in March 1971. In accordance with President Nixon's Phase I price freeze, a ceiling had been put on the price of milk from the dairy. The dairymen thought the floor was too low and in March entered a complaint with the Department of Agriculture. The USDA stood its ground and denied a change. On March 23, officials of the dairy co-ops (Middle America Dairies, Inc., Dairymen Inc., and Associated Milk Producers, Inc.) met with President Nixon in the White House. Two days later USDA suddenly reversed its decision and allowed milk prices to go from $4.66 to $4.95 per hundred weight. The decision was worth about $300 million a year to the dairy farmers, according to the general manager of Associated Milk Producers, Harold Nelson. Obviously, $422,500 was not a bad investment, even if it had to be delivered in $100 bills. The suit filed by Nader led to the inspection of all secret donations deposited before April 7 in the National Savings and Trust Company where CREEP had the fourteen dummy committees. The milk favor was only one of the many blatantly granted by President Nixon to large contributors that had now become public knowledge. Among the others: Walter Annenberg gave $250,000 and was appointed ambassador to England; Mr. George and Dr. Ruth Parkas, owners of the Alexander department store chain, gave $300,000 and Dr. Parkas was appointed ambassador to Luxembourg; V. John Krehbiel, an insurance broker, gave $30,000, which he called his "usual contribution," and wound up ambassador to Finland (The GAO estimated that $1.2 million collected by CREEP came from current or soon-to-be-appointed ambassadors.).

H. W. McCollum and Phillip Kramer, chairman and president respectively of Amerada Hess Oil Corporation of Houston, contributed a combined $50,000. On Jan. 8, 1973 the White House increased the quotas for oil imports from

the Virgin Islands by six million barrels. The largest oil refinery in the Virgin Islands belongs to Amerada Hess.

W. Clement Stone, chairman of the board of Combined Insurance Company of Chicago, contributed $1 million through dummy committees. Stone had dined at the White House on Dec. 7, 1971. The next day, his insurance company submitted a request to the price board asking for exemption from the restrictive ceiling put on insurance premium payments. Dec. 22 an exemption was granted to four insurance companies, including Stone's Combined Insurance Company. The $1 million donation arrived shortly thereafter.

All this was disclosed from only 14 dummy committees; there were 536 others whose records remain unexamined.

The April 7 date did not stop the money from rushing into CREEP. From April 7 to Aug. 31, a total of $11 million poured in. This figure is in addition to the secret $200,000 contribution of Robert L. Vesco, and untold numbers of other secret contributions. Vesco was being investigated by the SEC for looting over $200 million from a Geneva-based mutual fund complex and the contribution was intended to halt those hearings. The plan looked better on paper than in federal court where Vesco, Mitchell, Stans, and Sears eventually were indicted for conspiring to obstruct justice.

After the *Washington Post* reported that a $25,000 check found in Bernard Barker's Miami bank account was signed by Kenneth Dahlberg, CREEP's midwest fund raiser, the GAO started an investigation. Their report of Aug. 26 to the Justice Department cited five "apparent" and four "possible" violations committed by the Finance Committee for the Re-election of the President. Despite its protestations of innocence, the committee was later fined $8,000 on eight counts of campaign spending violations. It was the first time since a campaign finance law was instituted in 1925 that the GAO had found such illegal conduct.

A full investigation of CREEP misappropriations was requested on Oct. 3 by Wright Patman, Democrat from Texas and chairman of the Banking and Currency Committee. Patman pointed to massive discrepancies of at least $800,000 between CREEP's books and CREEP's actual cash on hand. The Justice Department said an investigation would interfere with the Watergate trial. CREEP called the charges "irresponsible."

Jan. 11 to Jan. 18/"Scorched Earth"

Jack Caulfield sat in his car nervously awaiting the arrival of James W. McCord Jr. Darkness had enveloped the city of Washington, and traffic was heavy on the George Washington Parkway. Caulfield had parked inconspicuously along the shoulder of the road. The experienced law enforcement officer and White House aide knew the message he was about to convey to McCord was expressly illegal, but he believed he was doing a service for someone no less than the President of the United States.

Officials in the White House wanted to make certain none of the seven men on trial for the Watergate break-in implicated anyone higher up in Administration echelons. Two days earlier, on Jan. 10, former White House aide E. Howard Hunt had pleaded guilty in the trial, ensuring his silence and obviating the calling of witnesses against him. It was rumored that more of the defendants would follow Hunt's lead. The White House wanted a wall of silence around Watergate. Caulfield was about to meet with the one man who might break that wall. It was a desperate, last-ditch effort to gain his full cooperation.

It all began the previous week when Caulfield attended a drug conference in San Clemente, California. Counsel to the President John Dean discussed with Caulfield what response might be made to the threatening letter Caulfield received from McCord the previous December. Dean had made a list of three concessions the White House was prepared to make: 1) "a year is a long time" (to spend in jail before receiving clemency), 2) "your wife and family will be taken care of" and 3) "you will be rehabilitated with employment when this is all over." The message, an assurance to McCord that he would be well rewarded for his silence and would in short order receive executive clemency, was then conveyed to the indicted Watergate conspirator by one of Caulfield's associates, Anthony Ulasewicz. It had not been enough. McCord had wanted to see Caulfield personally.

So, on Jan. 12, James McCord pulled up behind Caulfield on the Parkway, got into Caulfield's car, and confronted him. McCord was unhappy with the offer from the White House. "Jack," the nineteen-year CIA veteran said, "I am different from all the others. Anybody who knew me from the CIA knows that I always follow my own independent course. I have always followed the rule that if one goes [to jail] all who are involved must go. People who I am sure are involved are sitting outside with their families. I saw a picture in the newspaper of some guy who I am sure was involved sitting with his family. I can take care of my family. I don't need any jobs. I want my freedom."

Caulfield was sympathetic to his friend's desire to get off the Watergate hook. It was Caulfield, after all, who originally recommended McCord to be the head of security for the Committee to Re-elect the President. But there was little Caulfield could do now that McCord was indicted for a felony. He assured him that the offer of executive clemency had come from "the highest level in the White House."

McCord outlined an alternative that might give him his freedom. He told Caulfield that in the fall of 1972 he had made phone calls to the embassies of Chile and Israel, both of which he believed were subject to "national security wiretaps." On both occasions he had stated, without giving his name, that he was one of the men involved in

the Watergate scandal, and went on to inquire about visas and other documents necessary for travel to those countries. McCord believed that if his attorney asked the government to produce those wiretaps, and the government refused, he might go free. The first trial of Daniel Ellsberg had been blocked in much the same way in 1972. McCord wanted an assurance that the government would dismiss his case rather than reveal details of its surveillance of the two embassies.

But all Caulfield could do was renew the offer of executive clemency coming from "the highest levels of the White House." McCord wouldn't buy it. Nor would John Dean buy McCord's alternative proposal. The next day Dean called Caulfield into his office and gave him further instructions: "Jack, I want you to go back to him [McCord] and tell him that we are checking on these wiretaps, but this time impress upon him as fully as you can that this offer of executive clemency is a sincere offer which comes from the very highest levels of the White House."

"I have not used anybody's name with him, do you want me to?" Caulfield replied.

"No," said Dean, "I don't want you to do that but tell him that this message comes from the very highest levels."

"Do you want me to tell him it comes from the President?" Caulfield said.

("No," Dean responded, "don't do that, say that it comes from way up at the top."

Dean made certain that Caulfield understood the grav-

ity of the situation. If the lid were ever to come off the Watergate affair, the President and the government of the United States would be threatened. McCord was the only loose thread that could lead investigators to the Oval Office.

Caulfield met McCord again on Jan. 14 at the same spot on the George Washington Parkway. This time the two men got out of their cars and walked down a path toward the Potomac River. According to McCord, Caulfield told him, "You are not following the game plan. Get closer to your attorney. You seem to be pursuing your own course of action. Don't talk if called before the grand jury. Keep silent, and do the same if called before any Congressional committees." McCord still refused to follow the game plan. He wanted nothing less than his freedom, and he left the meeting with the certainty that the White House had the power to arrange that for him, but would not. Caulfield reported back to Dean, who said nothing. The following day Caulfield called McCord to "commiserate" with him, but to no avail. McCord was the wildcard in the Watergate deck. Many White House staffers nervously speculated on what action the grim-faced old CIA crony might take in the weeks that followed.

Hunt's guilty plea on the first day of the trial, followed the next day by an amended guilty plea to all counts of the indictment, imparted new importance to the Watergate grand jury. The questions the jury wanted answered might not even be touched at the trial itself. As soon as Hunt's guilty plea came in it was evident that the conspirators' intented to keep quiet. In response, the grand jury convened and announced Hunt would be the first person they would call to testify. It was a signal that if other conspirators refused to talk, they too would be called, and one way or another the grand jury would pursue an investigation until all those involved were brought to justice. The system, it seemed, would not tolerate any cover-ups.

On Jan. 15, Bernard Barker, Eugenio Martinez, Virgilio Gonzales, and Frank Sturgis all entered pleas of guilty in the Watergate trial. Judge Sirica, angered that only two defendants remained on trial, questioned the four men closely on whether they had been promised anything in return for their silence. "Has any person outside the courtroom today or in the courtroom promised that if you four men would plead guilty you wouldn't have anything to worry about, your families would be taken care of, would get so much a month, for example, has that been done?" The men emphatically answered no.

Sirica was convinced these men were hiding something. In a highly unusual maneuver, the judge questioned the defendants at length on their involvement in the Watergate break-in. He repeatedly questioned Bernard Barker about the source of the $114,000 dollars in his

Miami bank account, and Barker claimed that the checks had just arrived in the mail. At the end of the exhaustive questioning, Sirica announced to Barker in a quiet, exasperated voice, "I'm sorry, but I don't believe you."

The strange turn of events at the Watergate trial created a public clamor for some thorough examination into the affair. On Jan. 18, Attorney General Richard Kleindienst promised that the Justice Department would cooperate fully with the Senate Select Committee investigating Watergate and related charges of election misconduct. Kleindienst said he would allow the Senators to examine privately everything that the FBI had uncovered about the case, but he added that the ongoing criminal prosecution would limit the amount of material the Senators could make public.

Washington, meanwhile, was being prepared for the inauguration of Richard Nixon. Light poles along Pennsylvania Avenue were draped with red, white and blue bunting. Spectator stands were erected. Even the trees in Washington were sprayed with a special repellant so the birds would not be able to perch above inaugural spectators, dropping their feces upon them. Armed guards patrolled the streets in anticipation of protestors.

And on the same day, in Los Angeles, that most thorny of prosecutions, the trial of Daniel Ellsberg and Anthony Russo for releasing the Pentagon Papers, began for the second time.

The Plumbers Plug a Leak

The process of my prosecution was part of a scheme to affect the primaries and re-elect the President.
Daniel Ellsberg, May 16, 1973

And let me say, I think it is time in this country to quit making national heroes out of those who steal secrets and publish them in the newspapers.
Richard Nixon, May 24, 1973

An enormous crowd of people milled around outside the Los Angeles Federal Courthouse on Wednesday morning, Jan. 17, 1973 awaiting the start of the Pentagon Papers Trial. The courtroom was already overflowing with spectators. Among the people who anxiously waited for Judge William Matt Byrne to gavel the courtroom to order were twenty-three Vietnam veterans occupying the front rows, including one confined to a wheelchair because of injuries he suffered in Vietnam.

In his opening statement, the government's chief prosecutor, David Nissen said the government's case would be a "calm, unemotional presentation of the facts." The war, government information policies, and acts of conscience were "irrelevant," said Nissen. Instead, the trial was a simple matter of conspiracy and theft of what he described as "guarded" and "highly classified" documents, the Pentagon Papers.

Defense counsel Leonard Boudin took issue with Nissen and said the case was not so simple. There were going to be "minor differences between us and the government with respect to mechanical facts," said Boudin, and there would be "tremendous differences as to what the implications are." Boudin denied that any theft had taken place. He said the documents were not government property, and in any event, Ellsberg was fully authorized to have them. Boudin argued that the primary issue in the trial was "the whole problem of a government system of classifying documents . . . that is not a lawful governmental function." He characterized the government's case as one "based on the theory that somehow or other, if you take information . . . and you give it to the Congress of the United States, you are taking it away from the government, the theory apparently being that the President is the Government and Congress is not."

The defendants in this perplexing case, Daniel Ellsberg and Anthony Russo, were indicted by a Federal grand jury on Dec. 30, 1971 for conspiracy, theft, and espionage. The government did not charge Ellsberg and Russo with giving the secret forty-seven-volume Pentagon study to the newspapers. Specifically, Ellsberg was charged with theft of "the arrangement of the words on the pages" of the Pentagon Papers and the "ideas conveyed by that arrangement." The Government's indictment also charged Ellsberg with espionage for giving the Papers to Russo. Russo, in turn, was charged with theft and espionage for receiving the words, which were classified at the time. The Government argued that these words were arranged in a manner that related directly to the "national defense." Ellsberg and Russo were both accused of conspiracy to commit theft and espionage, and to "defraud the United States and an agency thereof by impairing, obstructing, and defeating its lawful governmental function of controlling the dissemination of classified Government studies, reports, memoranda and communications."

The indictment covered a period between March 1969 and September 1970, ending nine months before the Papers became public. If they were found guilty, Ellsberg and Russo could face a 150-year prison sentence and $160,000 in fines.

This was the second Papers trial. Judge Byrne had declared the first a mistrial on Dec. 8, 1972. The jurors hadn't even heard a word of testimony. They had sat on the case in the courtroom for an estimated three hours on the day they were sworn in and spent the next four months on call at home waiting for testimony to begin.

The mistrial resulted from an unprecedented stay caused by a defense appeal to the Supreme Court for disclosure of an electronic surveillance report. The government admitted the existence of the wiretap, but refused to supply any information about it except that it involved a government "foreign intelligence operation" intercepting a phone conversation between one of the defense attorneys or their consultants and an unknown party.

Justice William O. Douglas granted the stay in the first trial on July 29, 1972 so the Supreme Court could decide whether to hear the defense wiretap appeal after its summer recess. When the high court refused to hear the appeal, the defense moved for a mistrial on the grounds

the jury had become tainted and prejudiced by publicity about the trial, the Presidential election, and comments made by Vice-president Agnew comparing the release of the Pentagon Papers to the burglary of the Democratic Party's Watergate offices. Over national television on Oct. 29, 1972, Agnew had said "I also feel that whether a person steals Larry O'Brien's secret papers or steals the Pentagon Papers he should be punished."

The defense argued that the long delay precipitated by the Supreme Court stay might make the jury impatient with the nine-week case it intended to present after the government's four-week case. Judge Byrne denied the initial request for a mistrial. The defense appealed the decision and was rebuffed again. However, the Ninth Circuit Court of Appeals ruled that, "It appears to us as foolish to proceed to trial in the case with the jury selected four months ago." Since this laid the groundwork for a posttrial appeal, the opinion moved Judge Byrne to change his mind and rule a mistrial.

This was only one episode in the long, stormy trial triggered by Ellsberg's decision to make the war study public. Ellsberg was a forty-one-year-old Rand think-tank employee and Defense Department analyst who had prepared studies on the possibilities of various kinds of nuclear threats, strikes, counterstrikes, and projected holocaust casualties. In 1965, Ellsberg had accompanied Major General Edward Lansdale to South Vietnam to organize an independent intelligence operation. At that point in his life, there was little conflict between Ellsberg's conscience and American foreign policy in Indochina. But by the time of the 1968 Tet offensive, he began to despair of U.S. agression in Vietnam and his own involvement in war-making policy.

In Ellsberg's *Papers on the War*, he recalled a meeting he had in Saigon with General Lansdale and the prominent partner of a prominent Wall Street law firm, Richard Nixon. After shaking hands, Nixon asked, "Well, Ed, what are you up to?" Lansdale replied, "We want to help General Thang (Lansdale's Vietnamese counterpart) make this the most honest election that has ever been held in Vietnam." According to Ellsberg, Nixon replied, "Oh sure, honest, yes honest, that's right—so long as you win!"

Ellsberg was forced to leave Vietnam after he became ill with hepatitis in 1968. By then he had spent about eight

After xeroxing a copy of the study, Ellsberg delivered portions of the Papers to Senator William Fulbright, chairman of the Senate Foreign Relations Committee, in the spring of 1971. Fulbright was sympathetic to Ellsberg's cause, but refused to make the Pentagon study public. Ellsberg then made his historic decision to turn the Papers over to the *New York Times*.

Four years after the Vietnam History Task Force had been commissioned to write the Pentagon Papers, the war was still dragging on. On June 13, 1971, the *Times* began to publish portions of the study supplied by Ellsberg. Beneath an undemonstrative three-column headline, *Vietnam Archive: Pentagon Study Traces 3 Decades of Growing U.S. Involvement*, it launched a story that spilled over six full pages in the Sunday editions. It was an earth-shaking story and it was obviously based on what President Nixon would consider an earthshaking security breach.

All hell broke loose in the White House. Special Counsel to the President Charles Colson said he attended a series of meetings there in early July which he characterized to the FBI as "kind of panic sessions to determine what was going on and what was going to be published next by the newspaper." President Nixon was angered by the disclosure and ordered his subordinates to find out how they occurred. "There was every reason to believe this was a security leak of unprecedented proportions, "Nixon recalled on May 22, 1973, "It created a situation in which the ability of the Government to carry on foreign relations even in the best of circumstances could have been severely compromised."

The fear in the White House was exacerbated by widespread opposition in the country to the President's war policy in the summer of 1971. Also, Nixon was on the verge of his historic trips to Moscow and Peking and did not want to suffer any domestic embarrassments.

Nixon's reaction was twofold. On the level visible to the American public, the Justice Department fought a running court battle with the *Times* and other papers to stop publication of the Pentagon war study. The Papers evolved into the greatest freedom of the press issue since the Alien and Sedition Acts of 1798. Finally Nixon's own Supreme Court ruled in a split decision that prior restraint on the press is unconstitutional. Rebuffed, Attorney General John Mitchell promptly announced that the Justice Department would "prosecute all those who have violated federal criminal laws."

That was only the surface Administration reaction to the Papers. Beneath the official pronouncements, a second, clandestine attack was being mapped out. Nixon admitted in his May 22 statement, "I approved the creation of a Special Investigations Unit within the White House which came to be known as the 'plumbers.' This was a small group at the White House whose principal purpose was to stop security leaks and to investigate other sensitive security matters."

The Plumbers vigilante squad's first assignment, unknown to the Pentagon Papers defendants, was Daniel Ellsberg. The sinister activities of Nixon's intelligence squad toward Ellsberg were not to become public until after the second Papers trial was well underway.

Testimony in the government's new case began on Jan. 18, 1973. Prosecuting attorney Nissen said the government would prove that the defendants had conspired to "defraud the United States by impairing, interfering with or defeating its governmental function of controlling the dissemination of classified government materials" and that Ellsberg and Russo had committed offenses against the "United States regarding government property of over one hundred dollars and national defense documents." Nissen repeated his previous arguments, adding that the court should disregard "whether someone else had done something similar." This point may have been a

months on the Pentagon study ordered by Secretary of Defense Robert McNamara and was writing a draft of one volume. Historian Richard Ullman wrote that the purpose of the "Vietnam History Task Force" was not to get at the larger questions of right and wrong . . . but to present an account of how it all came about that in the middle of the year 1967 . . . half a million Americans found themselves in South Vietnam fighting a land and air war against a dedicated and intransigent Asian enemy."

Ironically, it was precisely the "larger questions of right and wrong" which came to preoccupy Ellsberg. A friend recalled first meeting Ellsberg in a Santa Monica restaurant and hearing terse answers to conversational questions:

"What do you do?"
"I work."
"What kind of work do you do?"
"I think."
"What do you think about?"
"Vietnam."
"What do you think about Vietnam?"
"How in God's name are we going to get out of there?"

passing reference to other government officials who leak classified documents to the press and the public. Even President Johnson had published portions of the Pentagon Papers in his memoirs, *Vantage Point.*

Nissen also argued that the documents in the case were "related to the national defense in 1969" and that they "could have been used" to the advantage of foreign nations and the disadvantage of the United States. Several times he contended that the Papers "could have hampered our efforts to negotiate a settlement of the war and to secure the return of the prisoners."

This strategy was attacked by the defense's Boudin, who argued, "there is no charge in the indictment that says that the defendants had any intention of injuring the United States" or "giving classified information to a foreign nation or communist organization." Boudin said the defense would prove that "this system of classifying government documents . . . is a system of keeping things secret, not only from the American citizens, but from the Congress."

The inability of the government to demonstrate that Ellsberg had jeopardized national security was eclipsed, however, when a series of mind-boggling revelations dragged the Pentagon Papers trial into the Watergate affair.

Judge Byrne shocked the court when he announced on April 27 that the office of Ellsberg's psychiatrist had been burlarized by White House Plumbers Hunt and Liddy. Before a Federal grand jury in Washington, Hunt had testified that the CIA outfitted him with electronic devices and disguises to execute the "bag job." The matter was further complicated when the President's chief domestic adviser, John Ehrlichman, admitted that he had learned of the burglary but did not report it, exposing himself to possible prosecution for obstruction of justice. An FBI report also revealed by the judge related that "Ehrlichman told him [Colson] this was a national security matter and not to be discussed with anyone."

The Watergate links with the trial were firmed up on April 30, when Judge Byrne admitted he had met twice with Ehrlichman. Following a *Washington Post* account which said Byrne had been offered the job of FBI director, the Judge confirmed that Ehrlichman had "suggested to me a possible future assignment in government." Byrne also said he met briefly with Nixon himself. Defense attorneys condemned the meetings as an unprecedented intrusion into the judicial process by the executive branch; or, more concisely, a bribe.

This was only a trickle in the Niagara of information the government had tried to shut off. Reluctantly, the FBI admitted it had overheard Ellsberg on a national security wiretap in late 1969 and early 1970, long before the Pentagon Papers were published. This surveillance had taken place during the critical period when Ellsberg was actually photocopying the documents, several months before he released them to the news media. It appeared Attorney General Mitchell had authorized the original bugging operation, which included thirteen taps on government officials and four taps on newsmen to investigate information leaks. Judge Byrne had asked the government a year before and at several other times during the course of the trial for a full accounting of all bugs, in addition to materials that might establish the innocence of Ellsberg and Russo. A preliminary FBI report admitted that Ellsberg had been overheard during a call he made from the home of Morton Halperin, a director of the Pentagon Papers study and then a consultant to Henry Kissinger's National Security Council. In fact, it was Kissinger who had relayed his fears about security leaks to J. Edgar Hoover. Supposedly, no record of the conversation could be found, although a

bureau employee recalled having seen it. Without any record of the tap, there was no way of telling exactly what Ellsberg had been overheard saying or whether anyone else in the trial had been recorded.

The missing logs of FBI wiretaps were eventually recovered in Ehrlichman's White House safe. "Investigators," the *Post* reported, "were told the files were turned over to the White House in the summer of 1971 out of fear they would be used against President Nixon or former Attorney General John Mitchell by Hoover who was then struggling to keep his job."

The Nixon Administration's use of wiretapping, the machine it used to enforce the law, had backfired. As a result of Nixon's personal directive for an urgent investigation into alleged national security leaks, Judge Byrne declared a mistrial and also dismissed all charges against Ellsberg and Russo on May 11, 1973. In his ruling Byrne declared angrily from the bench that "the conduct of the government has placed the case in such a posture that it precludes the fair and dispassionate resolution of these issues by a jury." This action brought an end to the trial's role in uncovering government misconduct. Defense attorneys claimed that the Administration had deliberately withheld the FBI wiretaps in order to rig the dismissal and prevent further embarrassing disclosures.

Testifying on May 16, 1973 before a panel of Senate subcommittees headed by Edmund Muskie, Ellsberg said he believed his prosecution was "part of a scheme" to re-elect Richard Nixon. Hunt's real assignment, Ellsberg said, was to "smear me" and find out if he could be turned into a "mud ball that would stick to a Presidential candidate." It stuck, all right, but to the wrong man and too late.

Jan. 19 to Feb. 17/"I Don't Believe You"

"I, Richard Milhous Nixon, do solemnly swear that I will faithfully execute the office of President of the United States, and will, to the best of my ability, preserve, protect, and defend the Constitution of the United States."

January 20, 1973

Inauguration day number two for Richard Nixon found an anxious crowd of dignitaries, Republican party workers, Congressmen, newsmen, and spectators milling about the Capitol grounds. They came to the morning swearing-in ceremonies not only for the pomp and majesty, but to hear a President who had not made a public statement in almost two months. It was not expected that Nixon would use his Inaugural Address to answer any of the questions put to the White House during his months of silence, but he might at least provide some clues.

Why, for example, had the President ordered the unprecedented Christmas bombing of Hanoi and Haiphong? What effect did Nixon expect the bombing to have on the Paris peace talks? How did Nixon hope to deal with what Congressional leaders were referring to as the impending Constitutional crisis? How would the President deal with charges of campaign misconduct in the past election, and, above all else, what did he have to say about the Watergate?

As the President took the speaker's podium, a hush

fell over the assembled throng. Mr. Nixon delivered a brief address, noteworthy only for its vagueness. He alluded to a coming ceasefire in Vietnam, but said nothing more about it. He hinted at broad changes in domestic policy, but merely told the American people to be more self-reliant. "Let each of us remember," said Nixon, "that America was built not by welfare but by work, not by shirking responsibility but by seeking responsibility. In our own lives, let each of us ask not just what will government do for me, but what can I do for myself?" He hadn't even bothered to make up his own lines.

Ambiguities in the face of concrete national dilemmas were enough to evoke rousing applause from the audience assembled, but not from the 100,000 or more demonstrators who filled Washington on that day to protest the ongoing war in Indochina. As the official inaugural parade wound its way up Pennsylvania Avenue later in the day, only two blocks away angry protestors were denouncing the man who had just been sworn in as President of the United States. Their slogan was a resounding chant of "peace now."

Never in the annals of antiwar protests were such

pleas answered so quickly. Only three days later, in a Jan. 23 televised address to the nation, Nixon announced an agreement to "end the war and bring peace with honor in Vietnam and Southeast Asia." By a strange twist of fate, the cease-fire announcement came the day after the death of former President Lyndon B. Johnson, the man most credited with escalating the Vietnam War out of reason and control. In his address Nixon told the American people:

"Your steadfastness in supporting our insistence on peace with honor has made peace with honor possible. I know that you would not have wanted that peace jeopardized. With our secret negotiations at the sensitive stage they were in during this recent period, for me to have discussed publicly our efforts to secure peace would not only have violated our understanding with North Vietnam; it would have seriously harmed and possibly destroyed the chances for peace. Therefore, I know that you now can understand why, during these past several weeks, I have not made any public statements about those efforts. The important thing was not to talk about peace; but to get peace and to get the right kind of peace. This we have done."

Nixon announced that the formal cease-fire would be signed in Paris at 7:00 P.M. on Jan. 27 by representatives of the United States, North Vietnam, South Vietnam, and the Provisional Revolutionary Government. The longest war in American history was apparently coming to a close, and the long-lost prisoners of war were coming home. It should have been a time of victory for Nixon. But it wasn't, not by a long shot.

The American people, long accustomed to receiving government rhetoric over an ever-widening credibility gap, felt some relief at the announcement of peace. Nevertheless, the majority of the people expressed only skepticism at best, concluding that time would be the test of Nixon's promises. They could do no less. Details on exactly how the government had concealed the true facts behind the Vietnam war were being highlighted daily as a result of the ongoing Pentagon Papers trial in Los Angeles. In addition, the unexplained Watergate affair and the bizarre events taking place in the Watergate trial then being conducted in Washington indicated that powerful people somewhere in government were once again hiding the truth behind government machinations.

On Jan. 19, the day before Nixon's inauguration, the key prosecution witness in the Watergate trial—former FBI agent Alfred C. Baldwin III—mysteriously forgot the names of the three officials of the Committee to Re-elect the President to whom he had delivered transcripts of wiretaps on Democratic National Headquarters in June 1972. Baldwin had told the *Washington Post* that he delivered the transcripts to William Timmons, Robert Odle and Glenn J. Sedam. Now, Baldwin was unable to testify in court to that crucial point.

On Jan. 22, during Baldwin's cross-examination, Judge Sirica excused the jury and began questioning Baldwin himself.

"What is the name of the party [to whom you gave the transcripts]?" Sirica asked.

"I do not know, your honor," Baldwin replied.

"When did you have a lapse of memory as to the name of that party?" Sirica asked incredulously. Baldwin continued to forget.

At the same time, revelations in the Watergate affair that would eventually lead investigators higher in their search for guilt had begun to surface. *Time* magazine reported that former attorney general Mitchell and presidential counsel Colson had approved the electronic eavesdropping of Democratic headquarters. *Time* quoted Howard Hunt as telling the four Cuban burglars that both Mitchell and Colson had authorized the clandestine mission. Colson threatened *Time* with a multi-million dollar law suit.

Gray didn't know how the Dita Beard memo he had given Dean had gotten back to ITT within a week.

At this time, a law suit brought by Ralph Nader against the Nixon finance committee uncovered the fact that Walter Annenberg, ambassador to England, led a list of secret Nixon contributors who gave substantial donations to the Nixon campaign in the month prior to the April 7 reporting deadline. A few days later, CREEP pleaded *nolo contendere* to eight counts of misuse of campaign funds brought against the Nixon committee by the General Accounting Office. CREEP's payment of the $8,000 fine marked the first time a presidential campaign organization was cited for illegal activity since the passage of the Corrupt Practices Act of 1925.

CREEP was in hot water at the Watergate trial as former officials of the organization took the stand to testify about the affair. Hugh Sloan, former treasurer of the Finance Committee to Re-elect the President, told the court that payments of $199,000 to G. Gordon Liddy had had the prior approval of campaign chairman Mitchell and finance chairman Maurice Stans. Sloan said that he knew the money was to be used in intelligence-gathering operations, but he was unaware of the nature of those operations. An increasingly incredulous Judge Sirica found it difficult to believe that such a large sum of money could have been disbursed without the treasurer keeping tabs on how the funds were spent.

Someone, obviously, was misdirecting funds somewhere along the line, and Sirica asserted that any responsible official surely would have known about it.

In what must have been an embarrassment to President Nixon, Jeb Stuart Magruder—former deputy director of CREEP and administrator in charge of the inaugural celebration—testified that $235,000 dollars was budgeted by CREEP for intelligence operations. The Committee wanted to gather information on radical groups they feared might disrupt Nixon rallies and the Republican National Convention itself. Clearly, the Democratic National Committee didn't fit into this category.

Furthermore, the testimony that was taken in the trial demonstrated that the conspirators planned far more than just the bugging of Democratic National Headquarters. A twenty-five-year-old college senior named Thomas Gregory testified that he had been recruited by Hunt to spy on the Muskie campaign and later on the McGovern campaign. Gregory had attended a meeting of six of the seven Watergate defendants where they planned a break-in of George McGovern's campaign headquarters. Gregory said he was paid $175 dollars a week by Hunt for his espionage activities. The student didn't say that he also received sixteen college credits in political science from Brigham Young University for working in the campaign.

Radicals were key to the defense offered in the Watergate trial. James McCord's attorney, Gerald Alch, argued that the former CIA agent had acted under duress, motivated by a fear of potential violence from radical groups linked to the Democrats. Alch said it would have been in McCord's purview as head of CREEP security, under the circumstances, to initiate the bugging. Judge Sirica, knowing a good one when he heard it, labeled that defense "ridiculous."

As the elusive Watergate litigation proceeded, Judge Sirica became more and more determined to get to the truth before the well of testimony ran dry. At one point Sirica read Hugh Sloan's testimony to the jury, which had been out of the courtroom when it was given, so they could determine if the former CREEP treasurer were telling the truth. Peter Maroulis, attorney for Liddy, objected that the judge was giving undue weight to Sloan's testimony in the eyes of the jury. Maroulis moved for a mistrial, bringing down the full weight of the judge's ire. "I exercise my judgment as a federal judge and as the chief judge of this court," Sirica told Maroulis. "As long as I'm a federal judge, I'll continue to do it. I could care less what happens to this case on appeal. I'll continue to do what I think is right at the moment," he fairly shouted.

While Judge Sirica was experiencing frustration inside his courtroom, Senator Sam Ervin announced the scope and form the Senate investigation into Watergate would take. The Senator from North Carolina said his committee intended to use its subpoena power to elicit testimony from top White House aides. Ervin said the investigation would cover not only the break-in of Democratic Headquarters, but also charges of campaign sabotage and spying, the receipt and use of campaign funds, and the practices of various government agencies during the campaign.

At the same time, demands for a special prosecutor in the Watergate investigation were voiced anew. Sirica's unorthodox actions in the course of the litigation had made it obvious that neither the prosecution nor the defense was concerned with uncovering the truth in the affair. It was obvious to most observers that some sort of elaborate cover-up was taking place. Suspicions were heightened on Jan. 28 when Dwight Chapin, President Nixon's appointments secretary, suddenly decided to leave the White House staff to join United Airlines. Chapin's name had previously been linked to acts of campaign sabotage.

On Jan. 30, a jury of eight women and four men took only ninety minutes to find Liddy and McCord guilty of all counts in the Watergate trial. Only three weeks after its start, the criminal litigation had ended, with the nation as much in the dark as ever. Case closed, or so it seemed. The seven guilty conspirators had yet to be sentenced, pending appeal of the conviction by McCord and Liddy. Jack Caulfield, meanwhile, was certain that wildcard James McCord, now facing a forty-five-year prison term, would soon spill his guts to Judge Sirica.

In the aftermath of the Watergate trial, bits and pieces of information emerged which increased Judge Sirica's determination to open Watergate by imposing maximum sentences on the seven defendants. On Feb. 7, Seymour Hersh reported in the *New York Times* that Gordon Strachan, a former staff assistant to H. R. Haldeman, had served as the contact between Liddy's intelligence operation and alleged agent-provocateur Donald Segretti. Strachan's name was the missing link in the Republican spy network, and it supplied added credence to charges of campaign espionage and sabotage. At the same time, Ehrlichman confirmed that he had been informed of possible White House involvement in the Watergate break-in soon after it occurred. "This is a routine kind of thing that is done if members of the White House staff are arrested or in trouble," Ehrlichman said in a statement. The finger of guilt in Watergate pointed ever upward.

The activities of Liddy and Hunt came under careful scrutiny after their guilt had been established. In mid-February, it was reported that Hunt had conducted an investigation into the private life of Senator Edward Kennedy shortly after the death of Mary Jo Kopechne at Chappaquiddick. It was also reported that both Hunt and Liddy had access to information obtained through national security wiretaps while both worked on the White House staff. It was becoming evident that Hunt and Liddy were involved in clandestine actions that extended far beyond the Watergate, although people could only guess how far.

On Feb. 17, President Nixon announced the appointment of L. Patrick Gray as permanent director of the FBI. "Mr. Gray was nominated because he's the best man [the President] can find to head up the FBI," Press Secretary Ziegler told a news conference. It was an appointment that both Gray and Nixon would come to regret.

The FBI

As suddenly and unexpectedly as a raid at dawn, John Edgar Hoover was dead. At seventy-seven, it was perhaps his final act of defiance, leaving leaderless a corps of nearly 20,000 over and undercover agents he had personally amassed, trained, and supervised. The Federal Bureau of Investigation had not known a single day in its forty-eight-year history without Hoover as the top G-Man. He was called by many the "godfather of Pennsylvania Avenue." J. Edgar Hoover was not only the FBI's creator, he *was* the FBI.

He had joined the Justice Department as a lawyer in 1917, and six years later, at the age of twenty-nine, was asked to take over the department's investigative bureau. Aware of the meaning of power even then, he consented on the condition that an entirely separate and a apolitical branch of government be established with himself as the almighty leader. From the beginning, he was bent on making the FBI the world's greatest law enforcement agency. By 1932, the FBI was ready to make an indelible imprint upon the American consciousness by solving the Lindbergh kidnapping case. The FBI was on the front page for the first time, and Hoover liked the image and the publicity.

The Bureau became a myth in the 1930s. John Dillinger, Pretty Boy Floyd, Ma Barker, Alvin Karpis, the Rosenbergs, Rudolph Abel: all legendary public enemies—all captured or killed by the FBI. The bigger the target, the better Hoover liked it. On a weekend in 1940, Hoover led a raid that netted no fewer than thirty-three Nazi spies.

Unlike most law enforcers, Hoover never shied away from the press; he was always eager to mug for the cameras and shoot the breeze with reporters. He knew the publicity could do no harm. Only lawyers and accountants were accepted for the rigorous training that Hoover devised. Image-maker Hoover quickly transformed his agents into "gangster-busting, spy-catching, straight-shooting, star-spangled heroes." Books, radio serials, backs of Wheaties boxes, comic strips and then a television series—all supervised by Hoover—would turn the G-Man, the Bureau, and its Director into elements of American folklore.

Hoover pioneered scientific law enforcement with the introduction of extensive fingerprint files, a national crime laboratory, and computerized files that could produce a criminal's history at the push of a button. Congress passed all his budget requests with only perfunctory examination. The press did not dare question any FBI releases. And the eight Presidents Hoover served under treated him with kid gloves.

Never actually a friend of any President, Hoover remained close enough to wield his special brand of power, yet distant enough to transcend partisan politics. Critics and supporters alike agreed that the man kept the FBI clearly separate from the White House—an achievement that may become regarded as his greatest.

Though he obviously loved the limelight, Hoover's personal life was a mystery, partly because that's the way he wanted it. He lived with his mother until her death in 1938 and then, never having married, lived alone. His favorite pastime was the race track. Friends said the ponies were an obsession, though they would quickly add that Hoover religiously patronized only the two-dollar window at Pimlico. It was a good thing: he lost consistently. But the race track was an integral portion of his Roaring Twenties, straw hat, tommy gun image until the end.

Hoover's final years, marred by scandals, gossip and even outright questioning of his ability and authority, were a far cry from the gang-busting days. When John F. Kennedy took office, bringing with him an aura of youth and vitality, his first appointment was the re-appointment of Hoover, aged 65. Ironically, it was during the Kennedy years that Hoover's power would at last be challenged. Attorney General Robert Kennedy started publicly denouncing the FBI's massive and growing dossiers on private citizens and even congressmen. It was Robert Kennedy who first accused Hoover of allowing ideology to interfere with efficiency. Since organized crime was one of Kennedy's main targets, it inevitably led to many confrontations with the FBI director, who had for many years refused to acknowledge the Mafia's existence. The obvious reason why was that if the Mafia existed, then the FBI was failing desperately in an area where it was needed most; Hoover just wanted to avoid any possibility of the FBI yielding to bribes or payoffs.

It was the FBI director—ever defiant—who was to telephone Robert Kennedy on Nov. 22, 1963, to coldly report, "The President is dead." Robert Kennedy and Hoover never spoke again.

Kennedy had opened the doors of confrontation, but the next AG, Ramsey Clark, was to rush through them often. Clark openly criticized Hoover for keeping files on blacks, civil rights leaders, leftist organizers, antiwar activists, and members of Congress. Hoover did not appreciate the charges and reacted with moments of pique, calling Clark "a jellyfish" and Martin Luther King "the

most notorious liar in the country."

Local police forces had become sophisticated and computerized, and there were constant complaints about the FBI overstepping its jurisdiction and actually interfering with apprehensions. Inefficiency and dissension at the Bureau were blamed on Hoover's insistence that he pass judgment on each memorandum, each request and each arrest. He reportedly fired one FBI agent whom he found reading *Playboy*, screaming that only "moral degenerates" read

such trash. The FBI and the CIA stopped communicating entirely when an FBI employee leaked some petty information to the CIA and the CIA refused to tell Hoover who the culprit was. Men on Capitol Hill were calling Hoover moody and inefficient—and even senile. The years had taken their toll. Hoover had outlived his righteousness.

From a time when right and wrong were as different as Eliot Ness and Al Capone, to an era of perplexing moral dualism symbolized by Dr. Ellsberg's widely accepted although perhaps illegal leak of the Pentagon Papers, Hoover's views remained rigidly black and white. Once the foremost defender of the American citizenry, he found himself spying on it. But an ironic turn of events would catapault Hoover back into his old role of stalwart protector.

In July 1970, President Nixon approved a plan for expanded domestic security, but, according to Nixon, he rescinded his approval five days after it was put into effect, "prompted by the opposition of Director Hoover." As reported by the *New York Times* on June 7, 1973, the intelligence plan was recommended to the President by an interagency committee of representatives from the FBI, CIA, Defense Intelligence Agency, National Security Agency, and the counter-intelligence arms of the Army, Navy and Air Force. A report to the President called for the organization of the Interagency Group on Domestic Intelligence and Internal Security (IAG). The recommendations sent to Nixon on June 6, 1970 were, in part, as follows:

"Present procedures [of electronic surveillance] should be changed to permit intensification of coverage of individuals and groups in the United States who pose a major threat to the national security . . . of foreign nationals and diplomatic establishments of interest to the intelligence community. At the present time, less than electronic penetrations are operative . . . Everyone knowledgeable in the field, with the exception of Mr. Hoover, concurs that existing coverage is grossly inadequate . . .

There is no valid argument against use of legal mail covers [opening mail] except Mr. Hoover's concern that the civil liberties people may become upset. This risk is surely an acceptable one and hardly serious enough to justify denying ourselves a valuable and legal intelligence tool.

Covert coverage is illegal and there are serious risks involved. However, the advantages to be derived from its use outweigh the risks . . .

Present restrictions [on surreptitious entry] should be modified to permit procurement of vitally needed foreign cryptographic material. Also, present restrictions should be modified to permit selective use of this technique against other urgent security targets . . . Surreptitious entry of facilities occupied by subversive elements can turn up information about identities, methods of operation, and other invaluable investigative information. This technique would be particularly helpful if used against Weathermen and Black Panthers . . . It is the belief of all except Mr. Hoover that the technique can still be successfully used on a selective basis . . .

The plan was submitted to President Nixon by Tom Charles Huston, then a junior staff member of the White House who was in charge of the interagency meetings. Huston addressed the report to H. R. Haldeman, saying, "We don't want the President linked to this thing with his signature on paper . . . all hell would break loose if this thing leaks out." The report included Huston's own "top secret analysis and strategy." It read, in part:

Having seen the President in action with Mr. Hoover, I am confident that he can handle this situation in such a way that we can get what we want without putting Edgar's nose out of joint . . .

I might add, in conclusion, that it is my personal opinion that Mr. Hoover will not hesitate to accede to any decision which the President makes, and the President should not, therefore, be reluctant to overrule Mr. Hoover's objections. Mr. Hoover is set in his ways and can be bull-headed as hell, but he is a loyal trooper. Twenty years ago he would never have raised the type of objections . . . but he's getting old, and worried about his legend . . .

On July 15th, a top secret White House "Decision Memorandum" approved the report and called for the IAG to go into operation on Aug. 1. It specified, in an attempt to placate Hoover, that the director of the FBI should serve as chairman of the interagency committee. It further stated that Tom Huston would participate in all activities of IAG as personal representative of the President.

Hoover remained rigid in his disapproval of both the report and the President's decisions. Hoover's motivations were unclear, for he had allegedly engaged in many similar illegal activities himself. He said he was fearful that the well-manicured image of the FBI would be tarnished if any agents were caught making surreptitious entries, and he was certainly displeased with the possible usurpation of FBI power.

On the other hand, sources said that the brazen lawlessness of the President's proposal, including burglary and the opening of mail, offended Hoover's alleged respect for civil liberties. During World War II, Hoover stood almost alone in his opposition, on constitutional grounds, to the internment of Japanese-Americans. Despite his reasons, it was the cranky, seventy-six-year-old Hoover who, again at odds with the rest of the intelligence community, single-handedly thwarted the President's plan to establish an illegal super-spy agency.

Many people were now urging Hoover's retirement. Nixon's closest advisers, especially Haldeman and Ehrlichman, wanted the "old man" out. But he had twice refused to retire, at 65 and at 70, and Hoover was not about to be sent out to pasture at age 76. Not even Richard Nixon could expire an American institution. Only destiny could do that, and on May 3, 1973, it did. Even though he was 77, it came as a surprise—most people thought him immortal. "People around here," said one congressional aide, "felt he had a dossier on Saint Peter."

While he lay in state in the Capitol Rotunda, previously reserved for Presidents, war heroes and distinguished Congressmen, 25,000 mourners paid their respects to the passing of the director of the FBI—and perhaps the FBI itself. With Hoover's departure a host of previously unnecessary questions arose: What exactly is the FBI and what should it be? In how much secrecy should it carry out its operations? What sort of checks and balances tempered its awesome power? And the last question, which might in part answer all other questions: Who would become the new director of the FBI?

The President was confronted with a decision that no President had ever faced before—filling Hoover's legendary shoes. With the taste of bitter Senate confirmation hearings fresh in his mouth, Nixon played it safe in this election year and named fifty-five-year-old Louis Patrick Gray III as acting director of the FBI. Gray had never raided a gangster hideout, had never made an arrest, and had never prosecuted a major case in court. As a lawyer, he specialized in tax and trust suits. He was by no stretch of the imagination a lawman. With Annapolis and twenty years in the Navy behind him, he hardly evoked the image of a G-Man.

Gray had only two apparent qualifications: his administrative skill and his unadulterated loyalty to Richard Nixon. He had met Nixon at a Washington party in 1947 and the two had been friends ever since. Gray left the Navy in 1960 to work under Robert Finch in Nixon's campaign against John F. Kennedy. In 1969, Gray was appointed executive assistant under Finch, who was by then secretary of Health, Education and Welfare. With that move, L. Patrick Gray officially joined the team. A year later he was transferred to the Justice Department as an assistant attorney general.

Immediately upon the announcement of Gray's appointment to the FBI, critics charged that it was purely political. Though Gray claimed nonpartisanship, most people on Capitol Hill could not believe that any Nixon appointee—especially Gray—could be apolitical. The previous month Gray had added his voice to the crescendo of Nixon Administration attacks on the press, which had increased in frequency and fury since Watergate. In a speech in Santa Ana, California, Gray accused journalists of "becoming too much a part of the culture of disparagement which threatens to destroy all respect for established institutions." He then singled out the *New York Times, Washington Post,* NBC, and CBS for sacrificing "accuracy and objectivity to partisan bias and prejudice."

For the first time in 50 years, an administration could conceivably control the FBI, and Nixon's instincts did not place him above that temptation. The memory of the recent intelligence superagency battles Nixon had lost to Hoover was probably still vivid in the Presidential mind. So L. Patrick Gray III, square-jawed, hard-working, ex-Navy captain who attended mass nearly every morning and wore an American flag pin in his lapel, entered the FBI under a barrage of criticism that would ricochet about his head until the end.

In his first months as acting director, the burly weight-lifter abandoned many of his predecessor's outdated rules and regulations. Agents no longer had to wear white shirts and they were allowed to grow mustaches and sideburns. Hoover had outlawed colored shirts and facial hair because, he claimed, they were contrary to the public's image of a G-man. He even chastised one FBI executive for hiring a bald-headed agent.

Gray opened lines of communication, revamped the Byzantine bureaucracy, and even tolerated a pinch of dissension in the ranks. He went out of his way to employ members of minority groups and hired the first female FBI agents. "I've tried to open the windows and raise the shades," he said. "I want to stimulate and stir all this talent."

Following Hoover's "Red Menace" footsteps, Gray refused to attack organized crime and drug trafficking and instead concentrated on subversives, blacks, and antiwar activists. He whole-heartedly endorsed the surveillance of radical groups before they committed any crimes. "The potential is there, the motivation is there," he said. "These people are virtually opposed to our constitutional society. Whether they have the capabilities or not is not for us to judge. We have to provide the intelligence about them."

Still, with revelations about Watergate proliferating, the question loomed larger than ever: Could Gray conduct an intensive investigation involving former friends, associates and employers? Speculators were uncertain if even Hoover would have insisted upon a thorough probe—not out of deference to the President, but because of the possible harm to the country. Gray's allegiances were not yet as well-defined.

When the campaign to re-elect the President was in full swing and CREEP needed information, they went to avowedly "nonpartisan" Gray. In September 1972, Gray ordered twenty-one agency field offices in fourteen states to file expert advice on how the President and his aides could best handle campaign issues related to criminal justice. At the same time, Gray himself went on the campaign trail for Nixon and delivered pro-Administration speeches in Butte, Montana; Spokane, Washington; Philadelphia and Cleveland. In one speech Gray exclaimed that the U.S. was "on the threshold of the greatest growth in our history." In another, he criticized "those who insist that our priceless liberties are being eroded—that freedom is increasingly in jeopardy across the United States."

Gray's conduct was indeed peculiar for an acting director of the FBI. Critics pointed to the speeches as examples of Gray's ties to the President, while one White House aide stated bluntly that "he's just another Nixon surrogate now." He was away from FBI headquarters so often that his first in-house nickname became "Two Day Gray." Later, Gray would describe his public rhetoric as simply "carrying the FBI's message to the people."

Another message he was carrying to anybody who would listen was his desire for the permanent post of FBI director. Ten months had gone by and Nixon was back in the White House but there still was no word on Gray's nomination. With the Watergate affair escalating, it was apparent that Nixon did not want to throw a juicy chunk of meat like L. Patrick Gray to the Democratic lions on the Senate Judiciary Committee. But Gray was looking forward to both the appointment and the Senate battle. "You can expect one hell of a confirmation fight," Gray said, with a twinkle in his eye.

On Feb. 17, Gray got his wish. The announcement of Gray's appointment as permanent director went off like the opening bell of a heavyweight championship match. The challengers struck first.

"Pat Gray, with his bullet head and pugnacious jaw had the look of an FBI director. It is now clear that he lacks the qualifications," wrote Jack Anderson. The suspicions voiced ten months before had mounted and Gray's "pugnacious jaw" was receiving more than its share of the critics' left hooks. He was accused of conducting a shallow and cursory investigation into Watergate and some even claimed that Gray was keeping the White House abreast of his findings, even though White House officials had been implicated. The momentum for a bloody confirmation battle was growing.

Sen. Sam Ervin of South Carolina headed the sixteen-man confirmation committee. It adjourned on February 8 and went after Gray with a vengeance. The questioning by Democratic senators like Ted Kennedy, John Tunney of California, Birch Bayh of Indiana, and Robert Byrd of West Virginia was brutal and direct. Watergate was the issue, plain and simple, and few questions were asked about Gray's views on law enforcement. He testified that he had resisted giving FBI files of the Watergate investigation to the White House, but legal advisers had told him he was obliged to accede to White House requests. Gray said that two days after the break-in, on June 19, he received a summary report that had "come up through FBI channels." Copies of the FBI report were addressed to Haldeman and AG Kleindienst. "I nixed that. 'No, we will not do that.'" But a month later, Gray testified, John Dean, who was allegedly conducting his own White House investigation, "asked us to give him what we had to date." Gray then gave the "raw files" to Kleindienst. "I have every reason to believe that it then went to the White House," he said.

The questioning was heated and Gray at one point became a bit ruffled. "I work for the President," he declared and then offered to show the FBI report to any congressman. Rather than appeasing the Senate committee, the unorthodox offer only added fuel to their anger. They wanted to know about the FBI interviews of alleged saboteur Donald Segretti. The Washington *Post* had reported that on Aug. 19, two days before the Republican Convention, Presidential aides flew to Miami and showed Segretti the files of two previous interviews he had had with the FBI. Segretti was preparing to appear before a grand jury on Watergate. Gray testified that the FBI interview of Segretti on June 26 had included no questions about Watergate because Segretti was obviously not involved. Then he went on to say that he could not guarantee that White House aides had not shown Segretti the FBI reports.

The Senators were stunned by these admissions and shifted their line of attack to establish Gray's relationship with the White House. Gray agreed that he had accepted a speaking engagement in August after a request from a campaign official, but he claimed that he had made up his own mind. Senator Byrd hammered away at the Gray-Nixon relationship, saying he feared the FBI was becoming a private detective agency for the White House. Gray vehemently denied the charges. The first day of hearings ended with Gray's "one hell of a fight" prediction coming true. But Gray was no longer the favorite.

Round two of the hearings opened with Gray admitting that the FBI had wanted to interview Martha Mitchell, but John had refused permission. Gray said he assumed the agents wanted to speak to Mrs. Mitchell because of her public statements about "all those dirty things going on." John Mitchell, in private law practice when the agents approached him, said his wife had nothing to contribute to the investigation and warned that the agents should not try to see her. The agents heeded Mitchell's warning.

Gray said it was "a matter of courtesy" extended to the former AG and CREEP chief. Senator Bayh replied, "that kind of double standard might be asking for trouble." Gray again contended that the FBI's investigation was complete and thorough. His further testimony contradicted his contention. FBI agents were denied an interview with former assistant AG Robert Mardian, a top official of CREEP, when Mardian claimed an attorney-client relationship with principals in the Watergate affair. Mardian was not bothered again. Although FBI agents interviewed John Ehrlichman, they did not speak with the President's chief of staff, Haldeman. And Gray swore he could find no evidence to support *Time*'s assertion that the FBI had tapped the telephones of newsmen and White House staffers. At the day's end, the committee was pleased, and a bit surprised, with Gray's candor—but it did little to repair the damage of these new revelations. The once bright chances of Gray's confirmation were fading rapidly.

(The disclosures of the next day further darkened those chances. Included in files supplied by the FBI at committee request was a memorandum from Patrick O'Donnell, a former presidential assistant, which advised that the City Club of Cleveland "had asked our assistance in attempting to secure your participation as a key speaker . . . With Ohio being crucially vital to our hopes in November, we would hope you will assign this forum some priority in planning your schedule."

The memorandum referred to the Cleveland speech Gray had delivered in August 1971—the same speech Gray insisted he made up his own mind about. The evidence of collusion was building. Gray testified during the third and fourth rounds of the hearings that John Dean had sat in on every FBI interview of White House officials. He did not want Dean there, emphasized Gray, but the only other option was to conclude "that there could be no investigation of White House personnel. I decided I could jolly well let the interviews be conducted with Mr. Dean sitting in." Jolly was not the mood of the senators as they continued to tear away any remaining shreds of Gray's claims of nonpartisanship. They were unimpressed when Gray called the Watergate probe "as aggressive and as exhaustive an investigation as the FBI has ever conducted or is capable of conducting within the four walls of its jurisprudence."

At this point a tiring Gray refused to answer any more queries about Watergate, saying, in effect, enough is enough. "I respectfully decline to answer that question," was his response over and over again until the committee sidetracked into other areas—like the Dita Beard memo. Gray testified that he personally gave the memo to John Dean after it had been submitted to FBI, but did not know how it got back into ITT hands within a week. He also stated that the FBI was fully aware that Colson dispatched Hunt to visit Dita Beard in the Denver hospital last March. No law had been broken, Gray insisted, and therefore the FBI did nothing about it.

Knowing that his confirmation was in serious trouble, Gray revealed more and more information in hopes that his honesty might salvage his image. He admitted that Herbert Kalmbach, Nixon's personal lawyer, told FBI agents last August that he had paid Donald Segretti be-

tween $30,000 and $40,000 on request of Dwight Chapin, the President's appointment secretary. This was the first official corroboration of the charges.

During the fifth round, on March 8, Gray's testimony brought the whole confusing Watergate mess closer to the White House. He accused John Dean of "probably" lying when Dean told FBI agents that he did not know whether or not Hunt had an office in the White House. In fact, Gray explained, three days after the Watergate break-in Dean had told two of his deputies to search Hunt's Room 338 in the old executive office building next to the White House. Not only did Dean know Hunt had quarters in the White House, but he knew exactly where they were. The Judiciary Committee was incredulous. They could not believe that in spite of this knowledge, Gray subsequently handed over all the FBI files Dean requested. Gray said he had sent the files to Dean "through the chain of command," a phrase he used often throughout the hearings. All eight Democratic senators were publicly saying they would not confirm Gray and they were sure they could muster at least one Republican nay. Nine was the knockout number.

Gray could not help but sense defeat. Formerly sturdy and confident, his demeanor became sullen. In a soft bass voice he admitted that it was Kleindienst who told him to stop testifying about Watergate midway in the hearings. Later, Gray told the committee that Dean and Ehrlichman had approached him at least fifteen times when Watergate news was being leaked to the press. "I resented it," Gray stated. But he continued to supply Dean with each new FBI finding, even though those findings had shown Dean to be the man who suggested the hiring of G. Gordon Liddy. The Senators were appalled by Gray's subservience to White House aides. Senator Byrd threw up his hands and told Gray, "Christ himself was betrayed by one of his chosen few."

An embarrassed White House began cutting as many ties with the acting director as possible. President Nixon, during a March 16 press conference, even condemned Gray's offer to show FBI files to members of the committee. "I believe that the practice of the FBI furnishing 'raw files' to full committees must stop with this particular one," said Nixon.

It was all over save the eulogies. The White House related that on April 4, in a 10-minute phone call to San Clemente, Gray asked Nixon to withdraw his name from nomination. With no argument and only a touch of regret, Nixon complied with the request.

The President had this to say about that: "Because I asked my counsel, John Dean, to conduct a thorough investigation of alleged involvement in the Watergate episode, Director Gray was asked to make FBI reports available to Mr. Dean. His compliance with this completely proper and necessary request exposed Mr. Gray to totally unfair innuendo and suspicion and thereby seriously tarnished his fine record as acting director and promising future at the bureau."

Gray's withdrawal avoided added embarrassment for the President. Whether Gray actually had fallen or had been pushed from confirmation was left to speculation. But the sacrifice of L. Patrick Gray III, the Administration's first lamb sent to slaughter, would prove futile, for Watergate was now a full-fledged scandal that would require the President to provide some answers to the growing list of questions.

Feb. 18 to Feb. 28/Mene, Mene, Tikal Upharsin

Had Nixon been looking at the handwriting scrawled on every White House wall in February 1972, he would have seen big trouble. An angry Congress was on the verge of taking drastic action to reassert its constitutional authority. Investigations into the Watergate affair and the financing of Nixon's re-election campaign were cracking the bulletproof shield about the Presidency. The Pentagon Papers trial, so crucial to Nixon's ends, was going poorly as past and present high government and military figures testified in Los Angeles that the release of the papers in 1971 had not damaged national security; a pending Congressional inquiry into the role of ITT in Chile did not chalk up any popularity points for the President either.

The congressional key to Nixon's crumbling house of cards was Senator Sam Ervin, chairman of the select committee appointed to investigate the Watergate affair. Writing in the *Washington Post* in mid-February, Ervin—an acknowledged expert on the Constitution—attacked what he termed Nixon's 'brazen seizure of power.'

"The question," said Ervin, is "whether the Congress will remain viable, or whether the current trend towards executive usurpation of legislative power will continue unabated until we have a presidential form of government.

"Executive impoundment of legally appropriated funds is only one in a long line of executive usurpations of legislative power which the Congress has condoned by its acquiescence. Indeed, the Separation of Powers Subcommittee [of the Senate Judiciary Committee] has investigated several of the most serious instances, including abuse of the pocket veto power, use of executive agreements to circumvent the constitutional role of the Senate in treaty-making, exercise of lawmaking power through the issuance of executive orders, and the refusal to provide information and testimony to the Congress under the guise of 'executive privilege.'

"The executive has seized power brazenly because the Congress has lacked the courage and foresight to maintain its constitutional position."

Nixon apparently had not read the handwriting on the wall. Instead, he'd appointed L. Patrick Gray permanent director of the FBI, providing a focus for all of Congress' anger, frustration, and curiosity. The President was not offering up Gray as a scapegoat. The FBI director-des-

Only four days after Nixon named Gray, a Bernstein and Woodward story in the *Post* revealed that convicted Watergate conspirator E. Howard Hunt had been sent to the bedside of Dita Beard in March 1972 to dissuade her from identifying the infamous ITT memo. After the visit, Ms. Beard issued a statement calling the memo a forgery. According to the *Post* story, this came out in an admission made by Charles Colson, special counsel to the President and Hunt's White House supervisor, in secret Watergate grand jury testimony. Colson earlier had given sworn public testimony that Howard Hunt did not work for him in 1972.

Another strange maneuver surrounding the Watergate mystery was also discovered. Hugh Sloan, the treasurer of the Finance Committee to Re-elect the President who quit in July 1972 over the Watergate bugging, had been rehired by the committee only four days before the start of the Watergate trial in January. Sloan supposedly was helping finance chairman Maurice Stans wrap things up and was being paid $100 to $150 a day for his efforts. Sloan's return to the re-elect fold seemed highly suspicious, especially in the face of his January testimony before Judge Sirica. The judge had accused Sloan of lying. Now, with Sloan rehired at a cushy fee, it appeared he ignate was simply the first of Nixon's fatted flock to be put on the block for inevitable slaughter. The Senate Judiciary Committee, which by law had to approve Gray's nomination, became the slaughterhouse.

Initial reaction to Gray's nomination had been mixed senatorial caution and outrage. Majority Leader Mike Mansfield said he was willing to give Gray the benefit of the doubt as to whether the FBI under his direction had become politicized. Democratic Whip Robert Byrd, on the other hand, charged Gray with being "openly partisan" in the FBI's failure to pursue the Watergate affair. Byrd, a Judiciary Committee member, had urged the defeat of Gray's nomination.

If Gray was to have succeeded in gaining Judiciary Committee approval, he would have had to play a cautious hand. He would somehow have to convince the senators of his detachment from President Nixon, whom he had served in both the 1960 and 1968 presidential campaigns. Unfortunately for Gray, the events immediately prior to his confirmation hearings had not done much in his favor. might have had some purpose for conveniently not having known how Liddy used the $199,000 Sloan gave him.

On Feb. 28, the Democratic Party filed another amended complaint in their civil suit against the Republicans. The Democrats doubled the stakes to $6.4 million damages; the Watergate conspiracy began to promise incredible dividends. They also named two additional CREEP officials as defendants—Jeb Magruder and Herbert Porter—making the list of defendants look like a who's who of the Republican party.

The same day the anxiously awaited confirmation hearings had gotten underway. The FBI director-designate had staunchly maintained that his investigation of the Watergate affair had been "non-political" and unrestricted. "We gave it a full-court press," said Gray, "I was not such a jackass as to think that the credibility of the FBI as an investigative agency would not be on the line in this thing."

The day before the Judiciary Committee confirmation hearings began, the testimony of New Jersey Republican Harry Sears had been made public, revealing for the first time his pre-trial deposition in an SEC suit. It was now known that Maurice Stans and John Mitchell had solicited a contribution of $250,000 from financier Robert Vesco while he was under securities investigation. Sears' testimony would be the first direct evidence of conscious wrongdoing on the part of top Nixon campaign officials. Even more damaging was the fact that both Mitchell and Stans had been cabinet officers. The writing was off the wall and in the headlines.

Vesco to King's Knight 4

Robert L. Vesco had just about anything anyone could ever want. He had best friends who were the heads of various governments. He had even stood on the podium with Richard Nixon at a 1968 campaign rally. He had ownership of some of the world's largest corporations. Some said he practically owned the Bahama Islands. He had more money invested in Costa Rica than any other single individual. He jetted around the globe in his own unmarked Boeing 707, equipped with sauna and discotheque. His personal fortune was nearing a billion dollars. He owned an eighty-acre estate in New Jersey where his wife and four children lived.

But in May 1973 there was something wrong. Uniformed guards in jeeps patrolled the estate around-the-clock. And Robert Vesco was not with his family, he was in seclusion in Costa Rica. There, too, armed guards surrounded his rented villa. Vesco said his life was in danger.

By Latin American terrorists and kidnappers? "No, by the agencies of the United States," he said. "The revolutionaries down here can't come near the viciousness of the American agencies."

The CIA or the FBI or the Pentagon? "It seems to me that they're all under the same roof now—and I know too much."

The story of Robert Vesco is a strange and sordid tale of high finance and international intrigue which lead to criminal acts at the highest levels of American government. Vesco was no stranger to politics. One of his closest associates, and a man who figured prominently in the story, was Harry L. Sears.

Sears had been a die-hard Republican since his days as a party committeeman in New Jersey. After becoming a state senator in 1961, he'd scratched his way to senate majority leader, where he remained until 1967. When CREEP needed a man to head up the Nixon re-election drive in New Jersey, Harry Sears was the logical choice. He was friendly with many GOP officials, and on a first-name basis with John Mitchell. At the time Sears was also the director of a large Jersey electronics firm, International Controls Corporation. The chairman of the board at I.C.C. was Robert Vesco.

At the time, Vesco was in Geneva, Switzerland, buying the controlling stock of a mutual fund complex called International Overseas Services from millionaire-founder Bernie Cornfield. At the time of purchase, many of Vesco's business associates condemned his move as foolish. "Cornfield's a financial wizard," said one of them, "and if he's pulling out, there's a sure disaster ahead." But another Vesco confidant explained how Vesco operated. "He's a chess player. The whole thing's a giant chess game to him and Vesco knows his opponent's next ten moves even before his opponent does."

Five months later, in June 1971, the Securities and Exchange Commission made a move Vesco had not planned on. The federal regulatory body started an investigation of International Overseas Services and Robert Vesco. They suspected him of looting many millions of dollars. The announcement of the investigation shook Vesco—but only momentarily. He sent Harry Sears to tell John Mitchell to hold up the SEC's probe. When there was no sign of this happening, Vesco the chess player started making his moves.

Vesco hired Nixon's errant nephew— "It can't do any harm," he remarked.

He hired Donald Nixon, the President's nephew, in July, just one month after the SEC investigation had gotten under way. The hiring was done through Gilbert Straub, then director of the European division of I.C.C., the Jersey electronics firm. Straub was a close friend of both Edward Nixon and F. Donald Nixon, Donald's father. When Straub was married, to a German woman, both Nixon brothers attended the wedding.

So in the summer of 1971, while under investigation by the SEC, Vesco peopled his side of the chess board with players such as Harry Sears (working for CREEP), Gilbert Straub (friend of the President's brothers), and Donald Nixon (the President's nephew). When he hired Donald, Vesco remarked slyly, "I'm doing the Nixons a favor, it can't do any harm. . . ."

In December, the pawns started to move into place. A small civil suit landed Vesco in a Geneva jail. Immediately, he got in touch with Sears. Sears went directly to Attorney General Mitchell and told him the story. The very next day, after a phone call from the U.S. embassy, Vesco was released from prison.

In January 1972, Daniel Hofgren, vice-chairman of the CREEP finance committee, solicited a contribution from Vesco. According to Hofgren's testimony, he went back to finance chairman Maurice Stans and said that Vesco was "really up there in the clouds back then. They were rolling in money, you know? So later I said to Morrie (Stans), 'Lookit, they're talking big numbers.' And he said, 'I'll take it from here.'"

A month later, with CREEP apparently ready to talk business, Sears went back to Mitchell and asked him to arrange a meeting between Sears and SEC chairman William Casey. The meeting never took place and the investigation continued. The time had come for Vesco to make a strong offensive move, to place the other side of the board in check.

The check was offered to Stans, and Vesco sent no surrogate this time—he went himself. He offered $500,000 if Stans and Mitchell would halt the SEC investigation. Stans said he would settle for $250,000—in cash and before April 7. And he would do what he could with the SEC. Vesco agreed and went straight to Mitchell's office to get his approval. Mitchell concurred. On March 8, according to grand jury testimony, it was all arranged.

Vesco needed $250,000 in cash in a hurry to beat the April 7 disclosure deadline. With this in mind, he flew to the Bahamas.

Vesco owns the Bahamas Commonwealth Bank, along with a string of other Bahama companies like automobile dealerships, liquor stores, travel agencies, and pharmacies. Of twenty one Bahama stocks quoted daily by brokers around the world, six were publicly associated with Vesco.

Vesco started making his big splurge in the Bahamas sometime in the beginning of 1971. The Bahamas Commonwealth Bank, for instance, was purchased "between November 1971 and March 1972," according to the bank's manager. During that same time span, Vesco had allegedly spirited away many millions from International Overseas Services.

While most banks in the Bahamas were lending money with great caution because of a slumping economy and a high-risk factor, the Bahamas Commonwealth Bank was writing mortgages as high as 100% for some properties. The largest loans were made to high-ranking government officials of the ruling Progressive Liberal Party. Vesco had reportedly dined with and befriended the Bahamas Prime Minister, Lynden O. Pindling.

Exactly how much Vesco owns in the Bahamas is purely speculative. The banking laws of the islands ensure much the same degree of secrecy as those in Switzerland. But a few things are clear: Vesco has pumped at least $10 million dollars into the sagging Bahamas economy, and the powers that be are exceedingly grateful; and Vesco is an economic powerhouse in the Bahamas.

But it took Vesco longer than he expected to get the $250,000 in cash from the Bahamas into the Barclay Bank in New York City. It was already April 10—three days beyond the cut-off date. With this new development, the original plans had to be slightly altered. The alteration was verified by no less a personage than Edward Nixon. According to grand jury testimony, Nixon instructed Vesco to deliver only $200,000 in $100 bills to Stans that day and contribute the other $50,000 to CREEP six months later in a more traditional fashion, by a check that would be reported. Vesco followed Nixon's instructions.

On the morning of April 10, Vesco sent an aide to withdraw $250,000 from the Barclays Bank and bring it back to him at his New Jersey estate. Vesco took out $50,000 and stuffed the remaining $200,000 into an old brown briefcase. He handed it over to Harry Sears and Laurence Richardson, former president of I.C.C. In a matter of hours, Richardson and Sears were in Washington, D.C. They went directly to Stans' office and handed over the briefcase. Stans told Hugh Sloan, finance committee treasurer, to put the $100 bills in the safe. Sloan knew nothing about the deal, he claimed later.

The stash in Stans' safe by this time reportedly had grown to $1.3 million in illegal funds. An estimated $235,000, according to Sloan, was paid to G. Gordon Liddy for the break-in at the Watergate. The rest of the stash financed other sabotage.

Three hours after the $200,000 was delivered, Harry Sears finally had an audience with William Casey, the SEC chairman, and G. Bradford Cook, counsel for the SEC who was in charge of the Vesco investigation. The rendezvous had been arranged earlier in the day by John Mitchell. The meeting was a $200,000 exercise in futility. The SEC was unrelenting and the investigation went on.

At this point, Vesco went off the chess board and brought in some reinforcement from abroad: Jose "don Pepe" Figueres, the President of Costa Rica. Vesco had met Figueres for the first time in May 1972. In July Figueres sent a diplomatic letter to Richard Nixon claiming that Costa Rica was a "showpiece of democratic development" and that the SEC investigation of Vesco would hurt the small, struggling country.

Robert Vesco, according to the SEC, made a loan that summer of $2.2 million to Sociedad Agricola y Industrial San Cristobal, a company founded and still partly owned by President Figueres. The loan was funneled through one of the mutual funds controlled by International Overseas Services. Another $60 million was reportedly plowed into Interamerica Capital, a Costa Rican investment firm which handled government bonds and was headed by a close confidant of don Pepe Figueres, Alberto Inocente Alvarez. Figueres also specified that Señor Vesco had broken no laws in Costa Rica and that he and his money were welcome. Still, the SEC investigation went on.

Something had to be done. The father of Vesco investigator Cooke had been a GOP fund raiser in the Midwest, and was an old friend of Stans. So Stans met with Cook and SEC chairman Casey on at least four occasions in May, June, July and August concerning the SEC investigation of Vesco, according to grand jury testimony. Cook told Stans he was aware of the $250,000 that Vesco had pulled out of the Bahamas because it was money allegedly stolen from IOS. Cook said he also knew that some of the money was in Stans' secret fund. Stans insisted in their meetings that the contribution had nothing to do with the SEC probe of the Vesco securities swindle and that it should not be included in the final report that Cook was drawing up.

Cook later admitted that after talking to Stans he had, in fact, deleted a detailed paragraph about the $200,000 contribution and replaced it with a general and vague account of the Bahama withdrawal, leaving no mention at all of the contribution to CREEP.

The election was drawing near and the SEC had not halted its probe. When Vesco's closest associates began to be called to testify, Vesco went for broke. He told Harry Sears to get in touch with Mitchell and warn him that Vesco would spill the beans if the SEC did not back off immediately. Mitchell implied that his hands were tied, but said not to worry. He told Vesco to sit tight, but Vesco was pacing nervously by then.

Ten days before the election, having failed to get any concrete results by going through the back door, Vesco decided to charge through the front. He sent a memorandum to F. Donald Nixon, the President's brother, who owed Vesco a favor for "babysitting" for his son Donald. Donald had lived with the Vesco family for seven or eight months by then and called Mr. Vesco a "best friend" and "mentor." Vesco had "adopted" the twenty-six-year-old nephew of the President; no one else had known what to do with him.

After Donald had completed a Navy stint in Vietnam, he traveled through India and returned to America where he joined a "hippie commune" in the Midwest. The Nixon family did not know what to make of Donald—Vesco did. Although never officially on the payroll, Donald said, "Mr. Vesco gave money out of his pocket from time to time . . . he's the one person who has never lied to me—ever. I put him up there with some heavies." The "favor" of hiring Donald two years previously was to be paid off.

In the memo to F. Donald Nixon, Vesco threatened to expose the whole underhanded deal with Mitchell and CREEP if the SEC did not cease investigations at once. The memo was communicated from F. Donald to Mitchell. It was returned to Sears, apparently having never reached the President, for whom it was intended.

Vesco boiled as Richard Nixon ran away with the presidential election, thanks in part, to money he had furnished. Twenty days after the re-election, the SEC filed a federal civil suit charging Vesco and forty one others with looting International Overseas Services for an astounding $224 million. The SEC brief stated that Vesco, who was in control of four mutual funds collecting money from investors to be re-invested in sound, secure companies around the world, had instead collected at least $224 million and started his own companies, funneled it into companies he already controlled, loaned it to friends, or deposited it in banks. The SEC cited some examples of where the money really went, including Costa Rica and the Bahamas. But the $200,000 contribution to CREEP

was not mentioned.

The *Washington Star News* reported on Dec. 26 that $200,000 of the looted Vesco money had been contributed to CREEP and never reported. It had become public knowledge and CREEP acted swiftly. On Jan. 31, 1973, all the money was returned to Vesco from CREEP with a letter saying, ". . . We believe it is in your best interest, as well as ours, that the contribution be returned." The refund came a little late, to say the least. And the SEC investigation continued.

On March 1, 1973 criminal proceedings were started against Vesco in U.S. District Court in New York by the SEC. United States Attorney Whitney North Seymour was in charge of the grand jury which, at the outset, separated itself from the allegedly illegal campaign contributions. The grand jury was to look into Vesco's swindle, not the contribution. The differentiation made by Seymour became more and more ironic as the grand jury proceedings got under way.

The next day, March 2, G. Bradford Cook became, at thirty seven, the youngest man ever appointed chairman of the SEC. He was appointed by Mr. Nixon. Soon he would become the youngest man to ever hold that office for less than three months.

Besides the criminal grand jury in New York, the GAO was holding its own investigation in Washington. On March 12, the GAO sent a report to the Justice Department of four illegal acts it suspected CREEP had committed. All four involved the Vesco-Stans payoff. The GAO had filed a similar report in August 1972, but the Justice Department did nothing with it, stating there was little real evidence. This time, the report was backed up with testimony from Hugh Sloan, the man to whom Stans handed the $200,000. Sloan's secret testimony opened the floodgates.

In New York, Seymour planned to subpoena Mitchell, Stans, Sears, and Vesco to testify. Interestingly, Seymour had conducted some of the investigation in private, months before it officially began. Based on what he had seen, since the bungling of the Watergate affair, he feared Justice would impede justice, according to the statements of informed sources. It was during that period of clandestine investigation that Harry Sears delivered the lengthy deposition which was to be the basis of the grand jury inquiry.

The witnesses who were subpoenaed arrived and testi-

fied—all but Vesco, who was in his rented home in Nassau, the Bahamas. On April 15, U.S. Attorney James Loew flew to Nassau to serve a subpoena. He walked up the driveway and saw Vesco; Vesco turned and fled, screaming, "Get him! Get him!" to his bodyguards. Loew threw the subpoena at Vesco on the run and hit him in the back. At that point, a group of bodyguards physically ejected Loew from the Vesco residence. In the road next to the shaken Loew lay a brown envelope containing the Vesco subpoena. "We don't want this," said one of the guards.

Even though Vesco did not appear, Mitchell, Stans and Sears did. Mitchell, after testifying, said he had "answered all questions freely, frankly and fearlessly." He did not say honestly.

March 1 to March 13/On the Altar

The strands of the Watergate puzzle that had been meandering about for months from accusation to smear to counter-charge to denial began to rewind, in early March 1973, into a tight, short fuse. Three leads to the bomb—FBI director-designate L. Patrick Gray, financier Robert Vesco, and the International Telephone and Telegraph Corporation—suddenly became focuses of public attention and exposure after months of rumor. Facts finally began to see the light of day.

As the three leads wound around each other, the high explosive called Watergate took on a completely new and different meaning for the American public. No longer did the word, once merely a prestigious Washington address, refer only to the break-in of Democratic National Committee Headquarters. Now, the term entered the English language as a catch-all meaning scandal, conspiracy and cover-up in the presidential administrations of Richard Nixon.

By far the biggest break in the whole affair had come in L. Patrick Gray's confirmation hearings when he testified that he had given FBI files on the Watergate investigation to the White House.

The Finance Committee to Re-elect the President filed a sworn statement that it had been ignorant of any federal investigation into the dealings of Robert Vesco until after the November elections, despite the fact that finance chairman Stans apparently did know about the SEC probe as early as April 1972. On March 1, 1973, U.S. Attorney Whitney North Seymour announced that he was initiating criminal proceedings against Robert Vesco in addition to the SEC's civil action already under way.

The Senate Foreign Relations Committee, meanwhile, was looking into the matter of Chilean President Salvador Allende. It had been suggested that ITT might have tried to influence that country's election against the Marxist ruler. San Diego and the American presidential election apparently hadn't been enough for the communications empire.

The underpinnings of the White House were clearly being shaken loose, and President Nixon sensed the tremor. It was at his press conference on March 2 that Nixon acknowledged for the first time that FBI files on the Watergate investigation *had* been given to his counsel John Dean. At the same time, the issue of executive privilege was thrust into the fore. The President said he would

certainly object to any member of his staff being called to testify before a congressional committee.

"It is executive privilege," said Nixon, "no President could ever agree to allow the counsel to the President to go down and testify before a committee. On the other hand, as far as any committee of the Congress is concerned, where information is requested that a member of the White House staff may have, we will make arrangements to provide that information, but members of the White House staff, in that position at least, cannot be brought before a Congressional committee in a formal hearing for testimony. I stand on the same position every President has stood on."

Instead of answering the embarrassing questions Gray had raised, attorneys for the Committee to Re-elect the President subpoenaed 10 reporters from four news publications to give depositions in the Republicans' $2.5 million counter-suit against the Democrats. The lawyers requested that the reporters, the same people who had unearthed the most damaging stories about CREEP, bring their notes with them to court so their "memory might be refreshed." The blatant attack on press freedom was aimed at finally discovering the identity of the White House leak. Fortunately, Judge Richey granted the newspeople a delay to prepare a plea to quash the subpoenas.

The leaks continued to spring. Even a plumber couldn't stop the torrent of revelations pouring from Gray to the Senate Judiciary Committee. In a written statement to the committee entered into the record on March 7, Gray admitted knowledge of a payoff to accused agent-provocateur Donald Segretti of between $30,000 and $40,000. Gray said that the funds were arranged by White House Appointments Secretary Dwight Chapin and transmitted to Segretti through President Nixon's personal attorney Herbert Kalmbach for "service to the Republican party." The admission virtually confirmed the electrifying *Washington Post* story of the previous October that was so viciously attacked by the White House.

At the White House, meanwhile, Press Secretary Ron Ziegler was busy issuing his daily, almost tape-recorded denials. He denied that John Dean had shown FBI reports to Donald Segretti, and claimed that Dean sat in on FBI interviews with White House staff only after staffers requested his presence.

The day following Gray's sensational admission, Ziegler finally felt the pressure of Watergate full force, almost causing him to yield before the onslaught. The young Ziegler was virtually astounded by the first question put to him at the morning White House press briefing. When does President Nixon plan to withdraw L. Patrick Gray's nomination to the FBI? a reporter asked. Ziegler took his time gulping a response, saying only, "there's no plan to do that." Ziegler's second question was another blatant shocker. When will H. R. Haldeman follow the lead of his former assistant Dwight Chapin and resign? Ziegler replied sharply that Haldeman planned no such thing.

It was just a case of bad breath for the President's mouthpiece. Another reporter asked Ziegler if he were prepared to apologize to the *Washington Post* for his past attacks. That question was followed up with another asking how Ziegler, presumably an intelligent individual, could possibly defend his past statements in light of L. Patrick Gray's testimony.

"I've reviewed the transcripts of what I've said in the past months," Ziegler responded. "I see nothing new and I have no further comment to offer on it. But I will say . . . that I stand firmly on my previous comments on questions that were put at that time in relation to stories and I stand firmly on the comments that I made in response to your questions and also on the reporting." Ziegler's coup of the session, though, was to admonish reporters not to jump to conclusions about "raw, unevaluated material from FBI files," meaning the information on Kalmbach, Chapin and Segretti.

The White House was standing on tenuous turf during early March. Judiciary Committee members had become markedly interested in the role of John Dean in any possible cover-up of the Watergate affair. Senator Kennedy speculated on possible legal assistance that Dean might have given conspirator E. Howard Hunt following the June break-in. Senator John Tunney revealed that Dean had recommended G. Gordon Liddy for his position at CREEP, apparently with the knowledge that Liddy was to direct clandestine activities. Grounds were being laid for the Judiciary Committee to subpoena Dean, in direct conflict with Nixon's stand on executive privilege.

The President and his re-election team were becoming the focus of attention as events built up to an ultimate confrontation with Congress. The Finance Committee to Re-elect the President admitted on March 9 that it had returned a total of $655,000 to three large contributors. The remittance of $100,000 sent to Texas oil magnate Robert Allen was revealed; another $305,000 dollars was returned to a Texas land speculator, Walter T. Duncan, who ac-

tually borrowed money to contribute to the Nixon campaign; and, finally, the return of Vesco's $250,000 dollars was confirmed by the committee.

While the Administration's credibility became increasingly subject to doubt, Nixon himself was bent on asserting his self-created role and provoking Congress. John Ehrlichman, Nixon's special assistant on domestic affairs, announced on March 9 that Nixon intended to veto fifteen spending bills before the Congress, including measures for flood control, the aged, vocational rehabilitation, veterans' burial benefits, veterans' hospitalization, veterans' drug rehabilitation and mental and physical retardation. Ehrlichman threatened that if the vetos were overridden by Congress, the President would impound the funds.

At the same press briefing, Ehrlichman revealed that he had personally asked John Dean to sit in on FBI interviews with White House staff the previous July. "I have always felt it appropriate to have counsel present at an interview of that kind," Ehrlichman said. "I just felt more comfortable." Ehrlichman also revealed that he "might have been in a little jeopardy with the employer" if he had refused to allow Dean's presence. Nixon's investigation into Watergate, apparently, had taken unprecedented form. No matter though—the next day President Nixon asked Congress to restore the death penalty.

The President found himself at a crucial juncture in his game plan against Congress. Both parties had reached an impasse, Nixon asserting unprecedented authority, Congress powerless to fight back except through uncovering the squalor underlying Nixon's strong hand. The President, the consummate gamesman, took a decisive step to undercut any possible Congressional advantage on March 11 by issuing a statement of policy on executive privilege.

Nixon declared the practice of executive privilege to be "a practical necessity." In this instance, it certainly was.

On the afternoon of March 13, the Senate Judiciary Committee met to consider "inviting" White House counsel Dean to testify in regard to his possible misuse of eighty-two FBI investigative Watergate reports that Gray gave him. The committee first received an accounting from Gray of some thirty-three contacts he had with Dean on Watergate, some on almost a daily basis following the break-in. Gray had also listed five contacts with John Ehrlichman concerning embarrassing "leaks" of information implicating high White House officials in the Watergate.

The committee then voted unanimously, 16 to 0, to "invite" Dean to testify in closed session. The invitation had a special senatorial R.S.V.P. "If the White House wants Patrick Gray," said majority whip Robert Byrd, "they will have John Dean come and testify."

High Noon on Capitol Hill

I will simply say the general attitude I have is to be as liberal as possible in terms of making people available to testify before the Congress, and we are not going to use executive privilege as a shield for conversations that might be embarrassing to us, but that really don't deserve executive privilege.

Richard Nixon, Jan. 31, 1973

A Constitutional crisis had been brewing between the President and Congress, and the pot boiled over when

Nixon refused to allow White House aides to testify before the Senate Judiciary Committee hearings on Gray's nomination.

The President was challenging Congress to a Constitutional duel. At stake was who would run the country.

The two had been squaring off for a long time. Every President since World War II had tried to invest more power in the executive branch and it was usually at the expense of Congress. Like his predecessors, Nixon said he believed the country needed a strong President. But this meant a head-on collision with a Congress that was already worried about its dwindling strength. Both Democratic and Republican members of Congress complained that Nixon had subverted the Constitutional authority of the legislative branch and that Congress had lost the power and facilities to deal with the Executive on an equal basis.

There were three major areas of contention: war and treaty powers, control of the purse and "executive privilege."

The Constitutional confrontation over executive privilege reached a crisis when Nixon refused to allow White House aide Dwight Chapin and counsel John Dean to testify before the Senate Judiciary Committee.

Senate Majority Leader Mike Mansfield had called for the Senate to suspend Gray's hearing until some of the matters connecting the Watergate burglary to the White House could be resolved. By bottlenecking the FBI nomination, Senate strategists had hoped to use Gray as a crowbar to pry Dean loose from the grip of the White House.

Nixon only squeezed tighter and issued the major policy statement on March 11, 1973 claiming that White House aides were protected beneath the umbrella of executive privilege, that unwritten law by which Presidents have traditionally refused to furnish information to Congress. Nixon defined executive privilege in terms of the doctrine of separation of powers "in which the President personally exercises his assigned executive powers is not subject to questioning by another branch of government. If the President is not subject to such questioning, it is equally inappropriate that *members of his staff not be so questioned, for their roles are in effect an extension of the Presidency* [emphasis added]." Nixon even anticipated his critics when he said, "Executive privilege will not be used as a shield to prevent embarrassing information from being made available but will be exercised only in those particular instances in which disclosure would harm the public interest."

As far as Nixon was concerned, "without such protection, our military security, our relations with other countries, our law enforcement procedures and many other aspects of our national interest could be significantly damaged and the decision-making process of the executive branch could be impaired."

Senate critics maintained they were less concerned about communications between White House aides and the President than they were concerned about relationships between staff members and people outside the White House. They suspected that Nixon was using national security as a smokescreen to protect his aides.

There was also concern that Nixon was attempting to override the traditional limits of executive privilege. In his policy statement Nixon said that the ". . . President must be able to place absolute confidence in the advice and assistance offered by members of his staff. And in the performance of their duties for the President, those staff members must not be inhibited by the possibility that their advice and assistance will ever become a matter of public debate, either during their tenure in government or at a later date."

The battle lines were drawn. If the executive and legislative branches of government were at war over the limits of presidential authority, it followed from the fact that executive privilege is never specifically mentioned in the Constitution. Nonetheless eighteen presidents have invoked it at one time or another to claim confidentiality.

While it has been a common tradition among American Presidents, there has been an equally strong tradition in Congress to restrict the President's use of executive privilege through legislation. Congress enacted a bill in 1912, and repassed it in 1966, making it a crime to inter-

fere with the right of government "employees to furnish information to either House of Congress." In the wake of the Teapot Dome scandal, Congress also passed a 1928 law which empowered the Senate and House government operations committees to obtain in writing virtually any information they wanted from the executive branch.

Nixon, himself, entered the debate over executive privilege as a Congressman during the Alger Hiss investigation in the Truman Administration. Hiss was a high State Department official who was accused of communicating government documents to Russia. The House Un-American Activities Committee had asked Truman to produce an FBI report said to have bearing on the Hiss case. When Truman refused to supply it, Congressman Nixon criticized the President on April 22, 1948 for issuing an order that "cannot stand from a Constitutional standpoint." Nixon said Truman's decision would mean "that the President could have arbitrarily issued an Executive order . . . denying the Congress of the United States information it needed to conduct an investigation of the executive department and the Congress would have no right to question the decision." As a result, Nixon strongly supported a 1949 bill which would make it a crime to intimidate anyone in or out of government called to testify before a congressional committee.

But apparently Nixon's philosophy changed when his job did. By his own count, Nixon has invoked executive privilege on three different occasions. However, the Library of Congress has estimated that Nixon used the doctrine to prevent aides from testifying before Congress on nineteen separate occasions. The difference in the figures flows from the White House's strict definition of executive privilege. According to the Administration, the doctrine was invoked only when it was announced it was being invoked. This left Press Secretary Ronald Ziegler in the awkward position of characterizing Henry Kissinger's frequent refusals to testify before congressional committees as mere statements, not formal invocations of executive privilege.

Congress became well-schooled in Nixon's formal invocation of executive privilege during the Senate Judiciary Committee hearings on the ITT affair and Kleindienst's nomination as attorney general in April 1972. Senator Sam Ervin had requested that three Presidential aides testify: Peter Flanigan, William Timmons and John Ehrlichman. Executive privilege was invoked by counsel John Dean. After several days of maneuvering, a compromise was arranged. Flanigan agreed to testify, providing questioning was restricted to four specific points. As a result, the committee learned nothing because the most interesting matters proved to be beyond the established boundaries.

While this exchange instructed Congress in what to expect from the White House, there is a corollary to the Flanigan incident which prefigured the imbroglio over Dean. After Flanigan's appearance, an interested citizen wrote a letter to Dean inquiring about the scope of executive privilege. Dean replied that Flanigan's testimony, along with "precedent and tradition," were evidence that no recent President, Nixon included, has "ever claimed a blanket immunity that would prevent his assistants from testifying before Congress on any subject." But it was precisely "blanket immunity" which Nixon used to prevent Dean from being interrogated by the Senate, a principle so "well established" that his own legal counsel had not known it existed eleven months earlier.

Nixon was not in conflict, however, with his ambition of consolidating greater power in the office of the Presidency. Executive privilege was only part of the game plan. He was equally determined to expand his control over the federal purse through impoundment of funds.

As with executive privilege, the Constitution makes

no specific mention of impoundment. However it provides that "no money shall be drawn from the Treasury but in Consequence of Appropriations Made by Law." At the same time the Constitution charges the President with making sure that "laws be faithfully executed." When Presidents impound money appropriated by Congress, they traditionally stand on this phrase for their legal authority; there are broad precedents for impoundment.

In the postwar era, Harry Truman impounded $735 million appropriated by Congress to create ten extra air force groups. Ironically, as a Congressman, Nixon voted to override Truman's veto and denounced him for not spending the money as directed. As President, Nixon came full circle, arguing that Truman had had every right to impound the funds.

With Nixon, though, impoundment was used to such an unprecedented degree that there was congressional doubt about its legality. The issue heated up in October 1972 when Congress killed Nixon's plan for a $250 billion spending ceiling. Nixon accused Congress of being fiscally reckless and said the ceiling was necessary to prevent a tax increase. Congress replied that Nixon's budget-cutting would not reduce the cost of government but would only put federal money into different areas. What infuriated Congress was that after it killed the spending ceiling, Nixon set out to impose the goal anyway by vetoing bills and impounding funds. The budget cuts totaled $10 billion. Nixon's impoundment seriously crippled and in same cases annihilated federal programs in housing, education, agriculture, conservation, pollution, health and poverty areas.

In an extraordinary attack on the President's impoundment strategy, the Senate voted on April 4 to set a $268 billion ceiling on federal spending, $18 billion more than Nixon proposed. The Senate approved a second measure on May 10 which underlined its determination by insisting that Nixon follow congressional directions on how funds are used.

Congress was not the only branch of the government that challenged Nixon's abuse of authority. Separate decisions in four federal courts held that the President had illegally withheld appropriated funds. In one decision, Judge Oliver Gasch ordered Nixon to release the funds because "the language . . . of the act clearly indicated the intent of Congress to require the administration to allot . . . the full sums authorized to be appropriated." Therefore, the court said, the President had no power to impound the funds, whatever his purpose.

But Nixon apparently was ready to ignore both the courts and Congress. Besides insisting that he had the power to withhold money that Congress had appropriated, Nixon claimed he could spend funds which Congress wanted to withhold. This was money Nixon wanted specifically for the bombing in Cambodia; the confrontation that developed around it was also a showdown over Presidential war powers.

When the 93rd Congress convened in January 1973, it launched a major battle to curtail the President's war-making policies by approving legislation that would plug Nixon's funding pipeline to Indochina. While it appeared that visible American involvement in Vietnam was ending, the air war over Cambodia was threatening to bring the United States to the very brink of military re-intervention in Southeast Asia. Liberal Republican Senator Jacob Javits maintained that Nixon's authority to take military action to liquidate the war ended when he signed the Jan. 27 ceasefire agreement. Secretary of Defense Eliot Richardson replied that if the President had the authority to negotiate the ceasefire, he had the power to force the parties of the treaty to comply with its conditions. Richardson also asserted that even if Congress withheld funds, the bombing in Cambodia would continue.

But Congress would not be steamrolled again. In a historic decision, the House voted 219 to 188 against transferring defense funds to pay for the Cambodian air war. It signaled the first time in six years that the House supported an antiwar amendment and the first time in the history of the war that it voted down a military appropriation. Congressional determination to limit Presidential war powers was made complete when the Senate also voted, 69 to 19, to cut off all funds for the bombing.

The President was under fire.

March 13 to March 23/A Matter of Privilege

When the Senate Judiciary Committee ignited the Watergate fuse by "inviting" Presidential counsel John Dean to testify, the White House instantly assumed a standard defense contingency. The probability that Congress would challenge President Nixon's blanket claim to executive privilege was well anticipated by the scheming, security-minded strategists around the Oval Office.

The very moment the Judiciary Committee voted to call Dean, White House Deputy Press Secretary Gerald Warren issued a statement denying that John Dean gave FBI reports on the Watergate investigation to Committee to Re-elect the President officials. The disclaimer was a response to former CREEP employee Judith Hoback who had given a signed affidavit to Senator Birch Bayh, a Judiciary Committee member, claiming that less than forty-eight hours after she supplied secret, confidential information to the FBI in July, CREEP attorneys asked for an explanation of her actions. The FBI report on Ms. Hoback,

who was an assistant to CREEP treasurer Hugh Sloan, was among those Patrick Gray gave John Dean.

Speaking for CREEP, Devan Shumway backed up Dean by saying CREEP learned of Hoback's action "from employees of the committee with whom she had discussed her separate interview" (with the FBI). Ms. Hoback said Shumway was lying. The proof, apparently, resided somewhere in John Dean's head which, at that moment, had a Presidential padlock on it.

The counsel to the President threw away the key the following day when he sent a two-paragraph letter to Senator James Eastland, chairman of the Judiciary Committee, refusing the committee's invitation to testify, and citing executive privilege. Dean did agree to answer written questions from the committee directly related to Gray's nomination but, in line with White House strategy, he reserved the right to determine which questions were related.

The Senate reacted to Dean's refusal with unmitigated outrage. Judiciary Committee members uniformly attacked Nixon's application of executive privilege, and their sentiments were echoed in Congress. Senator John Tunney argued that even if one were to assume executive privilege to be the President's constitutional right, it would apply only to communication between the President and the White House staff. The Judiciary Committee wanted to question Dean about his communication with Gray, not with Nixon.

Not surprisingly, the Judiciary wasn't the only Congressional committee whose requests to testify were refused by Dean. His absence before the Judiciary Committee, given Gray's sensational revelations about Watergate, at least made some sense if compared to his non-testimony before the Senate Foreign Relations Committee. That saga began on Jan. 25 when Senate Majority Leader Mike Mansfield entered a statement into the Congressional Record in which Dean said he would like to discuss "the recurring problem of leaks of classified information given in closed, executive sessions of Senate committees." Accordingly, William Fulbright, chairman of the Senate Foreign Relations Committee, wrote to Dean on Feb. 9 requesting "precise information in order to determine what steps should be taken." Fulbright's letter elicited a response on March 2 from Thomas Korogolos, deputy assistant to the President for congressional relations, saying that he and William Timmons would be happy to meet with the chairman on the matter. A perplexed Fulbright transmitted a letter to Dean on March 12 saying, "my inquiry was occasioned by a statement made by you." He informed the harried Dean that he was invited to appear before the Foreign Relations Committee. Dean never did.

The scrimmage lines were drawn in the superbowl of executive privilege, and John Dean had the good fortune of playing for the favored home team. His coach outlined the game plan at a March 15 press conference remarkable only for Nixon's ability to keep his team's signals secret.

Predictably, the first question put to the President was about executive privilege. Nixon responded calmly, with a straight face, that an irresponsible Congress was holding Patrick Gray hostage for a favorable disposition on the issue of Dean. Nixon declared it his Constitutional responsibility to uphold the principle of separation of powers, adding that Dean was protected by the "double privilege" of his lawyer-client relationship to the White House in addition to executive privilege. Nixon emphasized that Dean's willingness to provide written answers to proper questions from the Judiciary Committee proved that his administration was the most "forthcoming in history." John Dean would testify when hell froze over and not before.

In this assault on Congressional authority, Nixon revealed at least partly how he viewed the impending Senate investigation of the Watergate affair. Beginning by calling the inquiry of the Ervin committee proper, Nixon declined to comment on Gray's testimony that Dwight Chapin and Herbert Kalmbach gave Donald Segretti over $30,000 dollars. The President said the current investigation of the matter precluded any comment by him on it. In the next breath, though, Nixon said he intended to invoke executive privilege in forbidding White House staff from testifying before the Ervin committee.

The President's announcements on Watergate at the press conference had immediate repercussions in Congress. Acting under guidelines established by Nixon concerning "raw FBI files," Attorney General Richard Kleindienst rescinded an offer made by L. Patrick Gray to make the FBI files on Watergate available to all members of the Senate. Under the new arrangement only Senators Ervin, as chairman of the select committee, and Howard Baker, as committee vice-chairman and ranking minority

member, would be allowed access to FBI files on Watergate. The arrangement was bitterly criticized by other select committee members. Senator Daniel Inouye called Kleindienst's guidelines "an insult to the United States Senate," while Connecticut Republican Lowell Weicker said it was "essential that all seven members of the committee have access to the FBI's Watergate files." Was Kleindienst trying to hide something?

More to the point, was President Nixon trying to hide something by announcing two months before the Ervin committee was scheduled to hold hearings that White House staff members would not testify? Sam Ervin intended to find out. Speaking on the CBS news show "Face the Nation," the North Carolina Senator said that if any White House staff members invoked executive privilege, "I'd recommend to the Senate they send the sergeant-at-arms of the Senate to arrest a White House aide or any other witness who refuses to appear and let the Senate try him." Ervin had no intention of delaying his investigation while a Supreme Court fight lasting possibly two to three years went on over the Constitutionality of executive privilege. The White House called Ervin's threat "sensationalism," adding that any information the Ervin committee requested would be provided in writing "consistent with the doctrine of separation of powers."

The day before the Judiciary Committee hearings' on Gray scheduled resumption, Democratic whip Robert Byrd assailed Nixon's actions, summing up the Congressional view of executive privilege and Watergate. "I do not think that the Senate ought to have to stand, as it were, at the gates of the White House with its hat in its hands and beg, like Lazarus, for the crumbs of information that may be available to it through some tenuous and circuitous process of written answers and written questions," said Byrd. "A piece of paper cannot be cross-examined." Byrd added, "I think it is almost impossible to avoid the suspicion that someone at the White House, in preparing the statement [on executive privilege] for Mr. Nixon, was trying to cover up White House involvement in the ugly campaign of political sabotage and espionage which climaxed in the Watergate raid."

The fuse burned shorter and shorter, sputtering out details like sparks, until finally the Watergate bomb exploded with such force that its aftershock touched the most powerful men in America and its effect was predicted to be felt for years to come. Like a nuclear device which can only be detonated by a lesser explosion, the most immense scandal in American history blew up after the frustration suffered by Americans ignorant about Watergate reached a critical mass.

Almost as a prelude to the Watergate explosion, the nation's press won a dramatic victory for the First Amendment. CREEP attorneys, in an effort to discover the sources of information for news stories on Watergate, in connection with the Republican's $2.5 million countersuit against the Democrats, had subpoenaed ten reporters from the *Washington Post*, the *Washington Evening Star-News*, the *New York Times*, and *Time* magazine. Attorneys for the four publications moved before Judge Charles Richey that the subpoenas be quashed because they infringed upon the First Amendment guarantee of freedom of press.

"This court cannot blind itself to the possible chilling effect the enforcement of these subpoenas would have on the flow of information to the press and, thus, to the public," Judge Richey ruled. "This court stands convinced that if it allows the discouragement of investigative reporting into the highest levels of government, that no amount of legal theorizing could allay the public's suspicions engendered by its actions and by the matters alleged in this lawsuit."

The vindication in court of the investigative report-

ing that had uncovered so many sordid details in the Watergate affair was made even more potent the following day in the chambers of the Senate Judiciary Committee. The first trigger to the bomb went off when Gray admitted under questioning from Senator Robert Byrd that Dean had "probably" lied to him on June 22, only four days after the Watergate break-in. Byrd meticulously recreated a series of events that took place in the White House in the wake of the burglary of Democratic National Headquarters. Byrd said that after an address book on the person of one of the five men arrested in the Watergate connected E. Howard Hunt to the crime, Dean sent two aides to Hunt's office in Room 338 of the Executive Office Building. The contents of both Hunt's desk and safe were removed and taken to Dean's office where they remained until the White House counsel turned the material over to the FBI on June 26. Nevertheless, Dean was present at an FBI interview with Charles Colson on June 22 where he was asked if he knew of a Hunt having a White House office. Dean replied that he'd have to check.

Byrd then put the magic question to Gray. "Knowing all along that the office was there, that the safe was there ... he lied to the agents, didn't he?"

"Looking back on the details," said Gray, "I would have to conclude that judgement is probably correct."

The Judiciary Committee was incredulous at the disclosure. How could Gray, knowing that Dean had lied, continue to make FBI materials available to him? Gray answered that he not only gave FBI data to Dean but that he would continue to give Dean FBI data because "the man is counsel to the President of the United States." Both Senator Byrd and Senator Tunney contended that Gray should have gone to President Nixon directly and obtained assurance that FBI material wasn't being misused.

Gray's admission that Dean had probably lied to him made Nixon's forceful exercise of executive privilege in preventing Dean from testifying before the Judiciary Committee particularly suspicious. Again: was Nixon deliberately attempting to hide something? Not according to

the White House, which issued a statement calling Senator Byrd's questioning "reprehensible, unfortunate, unfair and incorrect." The statement maintained that the question put to Dean in June was whether the agents could visit Hunt's office, not whether he had an office. The statement said, "Mr. Dean flatly denies that he ever misled or ... lied to an agent of the FBI."

While the Judiciary Committee hearings were scheduled to continue for some time, Gray's testimony about Dean's lying ensured committee rejection of his nomination. All that Gray had to recommend himself for the position of director was his incredible, if late-blooming, candor. But as the long-time Nixon stalwart continued to make embarrassing disclosures about Watergate, White House support for his nomination diminished proportionately. Thus when Deputy Press Secretary Warren told the news conference on March 23 that "the President has submitted Mr. Gray's nomination and the President supports that nomination," a definite lack of enthusiasm on Warren's part was obvious to reporters.

What ' id begun as an apparent prank the previous June and became an election issue in the fall, now threatened to shake the very foundations of the Administration. The White House had hoped the matter would be forgotten with the trial of the seven men convicted of the break-in and a cursory investigation by the Ervin committee.

After all, Mr. Nixon had gone to great lengths, apparently, to make sure it would quiet down. Thirty-five meetings that John Dean had with the President between January and April reflect Nixon's concern. According to Dean, Nixon met with him shortly before the sentencing of the Watergate defendants. The President asked his counsel how much the seven men would have to be paid over the $460,000 dollars they already received in order to ensure their silence. Dean told the President it would cost about $1 million, and, according to Dean, Nixon replied that the amount posed no difficulty.

Dean evidently did not whip out his bankroll fast enough because when the Watergate defendants came before Judge John Sirica for sentencing on March 23, the lid blew off the cover-up, never to be replaced. Unexpectedly, Sirica ended up sentencing only G. Gordon Liddy—up to twenty years in prison for being the money man and apparent mastermind of "crimes by these defendants which can only be described as sordid, despicable and thoroughly reprehensible." The judge deferred sentencing on Hunt, Barker, Sturgis, Martinez and Gonzales for three months because "the court requires more detailed information before it can make a final determination of the sentences to be imposed." Sirica wanted the whole story of Watergate told, and for the first time in the long litigation he was certain that a compost heap of details remained to be known.

The judge opened the sentencing proceedings by reading a letter from James W. McCord Jr. he had received four days earlier. It admitted much of what people had been suspecting about the Watergate—and a good deal more.

"Certain questions have been posed to me from Your Honor through the probation officer," McCord's letter began, "dealing with details of the case, motivations, intent, and mitigating circumstances. . .

"Several members of my family have expressed fear for my life if I disclose knowledge of the facts on this matter, either publicly or to any government representative. Whereas I do not share their concerns to the same degree, nevertheless, I do believe that retaliatory measures will be taken against me, my family, and my friends should I disclose such facts. Such retaliation could destroy careers, income, and reputation of persons who are innocent of any guilt whatsoever.

"Be that as it may, in the interests of justice, and in the interests of restoring faith in the criminal justice system, which faith has been severely damaged in this case, I will state the following to you at this time which I hope may be of help to you in meting out justice in this case:

"1. There was political pressure applied to the defendants to plead guilty and remain silent.

"2. Perjury occurred during the trial in matters highly material to the very structure, orientation, and impact of the government's case, and to the motivation and intent of the defendants.

"3. Others involved in the Watergate operation were not identified during the trial, when they could have been those testifying.

"4. The Watergate operation was not a CIA operation. The Cubans may have been misled by others into believing that it was a CIA operation. I know for a fact it was not.

"5. Some statements were unfortunately made by a witness which left the Court with the impression that he was stating untruths, or withholding facts of his knowledge, when in fact only honest errors of memory were involved.

"6. My motivations were different than those of the others involved, but were not limited to, or simply those offered in my defense during the trial. This is no fault of my attorneys, but of the circumstances under which we had to prepare my defense.

"Following sentence, I would appreciate the opportunity to talk with you privately in chambers. Since I cannot feel confident in talking with an FBI agent, in testifying before a Grand Jury whose U.S. Attorneys work for the Department of Justice, or in talking with other government representatives, such a discussion with you would be of assistance to me. . .

"I give this statement freely and voluntarily. . . The statements are true and correct to the best of my knowledge and belief."

The bomb blew shrapnel of guilt throughout the Nixon Administration. The Watergate grand jury finally had grounds to pursue its investigation with determination. The Senate select committee received more than enough ammunition to blow executive privilege to pieces and uncover the complete cast of characters in the Watergate conspiracy. What Nixon and the re-elect committee had previously offered as defenses, explanations or counter-charges had now become the object of even more intense doubt and suspicion. Watergate was finally revealed for the predatory political animal that it was.

It was the beginning of the end as James W. McCord Jr. walked out of Federal District Court in Washington still a free man, the only one of the seven conspirators not to be incarcerated. The wildcard had been played.

Chapter IV

March 24 to April 3/The Wild Card

The cat named James McCord was out of the Watergate bag, never to return. Judge John J. Sirica had whetted McCord's appetite for freedom by declining to sentence the former CIA agent along with his co-conspirators; Sirica wanted to know everything that McCord knew abut Watergate, he wanted the investigating grand jury to know what McCord knew, and he wanted the Ervin committee to know as well. McCord turned out to be a docile house cat who was more than willing to purr soft evidence into the ear of anyone capable of helping him maintain his freedom.

McCord didn't waste any time either. Shortly after Sirica adjourned court on March 23, McCord contacted Samuel Dash, chief legal counsel to the Ervin committee, saying that he wanted to meet with Dash "in response to Judge Sirica's urging that he cooperate fully and freely with the Senate committee." Dash was more than happy to oblige his new witness, who was working against a March 30 deadline—the day he was scheduled to be sentenced by Sirica. Dash held two tape recorded interviews with McCord, one on the very day his letter was made public, the other on the following day.

In a highly unusual Sunday press conference, Dash told reporters that McCord had "named names," and that the witness was "able to provide documentation and other supporting evidence" to substantiate charges made in his

letter to Sirica. "I was ... impressed with McCord's sincerity in giving us a full and honest account," Dash said. "He's been very careful. His statements have been studied ... He's willing to go under oath." Dash declined to release any of the substance of McCord's disclosures.

Nevertheless, *Los Angeles Times* Washington bureau reporters Robert Jackson and Ronald Ostrow learned from reliable sources that McCord named Jeb Magruder and John Dean as having prior knowledge of the Watergate bugging. McCord supposedly told Dash that Magruder committed perjury in his testimony during the Watergate trial, that others—unnamed—also had prior knowledge, and that E. Howard Hunt had exerted pressure on the four Cubans to plead guilty. Naturally enough, Press Secretary Ziegler vehemently denounced the allegations: "the White House categorically denies this story. There is no substance or fact to it. Mr. Dean had absolutely no knowledge or any awareness whatsoever of the Watergate incident." Magruder issued a similar denial.

John Dean was fast becoming the Watergate man of the hour: refusing to testify before the Senate Judiciary Committee, allegedly lying to the FBI and, now, having prior knowledge of the Watergate bugging. Dean was in sore need of support, and he received it promptly from his boss. President Nixon phoned Dean from his Key Biscayne home on March 26 assuring his counsel that he had "absolute and total confidence" in him. Dean was later to allege that the real reason for Nixon's call was to tell him that he had been "kidding" when he suggested paying $1 million for the continued silence of the seven Watergate defendants.

For the moment, though, Nixon's support of Dean was no joke. Press secretary Ziegler reiterated Nixon's faith. "The President has complete confidence in Mr. Dean," Ziegler told newsmen, "and he wanted me here again this morning to publicly express President Nixon's absolute and total confidence in this regard." As a counter-offensive, Ziegler attacked the propriety of Dash calling the press conference concerning McCord's revelations. Incredibly, the press secretary went on to disclose that Dean had made a phone call to L. Patrick Gray shortly after the counsel was accused of lying to the FBI, asking Gray to retract his statement.

Meanwhile, Senate select committee members met for a briefing on McCord's interview with Dash, and voted to allow live television coverage of their hearings. The American public would finally have an opportunity to see and hear the men involved in this mega-scandal. It was hoped that witnesses before Ervin's select committee would be more cooperative than G. Gordon Liddy, who had declined to elaborate on his knowledge of the bugging by taking the Fifth Amendment twenty times during testimony before the grand jury. Government prosecutors then requested that Judge Sirica grant immunity from further prosecution for Liddy in order to compel him to testify.

Richard Nixon's doctrine of executive privilege was being worn pretty thin by the daily assaults unleashed by the Watergate probe. Ranking *Republican* members of Congress began to demand that the President come clean. Conservative Republican New York Senator James Buckley accused Nixon of making "less than a heroic effort" to get to the truth behind Watergate. "We are coming to a moment of truth about Watergate," Buckley said, "and I hope that we get that moment of truth. If there is a crime involved, I would like to see it exposed." Senator John Tower of Texas, chairman of the Republican policy committee, stated bluntly that it was "in the best interest of the White House that this whole thing be bared."

The most cogent plea for a relaxation on executive privilege came from the House Government Information Sub-committee. It was considering a bill designed to limit the use of executive privilege in denying information to Congress. Members of the sub-committee urged Nixon to allow John Dean to give "limited testimony" on the privilege question. The Subcommittee chairman, Republican William Morehead, accused the President of abusing the practice of executive privilege, calling it a Constitutional fantasy indulged by Congress as "a matter of courtesy between the two branches of government."

The Congress had almost reached the breaking point with Richard Nixon as the Select Senate Committee on Presidential Campaign Activities—the Ervin committee—met for its first official session on March 28. Behind closed doors, the Senators heard their first witness, James W. McCord, name more names in the bizarre Watergate conspiracy. McCord's testimony was to be secret, but within hours confidential sources revealed to newsmen that the bugging conspirator named Mitchell and former special counsel to the President Charles Colson as also having prior knowledge of the Watergate bugging.

McCord's fingering of the former attorney general elicited an immediate response from John's big-mouthed wife Martha, in one of her famous phone calls to the *New York Times*. "I fear for my husband," Martha confided, "I'm really scared. I have a definite reason. I can't tell you why. But they're not going to pin anything on him. I won't let them, and I don't give a damn who gets hurt. I can name names." Mrs. Mitchell also expressed the fear that someone might try to shut her up.

The Senate select committee was more concerned with shutting up leaks within its own body. The group was purposely meeting in closed session to receive testimony that would lay the groundwork for future public sessions. Leaks of new names implicated in the case, the fact that James McCord took the Fifth Amendment twenty times in an effort to gain immunity from further prosecution, and leaks of testimony transcripts themselves could only damage the overall success of bringing the Watergate culprits to justice.

The news leaks from the Ervin committee were particularly damaging insofar as new suspects named in the Watergate affair were concerned. It gave John Mitchell, for example, just cause to deny once again any involvement. "I deeply resent the slanderous and false statements about me concerning the Watergate matter reported as being based on hearsay and leaked out," Mitchell said. "I have previously denied any prior knowledge of or involvement in the Watergate affair and again reaffirm such denials." The Watergate grand jury, which was hearing extensive testimony from E. Howard Hunt after granting him immunity from further prosecution, was having more success in maintaining secrecy.

Just one week after Judge John J. Sirica had made James McCord's apocalyptic letter on the Watergate trial public, the first cracks in the White House defense appeared, cracks that would widen into chasms in the coming weeks. Press secretary Ronald Ziegler announced at a White House press conference that "any member of the White House staff called by the grand jury will be required by the President to testify." Nixon was conceding, apparently, that executive privilege, rooted in the Constitutional principle of separation of powers, applied only to an ideologically hostile Congress. Ziegler went on to say, "We are ready to cooperate to work out procedures to meet the needs of the [Ervin] committee without doing violence to the separation of powers." Ervin was demanding no less than complete testimony from White House staff.

Ziegler's announcement that Nixon wanted staff members to testify before the grand jury took on new meaning the same day when Judge Sirica informed prosecutor Earl Silbert that he wanted more witnesses called before the grand jury "in view of substantive developments" in the Watergate case. The President's announcement coupled with Sirica's edict could only mean that Nixon's boys were sinking fast. James McCord, who possessed the map of the Watergate swamp, was granted a three-month sentencing delay by Sirica.

Watergate was escalating rapidly, helped along in no small part by members of the Senate select committee with which Nixon wanted to make a deal. Committee member Lowell Weicker appeared on the CBS News show "Face the Nation" on April 1, accusing Nixon's chief of staff, H. R. Haldeman, of at least knowing about the Watergate cover-up. "Now the time has come for the chief of staff to step forward and explain," said Weicker. "I think it's absolutely necessary that Mr. Haldeman testify before the select committee. . . . Did he [Haldeman] have knowledge that there was a unit whose responsibility it was to have disruption and to have surveillance, and to have this type of action take place within the President's campaign? The answer is that he probably did. But this is what we've got to prove as a committee." Weicker was criticized for his statement by CREEP officials, but it was one more indication that testimony from McCord, Hunt and other sources was beginning to give the Ervin committee the upper hand in Watergate.

Sam Ervin played that hand on April 2, declaring, in response to Nixon's offer to allow White House staff to meet informally with the committee, that nothing less than

sworn testimony would be acceptable. Ervin said Nixon was "shooting the so-called executive privilege doctrine way out past the stratosphere . . . That is not executive privilege, that is executive poppycock. The President is conducting himself in such a way as to reasonably engender in the minds of the people the belief that he is afraid of the truth. Divine right went out with the American revolution and doesn't belong to White House aides." Official mouthpiece Ziegler said at a press conference, "I would encourage the chairman to get his own disorganized house in order so that the investigation can go forward in a proper atmosphere of traditional fairness and due process."

The White House was squarely on the defensive, finding every weak point in the select committee structure and hammering away in hopes of breaking its credibility. The Nixon team won a minor victory on April 3 when G. Gordon Liddy, having been granted immunity from further prose-cution, refused once more to testify before the grand jury and was sentenced to 18 months in jail for contempt. At the same time, though, the Ervin committee met in closed session, announcing afterward that it would no longer hold preliminary hearings to accept secret testimony before the full committee. The move was seen as a direct response to Ziegler's remarks, removing any basis for the White House to undermine the pending investigation.

Still, it was ironic that the press, which had done so much to uncover Watergate, was being made the scapegoat in this ongoing battle between Congress and the President. Given Richard Nixon's disdain for the fourth estate, he surely must have been gloating over the Ervin committee's apparent acknowledgement of the inherent damage of press exposure. To Nixon, it was probably one more nail in the custom-made coffin he had been designing for the nations' press.

Press: Making Himself Perfectly Clear

"It's time we once again had an open administration—open to the ideas from the people and open in its communication with the people—an Administration of open doors, open eyes, and open minds."

—Richard Nixon, 1968

After ten months of banner headlines, it appeared that the nation's press corps had been conservative in reporting the flood of scandals that gushed from Watergate. Each disclosure in the morning's papers was a wave washing Press Secretary Ronald Ziegler from his White House perch.

As the Washington press corps fired off questions with apparently unlimited ammunition, Ziegler had to duck the bullets. Sometimes he was wounded in these exchanges. One such bloodletting took place over John Dean's White House investigation into Watergate.

Q: Why did you refuse for eight months to tell us whether this report was written or oral?
A: Here, again, I don't think I should respond specifically to that question except to say that that was the guidance provided.
Q: Why won't you respond to it, Ron?
A: My response, to you, in relation to me . . . is when these questions came up, we sought guidance and the guidance we were provided was to respond as we did.
Q: Who did you seek guidance from?
A: We sought guidance from the counsel's office.
Q: Ron, when you say "the counsel's office," do you mean individuals other than Mr. Dean?
A: Well, Mr. Dean himself and members of Mr. Dean's staff.
Q: You were told it was written, and now discover it wasn't?
A: No, I said we never did indicate it was written.
Q: Why did you not tell us it was oral when we first asked?
A: As I said before, the guidance provided was to—
Q: Were you told to lie about it, or pass off the questions that you could have answered?
A: The fact of the matter is that we never indicated one way or another what form the Dean report took . . . the point I am trying to make is that the President called for an investigation. He wanted it thoroughly investigated [Laughter].

Long ago, the press had come to realize that getting information from Ziegler was like pulling teeth. At the tender age of twenty-nine, Ziegler had single-handedly raised newspeak to an art form. Evading another shot from a reporter concerning the Vietnam bombing of October 1969, Ziegler said, "I think I made it clear that when we were discussing the B-52 matter—the decision to delay flights of the B-52s for a period of 36 hours—that it related to the fact that the decision, when it was made, related to a period of 36 hours, and there was not a decision point after the decision to delay the flights for 36 hours to again order the resumption."

If Zeigler had an appitude for bending the language into pretzels, he had an equal capacity for unbending the same language to make himself perfectly clear, when he wanted to do so. When the *Washington Post* published reports connecting the White House to the Watergate burglary, Ziegler denounced them as "based on hearsay, character assassination, innuendo, and guilt by association."

A similar choice of words, though with quite a different meaning, appeared in a *Newsday* editorial in October 1971, after a long series the paper published exposing the business relationships of Richard Nixon's close friend Bebe Rebozo. After describing in some detail the quasi-legal way Rebozo milked the Small Business Administration for money, which he could have raised independently, *Newsday* concluded, "We are not suggesting any automatic guilt by association. We are suggesting, however, that the President has shown a lack of sensitivity, responsibility, and care in the choice of a friend." The Long Island paper was particularly concerned that Nixon might have sacrificed his moral authority as President in a suspicious stock transaction engineered by Rebozo.

Since press secretaries are commissioned not to make but to market White House policy, it would not have been Ziegler's decision to undertake a meticulous campaign to rebuke *Newsday* by undermining its Washington correspondent following the Rebozo series. Reporter Martin Schram suddenly noticed that "Ziegler wouldn't speak to me. If I was to go up and ask him something, he would tell me 'Not now, I'm too busy,' and walk away . . . I realized I was getting snubbed, so I made it a point to call once a week to ask for an appointment with Ron. His secretary would take down the information and I would never get a

·call back." Schram was informed by White House officials that he personally was not the target—*Newsday* was. Ziegler called Schram into his office on Feb. 7, 1972, and announced that *Newsday* would not accompany Nixon to Peking. Ziegler was quoted by Schram as saying, "I wanted to tell you personally that *Newsday* is not on the China list and that it doesn't have anything to do with the Bebe Rebozo series."

Schram's troubles were not the only ones *Newsday* suffered. While the paper was preparing the Rebozo series, the FBI called and wanted to know the publication date. Then the Internal Revenue Service audited editor David Laventhol's income tax. Then the IRS investigated the tax returns of both *Newsday's* publisher and the chief writer of the Rebozo series. Finally IRS accountants audited *Newsday* itself.

This was only one episode in Nixon's stormy relationship with the press. Every President since George Washington suspected he was the victim of a one-party opposition press, but Nixon made the adversary role a life and death affair. Nixon's feud with the press was cradled in the 1948 Hiss controversy. Congressman Nixon was pressing for conviction of Hiss, who was accused of transporting State Department papers to Moscow. What unsettled the young politician was the apparent reluctance of some of the seaboard papers to pursue the Hiss matter with proper zeal. In *Six Crises*, Nixon even suspected the *Washington Post* of conspiring to protect Hiss from official inquiries. He wrote that the *Post*, "which was typical of a large segment of the nation's news and of public opinion, had always taken a dim view of the Committee on Un-American Activities, and had launched an all-out assault on its procedures after Hiss first testified. It kept a drumfire of comment and criticism throughout the weeks in which the case developed. Its editorials called on the Committee to block its investigation and leave it to those with the proper 'Constitutional duty.'"

But if Nixon believed the newspapers were soft on Communism, he was abundantly certain they were not soft on him. When Nixon defeated Helen Gahagan Douglas in 1948, he was disturbed about newspaper caricatures which stereotyped him as a "red-baiter." He also resented the newspapers for jawboning the public about the "Nixon Fund" in 1952. Nixon defended his $18,000 slush fund as enabling "me to continue my active battle against Communism and corruption." But even the influential Republican *Herald Tribune* called for Nixon to resign from the Eisenhower ticket. The party prevailed upon Nixon to account for his improprieties in a nationally televised broadcast and the American public would decide Nixon's guilt or innocence. Nixon approached his crucible by deciding that "under no circumstances could I tell the press in advance what I was going to say or what my decision would be . . . this time I was determined to tell my story directly to the people rather than to funnel it . . . through a press account."

If the "Checkers" speech vindicated Nixon, it also vindicated for Nixon the notion that the press was a monkey on his back. That attitude was cemented in his first Presidential campaign when, according to historian Theodore White, in *The Making of the President, 1960*, Nixon viewed the press as a "hostile conspiracy." White even corroborated many of Nixon's fears when he conducted a quick poll of the reporters in Nixon's campaign entourage; 37 were Kennedy men, 13 were Nixon men.

The dam burst during the 1962 California gubernatorial campaign. Writing in *The Resurrection of Richard Nixon*, Jules Whitcover said the press was anxiously waiting for Nixon to concede defeat on the morning of Nov. 7 after it appeared that Pat Brown had won. Herb Klein was urging Nixon to make a statement to the press. Nixon replied, "Screw them."

But then Nixon sent Klein reeling by going downstairs and unleashing what he called "my philosophy with regard to the press."

"Good morning, gentlemen," he began. "Now that Mr. Klein has made his statement, and now that all the members of the press are so delighted that I have lost, I'd like to make a statement of my own . . . for once, gentlemen—I would appreciate if you would write what I say . . . For sixteen years, ever since the Hiss case, you've had a lot of fun—a lot of fun—that you've had an opportunity to attack me . . . I think that it's time that our great newspapers have at least the same objectivity . . . that television has. And I can only say thank God for television and radio for keeping the newspapers a little more honest.

"The last play. I leave you gentlemen now and you will now write it . . . But as I leave you I want you to know—just think how much you're going to be missing.

"You won't have Nixon to kick around any more, because, gentlemen, this is my last press conference and it will be one in which I have welcomed the opportunity to test wits with you . . . I hope that . . . the press . . . recognize that they have a right and a responsibility, if they're against a candidate, give him the shaft, but also recognize if they give him the shaft, put one lonely reporter on the campaign who will report what the candidate says now and then."

By the time of the 1968 Presidential campaign, however, Nixon had returned to active political life and to active combat with the press. After promising "an open administration," one month after the election Nixon had held no news conferences and planned none. Traditionally a President cultivates at least a few reporters, but Nixon kept the entire press corps at arm's length. Instead of reading newspapers, Nixon preferred to have his White House staff prepare brief summaries of the daily events.

Patrick Buchanan was one of the aides who telescoped news for the President. Buchanan's attitude toward the press is perhaps as neatly compressed as his news synopses in a 1973 Administration analysis he called *The New Majority*. Buchanan hypothesized that a "marriage of left-wing bias and network power" was conspiring to overthrow Americans' trust in their government. According to Buchanan, ". . . An incumbent elite, with an ideological slant unshared by the nation's majority, has acquired absolute control of the most powerful medium of communication known to man. And that elite is using that media monopoly to discredit those with whom it disagrees, and to advance its own ideological objectives—and it is defending that monopoly by beating its several critics over the head with the stick of the First Amendment." He asked critics of the press "not to be distracted by cries of repression and public tears over the death of the First Amendment."

Whether or not Nixon was the personal architect of the strategy, it originated in the White House. If there was some question of who drafted the blueprint, there was little doubt about its design. Said CBS anchorman Walter Cronkite, "What I object to in criticism from the White House is not in fact that there is criticism, not even the fact that they would try to raise their credibility by attacking ours. But what has happened is that this Administration, throughout what I believe to be a considered and concerted campaign, has managed to politicize the issue of the press versus the Administration to the point that now we come to the real crunch, which is the matter of our actual freedom to operate, our freedom to criticize, our right to do that."

During the Nixon Administration a growing number of journalists found themselves subpoenaed by federal, state and local prosecutors to supply evidence in court. Some reporters talked, some reporters appealed to higher courts, and some reporters went to jail.

The legal threat against the press crystallized in a Su-

1962: Herb Klein was urging Nixon to make a statement to the press. "Screw them," Nixon replied.

preme Court decision involving *Times* reporter Earl Caldwell. Caldwell was subpoenaed in 1970 to appear before a San Francisco grand jury to testify about a series of articles he wrote on the Bay area Black Panthers. He refused, arguing he would be effectively neutralized, regarded as an agent of the court, unless he could protect his sources of information. However, the Supreme Court ruled in a five to four decision in 1972 that journalists had no right to refuse to disclose confidential sources before a grand jury. The majority decision consisted of Nixon's four appointees, who were joined by swing Justice Byron White.

A year later, before a House judiciary subcommittee, Caldwell testified that the FBI "hounded" him for information about the Black Panthers. Caldwell said that FBI agents were calling and visiting him daily for a period of several weeks. Finally, when he refused to answer their calls, women began ringing the *Times* to ask for him, and when Caldwell answered their calls, FBI "agents would come on the phone."

A study of the Nixon Administration and the press conducted by the American Civil Liberties Union in 1971 concluded that "attacks on the press by officers of the government have become so widespread and all-pervasive, that they constitute a massive federal-level attempt to subvert the letter and spirit of the First Amendment."

After marshalling an unprecedented war on the print media, the Nixon Administration then proposed new structural changes in the laws regulating the broadcasting industry. In the summer of 1970, Clay Whitehead, Nixon's director of the Office of Telecommunications, out-Agnewed the Vice-president with a series of speeches criticizing the policies of the Federal Communications Commission as "obsolete," "footdragging," and "meddlesome." Then Whitehead admitted in the fall of 1971 that his office had drafted new guidelines to combat "consistent bias" in the television and radio industry. Whitehead's proposals included abolishing the Fairness Doctrine, which required broadcasters to strike a rough balance between conflicting views. Instead, the former Rand thinktanker recommended that the industry sell time on a first-come, first-serve basis. Whitehead had also alienated local community organizations by suggesting that broadcasting licenses be extended from three to five years, effectively reducing the threat of challenges to existing licenses by citizen groups. Since radio and television stations are licensed by the federal government, they are accountable to the FCC which, in turn, is supervised by Nixon's appointee Dean Burch, Barry Goldwater's 1964 campaign manager. This was the carrot and stick approach to reorganizing the media. The carrot was the five-year license; the stick was that local stations would become responsible for the network news that they broadcast. This meant that if the White House was upset with a particular story, it no longer had to fight a team of CBS lawyers. Instead, it could subpoena the news director of a small station in Altoona, Pennsylvania, who was not armed with the vast resources of a giant corporation and would feel intimidated.

Public broadcasting was another target for reorganization. Under Whitehead's new funding arrangement, 50 percent of the government's appropriations would go directly to local outlets, radically diminishing the Corporation for Public Broadcasting's independence and strength.

There was an immediate reaction from broadcast journalism. CPB official John Witherspoon wrote that "Whitehead has declared that until public broadcasting shows signs of becoming what this Administration wants it to be, this Administration will oppose permanent funding (of non-commercial television)."

In the words of FCC Commissioner Nicholas Johnson, "Whitehead is scaring the holy bejesus out of the industry."

The "bejesus" also involved calling individual journalists onto the White House carpet. Superaide Bob Haldeman and John Ehrlichman invited CBS reporter Dan Rather to the White House in April 1971, to discuss his "objectivity." According to Rather, Ehrlichman said, "I think you're slanted. I don't know whether it's just sloppiness or you're letting your true feelings come through, but the net effect is that you're negative. You have negative leads on bad stories."

Ehrlichman entered the fray again during an interview broadcast over KNBC in Los Angeles in June 1972. Ehrlichman was elaborating on why Nixon was so sparing with his news conferences. "He goes in there for half an hour and he gets a lot of flabby and fairly dumb questions, and it really doesn't elucidate much."

Perhaps as a result, Nixon has had only thirty-one news conferences during his first 222 weeks in office, which averages out to one every seven weeks. The previous three presidents averaged a press conference every two and a half weeks. President Harry Truman had a news conference almost every week. Franklin D. Roosevelt held more than one news conference a week.

While Nixon has insisted, "I am never concerned about opinion," his campaign aides have suggested the opposite. In *The Selling of the President* Joe McGinniss quoted Nixon television adviser Roger Ailes as having said, during the 1968 campaign, "Let's face it, a lot of people think Nixon is dull . . . They look at him as the kind of kid who always carried a bookbag . . . Now, you put him on television, you've got a problem right away. He's a funny-looking guy. He looks like somebody hung him in a closet overnight and he jumps out in the morning with his suit all bunched up and starts running around saying, 'I want to be President.' I mean, this is how he strikes some people. That's why these shows are important. To make them forget all that."

Nixon unclosed himself during a Jan. 31, 1973 news conference, to explain the details of the Vietnam peace agreement. The President was secure, perhaps over-confident of his page in American history, and used the opportunity to unearth some of the ghouls that haunted him during his last "press conference" in 1962. Nixon said, "We finally have achieved a peace with honor. I know it gags some of you to write that phrase, but it is true. . . ."

In terms of the Watergate scandal, Nixon has been even more remote from the press than usual. But the White House surrogates who harassed and publicly villified the *Washington Post* as it developed the story were legion. In the vanguard of the attack was former special counsel Charles Colson, who branded the *Post's* Watergate reporting "unconscionable."

Equally anathematizing to the press was the unsuccessful attempt by the Committee to Re-elect the President to compel reporters and news executives to turn over notes and other unpublished material on the Watergate case. The subpoenas were so broad that if honored, they would have provided Nixon campaign aides with the name of every confidential source, details of every interview, every scrap of information—including unpublished hearsay—collected by newsmen in their Watergate investigation. In quashing the subpoenas on March 21, 1973, Judge Charles Richey said "this court cannot blind itself to the possible chilling effect the enforcement of . . . these subpoenas would have on the press and public."

But things were not all coming up roses in Nixon's stink with the press. Ziegler had been forced to declare his previous Watergate statements "inoperative." And even the President himself had to bow a bit in recognition of the power of the press.

After his national television address of April 30, 1973, Nixon surprised the press corps by showing up unexpected in the press room. "Ladies and gentlemen," he said, in what must have been a distasteful moment, "we have had our differences in the past, and I hope you give me hell every time you think I'm wrong." They did.

April 4 to April 30/April Showers

Ten months to the day after the break-in of Democratic National Headquarters, President Nixon called a hasty press conference to announce that what most of the nation had come to suspect was probably true. After first announcing that he had reached agreement with Senators Sam Ervin and Howard Baker on ground rules whereby White House aides could testify before the Select committee while reserving the right to executive privilege, the President went on to acknowledge Watergate as the major scandal it was.

"On March 21, as a result of serious charges which came to my attention, some of which were publicly reported, I began intensive new inquiries into this whole matter," said Nixon.

"I can report today that there have been major developments in the case concerning which it would be improper to be more specific now, except to say that real progress has been made in finding the truth.

"If any person in the executive branch is indicted by the grand jury, my policy will be to immediately suspend him. If he is convicted, he will, of course, be automatically discharged. . . .

"As I have said before and I have said throughout this entire matter, all government employees and especially White House staff employees are expected fully to cooperate in this matter. I condemn any attempts to cover up this case, no matter who is involved."

Following Nixon's reading of his brief, startling statement on Watergate, press secretary Ron Ziegler fielded questions from a press corps vindicated by the announcement. Ziegler told them all previous statements on Watergate—ten months of invective, accusation and bitter denial marked by Ziegler's peculiar revulsion for the White House press corps—were "inoperative." "The statement today is the operative statement," said Ziegler, hoping to restore the nation's confidence in the President and the press' confidence in himself through one bold rhetorical stroke. It didn't work.

The days prior to Nixon's April 17 statement were marked by news leaks claiming convicted Watergate conspirator James McCord had named a gaggle of Nixon officials involved in the conspiracy in testimony before the grand jury. McCord's damaging revelations came after Judge John Sirica granted him immunity from further prosecution on April 5. McCord testified that his hiring by the Committee to Re-elect the President was cleared through John Dean, the same man who had hired Gordon Liddy, and who had become the focus of so much attention in the Watergate affair. Chuck Colson, who was also fingered by McCord, went so far as to take a lie detector test on April 7 which he claimed was proof that he had no prior knowledge of the Watergate bugging. Nixon officials were suddenly going to great lengths to assert their innocence, but in the public eye, such action only indicated a greater effort to hide their guilt.

McCord continued naming names while GOP powers in Congress and elsewhere stepped up pressure on Nixon to come clean. McCord testified on April 8 that CREEP attorney Kenneth Parkinson had channeled money to the seven Watergate defendants and had applied pressure on them to plead guilty in January. The former CIA agent said he had received $3,000 a month from Dorothy Hunt, wife of conspirator E. Howard Hunt, to remain silent about his role in the Watergate bugging. McCord testified that the $10,000 Mrs. Hunt was carrying at the time of her death in a December plane crash was part of the payoff money she received from Parkinson for distribution.

McCord's most damning revelation came as former White House aides Dwight Chapin and Gordon Strachin appeared to testify before the grand jury along with accused *agent provocateur* Donald Segretti. McCord reportedly told the grand jury he had learned through Gordon Liddy that transcripts of wiretapped conversations from Democratic National Headquarters were hand-delivered to Mitchell, former attorney general and director of CREEP. Liddy also informed McCord that Mitchell had ordered a list of priorities for bugging various Democratic party offices.

None of these accusations against the Nixon Administration and the Nixon re-election committee went unnoticed by Republican leaders. Senator Barry Goldwater, one of Nixon's strongest supporters, challenged the President to clear the air about Watergate. "The Watergate. The Watergate. It's beginning to sound like Teapot Dome. I mean, there's a smell to it. Let's get rid of the smell." Goldwater was joined in his request by most of the Republicans in Congress who began to see their political futures tainted by the Nixon Administration's handling of the Watergate affair.

It became apparent that Nixon was about to give in to the mammoth pressure generated by Watergate when he reportedly met with Mitchell on April 14. After supposedly conferring with the President, Mitchell announced to reporters that he was eager to testify before the Ervin committee, and that he was confident the President would authorize any White House staff member remotely involved to testify also. "I think that everybody who's involved, or has been stated to be involved, will come forward," said Mitchell. "I don't think it will hurt the presidency or the Republican Party . . . The White House, as I understand it, doesn't have anything to come clean about." White House deputy press secretary Gerald Warren later denied that Mitchell had met with the President, saying that he had talked with aides.

John's wife called Warren a "god-blessed" liar the next day, lending an eerie foreboding to the whole Watergate mystery. "They're lying from beginning to the end," said Mrs. Mitchell. "They're trying to hang this on my husband." The pall of gloom surrounding Watergate was further expanded by Attorney General Richard Kleindienst who was quoted by a reporter as saying the "Watergate case is going to blow up." On April 17, it did.

In the aftermath of Nixon's announcement of new "major developments" in the Watergate case, the American people were treated to a passion play of cover-up, denial and in-house backstabbing on the part of Nixon officials unprecedented even by previous efforts to mask the grandiose conspiracy. The White House moved immediately to settle—out of court—two lawsuits connected with Watergate that had been plaguing it for months. CREEP lawyer Kenneth Parkinson offered the Democrats $525,000 in settlement for their $6.4 million suit against CREEP. Maurice Stans, meanwhile, met with attorneys for Common Cause in an effort to reach accord in their lawsuit aimed at disclosing the sources of more than $10 million in secret contributions CREEP had received. Neither was successful.

Attorney General Kleindienst announced on April 18 that he was disqualifying himself from further involvement in the Watergate investigation because of the possibility that he would have to prosecute former close associates. The *Washington Post* reported that Jeb Magruder had met with Watergate prosecutors the previous Saturday, outlining details of a meeting in February 1972 with Mitchell, Dean and Liddy where the Watergate break-in was planned. Magruder was also reported to have said that Mitchell and Dean arranged for cash payments to the seven convicted conspirators after they were apprehended in Democratic National Committee Headquarters. A noose of accusations was closing in now, drawing ever tighter around very high figures in the Nixon Administration.

A strange game of point the finger and pass the bug began to be played in the higher echelons of government. John Mitchell was reported to have admitted attending three meetings in early 1972 where plans to bug Democratic headquarters were discussed, but he denied ever approving such plans. Mitchell's admission contradicted what he had been saying for the previous ten months, that Watergate was a complete surprise to him, but the time had come for contradictions in the intricate Watergate web of deception and deceit.

Less than twelve hours after the *Post* reported Jeb Magruder had fingered John Dean before federal prosecutors, Dean issued a statement, without going through normal White House press channels, that he was not going to be made a scapegoat in the Watergate fiasco. "Some may hope or think that I will become a scapegoat in

the Watergate case," said Dean. "Anyone who believes this does not know me, know the true facts, nor understand our system of justice." Dean was reported to be prepared to meet with federal prosecutors himself to finger H.R. Haldeman in the conspiracy. New mystery was added to the Watergate case the same day as Washington attorney Peter Wolf announced that a client of his had eight cartons of documents in his possession taken from E. Howard Hunt's office the day after the Watergate break-in. Wolf said the documents included plans for the Watergate operation and lists of secret contributors to CREEP. The name of the client remained unknown.

John Mitchell testified "fully, freely and openly" before the Watergate grand jury on April 20 reportedly acknowledging that he had approved the payment of Nixon campaign funds to Watergate conspirators after their arrest on June 17, but he maintained that the money was for legal fees, not to buy their silence. Mitchell was also reported to have told the grand jury that Jeb Magruder had gone over his head to the White House to get approval for the bugging plans which he himself disapproved.

The recriminations were coming full circle. Seymour Hersh reported the same day in the *New York Times* that John Dean had supervised cash payments of more than $175,000 in $100 bills to ensure the silence of the Watergate conspirators—some payments continuing into January of 1973.

The President seemed to be taking the exploding crisis in stride, declaring to a cabinet meeting, "We've had our Cambodias before." Nixon remained strangely silent throughout what was seen as the greatest crisis for presidential leadership since the Civil War. The Democrats, though, merely sat by as spectators, watching the Republican leadership discredit itself. Perhaps as a safeguard, the Democratic National Committee moved its headquarters from the Watergate hotel and office complex on April 20. The Watergate complex promptly put an ad in Washington and New York journals reading, "don't be bugged with the commonplace—this spring indulge yourself. Rent an office in the Watergate."

The Watergate scandal became the national joke, the national game, and the national tragedy combined. Accusations came so swiftly that people couldn't keep track of new characters being introduced. Nixon's popularity dropped dramatically in national polls while any credibility he may have enjoyed evaporated. Some observers called the White House bloodshed the result of an angry battle between two factions surrounding Nixon, one headed by Haldeman and Ehrlichman, the other by Mitchell and Dean. To most people, it was at once expected given the nature of politics but at the same time bewildering. It was obvious now that an immense cover-up had taken place to hide the real guilt in Watergate. The question became, did Nixon know?

The President came under constant attack for his silence on Watergate. Speaking on NBC's "Meet the Press" on April 23, Republican Senator Edward Brooke said "it is difficult to understand how persons working with the President would not make known to him an enterprise of this magnitude involving hundreds of thousands of dollars and involving such a potential risk. It is inconceivable to me that they would not have told the President about this matter. In fact, that they wouldn't have asked for his approval or disapproval." Nixon, meantime, phoned John Dean, H.R. Haldeman and John Ehrlichman from his Key Biscayne home wishing them all a happy Easter. To Dean, sweetly, he said, "You're still my counsel."

New disclosures persisted in the Watergate case, coming in such a torrent that the news media spoke only of Watergate. Two of the unknown secret Nixon campaign funds were revealed—the one controlled by Haldeman,

and the other one controlled by Nixon's West Coast henchman and personal attorney, Herbert Kalmbach. Three cartons of Nixon campaign financial documents finally found their way to a federal court where Common Cause was suing to have the identities of Nixon contributors made public. In the midst of it all, Nixon's foreign policy advisor, Henry Kissinger, warned an Associated Press luncheon against an "orgy of recrimination" aimed at those implicated in Watergate.

The orgy continued, however, as the trail of the elusive wiretap logs codenamed Gemstone led straight to the White House offices of Ehrlichman and Haldeman. President Nixon met for a full hour with John J. Wilson, the lawyer representing Haldeman and Ehrlichman in the Watergate affair, on April 24. The matter had become deadly serious. Observers expected a White House shakeup was imminent, and their suspicions were confirmed when Nixon offered former Defense Secretary Melvin Laird the job of cleaning the Waterbuggers out of the Oval Office. Laird declined. Jeb Magruder became the second casualty of Watergate on April 26, resigning his post as Assistant Secretary of Commerce.

The disparate parts of the Watergate puzzle dramatically began to piece together on April 27 when two revelations proved that Watergate was much larger than it had seemed. In Los Angeles, Judge William Matthew Byrne announced that he had received information that convicted Watergate conspirators Hunt and Liddy had burglarized the office of Daniel Ellsberg's psychiatrist in September 1971. In Washington, L. Patrick Gray resigned as acting director of the FBI amid disclosures that he had destroyed the documents belonging to Hunt at Dean's request. Within hours, President Nixon appointed Environmental Protection Agency director William D. Ruckelshaus to replace Gray. Ruckelshaus promptly announced that he had no desire to become permanent FBI director,

adding that he had asked for and received from Nixon assurances that no one would be spared in the Watergate investigation "no matter who is involved."

Watergate now transcended the boundaries of science fiction. What did the bugging of Democratic National Committee Headquarters have to do with the office of Daniel Ellsberg's psychiatrist? How could the director of the Federal Bureau of Investigation destroy evidence having a direct bearing on a case then under investigation? There seemed to be more to the White House than met the eye. Former Republican National Chairman Robert Dole, who had shrugged off Watergate the previous fall, recommended that Nixon fire his two top aides, Haldeman and Ehrlichman. "Right now the credibility of the administration is zilch, zero," said Dole. "If they have any dedication and loyalty to the President, they can show it by resigning."

The finger of guilt pointed higher and higher. John Dean was reportedly prepared to name Haldeman and Ehrlichman as the supervisors of the Watergate cover-up, contingent upon being granted immunity from prosecution. The Katzenjammer Kids were already scheduled to meet with federal prosecutors. The White House was crumbling pilaster by pilaster.

On April 30, President Nixon took to the airwaves to explain away Watergate. He announced the resignations of Attorney General Kleindienst, aides Haldeman and Ehrlichman, and John Dean, whom he fired. Nixon took great pains not to imply wrongdoing on the part of his former aides. Instead, Nixon took all blame upon himself. He failed to mention guilt.

Amidst the turmoil and furor of the most wholesale shake-up in American government on record, observers couldn't help noticing how much the speech resembled another speech delivered 21 years before by a Vice-presidential candidate named Richard Nixon, who himself was then being asked to resign.

The Child is the Father to Man

"Life for everyone is a series of crises."

Richard Nixon

"Senator, what is this 'fund' we've heard about? There is a rumor to the effect that you have a supplementary salary of $20,000 a year, contributed by a hundred California businessmen. What about it?"

The question was asked by veteran columnist Peter Edson and Richard Nixon, the thirty-nine-year-old Republican candidate for Vice-president, was not disturbed by the query, at least not yet. That was on September 14, 1952. Within a few short days, Democratic critics and even Republican loyalists were demanding a full accounting of the "Nixon Fund." The howling vaulted the young candidate into his first major public confrontation.

Nixon's Golgatha began when Eisenhower commanded his running-mate to make a full public disclosure of the slush fund on a nationally televised broadcast. Nixon reluctantly agreed, realizing that his political future would be marked with gravestones if he could not convince the television audience that he were "clean as a hound's tooth." It was an unparalleled crisis in Nixon's early career—and ultimately the prototype for his adult political life.

Nixon's primary concern was to rescue his candidacy from the jaws of partisan mudslinging. In Nixon's mind, the fund controversy was artificially created by Democrats, liberals, and unscrupulous newspaper propagandists. In *Six Crises*, Nixon concluded that "Every public figure, whose most important asset is his reputation, is at the mercy of the smear artists and rumormongers. No one can keep pace with a concerted smear campaign. . . A charge is usually put on the first page of the newspaper; the defense is buried among the deodorant ads." In effect, silence was a virtue; to answer criticism would be to dignify it by recognizing that it existed.

But Eisenhower's mandate precluded silence, so Nixon concentrated on marshalling his energies for a strong counterattack. The decision to reject a defensive posture followed logically from Nixon's earlier experience in political combat. "One of the most trying experiences an individual can go through," Nixon wrote, "is the period of doubt, soul-searching, to determine whether to fight the battle or fly from it. It is in such a period that almost unbearable tensions build up, tensions that can be relieved only by taking action one way or the other. And significantly, it is this period of crisis conduct that separates the leaders from the followers. A leader is one who has the emotional, mental, and physical strength to withstand the pressures and tensions created by necessary doubts and then at the central moment, to make a choice and to act decisively. The men who fail are those who are so overcome by doubt that they either crack under the strain or flee to avoid meeting the problem at all."

Nixon's Checkers speech was organized to conform exactly to these principles. It was broadcast on Sept. 23, 1952 to the largest audience that Nixon had ever addressed. Nixon was taking his case to the common man, not to the newspapers or to the Republican bigshots who were advising Eisenhower to find a new Vice-presidential candidate.

The fact that his speech was being televised made Nixon sensitive to the need for a good performance. At Whittier, Nixon had been a dramatic actor in student productions. His mentor, Dr. Albert Upton, professor of English and drama, watched when his former student cried over the fund disclosures back in 1952. Upton said, "I taught him how to cry in a play by John Drinkwater called *Bird in Hand*. He tried conscientiously at rehearsals and he'd get a pretty good lump in his throat and that was all. But on the evenings of the performance, tears just ran right out of his eyes. It was beautifully done, those tears."

Like his other performances, Nixon's Checkers speech was masterful. He opened by arguing that his slush fund was both legally proper and morally sound.

"I am sure that you have read the charge, and you have heard it, that I, Senator Nixon, took $18,000 from a group of my supporters. Now was that wrong? . . . It isn't a question of whether it was legal or illegal, that isn't enough. The question is, was it morally wrong? I say it was morally wrong if any of that $18,000 went to Senator Nixon for my personal use. I say it was morally wrong if it was secretly given and secretly handled. And I say it was morally wrong if any of the contributors got special favors for the contributions that they made. And now to answer those questions, let me say this: not one cent of the $18,000, or any other money of that type ever went to my personal use. Every penny of it was used to pay political expenses that I did not think should be charged to the taxpayers of the United States."

This was neither the first nor the last time Nixon was accused of impropriety. He was criticized for using "red-baiting" tactics against two early political opponents, Helen Gahagan Douglas and Jerry Voorhis. As a law student at Duke University, Nixon had indiscreetly broken into the Dean's office to find out his academic standing. Nixon was on scholarship and needed to maintain a particular grade average to keep his financial aid. After surreptitiously examining his file, Nixon found that his grades had not dropped enough to lose the scholarship. The money he would have lost was penny-ante compared to the sweepstakes at stake in the Checkers speech.

"There are some that will say, 'Well, maybe you were able, Senator, to fake this thing. How can we believe what you say—after all, is there a possibility that you might have feathered your own nest?' And so now what I am going to do, and incidentally, this is unprecedented in the history of American politics—I am going at this time to give this television and radio audience a complete financial history, everything I have earned, and everything I have spent, everything I own."

It was "unprecedented" and it was a surprise. Nixon had sucked the rubes into the tent. As a boy Nixon had worked as a barker for a wheel of chance at the "Slippery Gulch Rodeo" in Prescott, Arizona for six weeks. The concession stand was just a front, however, for an illegal back room poker and dice game. Nixon's salary included a cut from the back room profits.

Nixon used the technique of surprise on numerous other occasions, including a more volatile one when he was challenged by "Communist hecklers" in Uruguay during his 1953 Latin American goodwill mission. "By taking the offensive," he said, "and making maximum use of the element of surprise, I had been able to turn potentially antagonistic crowds against Communist agitators who were attempting to inflame them against me.

"Since those who make up a mob are basically cowards, one must never show fear in the face of a mob. Since a mob is not intelligent, but stupid, it is important whenever possible to confront it with an unexpected maneuver."

After calling upon his dog Checkers, his wife's "good Republican coat," and his two daughters, Nixon concluded his speech by invoking the will of the people. "The decision,

my friends, is not mine. I would do nothing that would harm the possibilities of Dwight Eisenhower to become President of the United States. And for that reason I am submitting to the Republican National Committee tonight through this television broadcast the decision which is theirs to make. And I am going to ask you to help them decide. Wire and write the Republican National Committee whether you think I should stay on or whether I should get off."

In poker, this is called a bluff. Eisenhower had already dealt Nixon a losing hand by forcing the television appearance on him. He could only win the pot by conning his way into the hearts of the public. Nixon had perfected his poker game while he was in the Navy during the Second World War. He had a reputation for being the only sane and sensible poker player in the South Pacific. But he did not play the game for its own sake—he abandoned it after the war. Nixon used it as a way to earn money and his profits were actually sizable enough to partially bankroll his political career when he left the Navy.

With the Checkers speech, Nixon had gambled and won also. "It was the crisis, itself, more than the merits of the engagement which rallies people to a leader," he said. "Moreover when the leader handles the crisis with success, the public support he receives is even greater." The size of Nixon's victory was measured in the overwhelming groundswell of public approval that followed his televised address. Instead of being fed to the wolves, Nixon was feeding the wolves his enemies.

Nixon had gone on the campaign trial by denouncing Adlai Stevenson as "Adlai the appeaser . . . who got a Ph.D. from Dean Acheson's College of Cowardly Containment." Nixon fired broadside after broadside into the Truman Administration as well. "We can assume because of the cover-up of this administration in the Hiss case that the Communists, the fellow travelers," Nixon said, "have not been cleaned out of the executive branch of government."

Alger Hiss was a State Department official who had organized the Dumbarton Oaks world monetary conference, the U.S. side of the Yalta Conference, and the meeting at San Francisco where the U.N. Charter was written and adopted. During testimony before the House Un-American Activities Committee in 1948, Whittaker Chambers, an editor of *Time* magazine, said that Hiss was one of four members of an underground Communist cell which was committed to "Communist infiltration of the American government."

Nixon's commie suspicions were not restricted to Truman, they extended to the government agencies investigating Hiss as well. In fact, Nixon criticized the Justice Department for having become politicized. "I had no confidence in some of their superiors who were under great political pressures and who so far had made a record which, to put it politely, raised grave doubts," Nixon said. "Did they intend to bring out any facts that might be embarrassing to the national Administration?" Apparently a similar political philosophy would govern the Justice Department's investigation of the Watergate burglary.

Nixon would come to believe that Hiss, who had leaked secret government documents, was an ancestor of Daniel Ellsberg, the man who was to leak the Pentagon Papers. For Nixon, "Hiss was clearly the symbol of a considerable number of perfectly loyal citizens whose theatre of operations are the nation's mass media and universities, its scholarly foundations, and its government bureaucracies. This group likes to throw the cloak of liberalism around all its beliefs. . . . They are not Communists, they are not even remotely disloyal . . . but they are of a mind-set as doctrinaire as those of the extreme right."

For other politicians, crises were their political epitaphs. But for Nixon, they were endurance tests, trial balloons for gauging his own strength, and tools for rebuilding the debris for other Babylons. Nixon had lived too close to the edge for too long to fall over it. Instead, he enlisted his own weaknesses and failings as grudging allies and converted defeat into a personal formula for triumph.

Nixon's political history is the record of a man unwilling to surrender to defeat, but it is also the record of a man unwilling to surrender to the truth. The internal forces that finally propelled Nixon to the Presidency were the same forces that trapped him in the Watergate.

Ironically, Nixon's failures often stemmed from the same weaknesses he attacked in other politicians. Nixon's refusal to investigate the crimes of his White House aides paralleled Truman's failure to investigate Alger Hiss. Just as Nixon criticized Truman for narrowly viewing the Hiss case "only in terms of political consideration," Nixon himself was criticized for reducing the Watergate burglary and its attendant public outcries to "espionage by one political organization against another."

Nixon even uncloseted some of his early political strengths to combat the growing chorus of criticism. In the Pentagon Papers Trial, though, Nixon dressed up the Communist spectre formula and marketed it as national security. Instead of Hiss leaking secret government documents to the enemy, this time it was Daniel Ellsberg leaking documents to the newspapers. Apparently, the enemy had become the American people. It was the old Nixon with a difference.

When Nixon ultimately confronted his seventh crisis on April 30, 1973—expecting to outmaneuver the American public with a surprise admission of White House accountability—too little was said and nothing done.

May 1 to May 7/Trees in the Forest

It wasn't enough. The government of the United States entered a state of near paralysis, incapable of recovery until the Watergate cancer had been removed completely. The President's "earnest" television disclaimer turned out to be bad medicine. Nixon could not cure the Watergate ills by saying "God bless America and God bless each and every one of you." The President had taken the responsibility of Watergate upon himself and accepted the burden of bringing the guilty to justice with all deliberate speed. It was obvious already that many of them were Nixon's friends; if he wished to avoid impeachment—now a topic of open conversation on Capitol Hill—he had to prove that he did not do as they did. The Watergate break-in, the Ellsberg burglary, and the massive cover-up had proved fatal to so many close to Nixon.

But instead of trying to convince America of his innocence, Nixon attended to business as usual, as if Watergate did not exist. His credibility as chief executive crumbled, a White House of cards tumbling under the weight of a stacked deck.

Rather than giving the Administration transfusions of new blood, Nixon announced the appointment of Elliot Richardson as attorney general and Leonard Garment as counsel to the President. For Richardson, the appointment to head the Department of Justice was his third cabinet post in as many months. Nixon, in his April 30 speech, delegated the power to appoint a special Watergate prosecutor to Richardson, but it soon became evident that the former secretary of defense was reticent to use the power. And Leonard Garment, as a former special counsel to

Nixon could not cure the Watergate ills by saying,"God bless America."

Nixon, already had some marginal involvement in the Watergate affair.

Remarks coming from Nixon stalwarts did not help the President's image in time of crisis either. Former defense secretary Melvin Laird told newsmen he was "totally confident the President just would not be involved in any way in this kind of operation, but if he were, it would be very bad for the country—that kind of disclosure." Operating under the premise of hear no evil, see no evil, Laird said he would not want to know that kind of truth. Republican law and order Governor Ronald Reagan commented that the Watergate conspirators should not be regarded as criminals because they are "not criminals at heart." For Reagan, the remark broke new ground in legal philosophy. Julie Nixon Eisenhower took time out from her tour of Disney World in Florida to comment on her father's new crisis. "I think that the G.O.P. and the rest of the nation will realize that this was just seven men who made a mistake, and others made a mistake by trying to cover it up." Julie described her father's televised speech as "very heartfelt."

Unfortunately for the President, others in government disagreed. FBI agents occupied the White House on May 1 to safeguard whatever remained of the files of Haldeman, Ehrlichman and Dean—and scuffled with Secret Service agents. Acting FBI Director William Ruckelhaus wanted no repetition of those past incidents when crucial evidence met the paper shredder. In Los Angeles, more damning revelations gushed forth from the Ellsberg trial, Ehrlichman to make the independent investigation of Daniel Ellsberg which led to the 1971 burglary. Judge Byrne confessed that Ehrlichman, with full knowledge of the clandestine investigation of Ellsberg, had met at length with the judge on April 5 to discuss the possibility of a nomination as permanent director of the FBI. Ellsberg's defense attorney, quick to point out the extraordinary interest of the White House in Ellsberg, moved for dismissal of the case. Leonard Boudin charged that "the conduct from the White House is so shocking that no alternative, no investigation, could palliate it. I really don't know of any parallel to the misbehavior involved. . . We are not dealing with an individual prosecutor named David Nissen, or the FBI, we are dealing with the highest authority in the country, the President of the United States." At the same time, Seymour Hersh reported in the New York Times that federal prosecutors had enough evidence to indict Haldeman, Ehrlichman, Mitchell, Dean, LaRue and Magruder.

now indicating that Nixon had personally ordered John

Congress was in a frenzy: Democrats had partisan gripes, Republicans resented the bad name Watergate gave them—and this from a President who disregarded the efforts of his own party's Congressmen to get reelected. Their voices were nearly unanimous in the demand for a comprehensive investigation. On May 1, the Senate approved by voice vote a resolution made by Republican Charles Percy that the President himself appoint the Watergate special prosecutor. But the resolution was not likely to have much effect on a President who wanted so desperately to stay as far above it all as possible. So the task fell by default to Richardson—and the Senate Judi-

ciary Committee made it plain that his nomination would not be approved unless he promised to appoint a prosecutor, and a good one. The improprieties of executive self-investigation had been tolerated long enough.

The aftermath of Nixon's April 30 speech brought another miracle to pass. Ron Ziegler apologized to the Washington Post. "We would all have to say that mistakes were made in terms of comments," said Ziegler. "I was overly enthusiastic in my comments about the Post, particularly if you look at them in the context of developments that have taken place. When we are wrong, we are wrong, as we were in this case."

Other men named in the Watergate case also saw the error of their ways, and left government service. David Young, former head White House Plumber, resigned his position on the National Security Council. Egil Krogh, another prominent Plumber, took a "leave of absence" from his position as Under-Secretary of Transportation. Former Secretary of the Treasury John Connally was so moved by the crisis that he announced his switch from the Democratic to the Republican Party. It was probably the most poorly timed move in Connally's well-planned career.

The Watergate crisis grew rather than diminished following Nixon's televised speech in which he had announced of the big four resignations—Bob and John and Dick and John. Undoubtedly, President Nixon had wished otherwise. The General Accounting Office accused CREEP' of an apparent violation of federal law for publishing an ad in the New York Times supporting Nixon's decision to mine Haiphong harbor and purporting to show citizen support for the mining. Further revelations in the Ellsberg case prompted Judge Byrne to demand a full transcript of Howard Hunt's testimony before the Watergate grand jury. Meanwhile, fallen aides Haldeman and Ehrlichman testified before the grand jury themselves.

Nixon was clearly losing ground. A Gallup poll published on May 4 showed that half the American people believed that the President had participated in the Watergate cover-up; forty percent thought that Nixon even had prior knowledge of the bugging of Democratic National Committee Headquarters.

The public's suspicions were further aroused the same day when John Dean gave Judge Sirica the keys to his safety deposit box. Dean told Sirica that the box contained classified documents that he felt had a bearing on the Watergate case. It was also disclosed that Dean had in his possession a written history of the Watergate operation and a detailed account of how White House aides attempted to whitewash it. The admission by Hugh Sloan that CREEP had collected $2 million secretly in early 1972 and had destroyed all records identifying the contributions did not help Nixon's credibility very much either. And Common Cause announced that its research indicated the Republicans had secretly amassed about $22 million for the 1972 campaign. The citizens' watchdog group continued to press its suit for full disclosure of all contributions.

Throughout the turmoil, President Nixon continued to react as a disaffected being, moving flaccidly through the ether of public non-confidence. On May 4, the President announced the interim appointment of General Alexander Haig as H.R. Haldeman's replacement. It was entirely un-

precedented for an active military officer to assume the civilian role of White House chief of staff, but the inconsistency apparently was inconsequential to Nixon, who remained ensconced in silence at Key Biscayne. (Later, though, Haig resigned his military commission.)

Meanwhile, in Orlando, Florida, *agent provocateur* Donald Segretti was indicted for forging the Florida primary letter alleging sexual misconduct by Senators Jackson and Humphrey. Segretti and George Hearing of Tampa, Florida were charged with two counts connected with that act of campaign sabotage. Senator Jackson asked the Ervin committee to look into the Florida investigation of the incident for possible obstruction of justice. The Ervin committee already was concerning itself with questionable investigations of the Watergate affair, most notably that of the Justice Department which had failed to find any evidence at all in the case except against the seven break-in conspirators.

The unearthing of the White House plumbing office had inexorably led to an investigation of the conduct of the CIA, which had cooperated to some degree with the Plumbers. Congressional probers learned from General Robert E. Cushman, former deputy director of the CIA, that the White House had made a concerted effort to involve the intelligence agency in domestic security operations in direct violation of federal law.

John Dean continued to assert that he could give very damaging testimony to federal prosecutors, evidence that would show President Nixon was well aware of a full-scale Watergate cover-up. Dean was the mystery within the mystery in the whole Watergate mess. The young counsel

was the only one of Nixon's inner-circle who seemed anxious to talk.

Events were now closing in on Mr. Nixon. Seymour Hersh reported that the President attempted twice to prevent the release of details on the burglary of Daniel Ellsberg's psychiatrist's office for reasons of national security. Exactly why the disclosure of details on illegal activity by the White House was a matter of national security remained a mystery, but around the country the words resignation and impeachment came more into vogue. Even Martha Mitchell told UPI reporter Helen Thomas that Nixon should resign. The Library of Congress reported a run on impeachment treatises. Martha said Nixon ought to step down "in order to give credibility to the Republican Party and credibility to the United States. I think he let the country down." On May 7, the first of the frantic Presidential denials was issued by the White House. "Any suggestion that the President was aware of the Watergate operation is untrue," said spokesman Gerald Warren. "Any suggestion that the President participated in any cover-up activities is untrue. Any suggestion that the President ever authorized the offering of clemency to anyone in this case is also false." Even if the President's assertions of innocence were accurate, many people were finding his judgement guilty, or absent. After all, his most trusted aides did, in fact, have the knowledge that he claimed to be lacking.

The same day as Nixon's protestation of innocence, Elliot Richardson announced that he intended to exercise the prerogative given him by the President and appoint a special Watergate prosecutor. In a conciliatory gesture,

Richardson invited the Senate Judiciary Committee to evaluate the qualifications of his selection and express "its confidence in him." The attorney general-designate stressed that the stringent qualifications for special prosecutor required an individual of "the highest honesty and integrity." It seemed that at last, the Justice Department's Watergate investigation might be put in the hands of someone capable of scraping eleven months of whitewash off the hallways of government. So it seemed.

Whitewash in the White House

The Watergate whitewash was painted with a broad brush, made possible by collusion among intelligence agencies, departments of the federal government, powerful corporations and the White House itself. Government officials lied, deceived, forged, concealed, conspired and otherwise committed high crimes and misdemeanors. Members of the Nixon Administration reached new heights in official lawlessness and new lows in official deception. Indeed it appears that, from all the evidence, the greatest crimes took place after the Watergate burglary.

Obstruction of justice is a crime. It is not a "technical violation" of a campaign act; in the eyes of the law it is a crime which theoretically can be as serious as murder. Generally speaking, the law provides that a person who obstructs the apprehension of a criminal is as guilty as or even guiltier than the criminal himself. Penalties for obstruction of justice often parallel the penalties for the given crime. So if Dean really lied to L. Patrick Gray by saying he did not know Hunt had a White House office, he made himself as guilty as burglary conspirator Hunt. If Ehrlichman really summoned CIA director Helms and Deputy Director Walters to his White House office and asked them to convince the FBI's Gray that the Mexican Connection investigation was interfering with national security, he was as guilty as Bernie Barker, or Robert Allen, or any of the many others involved there.

Like obstruction of justice, conspiracy is generally taken to be as serious a crime as the subject of the conspiracy. Such would be the case with the conspiracy, so strongly suspected by Judge Sirica, involving Douglas Caddy, the corporate lawyer who mysteriously showed up the morning of the Watergate break-in to represent the defendants. Like spoiled manna from heaven, Caddy showed up at the police station even though McCord and the Cubans repeatedly refused to make phone calls. Caddy refused to divulge how he knew they were caught, and was held in contempt of court. As it turned out, Hunt had called Caddy from the Howard Johnson's across the street from the Watergate where Baldwin had monitored the movements of the five burglars before their capture. Caddy might have had reason to keep quiet; Hunt's name was too easily traced to the White House to be mentioned.

Conspiracy, obstruction of justice and just plain cover-up were the mix which made the whitewash. The moment news of the Watergate burglary broke, the White House released a statement which claimed Hunt had not been employed there since March 29. The late Dorothy Hunt told a different story: she said her husband was a White House employee at the time of the break-in. For many months, the White House would not disclose the true details of Hunt's role in the White House—and then only when forced to do so. Mendacious and misleading statements such as these by officials are not crimes in the sense of being against the law—but they are crimes against the people who in a representative democracy have no choice but to place their trust and faith in those officials. President Nixon stated flatly that, ". . . the White House had no involvement whatever in this particular incident," and he would put the lie to those words many times in the pursuant months. Ziegler brushed off Watergate as a "third-rate burglary," a statement which, even assuming he is as ignorant as he later appeared to be, was patently absurd—just what one might expect of an ad man.

The whitewash, in all its aspects, began on June 17, 1972—the same day the Watergate was busted. According to statements of Chuck Colson, as soon as John Dean found out about the incident, he ordered Hunt to flee the country. When Colson heard of it, he screamed, "You will have the White House party to a fugitive from justice." Colson said the order was then rescinded; but nevertheless Hunt did flee to parts unknown.

Conspiracies to whitewash came quickly, too. The day after the break-in, the White House put into action a plan to place full responsibility on the CIA. After Ehrlichman bade Walters and Helms to invoke national security, Walters thought about it. Technically, a tenuous case could be made because Mexico was not usually FBI territory. But, Walters realized in short time, the CIA did not have a single covert activity taking place in Mexico, so there would be no national security problem and no violation of territorial jurisdictions. Walters called up Dean and told him his feelings. Dean replied with clumsy prodding. "Dean asked whether the CIA might have taken part in the Watergate episode without my knowing," Walters told the Armed Services Committee of the Senate. After assuring Dean that was not possible, Dean asked "whether there was not some way in which the agency might have been involved." Walters later concluded that these flimsily veiled threats were supposed to remind Walters that the CIA had been involved in the illegal breaking and entering of Dr. Ellsberg's psychiatrist's office a year before. But Walters had joined the agency after these events and said he knew nothing about it at the time of Dean's call.

Dean, exasperated by Walter's uncompromising attitude, finally asked "whether I had any idea of what might be done, and I replied that those responsible ought to be fired. He seemed disappointed." At that point, the thing went beyond cover-up to obstruction and conspiracy, according to Walters. "He asked if the CIA could not furnish bail and pay the suspects' salaries while they were in jail, using covert-action fund for this purpose." Walters said he refused to have any part of it.

By this time, old Gray had been dragged into the cover-up. He arranged to meet with several CIA officials concerning the Mexican Connection. The morning of the planned meeting, Ehrlichman called up Gray and told him to "cancel it." "Who decides on these things?" the perturbed Gray wanted to know. "You, Pat" Ehrlichman responded facetiously. At that point, Gray related, it became obvious to him that the law and order administration's officials did not want their law and order agency to uphold law and order.

When the plan to blame the CIA fell through, the whitewash became a much more difficult matter, requiring more liars and more concealments—but the Administration was prepared to pull out all the obstruction, conspiracy and cover-up stops.

"Obstruction of justice: the act by which one or more persons attempt to prevent or do prevent the execution of lawful process."

"Within my own staff, under my direction," the President said in his Aug. 29, 1972 speech, "counsel to the President, Mr. Dean, has conducted a complete investigation of all leads which might involve any present members of the White House staff or anybody in the government. I can say categorically that his investigation indicated that no one in the White House staff, no one presently employed, was involved in this very bizarre incident." Events later put the lie to those words too. Whether Nixon lied consciously is a matter yet to be determined; although he did say "categorically." One category he left out was the matter of Mr. Dean, who claimed later that he never had been told to carry out an independent investigation.

The President had, in his carefully worded speech, pointed to four possible scapegoats who were not "presently employed:" Mitchell, Liddy, Hunt and Hugh Sloan, the former CREEP finance treasurer who resigned six weeks before. Nixon also put full responsibility for the investigation on the shoulders of Dean; in case someone doubted the authenticity of the investigation at some later date, another scapegoat was ready to be shorn.

One lamb who wouldn't be led to the sacrificial slaughter was James McCord. Shortly after he was released from jail, McCord found a note in his mailbox instructing him to "Go to the phone booth on Route 355 near your home." It was signed *Jack*. "I'm a friend of Jack's" said the anonymous voice in the phone booth. "I formerly worked with him. Jack will want to talk with you shortly."

Jack's last name was Caulfield. And he called McCord to explain the secrecy and to offer any assistance if McCord needed it. Caulfield requested that when he was called at home, McCord should ask for Mr. Watson.

The day the Watergate trial proceedings began, Jan. 8, the mysterious voice told McCord that Caulfield wanted him to "plead guilty . . . you will get executive clemency. Your family will be taken care of and when you get out you will be rehabilitated and a job will be found for you. Don't plead immunity when called before the grand jury." A few nights later, McCord testified, the voice told him to drive to a Potomac River overlook on the George Washington Memorial Parkway, where he met with Caulfield. "Caulfield stated that he was carrying the message of executive clemency to me 'from the very highest levels of the White House.' He stated that the President of the United States was in Key Biscayne, Florida that weekend, had been told of the forthcoming meeting with me, and would be immediately told of the results of the meeting . . . He further stated that 'I may have a message to you at our next meeting from the President himself.'"

McCord didn't follow the orders but the other defendants apparently did. All but Liddy pleaded guilty, and have kept their lips tightly zipped. Liddy pleaded not guilty, but during the Watergate trial and since, he has been as communicative as a mummy.

"Obstruction of justice [also means] to impede or hinder, to interpose obstacles or impediments to the hindrance or frustration of some act or service as to obstruct an offi-

cer in the execution of his duty."

Thus, when Gray started telling the unexpurgated truth before the Judiciary Committee, Ehrlichman ordered him to shut up. Thus, Stans, who would later be indicted for obstruction of justice in connection with the Vesco case, filed a $5 million libel suit immediately after a House Banking and Currency Committee staff report said he had approved of the Mexican money laundry. Thus, Ehrlichman visited Judge Byrne with a carrot of an FBI appointment on his serpentine stick when it appeared that the Papers trial could by another Watergate embarrassment. Thus U.S. Attorney Earl Silbert, the prosecutor in the trial of the Watergate burglars, was stricken with tunnel vision when it came to the nitty gritty of cross-examining—so much so that Judge Sirica had to take the extraordinary step of questioning witnesses himself. Thus Gray bowed before the wishes of ex-attorney general Mitchell when he refused to allow FBI agents to interview Martha in connection with her intriguing statement about all "those dirty tricks that go on." Thus Bob Haldeman was never interviewed by the FBI. And so it goes.

"Obstruction in this sense [also means] to block up, to interpose obstacles, to render impassable, to fill with barriers or impediments as to obstruct a road or way."

Often enough, it was not so much a matter of interposing obstacles as it was of eliminating the roadway. Stans, for instance, burned CREEP's books.

Just how big an obstacle to justice the White House would be willing to erect was hinted at by an event related by McCord. Five days before his conviction, on Jan. 25, he drove with Caulfield to Warrentown, Virginia. During the trip, Caulfield warned, "You know that if the administration gets its back to the wall, it will have to take steps to defend itself."

"I took that as a personal threat," McCord testified. "And I told him that I had had a good life, that my will was made out and that I had thought through the risks and would take them when I was ready."

Some of the obstacles were erected by Mr. Nixon personally. Twice he thwarted disclosure of evidence concerning the burglary of Ellsberg's psychiatrist's office on the spurious grounds that it might endanger national security—by the time the trial was going on, the Pentagon Papers were into second and third printings. Dean, in mid-April, had told Watergate investigator Petersen about the burglary. Petersen had urged the President to report the information to Judge Byrne, then presiding over Ellsberg's second trial out in L.A. Twice Nixon refused. AG Kleindienst quickly muzzled Petersen and advised him to stop telling the President things he did not want to hear.

When it became apparent that Egil Krogh, the Plumber leader who had cleared the burglary, would be called to testify, Defense Secretary Richardson warned Nixon that he would resign if Judge Byrne were not informed. If Richardson quit at that point, the master whitewash would run thin, so Nixon obliged and a "mysterious envelope" arrived in Byrne's office on April 26. The letter was from Henry Petersen. Two days later, Kleindienst resigned, and the President appointed attorney general the man who had threatened him.

" 'Obstruction' is also a very general word in law being applicable to every hinderance of a man in the discharge of his duty, whether official, public or private."

The greatest crimes in the Watergate whitewash might well be considered those which are least obviously crimes, the ones which would fall in the category of cover-up. They are crimes deriving from a betrayal of the trust that is the underpinning of democracy. There used to be an assumption of honesty and truthfulness automatically accorded to public officials. That was before the Watergate.

It did not take much for the American people to see that the most thorough-since-the-assassination-etc. investigation made by Attorney General Kleindienst prior to the elections had succeeded in turning up evidence against only the seven burglars and their accomplices. As Ervin remarked, a back country magistrate could have prepared the case against those fellows.

Throughout the entire affair, there was an incredible disingenuousness to announcements of Administration resignations. Rather queer, it seemed, when John Mitchell cut out of CREEP so shortly after the Watergate. Martha put on a gallant show, but after John was indicted for obstruction of justice, it all seemed rather contrived. On Jan. 30, Seymour Hersh of the *Times* reported that the White House had become an unfriendly environment for Dwight Chapin, the President's appointments secretary, because of the recent charges that he headed that sabotage apparatus. Later that day, Chapin resigned to join the friendly skies of United Airlines. Naturally, it was maintained that he resigned to go into private industry, and all that rot. Even when Haldeman and Ehrlichman went down, neither they nor the President directly admitted it was due to the Watergate and the heavy rations of implicating disclosures taking place concurrently. Haldeman and Ehrlichman both laid their resignations to the irresponsible and innuendoed accusations appearing in the press.

The taint did not leave the Administration's investigation of the Watergate affair, even after the lengths Richardson was put to by the Judiciary Committee. The man finally chosen as special prosecutor, Archibald Cox, went to federal court in an attempt to keep the Ervin hearings closed to the public, or at least off the television sets. "I condemn any cover-up in this case," the President had said April 17, "no matter who is involved."

Obstruction of justice and sundry conspiracies were not the only actual crimes committed in the manufacture of the Watergate whitewash.

Herbert L. Porter, a CREEP aide, was to testify at the Ervin hearings that he had lied in his testimony at the first Watergate trial, before the Watergate grand jury and to the FBI in explaining why G. Gordon Liddy was given so much money from the Re-elect coffers. That is called perjury.

Porter said that Jeb Stuart Magruder had asked him to make up a story about how $100,000 of the money given to Liddy was spent. That is called subornation to perjury.

And, according to McCord, Kenneth Parkinson channeled large sums of money to the convicted Watergate burglars to keep quiet at the trial. That is called bribery, obstruction of justice, and conspiracy.
(According to Dean, Mr. Nixon himself was involved in arranging these pay-offs. Dean said Nixon asked how much the tab would be for silence, and was not worried about spending $1 million to buy it. Conspiracy to commit bribery: a high crime.

At a press conference on March 15, the commander-in-chief made it clear that the investigation of Watergate was a strictly domestic matter. "Now, this investigation does not involve espionage against the United States," he stated matter of factly. "It is, as we know, espionage by one political organization against another . . . the Congress would have a far greater right and would be on much stronger ground to ask the government to cooperate in a matter involving espionage against the government than in a matter like this, involving politics." Two months later, invoking executive privilege to prevent Dean from testifying, the commander-in-chief of cover-up would do a 180-degree reversal and excuse misconduct and illegalities of his Administration members on grounds of "national security." Add obstruction of justice, just for good measure. It too is a high crime.

Article II, Section 4. The President, Vice President, and all civil officers of the United States shall be removed from office on impeachment for and conviction of treason, bribery, or other high crimes and misdemeanors.

So it all came to pass, in the year of our lord nineteen hundred and seventy-three, on the last day of April, that Mr. Nixon had his second Checkers.

Again, he was at bat for himself in a nationally televised speech in which he was to explain how much he knew and did not know about a reigning scandal. The general consensus was that, this time, he struck out.

The speech was different from other Nixon speeches. He spoke slowly and heavily, the words carried the sort of extra baggage that had rarely encumbers a critical Nixon address. The weight was emotion. His customary military rigidness gave way to a slightly bowed head, hinting at a new-found humility. His paper maché television visage had cracked and the man—the man hidden behind the Presidency—could be seen through those cracks.

He accepted the responsibility for Watergate, but not the blame. He was too busy catching peace with honor to worry about American politics, to be concerned with his "closest friends and most trusted advisors" who were warping the American political system beyond recognition. He read his Christmas list like an old-aged Tiny Tim and then ended the night's address, appropriately enough, with another Dickensian phrase.

It was an unsatisfying speech all around. Nixon had lost his two palace guards to the gutting fire of Watergate, but insisted they were decent and honorable. He excused the behavior of his staff by labeling them zealots with a just cause. He answered no questions about Watergate and revealed nothing of what he knew.

The press brickbatted the speech as a sham. Congressmen complained bitterly that it had evaded the issues. A Gallup poll the following week showed that 41% of the American populace believed that Nixon knew of the cover-up, if not of the entire affair. The nation had swallowed Checkers and digested it well, but the Son of Checkers stuck in the throat.

May 8 to May 17/The Ides of May

During the second week following Nixon's April 30 staff purge, patterns of activity, scope, and reaction tenuously emerged from the tangle of scandal. It was obvious by now that the Watergate cover-up shielded much more from view than mere details surrounding the break-in of Democratic National Headquarters. Rather, the hidden culprit was the very alter ego of the Nixon Administration itself: clandestine activities involving the CIA, a White House "mission impossible" squad, the FBI, and a whole plethora of government bureaucrats playing national security games. Equally obvious was the incredible fact that illegal activities perpetrated by the alter ego, far from being the actions of a few overzealous Nixon campaign workers, were actually the result of Nixon policy.

Instead of professing his innocence, President Nixon seemed to be enveloping the White House in a cloud of guilt. The time had come for reconciliation, for the President to repudiate his claim to unprecedented executive authority and to dispel any doubts about his ability to lead the nation. Nevertheless, the White House remained a lofty pinnacle, its occupants issuing edicts from on high.

The White House announced on May 8 that it was relaxing its guidelines for testimony by White House aides called before the Ervin committee, which planned to begin nationally televised hearings on May 17. Under the new guidelines, drafted by Counsel to the President Leonard Garment, federal prosecutors were given White House approval for seeking immunity from prosecution for former high Nixon officials. Executive privilege was reserved only to the White House counsel who was to accompany any witness formerly entitled to use the questionable power. Senator Edmund Muskie immediately charged that the guidelines appeared to be designed to protect the President from incrimination. The rules were hardly a concession to the Ervin Committee, which announced the same day, prior to receiving the guidelines, that it intended to move to grant key witness John Dean immunity.

The new Nixon staff seemed to have a frenzied interest in former counsel Dean, who emerged from the Watergate fiasco as the most damaging witness against the President. The White House reportedly was attempting to retrieve nine documents in Dean's Alexandria safe deposit box. It was the keys to that box that Dean had turned over to Judge John Sirica to ensure that the classified documents—which alleged that Nixon knew of illegal activity carried out in his behalf—would make their way to the grand jury. White House efforts to intercept the material were foiled on May 14 the documents, bearing a *Top Secret—handle via COMINT channel* classification, were delivered to Sirica.

The President spoke during this period only under very guarded circumstances, fully aware that the nation looked to him for an explanation of Watergate. Nixon addressed a Republican fund-raising dinner on May 9, vowing, "I didn't get where I am by ducking tough issues." Nixon assured the friendly audience that he would "get to the bottom of this very deplorable incident." Still, even a G.O.P. fund-raising gala felt the effect of the scandal. The affair raised only $750,000 against an anticipated $2 million.

Events were unfolding that the President couldn't brush aside with timeworn reassurances that he would get to the bottom of things. Watergate had gone on too long already. Nixon had to do something immediately.

As the Central Intelligence Agency was coming under Congressional scrutiny for its role in the 1971 burglary of Ellsberg's psychiatrist's office, Watergate conspirator McCord gave a memorandum to the grand jury and the Ervin Committee in which he charged there was a plot to blame the Watergate bugging on the CIA, even though there had been no CIA involvement. CIA director James Schlesinger admitted to a Senate panel on May 9 that the CIA's role in the 1971 Ellsberg burglary had been an "ill-advised act," apparently in violation of the statute which established the CIA in 1947. Schlesinger went on to testify that the CIA's director then, Richard Helms, had ordered

agency participation in the operation at the express request of former White House adviser John Ehrlichman. For the CIA director to testify that someone as close to Nixon as Ehrlichman had made the improper request brought still graver questions about the President's own role into the affair.

Those questions were serious enough for Judge Byrne to dismiss all charges against Daniel Ellsberg and Anthony Russo, in addition to declaring a mistrial, on May 11 in Los Angeles. Byrne declared angrily from the bench that "the conduct of the government has placed the case in such a posture that it precludes the fair and dispassionate resolution of these issues by a jury." The government was probably relieved at the dismissal, which was precipitated by its failure to produce transcripts of wiretapped Ellsberg phone conversations, because the celebrated case had become a well-spring of Watergate disclosures. The missing wiretap transcripts were found a few days later, interestingly enough, in Ehrlichman's White House safe.

Uniform demands were voiced for the White House to take stronger steps to re-establish its credibility. Nixon attempted such a move on May 10, announcing another major shake-up. Former Treasury Secretary John B. Connally was named a special adviser to the President; CIA director James Schlesinger was named Secretary of Defense to replace Elliot Richardson; William Colby was named CIA director to replace Schlesinger; and J. Fred Buzhardt, general counsel of the Defense Department, was named special counsel to the President on a temporary basis to advise on Watergate matters. The White House also announced that the supercabinet system, which had been established in January to centralize bureaucratic control in the Oval Office, was being scrapped in favor of the traditional cabinet system in which the president met directly with department heads. Nixon's predilection for appointing old, familiar faces to new power positions within his administration did little to restore his credibility. Too many of those old faces were coming under the scrutiny of grand juries.

A grand jury in New York on May 10 indicted former Attorney General John Mitchell, former Commerce Secretary Maurice Stans, New Jersey CREEP official Harry Sears, and financier Robert Vesco on charges stemming from Vesco's illegal $200,000 contribution to CREEP. Part of the 46-page indictment read: "The defendants unlawfully, willfully, and knowingly did combine, conspire, confederate, and agree together and with each other to commit offenses against the United States . . . to defraud the United States and agencies thereof . . . interfering with and obstructing lawful governmental functions by deceit, craft, trickery, and means that are dishonest." Mitchell and Stans were also charged with six counts of perjury stemming from previous grand jury testimony.

Even though both Mitchell and Stans professed their innocence, they were the first cabinet members to be charged with criminal acts since the Teapot Dome scandal fifty years before. The chairman of the Securities and Exchange Commission, G. Bradford Cook, resigned from his post five days later, after serving only three months, because his name had been linked to a possible cover-up of Mitchell's and Stans' misconduct.

Nixon's government appeared to be toppling. An outraged Congress voted to cut off all funds for the bombing of Cambodia, tired of listening to aphorisms like "peace with honor" while the President bombed another country in Indochina back into the Stone Age in order to maintain that peace. Meanwhile, more Watergate revelations stoked the fires of Congressional and national anger. CIA deputy director Vernon Walters testified about the attempt by Dean, Ehrlichman and Haldeman to persuade the CIA to talk the FBI into calling off the Mexican laundry investigation. At the same time, it was revealed that L. Patrick Gray attempted to warn the President of a possible Watergate cover-up by high level aides, two weeks after the June 17 break-in.

Nixon remained silent now that the public knew he probably had just cause to believe that some sort of cover-up was taking place shortly after the Watergate burglary. Nixon remained silent too when former counsel John Dean, the man Nixon named on August 29 as having made a thorough investigation of the Watergate affair, announced that he had never made such an investigation. The only rebuttal the White House could muster came on May 15 when beleaguered Ron Ziegler announced the only Watergate report Nixon received was given to him orally by Ehrlichman. The President supposedly had assumed the information came from Dean.

With most of his former staff facing probable indictment, in some cases from more than one grand jury, Nixon's cherished image was in serious jeopardy. How could a distinguished world statesman surround himself with so many bunglers, liars, authoritarian paper shufflers and adolescents envious of James Bond? How could the President who promised to bring America together, allow such a major scandal to shatter it into fragments? How was Watergate possible?

In the meantime, electricians prepared the Senate Caucus room for the beginning of the Ervin Committee hearings. The same chamber had housed such vehement investigations as the Teapot Dome Hearings, the Kefauver organized crime hearings, and the Army-McCarthy hearings—which had been the first Senate inquiry ever broadcast on nationwide television. An anxious and perplexed nation awaited the start of the Ervin sessions. The nation wanted to see the faces behind the names that had been gracing headlines for months. People wanted to hear from the mouths of these men what Watergate was, what sinister motives had compelled them to so abuse the government they were supposed to serve. But most of all, overriding any simple curiosity, the American people desired to hear some modicum of truth amid the cacophony of Watergate.

Sam Ervin's gavel bringing the first session to order at 10:00 AM on May 17 was the beginning of that process.

The Price of Truth

Witnesses appearing before the Senate Select Committee on Presidential Campaign Activities

May 17: Robert Odle, Director of Administration for the Committee to Re-elect the President

May 18: James McCord, Security Director for the Committee to Re-elect the President

May 23: Gerald Alch, former Attorney for James McCord

May 23: John Caulfield, White House aide

May 24: Bernard Barker, convicted Watergate burglar

June 5: Sally Harmony, Secretary to Gordon Liddy

June 5: Robert Reisner, former Assistant to Jeb Stuart Magruder

June 6: Hugh Sloan, Treasurer for the Finance Committee to Re-elect the President

June 7: Herbert Porter, Director of Scheduling for the Committee to Re-elect the President

June 9: Maurice Stans, Chairman of the Finance Committee to Re-elect the President

June 14: Jeb Stuart Magruder, Deputy Director for the Committee to Re-elect the President

June 26: John Dean, former Counsel to the President

July 10: John Mitchell, former Attorney General and former Director of the Committee to Re-elect the President

July 13: Richard Moore, White House Special Counsel

July 16: Alexander Butterfield, White House aide and Federal Aviation Agency Administrator

July 18: Anthony Ulasewicz, former New York City policeman

July 19: Fredrick LaRue, former White House Counsel

July 19: Robert Mardian, former Assistant Attorney General

July 23: Gordon Strachan, aide to H. R. Haldeman

July 24: John Ehrlichman, adviser for domestic affairs to Richard Nixon

July 30: H. R. Haldeman, chief-of-staff for Richard Nixon

August 2: Robert Cushman, former Deputy Director of the CIA

August 2: Richard Helms, former Director of the CIA

August 3: Lt. General Vernon Walters, Deputy Director of the CIA

August 3: L. Patrick Gray, former Acting Director of the FBI

August 7: Richard Kleindienst, former Attorney General

August 7: Henry Petersen, Assistant Attorney General in charge of the Criminal Division

Whereas the Lord finally rested on the Seventh Day, Sam Ervin had to wait out thirty-seven uneasy and exhausting days before he gaveled an end to the first phase of the Senate's Watergate Investigation. As far as the television audience was concerned, the public hearings might have been a stock car demolition derby as White House ambassadors violently collided with Nixon critics. The smoke and fire of the confrontations were as real as the public wreckage of private lives.

As a word-weary American public served jury duty through the electronic and print media, Ervin piloted his committee through thirty-three witnesses, 7,573 pages, comprised of nearly 2 million words, of testimony. The volcanic outpouring of evidence has certainly embarrassed the Nixon Administration; with few exceptions, the testimony has been distinguished by self-serving platitudes,

"They don't act like innocent people," said Petersen.

evasions, and outright lies.

If the Watergate hearings have been socially useful in exposing high government corruption, they have none-theless generally failed to resolve many of the serious conflicts in testimony. Witnesses hostile to the President, particularly John Dean, have argued that Nixon authored or participated in a White House strategy to conceal the truth from the public. Nixon loyalists have contradicted Dean's interpretation and defended the President's innocence and unswerving commitment to full disclosure of the facts.

It is important to note that the distance separating the White House loyalists and the Nixon rebels has often been caused not by a division over facts, but by differing interpretation of commonly shared facts. The price of reconciling the disparities in the Watergate testimony has become the price of truth.

In an attempt to answer the question of who did what and when, the Senate Watergate investigators have naturally focused on the question of who committed the original sin of the 1972 campaign by authorizing the White House intelligence operation which included bugging Democratic National Committee Headquarters. There is no dispute that convicted Watergate burglar, Gordon Liddy, prepared an elaborate battle strategy to sabotage the Democratic campaign. John Mitchell, John Dean, and Jeb Magruder have all testified that Liddy's $1 million blueprint, which included blackmail, call girls, kidnapping, and wiretapping, was presented on two separate occasions and rejected each time by Mitchell. At a third meeting in Key Biscayne, Liddy presented a streamlined version of his original master plan which focussed on bugging the Watergate and other key Democratic offices. This customized plan was eventually bankrolled by CREEP and partially implemented. Those facts were unchallenged by witnesses at the hearings. However, when pressed for further details, all the active parties started a game of musical chairs with the truth.

Magruder testified that the then Attorney General John Mitchell grudgingly approved the Liddy plan and personally received wiretapping data from Democratic National Headquarters. Erupting like a medieval dragon, Mitchell denied he authorized the bugging or received wiretapping logs. He characterized Magruder's testimony as "a palpable, damnable lie." Committee Counsel Sam Dash asked Mitchell why Liddy had not been thrown out of his office for suggesting that the Attorney General approve obviously illegal wiretapping. With no small measure of bravado, Mitchell answered "I should have thrown him out the window."

Fred LaRue, another CREEP official and personal friend of Mitchell, attended that controversial Key Biscayne meeting, and testified that Mitchell neither approved nor disapproved the bugging plan. But when asked whether Mitchell had rejected the program "out of hand," LaRue admitted "Not to my recollection, no sir."

Mitchell stubbornly pumped up his own innocence by suggesting that "there may have been pressures from collateral areas in which they decided that this [wiretapping] was the thing to do. I can't speculate on who they might be." John Dean, without vindicating Mitchell by any

means, testified that Magruder said H. R. Haldeman, using Gordon Strachan as his mouthpiece, had authorized the Liddy fiasco. Both Strachan and Haldeman have denied it. But in a confessional tone of near-perfect altar boy purity, Strachan admitted that Magruder communicated Mitchell's approval to him. Strachan says he included this information in a "talking paper" for Haldeman who, in turn, failed to recall reading it.

Nixon's former White House straw boss also said he did not remember if Dean, as the former White House lawyer has alleged, reported the first two Liddy strategy sessions to him. No one, including Dean, has implicated Nixon in the prebreak-in conspiracy, although Dean has argued that if Haldeman knew, the President knew. Nixon has incontrovertibly denied this on several occasions. This area of the testimony has been a swamp of contradiction, but it is clear that neither Liddy nor Magruder could have authorized the invasion of Democratic National Headquarters without high level direction.

One of the fundamental factors that has preserved the muddy confusion on the wiretapping burglary is the wholesale destruction of evidence and records that might have otherwise indicted the guilty or exonerated the innocent. Within days of the June 17, 1972 break-in, the methodically loyal members of Nixon's staff undertook a paper-shredding and burn-bagging marathon that rivalled Mrs. O'Leary's cow for efficiency.

What the Watergate hearings confirmed was that Liddy shredded any documents relating to his perverted Disneyland of wiretapping, burglary, and sabotage; Magruder destroyed his eavesdropping reports from Democratic Headquarters; Strachan disposed of any incriminating documents in Haldeman's office; Kalmbach, LaRue, and Porter eliminated sensitive financial information from their respective files; Maurice Stans and Hugh Sloan destroyed their reports of campaign contributions collected before the financial disclosure law went into effect April 7, 1972; and former Acting FBI Director Pat Gray burned politically sensitive documents from Howard Hunt's safe along with his Christmas garbage. Assistant Attorney General Henry Petersen understated the case somewhat when he testified that "they don't act like innocent people. Innocent people come in and say 'Fine, what do you want to know?' It was not like that."

Ehrlichman was unmoved and stridently denounced charge after charge, including testimony that he assured Kalmbach of the propriety of raising money for the seven Watergate defendants. Nixon's personal attorney had vouched that he confronted Ehrlichman and said "I am looking right into your eyes...and it is absolutely necessary, John, that you tell me that John Dean has the authority, that it is a proper assignment and that I'll go forward on it." According to Kalmbach, Ehrlichman assured him the payments were proper and legal. Ehrlichman only returned the fire and said Kalmbach acted under Dean's instructions, not his.

But Dean implicated more than Ehrlichman in the money raising scheme. The former White House lawyer accused Nixon himself of being the principal architect of a strategy to buy the silence of the Watergate defendants. The Senate hearings have documented the fact that

$420,000 was disbursed to the families and lawyers of the convicted burglars. Speaking in crisp, deliberate sentences, Dean said Ehrlichman, Haldeman, and Mitchell all approved the payments. Dean also testified that during a hotly contested meeting with Nixon on March 13, 1973, "I told the President about the fact there was no money to pay [the defendants] to meet their demands. I told him it might be as high as $1 million or more. He told me that

was no problem and he also looked over at Haldeman and repeated the same statement."

Nixon's virtue was fastidiously defended by Haldeman during his Senate testimony. Unofficially serving as the White House emissary, Haldeman said "I seriously doubt that the conversation John Dean has described actually took place on March 13. A discussion of those matters actually occurred during a meeting on March 21. I did

raise the money," adding that it would be wrong.

During the same press conference, advertised as Nixon's rebuttal to charges made thus far during the then recessed Senate hearings, Nixon also denied that he ever extended an offer of executive clemency to any of the Watergate burglars, contrary to Dean's sworn testimony.

In his testimony, Dean insisted that during the March 13 meeting "the President then referred to the fact that Hunt had been promised executive clemency. He said that he had discussed the matter with Ehrlichman and, contrary to instructions that Ehrlichman had given Colson not to talk to the President about it, Colson had also discussed it with him later." Haldeman maintained that "the only mention of clemency was Dean's report that Colson had discusses clemency with Hunt and the President's statement that he could not offer clemency and Dean's agreement."

Too little has been explained at the Watergate hearings. Tension and uncertainty still surround the President. There has been a general collapse of public faith: According to a late August 1973 Gallup Poll, only 31 percent of the American people approved of the way Nixon has discharged his responsibilities, making him the least popular President in twenty years. The Oliver Quayle Poll indicated that if the 1972 election had been held ten months later, George McGovern would be President of the United States. The impact of Watergate on government has been a disaster of Biblical proportions and it remains to be seen if Nixon can restore faith in the White House.

John Dean has been undercut, but not totally discredited. Nor will he be until the President or the Watergate Committee reconciles the dramatic friction that divides the manifold accounts of the burglary and the subsequent efforts to conceal it. Although Nixon has finally attempted to heal some of the country's wounds, too often the President's explanations only provoke more questions. It is disturbing, for example, to believe Nixon forgot if Gray used the words "mortally wound" in describing the activities of his close aides during the Watergate investigation.

Clearly these people were not innocent. Magruder said that Mitchell did everything except give him a book of matches. LaRue corroborated Magruder and testified that Mitchell recommended "a bonfire." Mitchell repudiated both accounts, but confessed that he reluctantly participated in a cover-up. "We sure as hell weren't volunteering anything," Mitchell choked out. That included not volunteering anything to the President who would have "lowered the boom" on his White House aides, according to Mitchell, unlocking a Pandora's Box of "horror stories." There was no little irony in the former Attorney General's remedy for lawlessness among the White House staff which was "to take them out on the White House lawn and shot (sic) them all." On his own lawless silence about Watergate crimes, Mitchell rationalized his activities as the high cost of re-electing Nixon. The President's former law partner testified he would have reported "chapter and verse" what he knew about the conspiracy if Nixon had asked him, but Nixon never did.

Other testimony by Gordon Strachan indicated that Haldeman ordered his young assistant to "make sure our files are clean" of political intelligence memorandums. Strachan complied and reported so back to his Chief of Staff. Haldeman refuted Strachan and said he could not recall instructing him to destroy evidence. His memory similarly failed to pinpoint the moment he first learned of the Watergate burglary, whether Dean ever warned him about Liddy, and how a $350,000 cash fund he himself controlled was used to pay lawyers' fees for the seven Watergate defendants.

No memory breakdown interfered with Gray's volatile testimony. He told the Senators that Dean and Ehrlichman ordered him to destroy "political dynamite" from

listen to the tape of the entire meeting. The President said 'There is no problem in raising a million dollars; we can do that, but it would be wrong.'"

Nixon himself publicly upbraded Dean on May 22, 1973 by saying "I did not know, until the time of my own investigation, of any effort to provide the Watergate defendants with funds." But during a rare press conference on August 22, Nixon acknowledged that he used the words "we could wiretapper Hunt's White House safe. Dean had been quick to hang the Gray albatross around Ehrlichman's neck when he claimed Nixon's Domestic Policy Czar originally suggested Hunt's files be "deep-sixed" in the Potomac. Dean advised Ehrlichman to give the material to Gray who, after holding it for six months, burned it along with the trash during Christmas week.

Ehrlichman contradicted both Gray and Dean just as he vigorously denied every illegal or improper act attributed to him. Brilliantly and arrogantly, Ehrlichman refuted the twin testimony of Richard Helms and Vernon Walters of the CIA that he attempted to delay the FBI investigation into campaign money in Mexico on grounds it would have exposed covert CIA activities. All that was uncovered, curiously, was the laundering process by which CREEP money was washed of its identity and used to finance the Watergate burglary.

Ehrlichman's five-day appearance before the Senate Watergate Committee, the longest by any witness, was marked by a series of dramatic eruptions and debates over the limits of presidential authority and campaign practices. Ehrlichman argued that a President could authorize burglaries to protect national security, that there was no impropriety in discussing a government job with a judge presiding over a politically sensitive trial, that investigating the sexual and drinking habits of political opponents was a necessary and proper part of campaigning, and that it was appropriate to try to prevent a former Cabinet official, Maurice Stans, from suffering the disgrace of appearing before a grand jury looking into the 1972 election.

Eager to promote his own innocence, Ehrlichman was equally quick to indict the moral vicissitudes of others. The Senate Committee was frustrated and chilled by Ehrlichman. Hawaii Democrat Daniel Inouye was overheard, much to his embarrassment, when he said into a live microphone, "What a liar." Inouye retracted his remark but another committee member, Senator Herman Talmadge, went on record declaring "It's hard to believe that a man of your intelligence could have been so involved in so much complicated complicity and knew nothing about it."

The matter is further aggravated by the fact that Nixon steadfastly refuses to release the secret White House tapes which could move the nation closer to the truth. Until he does, the public cries that Nixon might have violated his oath of office and might be guilty of "high crimes and misdemeanors," defined by the Constitution as the basis for impeachment, must stand.

Tapes

The anxious whispering between the seven Senators listening to the concluding testimony of former White House Special Counsel Richard Moore on the morning of July 16 seemed unusual for the normally attentive and decorous members of the Ervin Committee. Later in the day a surprise witness at the hearings on 1972 Presidential campaign practices, FAA administrator Alexander Butterfield, provided the reason for the Committee's abnormal agitation before a national television audience. Butterfield, a former staff aide to deposed White House chief-of-staff H. R. Haldeman, revealed the existence of an elaborate White House electronic eavesdropping system that allowed President Nixon to tape record virtually every meeting and telephone conversation he had at the White House since the system's installation in June 1971. The taping system was so secret that its existence was known only to Mr. Nixon, Haldeman, Butterfield—who supervised the office of presidential papers—White House aide Laurence Higby, and select members of the Secret Service who kept the system in working order.

The existence of the secret White House tapes had been disclosed two weeks before Haldeman appeared before the Watergate Committee revealing that he had listened to some of them. The announcement literally unglued both the Senate panel and the nation. After Nixon refused to permit either Congress or the Special Watergate Prosecutor to have access to the tapes, arguing they were protected by the separation of powers, Haldeman's bland admission left even Bible-quoting Sam Ervin speechless. In effect, the White House had marshalled its armies on the field with the intention of vaporizing Dean's credibility as a witness.

While Butterfield testified that the eavesdropping system was undoubtedly installed "to record things for posterity for the Nixon Library," both the Ervin Committee and special prosecutor Archibald Cox immediately sought access to the tapes for a more immediate use. Perhaps unwittingly, President Nixon himself had created the ultimate Watergate witness, tape recordings that presumably would spell out word for preserved word what exactly Nixon's role, if any, had been in the Watergate cover-up. The tapes seemed to provide the President with incontrovertible evidence to refute the charges of his former White House Counsel John Dean that the President had been aware of the Watergate cover-up as early as September 15, 1972; that the President had been willing to raise over $1 million in "hush money" for the seven convicted Watergate burglars; and had offered to grant executive clemency to at least one of the burglars, E. Howard Hunt. But if the tapes did support Nixon's claim to innocence, why had he chosen to keep them secret?

The Ervin Committee had already sought to have the President testify before it in some form and to gain access to presidential papers. Writing in response to the Committee on July 6, President Nixon refused to comply with the Select Committee's request. "The pending requests," Nixon said, "would move us from proper presidential cooperation with a Senate Committee to jeopardizing the fundamental constitutional role of the presidency. This I must and shall resist. No President could function if the private papers of his office, prepared by his personal staff, were open to public scrutiny." Nixon's letter set the stage for a constitutional confrontation between himself and Congress that the Ervin Committee sought to avoid at all costs. On July 12 the Committee resolved to authorize chairman Ervin to meet with the President to reach some compromise whereby presidential papers pertaining to the Watergate investigation could be released to the committee.

But the Butterfield revelation about White House tapes ended all possibilities of compromise. Throughout its investigation, the Ervin Committee urgently attempted to uncover any possible presidential involvement in the Watergate cover-up as its first priority, or in Senator Baker's words, to ascertain "what did the President know, and when did he know it." With vital evidence available, actual tape recordings of key meetings where improprieties were allegedly discussed, the presidential shield of executive privilege was bound to be assaulted by the Ervin Committee, by Cox, and by "the public's need to know."

The Nixon response was to assert executive privilege more forcefully than ever. The President ordered that no member of the Secret Service give testimony before the Ervin Committee on any aspect of his White House duties, after the Committee attempted to learn more about the care and handling of presidential tapes. On July 17, the Ervin Committee officially requested that it be allowed access to the tapes. Public sympathy seemed to be with the Ervin Committee while many members of Congress who had supported the President expressed outrage that their private conversations with Nixon had been taped. The administration, for its part, was quick to point out that both Presidents Kennedy and Johnson had also used taping systems, although on a much reduced scale. Nixon's only statement in the week following Butterfield's disclosure was to "let others wallow in Watergate."

The Watergate investigation seemed to have gone as far as it could without a possibly fatal impasse between Nixon, the Ervin Committee, and Cox. If the President chose not to release the tapes of crucial meetings with Dean and others, the committee and the special prosecutor would have no recourse but to subpoena the President. It appeared that President Nixon might have some justification for denying the presidential papers and tapes to the Ervin Committee, based on the constitutional guarantee of separation of powers. But what justification could Nixon offer Cox, himself a part of the executive branch of government, immune from the ordinary chain of command by right of his special prosecutor status?

(The incredible tension created by the impending confrontation was emphasized on July 19 when someone posing as Treasury Secretary George Shultz, the man in charge of Secret Service operations, telephoned Senator Ervin, informing him that the President had decided to turn the tapes over to the Senate Committee. "I think it was a very wise decision on the part of the President," Ervin told his national television audience, obviously relieved an impasse with the White House had been avoided. Minutes later, after speaking with White House Counsel Leonard Garment, a saddened Ervin, his face glowing with embarrassment or outrage, announced that someone had played "a right dirty trick" on the Committee.

A confrontation was not to be avoided. Replying to the Ervin Committee's request for the tapes on July 23, Nixon stated: "The fact is that the tapes would not finally settle the central issues before your Committee.... The tapes are entirely consistent with what I know to be the truth and what I have stated to be the truth. However, as in any verbatim recording of informal conversation, they contain comments that persons with different perspectives and motivations would inevitably interpret in different ways." In a separate letter delivered on the same day as Nixon's message to the Ervin Committee, Special White House Counsel Charles Allen Wright informed Archibald Cox that his request for eight specific tapes was being declined on similar grounds. Wright added, "if you are an ordinary prosecutor and thus a part of the executive branch as well as an officer of the court, you are subject to the instructions of your superiors, up to and including the President, and can have access to presidential papers only as and if the President sees fit to make them available to you."

The President drew his battleline forcefully over the issue of executive privilege and the confidentiality of presidential papers and tapes. Both the Ervin Committee and Cox responded to the challenge by issuing subpoenas for the tapes, which had come to be the embodiment of an exasperating conflict between a nation eager to get at the truth behind the squalor infecting its political processes, and a President willing to assume blame for the unprecedented scandals within his administration, but unwilling to relinquish any of his presidential prerogatives as a consequence. Ironically, the Watergate scandal that began with a bugging incident reached an impasse because of still another bugging incident, the President of the United States secretly recording his private conversations.

Archibald Cox replied to the President's response in strictly legal terms, outlining his justification for issuing a subpoena for the tapes. "Careful study before requesting the tapes," Cox said in a prepared statement, "convinced me that any blanket claim of privilege to withhold this evidence from a grand jury is without legal foundation. It therefore becomes my duty promptly to seek subpoenas and other available legal procedures for obtaining the evidence for the grand jury.... Happily, ours is a system of government in which no man is above the law."

Chairman Sam Ervin, after his committee voted unanimously in executive session to subpoena the President, delivered a much more emotional response over national television. The seventy-six-year-old Chairman, who had by then reached the stature of a folk hero in the public eye, seemed to be explaining in a grandfatherly way to a perplexed nation the magnitude of the action his committee was embarking upon. "This is a rather remarkable letter," Ervin said of Nixon's message refusing to supply the tapes. "If you will notice, the President says he has heard the tapes or some of them, and they sustain his position. But he says he's not going to let anyone else hear them for fear they might draw a different conclusion.... I am certain that the doctrine of separation of powers does not impose upon any President either the duty or the power to undertake to separate a congressional committee from access to the truth concerning alleged criminal activities.... I love my country. I venerate the office of the President, and I have the best wishes for the success of the incumbent because he is the only President this country has at this time.... I deeply regret that this situation has arisen, because I think that the Watergate tragedy is the greatest tragedy this country has ever suffered. I used to think that the Civil War was our country's greatest tragedy, but I do remember that there were some redeeming features in the Civil War in that there was some spirit of sacrifice and heroism displayed on both sides. I see no redeeming features in Watergate."

The long Watergate scenario, which had been dramatically unfolding for thirteen months, was destined to be prolonged for at least another three while the question of the tapes proceeded through the courts, to be ruled upon ultimately by the Supreme Court. Although President Nixon was quick to state that he would abide by a "definitive" ruling of the Supreme Court on the question of executive privilege, legal scholars were equally quick to note that Supreme Court decisions are more often than not less than definitive. In addition, since a large part of the President's case was based on the constitutional provision for a separation of powers between the three branches of government, it appears quite possible that the President has reserved the right to refuse to comply with a Supreme Court ruling unfavorable to himself. He could conceivably claim that the judicial branch of government was infringing upon his powers as chief executive.

Still, once the legal process had been entered to resolve the dispute, the process had to run its course. Presi-

dent Nixon was given until July 26 to produce the evidence requested by Cox and the Ervin Committee. In a letter to Judge Sirica on the twenty-sixth, Nixon again declined to produce any tapes, while turning over two documents to prosecutor Cox. The President, citing an obscure opinion by former Attorney General James Spred written in 1865, said flatly that "it would be inconsistent with the public interest and with the constitutional position of the presidency to make available recordings of meetings and telephone conversations in which I was a participant." Judge Sirica immediately issued a "show cause" order, giving attorneys for President Nixon until August 7 to prepare arguments justifying Nixon's refusal to comply with the subpoena.

In a separate letter to the Ervin Committee on the twenty-sixth, Nixon again refused to comply with the Committee's subpoenas, but offered to make available specific documents requested to the Committee. Ervin became indignant over President Nixon's offer, stating bluntly to the television audience that his Committee was not clairvoyant. "Since we have never seen the documents," Ervin said, "the President puts on the Committee a manifest impossibility in receiving the documents.... I think the President could comply with the request of the committee and the Constitution would not collapse, and the heavens would not fall, but the committee might be aided by the President in determining the truth of his involvement."

If Sam Ervin and the Senate Watergate Committee were angry over President Nixon's toying with them, it was nothing compared to the anger engendered by former White House chief-of-staff H. R. Haldeman when he revealed to the Senators on July 30 that he had listened to the tape recording of the March 21 Nixon-Dean meeting in April while still on the White House staff. But, Haldeman testified, he had listened to the tape of the September 15, 1972 Nixon-Dean meeting in July, while a private citizen, shortly before the existence of the tapes was made

public. Haldeman told the startled Watergate Committee the President himself had requested that he listen to the tape, and that both recordings were completely consistent with the President's statement on his alleged complicity in the Watergate cover-up.

In his opening statement before the committee, Haldeman maintained that the President had been playing devil's advocate with John Dean on March 21, attempting to "smoke out what was really going on" in the Watergate affair. "He asked how much [hush] money would be involved over the years, and Dean said probably $1 million—but the problem is that it is hard to raise. The President said there is no problem is raising $1 million, we can do that, but it would be wrong.... He was trying to get Dean's view, and he was asking him leading questions in order to do that. This is the method the President often used when he was moving toward a determination." Haldeman's version matched John Dean's version almost word for word except for the phrase "but it would be wrong."

It quickly became obvious that the Ervin Committee felt it was wrong for the President to allow Haldeman to listen to the tapes, especially after his dismissal from the White House. Chairman Ervin, calling Haldeman's testimony on the tapes "counterfeit evidence," accused him of collaborating with White House attorneys on the official version of the tapes' content. "What's wrong with that?" Haldeman's lawyer John J. Wilson asked. "That's what we call in North Carolina colludin' together," Ervin answered. "The clear indication is that the White House counsel wanted Haldeman to reveal his interpretation of the tapes to the public." Senator Daniel Inouye probably capsulized the indignation felt by the committee when he said, "I would think that if a private citizen of the United States can get permission to listen to the tapes in private, at home, the Senate select committee should be able to hear them."

The White House expressed only mild consternation over Haldeman's testimony about the tapes, despite the apparent contradiction with President Nixon's July 23 statement that "none [of the tapes] has been transcribed or made public and none will be." Presidential press secretary Gerald Warren announced the guidelines by which Haldeman had been allowed to listen to the tapes. "The question of access has been decided by the President based on the President's judgement of who could best assist him in determining the facts of the Watergate matters, without jeopardizing the confidentiality of the tapes." It became patently obvious, however, that Haldeman's testimony was a veiled attempt by the White House to completely discredit the testimony of John Dean.

Throughout the long ordeal over the tapes and related presidential documents, President Nixon's refusal to comply with subpoenas and requests that he himself testify were punctuated with a promise to address the nation on Watergate, offering his side of the controversy sometime after the Ervin Committee recessed. While an anxious nation awaited Nixon's pronouncement on Watergate, the President's attorneys went into court on August 7, the same day that the Ervin Committee recessed, to file a legal brief in response to Judge Sirica's "show cause" order. The President frankly argued that he was "answerable to the nation but not to the courts." The brief maintained that "the threat of potential disclosure of any and all conversations would make it virtually impossible for President Nixon or his successors in that great office to function. Beyond that, a holding that the President is personally subject to the orders of a court would effectively destroy the status of the executive branch as an equal and coorinate element of government."

Special prosecutor Cox filed his rebuttal to the presidential brief on August 13 saying that "the President has an enforceable legal duty not to withhold evidence from a grand jury. The grand jury occupies a fundamental position in the administration of public justice. There is no exception for the President from the guiding principle that the public, in the pursuit of justice, has a right to every man's evidence." Cox further argued that even if the presidential tapes were protected by executive privilege, the President had waived that right by allowing Haldeman, as a private citizen, to listen to the tapes and testify as to their content.

When President Nixon finally did address the nation on Watergate on August 15, he admonished that "the time has come to turn Watergate over to the courts and for the rest of us to get on with the urgent business of our na-

tion." The President devoted a considerable portion of his talk to the question of the tapes and his justification for withholding them from public scrutiny. The "principle of confidentiality is at stake in the question of these tapes," Nixon asserted. "I must and I shall oppose any efforts to destroy this principle, which is so vital to the conduct of this great office."

President Nixon's statement on the tapes, as well as his comments on them at his August 22 press conference, clearly demonstrate his determination to allow the matter to be dealt with in the courts and only in the courts. The question remains dangling, however, whether or not the President will comply with a Supreme Court ruling on the issue that he and his attorneys perceive to be less than definitive.

In many ways, the presidential tapes have come to personify the entire morass of government scandal called Watergate. The President could have easily ended the controversy by releasing the sought-after tapes and at the same time remained wholly consistent with the only precedent for such a matter. In 1807, when Chief Justice John Marshall was presiding over the Aaron Burr treason trial in Richmond, he subpoenaed President Thomas Jefferson and ordered him to turn over to the court certain presidential documents relating to the Burr case. Jefferson refused to testify but produced the requested documents. In much the same way, President Nixon could easily have turned over requested tapes while doing so at his own discretion, without a court order, thereby reserving his privilege and avoiding the establishment of what he regards as a dangerous precedent.

But the President chose instead to turn the issue over to the courts, fully aware that the outcome could go against him, setting the precedent he fears, and possibly precipitating an even more complex constitutional crisis by not resolving the tape issue with the Supreme Court, thereby giving Congress no alternative but to begin impeachment proceedings.

Great forces are at work reshaping the balance of constitutional power in the federal government. A President who became so powerful that his administration could be irrevocably corrupted by that power now attempts to cling to as many of his prerogatives as possible. Congress, meanwhile, is forcefully reasserting its authority while the courts serve the function of a reluctant arbiter in the dispute. At the fulcrum of the apparent readjustment of federal power sit the tapes, reduced to poker chips in the Watergate game of chance.

APPENDICIES

Appendix I

Who's Who In Watergate

Alch, Gerald. First attorney for McCORD. He defended McCORD's right to initiate the bugging, for God and country. Replaced by FENSTERWALD.

Allen, Robert. President of Gulf Oil and Resources, and Republican campaign finance director for Texas. Allen funneled funds across the border, laundered them in Mexico banks and delivered them to STANS, whence they ended up in the Miami bank account of BARKER. Allen said he did not think he did anything wrong, even though corporate and foreign donations are expressly illegal.

Anderson, Jack. Syndicated columnist. He disclosed ITT's $400,000 donation made to the Republicans in exchange for dropping an anti-trust suit which resulted in a bitter fight over KLEINDIENST's nomination as attorney general.

Andreas, Dwayne. Millionaire "soybean king." He funneled money to Stans, trying to beat or cheat the contribution reporting deadline last year. He was director of a bank which, after he made the contributions, was mysteriously awarded a federal charter.

Baldwin, Alfred C. III. Former FBI agent. He is alleged to be behind-the-scenes participant in the Watergate bugging, delivering eavesdropping logs to CREEP officials. He was granted immunity from prosecution and reportedly has been singing like crazy to the Watergate grand jury.

Barker, Bernard L. Cuban-born, 55-year-old former CIA agent who served as an aide to HUNT in the Bay of Pigs invasion of Cuba. He was convicted as the paymaster for the Watergate burglary and bugging team. Previously, he was Bay of Pigs paymaster. Money given to Stans by ANDREAS, ALLEN and others ended up in his bank account in Miami—he told the Watergate judge he did not know where it was coming from, and did not ask. Barker also is a business associate of Bebe REBOZO, the President's closest friend and confidante.

Barrett, John. Member of Washington Metropolitan Police tactical squad, the one which caught the Watergate burglary and bugging squad red-handed.

Beard, Dita D. Lobbyist for International Telephone and Telegraph. She wrote a memorandum saying that MITCHELL was trying to fix a Justice Department antitrust action against ITT. After its publication, HUNT visited her bedside and she changed her story to a denial that she ever wrote the memo.

Bernstein, Carl. One of a pair of Pulitzer-prize winning *Washington Post* reporters who disclosed much of the dirt under the Watergate rugs.

Byrne, William Matt. U.S. District Court judge in Pentagon Papers trial. He was approached by Ehrlichman in an apparent attempt to fix the Ellsberg case.

Caddy, Douglas. Member of Washington law firm of Gall, Lane, Powell and Kilcullen, and first executive director of Young Americans for Freedom back in the 1960's. CADDY mysteriously showed up at police headquarters the morning the Watergate burglars were busted—even though none of them had placed a call for him. Later ran afoul of a federal judge, who wanted to find out what he was up to, and was found in contempt for refusing to say.

Carter, Frank. Alias of BARKER.

Casey, William. Securities and Exchange Commission chairman. He refused to halt investigations of VESCO, but failed to keep his hands washed. Resigned.

Caulfield, John J. (Jack). New York cop hired to work in EHRLICHMAN's Domestic Affairs Office at the White House, ostensibly as a liaison with local and state law enforcement agencies. Instead, he did Ehrlichman's dirty work, like hiring McCORD for a position with CREEP. Testified that he was offered clemency from the President if he kept his trap shut. He didn't.

Chapin, Dwight. Nixon's appointments secretary—until forced to quit due to his part in events related to the Watergate. Landed a job as an executive of United Airlines. It was a United Airlines jetliner which crashed killing Mrs. Dorothy HUNT. According to the FBI's GRAY, Chapin sent funds to SEGRETTI, through KALMBACH, for political sabotage efforts.

Clawson, Ken. Ex-reporter for the *Post,* former deputy

director of White House communications and communications director for CREEP. He wrote the "Canuck" letter, and lived to regret it.

Colson, Charles W. Special counsel to the president, also forced out by the Watergate. He is a fellow you wouldn't want your daughter to go out with. Known as "Nixon's hatchet man" and "Mr. Dirty Tricks." He has been named as the direct supervisor of HUNT, and the supervisor of the "attack groups" which carried out campaign sabotage from their White House base. If you're his grandmother, watch out.

Connally, John B. Nixon's Secretary of the Treasury, he used to be a Democrat from Texas, but now is a Republican. Headed up Democrats for Nixon during the reelection campaign.

Cook, G. Bradford. Counsel for the Securities and Exchange Commission. He attended the meeting with SEARS and CASEY to halt SEC investigation, later became SEC chairman, and resigned in record time. His old man was a CREEP crony.

Cushman, Gen. Robert. CIA deputy director and personal aide to Nixon. He supplied Hunt with false identification and disguises, like a red wig.

Daguerre, Manuel Ogarrio. A wealthy Mexican lawyer who was part of ALLEN's money laundry operation. He processed the $89,000 check from ALLEN through Banco Internacional S.A.

Dahlberg, Kenneth H. Midwest finance chairman for the Nixon campaign. He funneled at least $25,000 in secret contributions to STANS. Along with ANDREAS, he was director of a bank which later got a mysterious charter.

Dean, John Wesley III. Chief White House counsel to the President, he was fired by Nixon, or forced to resign, or something like that. His testimony has implicated the President himself. Ostensibly, Dean was fired for what he knew and didn't tell about the Watergate. After the burglary took place, Dean was allegedly appointed to conduct a no-holds-barred investigation of the incident for the White House. What he made was a no-holds-barred coverup; and since then his name has come up repeatedly as a culprit himself. Dean says he never was ordered to make an investigation, that Nixon just made that up. Somebody's lying.

DeDiego, Felipe. Anti-Castro Cuban working part-time for CIA. Drafted by BARKER for an antiwar counter-demonstration, along with Reinaldo PICO.

Diem, Ngo Dinh. President of South Vietnam, until the CIA murdered him in 1963. HUNT said Kennedy ordered him murdered, and he forged cables to prove it.

Dole, Robert. Former Republican national chairman. Got red in the face over Watergate, but has not himself been implicated. He said, "We deplore action of this kind in or out of politics." But then again, he said Mitchell had nothing to do with the dirty campaign tricks.

Dulles, Allen. Former director of the Central Intelligence Agency. He introduced McCORD to L. Fletcher Prouty, then the CIA's director of military operations, as "my top man."

Duncan, Walter I. Texas land speculator. Borrowed $305,000 to donate to Nixon campaign. Shows how far folks would go to get CREEP hands in their pockets.

Eduardo. HUNT's Cuban nickname.

Ehrlichman, John D. A Seattle lawyer who was, until his resignation under fire on April 30, 1973, the top domestic affairs adviser to President Nixon. The heat turned on him when Dean was reported on the verge of testifying that Ehrlichman and other higher-ups were involved in the Watergate. He conceded that he ordered a secret White House investigation of Ellsberg resulting in a break-in at his psychiatrist's office. He presided over the Plumbers, and welcomed the likes of McCord, Hunt and Liddy to his domestic affairs office—according to the President.

Ellsberg, Daniel L. The former Pentagon analyst who had a change of conscience and released the Pentagon Papers, a secret study of the Vietnam War, to the *New York Times*. He was the principal defendant in the Pentagon Papers trial which was dramatically ended by a dismissal of all charges when the judge found "shocking" conduct on the part of government officials in the case.

Ervin, Sam Jr. Seventy-six year old Democratic Senator from North Carolina chosen to head the Senate's Watergate investigation. He is a conservative but noted for his strong views on constitutional liberties; generally considered the Senate's expert on the Constitution, and widely respected in his post as chairman of the Senate select committee investigating campaign practices during the 1972 election, i.e., Watergate. He is a portly, white-haired man with a strong Southern drawl who is fond of illustrating his points with anecdotes and Shakespearean and Biblical quotations.

Fensterwald, Bernard. Second lawyer for McCord. He is a founder of the Committee to Investigate Assassinations.

Fielding, Lewis. Daniel ELLSBERG's psychiatrist. His office was burglarized by HUNT, LIDDY and some Cuban henchmen in an attempt to find dirt on ELLSBERG.

Figueros, Jose "Don Pepe". President of Costa Rica. He sent a letter to Nixon claiming SEC investigation of VESCO would hurt his country—not to mention his company.

Flanigan, Peter. Presidential aide. He invoked executive privilege when called to testify before the Congressional committee concerning the Dita BEARD memo.

Garment, Leonard. After DEAN was forced to resign, Garment was named to replace him as chief counsel to the President. No sooner was he hired than it became known that he earlier had torpedoed investigations made into questionable Administration activities.

Geneen, Harold. President of ITT during the Watergate days. He has been involved in questionable campaign donations to Mitchell and Magruder, arranging the $400,000 contribution to the Republicans for their convention in San Diego and also in an attempt to use the CIA to tamper with Chilean politics.

Godoyn, Raul. Alias of Virgilio R. GONZALES.

Gonzales, Virgilio R. Former CIA operative, active in right-wing, anti-Castro groups in Florida. A locksmith by trade, he also participated in the abortive Bay of Pigs invasion. He was arrested in the Watergate, and convicted of burglary and related charges along with the six others.

Gray, L. Patrick 3d. Acting director of the FBI, until he resigned suddenly on April 27, 1973. Gray, not a career FBI man, was on the stand for his confirmation as director before the Senate Judiciary Committee, when he started making embarrassing statements, such as declaring that DEAN had probably committed a cover-up. Under heavy fire on other issues, Gray then had his nomination yanked out from under him by the President. He remained as provisional director, until April 27, when Mr. Nixon yanked that out from under him. He admitted burning documents given him by Dean—and that's a criminal offense.

Gregory, Thomas J. A college student, one of many, drafted by HUNT to infiltrate the Muskie and McGovern campaigns.

Greigg, Stanley. Deputy chairman of Democratic National Committee. Watergate burglars were nabbed in his office.

Haldeman, Harry Robbins. Former J. Walter Thompson advertising and PR man, who rose to become the powerful White House chief of staff. He had complete control over who got in the door of the Oval Office to see Mr. Nixon—that is, until he resigned under fire on April 30, along with EHRLICHMAN and KLEINDIENST, amidst revelations of his role in the Watergate and related campaign illegalities. Crew-cut, Spartan, self-described

"S.O.B." He was so close to the President that he is reputed to once have said, "Even John Mitchell comes through me." Not anymore.

Hamilton, Edward. Alias Frank STURGIS.

Harmony, Sally. Secretary to LIDDY, she is rather reminiscent of Miss Moneypenny of James Bond fame.

Hart, Gary. National campaign manager for McGovern. False message sent in his name to George Meany by the tricky dickers.

Helms, Richard. Director of the CIA, until his resignation at the President's request last year to become ambassador to Iran. He refused HALDEMAN and EHRLICHMAN requests for the CIA's help in the Watergate affair. He said he also was asked by GRAY to claim that an FBI investigation of the Mexican laundry operation would interfere with "national security." He refused.

Holback, Judith. Administrative assistant to SLOAN. She supplied secret confidential information to the FBI, which gave it to DEAN, who gave it to her good.

Hofgren, Daniel. Vice-chairman of the Nixon finance committee. He was the one who solicited a donation from VESCO.

Hoover, J. Edgar. Dead Director of the FBI. He opposed the domestic superspy agency, forcing Nixon to form the Plumbers.

Hunt, E. Howard Jr. Long-time CIA agent, chief operations officer at Bay of Pigs. Served as $100-dollar a day White House consultant. He was convicted as being one of the three leaders in the Watergate break-in plot. At the time of the raid, he served as security chief for CREEP. He was the first of the seven Watergate defendants to plead guilty to the burglary.

Hunt, Dorothy. E. Howard's wife, she died in a United Airlines plane crash in December 1972, carrying $10,000 in $100 bills in her purse. Allegedly the money was to pay the Watergate defendants for keeping their mouths shut. There was plenty more wherever that came from.

Huston, Thomas Clark. Junior staff member of the White House in charge of super-spy agency committee meetings. He submitted domestic security plan to Nixon, and bad-mouthed the Hoove.

Kalmbach, Herbert W. 51, a California real estate dealer and President Nixon's personal attorney. Served CREEP as associate finance chairman under STANS. He allegedly had control over a $500,000 secret campaign fund used to finance the campaign sabotage operations of SEGRETTI.

King, Steve. Martha MITCHELL's personal bodyguard, and a CREEP security person, he ripped the phone off the wall while Martha was in the middle of spilling the beans to a newspaper reporter.

Kleindienst, Richard G. Attorney General of the United States until April 30, the day of reckoning. An Arizona lawyer who worked long and hard for Goldwater, he became deputy attorney general after Nixon was elected President in 1968. He played active roles in Supreme Court nominations, May Day anti-war protests and mass arrests, and finally was appointed Attorney General in spite of his involvement in the ITT affair, a corollary scandal to the Watergate. Explaining his sudden resignation, he said, "Those disclosures inform me, for the first time, that persons with whom I had close personal and professional associations could be involved in conduct violative of the laws of the United States." Prophetic words.

Korogolos, Thomas Deputy Assistant to the President for Congressional Relations. He agreed to meet with Fulbright on security leaks, in place of DEAN. Fulbright spat on the idea.

Krogh, Egil Jr. Undersecretary of the Department of Transportation, until his resignation May 9. Ehrlichman assigned him and David YOUNG the task of running a "special national security project" which would become better known as the Plumbers.

LaRue, Frederick C. Described as once-attorney general MITCHELL's right-hand man, he is named as having received $350,000 from STRACHAN for distribution to the dirty trick boys in the Republican organization. He is a former White House aide and allegedly one of the re-elect officials who directed a "house-cleaning" to destroy CREEP financial records following the Watergate arrests.

Leary, Timothy. Former Harvard University professor whose heretical advocacy, "drop out, tune in and turn on" and Millbrook, N. Y. bust became prime targets for LIDDY's hallucinatory campaigns against drugs when running for office in the state. He lost.

Leper, Paul. Member of the Washington Metropolitan Police squad which apprehended the Watergate burglars.

Liddy, G. Gordon. Former FBI officer, treasury department aide, and most recently White House staffer. He served as a counsel to Finance Committee to Re-elect the President, and was fired from that post by MITCHELL, allegedly for refusing to answer FBI agents' questions about the Watergate affair. Shortly later, Mitchell himself resigned from his post as chairman of the re-election campaign. Liddy owed his appointment to DEAN, and worked closely with EHRLICHMAN. He is frequently described as the "spy-master" for the Republicans. He pleaded guilty to the Watergate, and has kept tightly sealed lips throughout the entire affair, even to the point of refusing to testify before the Watergate grand jury.

Liedke, William. President of Pennzoil United Oil and Gas empire and Southwestern U.S. finance chairman for the Republican campaign. Ran a laundry.

Loew, James. U.S. Attorney physically ejected from VESCO residence in the Bahamas while serving subpoena.

MacGregor, Clark. Formerly a Nixon assistant for Congressional liaison. He became the director of CREEP when Mitchell resigned his post.

Magruder, Jeb Stuart. Formerly a cosmetics merchandiser, he became a special assistant to the President, in the Haldeman clique. He resigned April 26, after being fingered as the man who gave LIDDY his orders. His campaign post was as chief of staff and deputy director of CREEP.

Mardian, Robert. Before the campaign, he was the assistant attorney general in charge of the Internal Security Division of the Justice Department. In that capacity, he zealously worked at prosecuting alleged subversives and protestors. As political coordinator for CREEP, he received transcripts of electronic surveillance of Democratic National Headquarters, according to McCORD.

Maroulis, Peter. Attorney for LIDDY. He protested the reading of SLOAN's testimony by SIRICA and asked for a mistrial. Motion denied.

Martin, Edward. Alias James W. McCORD Jr.

Martinez, Eugenio R. A CIA operative and real estate dabbler who, along with BARKER, had business relations with a Bebe REBOZO firm. He was one of the four Cuban peons caught with his pants down inside the Watergate, and convicted for it.

McCord, James W. Jr. Twenty-year veteran of the CIA and security coordinator of CREEP, McCord was one of the three biggies convicted of leading the four Cuban peons into the Watergate. McCord was the only one of the three actually apprehended inside the Watergate. He was hired to his post with CREEP by DEAN. Once worked on a system of national "contingency" censorship of newspapers and broadcast media. Reportedly a homebody, McCord freaked when the Watergate judge slapped a heavy jail sentence on him, becoming the biggest songbird in the entire affair. He is 55, if you believe him, or 49, if you believe the *New York Times*.

Melloy, Doctor Bernard. Headed a CIA mental unit.

He was asked by HUNT to produce a file on ELLSBERG's psychiatric problems after the burglary attempt failed.

Merriam, William. Vice-president of ITT for Washington. He was the recipient of the Dita BEARD memo.

Mitchell, John N. 59, Former attorney general under Nixon, later former chairman of CREEP, now nothing—except indicted for conspiracy and obstruction of justice. Mitchell has been linked to the ITT scandal, to the VESCO scandal, and to numerous other foul deeds of the campaign team he presided over. He is a close personal friend and former law partner of the President. He used to be known as "Mr. Law and Order."

Mitchell, Martha. Wife of Mr. Law and Order. Martha already had gained a reputation for having the biggest mouth in D.C., when she came to play a pivotal although uncertain role in the scandal. She threatened, in a phone call to a reporter, to expose her husband's dirty deals if he did not resign from CREEP and come home to her and the kids. In the middle of the conversation, her phone was ripped off the hook. However, after Mitchell's resignation turned out to be very convenient, the theory was advanced that Mrs. Mitchell was only playing Republican games.

Mullen, Robert. President of Robert Mullen Associates, an advertising agency which employed HUNT and CADDY at the time of the break-in. Later, the agency was named as a front for the collection of over $10 million in Nixon campaign contributions prior to the April 7 disclosure deadline. Allegedly, businessmen donated the money, then wrote it off as an advertising or public relations business expense.

Nixon, Donald Klutzy nephew to the president. He was supported by VESCO when Nixon family did not know what to do with him.

Nixon, Edward C. Brother of President Richard Nixon.

Nixon, F. Donald. Brother to the president. He received message from VESCO threatening to reveal the deal with MITCHELL and CREEP if the SEC's investigation did not cease.

Nixon, Richard Milhous. President of the United States. He has been implicated in the Watergate cover-up by John Dean, his own former Presidential counsel.

O'Brien, Lawrence F. Democratic National Committee chairman until 1972, and titular head of the McGovern campaign. Noted for his denunciations of the Nixon administration's campaign activities.

Odle, Robert C. Jr. Director of personnel for CREEP. He was one of the recipients of the eavesdropping tapes from the Watergate surveillance. He directed Liddy to a paper shredder after the arrests took place.

O'Donnell, Patrick. Former presidential assistant. He sent a memorandum to Gray asking the then FBI director to speak in Ohio on behalf of the President.

Patman, Wright, Chairman of House Banking and Currency Committee. He accused the White House of engineering the committee's vote not to investigate Watergate before the election.

Petersen, Henry E. Assistant attorney general in charge of the original Watergate investigation. No one has accused him of pursuing the matter—shall we say—zealously.

Polizzi, "Big Al." A convicted black marketeer named by the Federal Bureau of Narcotics as "one of the most influential members of the underworld in the United States." Had business dealings with Bebe REBOZO, the president's closest confidant.

Pico, Reinaldo. Anti-Castro Cuban working part-time for the CIA. Drafted by BARKER for the antiwar counter-demonstration, along with deDiego.

Porter, Herbert L. A protege of White House communications secretary Herb Klein, Porter was one of the few men—including also Stans, Sloan and Mitchell—who had access to the safe in Stans office which contained the secret cash fund allegedly used to finance dirty deals.

Rafferty, Joseph A. Jr. The criminal lawyer summoned by CADDY to speak for the five men arrested in the Watergate at their arraignment.

Rebozo, Bebe. The mystery man from Miami, U.S.A. Of Cuban descent, he dabbles in real estate in Florida and California. An associate of the likes of Bernard Barker and Martinez, and who knows who else. In 1960, he established the Key Biscayne Bank, which in 1968 became a haven for stolen stocks channeled there by organized crime. He is better known for being the President's best friend and closest confidante.

Reisner, Robert. Youth coordinator for the Committee to Re-elect the President.

Richardson, Laurence. Former president of I.C.C. He carried money from VESCO to STANS. Just call him "boy."

Rietz, Ken. Thirty-two, headed President Nixon's youth campaign in 1972. Later named director of the Republican National Committee's "New Majority Campaign for 1974." Rietz's deputy on the campaign staff, George C. Gorton, has reportedly admitted that he hired and paid a college student to infiltrate radical groups such as the Muskie campaign team.

Rohatyn, Felix. ITT lobbyist and trusted friend of Secretary of Commerce Peter Peterson—so trusted that he was trustee for Peterson's money.

Russo, Anthony J. Jr. Co-defendant of Daniel ELLSBERG, and also a Rand think-tank veteran.

Sears, Harry L. Shrewd, diplomatic lawyer for Robert L. VESCO. He gained special favors from Mitchell for his wealthy client, who had contributed many thousands to the Nixon campaign. Sears formerly had been majority leader in the New Jersey legislature. He was indicted, along with MITCHELL, VESCO and company.

Sedam, J. Glenn Jr. General counsel of the CREEP, Sedam is also one of those who received tapes of the Watergate bugging.

Segretti, Donald H. 31, California lawyer and classmate of Chapin and Strachan. He has been named repeatedly as the man who personally directed a campaign of political character assassination, sabotage and spying by cadres of agents recruited from across the land. He received large and unexplained sums of money from CHAPIN, as well as $30,000 from Nixon's personal lawyer, KALMBACH. Segretti was the West Coast Mr. Dirty Tricks.

Seymour, Whitney North. U.S. Attorney in New York in charge of the grand jury investigating the VESCO swindle.

Shollfer, Carl. That's Officer Shollfer. He was part of the tactical squad of the Washington Metropolitan police which apprehended the Watergate burglars.

Silbert, Earl. U.S. Attorney for Washington, D.C. He prosecuted the Watergate burglars. The judge thought he didn't prosecute very hard, for some unknown reason.

Sirica, John J. One of the heroes of the Watergate. He is a judge for the U.S. District Court for Washington, D.C. He presided over the Watergate trial, and also over the continuing Watergate grand jury investigation, proving himself a hard-nosed old Republican by imposing stiff penalties which apparently started loosening some tongues—particularly McCord's.

Sloan, Hugh W. 32-year-old treasurer of the Finance Committee to Re-elect the President. After a visit from the FBI in the wake of the Watergate, he resigned his post. He was one of those who had access to Maurice STANS' safe, and he admitted in court that he gave $200,000 to LIDDY. He says he did not know what the money, approved by STANS and MITCHELL, was used for. After all, he was only treasurer.

Smathers, George. U.S. Senator from Florida, adviser and ally of Nixon, member of Small Business Administration committee. He regained citizenship for STURGIS and interceded in SBA loan for REBOZO.

Stans, Maurice. Director and chairman of the Finance Committee to Re-elect the President. Formerly, he had served as Secretary of Commerce. He has been tied to the passage of several hundred thousands through Mexican laundries. He had a safe in his office, out of which Bernard BARKER was paid, containing a secret fund of $350,000 or more. He claimed, before being forced to resign from the CREEP and the government, that he didn't know what was in the safe.

Strachan, Gordon. 29, White House consultant and courier boy. He was the link between Donald SEGRETTI and CHAPIN & Co. He also was allededly the White House contact for the Watergate break-in squad. A protege of Herb Klein, director of communications for the White House, who still survives the turmoil. Strachan has been named as one who carried $350,000 from HALDEMAN to LaRUE to pay the conspirators to keep their mouths shut.

Sturgis, Frank. Another CIA operative, and a former gun runner to Cuba—first for Castro, then against him—who formed a group called Cubans for Nixon in 1972. He was one of the four peons found guilty of carrying out the Watergate raid.

Timmons, William E. Nixon's special assistant for Congressional relations, he had managed to survive the swinging scimitar. But he was named as one of the select who got copies of the eavesdropping tapes made of Watergate conversations.

Tydings, Joseph. Democratic Senator. He was framed by COLSON and became ex-Senator.

Ulasewicz, Anthony. Associate of CAULFIELD. He carried message from DEAN to McCORD, provided comic relief at Ervin hearings.

Valdez, Jean. Psuedonym of Eugenio R. MARTINEZ.

Vesco, Robert L. International financier. Indicted in absentia for trying to fix a SEC investigation into his affairs, along with SEARS, MITCHELL, et al. Nearly a billionaire, he is the owner of conglomerate interests, and has been implicated in a $200 million mutual funds theft scandal. Owns most of the Bahamas, some say. Last known address: Costa Rica.

Walters, Vernon A. Deputy director of the CIA. He refused, along with HELMS, to intervene in the Watergate affair—according to his testimony.

Wills, Frank. Watergate security guard who blew the whistle on the burglars.

Winchester, Ray. Pennzoil's vice-president, and a courier for illegal campaign funds.

Woodward, Bob. *Post* Pulitzer prize winning reporter who, with BERNSTEIN, broke open the Watergate.

Young, David. National Security Council aide who ran the Plumbers and other campaign activities. He resigned May 2.

Ziegler, Ronald L. 33, White House press secretary and former ad man in the Disneyland game. He has been the only person in the administration who has been speaking about Watergate on a daily basis and in public. Reporters stopped believing him long ago.

Appendix II

The Watergate Trial

The following are excerpts from the official court transcript of the trial of the Watergate seven in U.S. District Court in Washington, D.C. The trial was presided over by Judge John J. Sirica and ran from January 8 to January 30. The final excerpt is from the sentencing proceedings in Judge Sirica's court, held on March 23, 1973.

Throughout much of the trial, Judge Sirica, in an unusual although not improper legal departure, handled the questioning of witnesses himself, very obviously dissatisfied with the efforts of the government prosecutor.

Only defendants Liddy and McCord entered pleas of not guilty and stuck to them. The other five—Hunt, Sturgis, Gonzales, Martinez, and Barker—changed their pleas to guilty. All seven were found guilty.

Hunt's Attorney: I just believe, Your Honor, that it is a very fair disposition of Mr. Hunt's case to plead guilty to three felonies at this time.

I think in the ends of the justice, we respectfully ask Your Honor to accept that plea.

The Court: Well, I think I should tell you this, and your client, I haven't definitely made up my mind yet what I am going to do.

I may take this under advisement and think about it and meet again with you in the morning, but I think you know this and this is for the benefit of Mr. Hunt or any other Defendants if they ever get to the point where they might want to enter a plea.

I can't see that I can make any exception.

Now, for Mr. Hunt's information, before this is done. And for the information of any other Defendants, if there comes a time when any other Defendant might want to change his plea, I wish to acquaint them with the Court's policy regarding commitment following a guilty plea, a plea of guilty or conviction, pending sentence.

It has been this Court's practice to commit a Defendant to jail in practically all cases whether white collar crime, or crimes of violence, following any plea of guilty which is accepted by the Court or conviction.

In a great many instances, the Court has committed the Defendant pending sentencing regardless of the crime or type of crime involved. That has been the Court's practice. See?

Now, you ought to have those things in mind. Mr. Hunt ought to have them in mind.

The Court: Now, I will take Mr. Martinez first and I will ask you

They will want to know where this money came from, who was the money man, who did the paying off, who paid Mr. Barker, how much was paid.

some questions. As I indicated some time ago, I think I indicated this, I posed certain questions to the Government during the pretrial hearing of this case and I think some of you were present and undoubtedly you heard it. I do not have a jury in the jury box now and I purposely sequestered them, had them locked up, so they couldn't hear any of the things going on in this courtroom.

I indicated more than once, and I am going to say it again, I want you each to listen carefully. This jury is going to want to know somewhere along the line what purpose did you four men go into the Democratic Headquarters for. You understand that question?

Mr. Barker: Yes, sir.

The Court: They are going to wonder who, if anyone, hired you to go in there, if you were hired. I am just assuming they will be asking themselves these questions. They are going to want to know if there are other people, that is, higher up in the Republican Party or the Democratic Party or any party who are mentioned or who are involved in this case and should be in this case, you understand that?

The question will arise undoubtedly what was the motive for doing what you people say you did by going into the Democratic Headquarters as outlined by Mr. Silbert in his opening statement.

The Court: Who are those persons that you refer to?

Mr. Barker: This would be only an assumption, sir—Mr. Hunt.

The Court: Are you trying to have me believe—I have to find out all the facts about this plea—that you received an envelope and finally they traced this $25,000 to your account, or your trust account, I believe there was another item of $89,000, how did that happen to get in there?

Mr. Barker: Your Honor has asked me to give you the facts as I know them, and I am saying the facts as I know them, no more, no less. I can only make assumptions which because of my background and other people involved you can understand that this is not a new thing with us.

The Court: Who are the other people involved?

Mr. Barker: As far as I know, Mr. Hunt.

The Court: He is the only one that is involved so far as you know?

Mr. Barker: As far as I know, Mr. Hunt is the only one that I, up to where I reach, I have also known Mr. Liddy—

The Court: Were you working under the direction of Mr. Hunt or other people in this job that was pulled off?

Mr. Barker: I was working with Mr. Hunt and I wish to state that I was completely identified with Mr. Hunt. What I am trying to say to you is that this, and I hope I don't sound arrogant, I cannot state I worked for a man and I am stupid enough to know what he wants—I have worked for Mr. Hunt and I have the greatest honor and distinguish him, and anything that I worked with him as my superior I am completely identified with all of that, and I have known exactly what my responsibilities are and I will face to all of my responsibilities.

The Court: You heard Mr. Hunt freely admit his guilt in this case the other day, didn't you?

Mr. Barker: I did so.

The Court: To the counts that involved him, correct?

Mr. Barker: Yes.

The Court: I want to know if you will tell me where did this money come from that was traced to your account—the trust account or your personal account—where did you get this money, these hundred dollar bills that were floating around like coupons?

Mr. Barker: I have nothing to do with hundred dollar bills floating like coupons, Your Honor, to my knowledge. I have stated that an amount of money in checks came to me with orders to change them—

The Court: —Wait a minute. An amount of money came to you with orders to change what?

Mr. Barker: To make them cash, sir.

The Court: Who gave you the orders?

Mr. Barker: I said they arrived by mail.

The Court: When did they arrive by mail?

Mr. Barker: Oh, about, I would say three or four days before I presented them to my bank for collection. I would refer to that date to Your Honor.

The Court: You presented what to your bank?

Mr. Barker: I passed this through my bank account.

The Court: You mean the $25,000 check?

Mr. Barker: And the $89,000 check—four checks that apparently came from Mexico.

The Court: Didn't you think it was strange that amount of money coming through the mail without being registered or anything?

Mr. Barker: No, I don't think it is strange, Your Honor. Like I said, I have previously before this been involved in other operations which took the strangeness out of that as far as I was concerned.

The Court: All right. I take it this is as far as you want to go in connection with your statement to the Court as to the money—talking about the money now?

Mr. Barker: Yes, sir.

The Court: Where it came from, what it was used for?

Mr. Barker: Yes, sir.

The Court: How much of that money did you actually use? We are talking about a lot of money. We are talking about $25,000 which was converted into cash, wasn't it?

Mr. Barker: Your Honor, it was $114,000. $89,000 were four Mexican checks. Another $25,000 was the famous Dahlberg check that was sent down to my case in Miami where I was tried for many things and eventually it turned out to be a misdemeanor.

Now, as the District Attorney has stated, sir, in his statement of this money I deposited in a trust account and it went to the place of its precedents—

The Court: —How was the check made out, who was the payor of the check and the payee?

Mr. Barker: I don't remember what it was but there are copies of that check available. I remember one of them was Dahlberg. I remember four of the other checks involved were some Mexican name that I cannot recall at this time, but as answer to your statement where that money went, that money passed in that manner to my account where it was supposed to be, and I have never at any time had in my possession or used one cent of that money.

The Court: Look, Mr. Barker, it takes quite a lot of money to stop at a place I imagine like the Watergate, although I have never stopped there, and it takes money to feed people, it takes money to travel by airplane from Miami and back, hotels and so forth.

Where did you get that money that you used to pay those men's expenses?

Mr. Barker: Your Honor, I got that money in the mail in a blank envelope.

The Court: I am sorry, I don't believe you. All right.

The Court: Listen to these questions before we proceed.

Now, have each one of you who have entered these pleas of guilty been induced by any promises or representations by any-one—lawyers or anybody else—as to what sentence will be imposed by me? Have any promises of any nature—

The Defendants: (In chorus.) No.

The Court: All say, no.

Has anyone threatened or coerced you into making this plea of guilty as to these counts?

The Defendants: (In chorus.) No, Your Honor.

The Court: Has any person outside of the courtroom today or in the courtroom promised that if you four men would plead guilty you wouldn't have anything to worry about, your families would be taken care of, would get so much a month, for example, has that been done?

The Defendants: (In chorus.) No, Your Honor.

The Court: I want to tell you what the possible sentences are. I am not saying what the sentences will be.

Now, under the conspiracy count, number one, upon conviction of the above offense the fine could be as much as $10,000 or imprisonment for not more than five years or both. Under count two, the burglary count, the sentence could be not less than two years nor more than fifteen years. Under count three, the burglary in the second degree, the sentence could be not less than two years nor more than fifteen years each of you. Under count four, the sentence could be not more than $10,000 fine or imprisoned for not more than five years or both. Under count five, upon conviction the sentence could be not more than $10,000 or imprisonment for not more than five years. Under count six, the sentence could be not more than $10,000 or imprisonment for not more than five years. Under count seven, the sentence could be a fine of $10,000 or imprisoned for not more than five years. Do you understand that?

The Defendants: (In chorus.) Yes.

The Court: Has anyone promised any of the four of you if you plead guilty to any one or all of the counts that you will serve a short term or get executive clemency or commutation of sentence?

The Defendants: (In chorus.) No, Your Honor.

The Court: Are you sure of that?

The Defendants: (In chorus.) Yes, sir.

The Court: Mr. Sloan, I want to ask you a few questions. I am interested in these checks—Mexican checks. Let's go back there a few minutes. The one for $15,000, one for $18,000, one for $24,000, one for $32,000. We call them the Mexican checks, Government Exhibit 112A, total of $89,000, correct?

A Yes, sir.

Q You turned these over to Mr. Liddy, is that your testimony?

A Yes, sir.

Q What was the purpose for turning them over to him?

A My concern in this case as with the subsequent Dahlberg check was the fact that under the law and our interpretation the way we normally handle our affairs, there is a gift tax contribution but it would raise questions for instance if a $15,000 check were deposited in any particular account, the intent of the donor was for us to handle his donation in such a way we would not incur for him any gift tax liability; therefore, the conversion to cash was an administrative method of breaking these checks down into the elements that would fall beneath the contribution limit.

Q Did he tell you how he was going to convert them to cash?

A No, he just indicated he would convert them.

Q What made you believe he could convert these checks to cash?

A He had previously when I discussed the general question whether there was any problem with these foreign checks as I had not handled any similar to this, and at that time I asked him what the best way to handle this would be and we mutually agreed to conversion to cash. And he merely offered at that point and indicated he had some friends who would do it.

Q Tell me about the $25,000 check, the Dahlberg check?

A This was presented to me by Secretary Stans in his office sometime the week following April 7. He indicated to me at that time it represented a contribution pre-April 7 from a donor whose name he gave me and the conversion to cashier's check was just a method of transporting it from Florida to our offices.

Q You said, I think and correct me if I am in error, that you turned over a total of about $199,000 in cash?

A That is the best of my recollection.

Q Where did you get that money from?

A Cash fund contributions to the President's campaign.

Q What was the purpose of turning over $199,000 to Liddy?

A I have no idea.

Q You have no idea?

A No, sir.

Q You can't give us any information on that at all?

A No, sir. I was merely authorized to do so. I was not told the purpose.

Q Who authorized you to turn the $199,000 over to Mr. Liddy in cash?

A Jeb Magruder.

Q For what purpose?

A I have no idea.

Q This is a pretty sizable piece of money.

A In and of itself, but not in the context of the campaign.

Q You didn't question Mr. Magruder about the purpose of the $199,000?

A No, sir. I verified with Mr. Stans and Mr. Mitchell he was authorized to make those.

Q You verified it with who?

A Secretary Stans, the Finance Chairman, and I didn't directly but he verified it with John Mitchell, the Campaign Chairman.

Q This $199,000 could be turned over to Mr. Liddy is what you are saying?

A Not the specific amount but Mr. Magruder, his authorization was authorization enough to turn over the sums in question.

Q Did anybody indicate to you by their action or by words or deed what this money was to be used for?

A No, sir.

Q You are a college graduate, aren't you?

A Yes, sir.

Q I think you majored in history, is that correct?

A That is correct.

Q What did you know about Mr. Liddy before the time all this cash was turned over to you?

A I just had known him through hearsay, that he had been an employee with the Treasury Department, a former FBI agent, a former consultant at the White House.

Q You said you got some receipts, didn't you, for this money you turned over to him?

A No, sir, I did not say that.

Q Did you ever get any part of the $199,000 back?

A No, sir.

Q You don't know what Mr. Liddy used it for?

A No, sir.

Q No idea?

A No, sir.

Q He was never questioned by you or anybody else what he did with the $199,000?

A No, sir.

Q You said you saw him come into headquarters, I suppose near you, on the morning that these five men broke into the Democratic Headquarters, is that correct?

A Yes, sir.

Q You knew, did you not, Mr. Liddy was a former FBI agent, correct?

A Yes, sir, I heard that.

Q You know, don't you, it is common knowledge at least before you can be appointed as an FBI agent you must be a member of the Bar?

A Yes, sir.

Q Still you tell this Court and the lawyers you saw him passing you, went by you—yes or no?

A Yes, sir, that is correct.

Q And he said something like—repeat what you claim he said?

A To the best of my recollection what he indicated was: my boys were caught last night; I made a mistake by using somebody from here which I told them I would never do. I'm afraid I'm going to lose my job.

Q What did you say to that?

A He was in a hurry and just passed on. I don't believe I responded.

Q Here is a man, a former FBI agent, makes a remark to you, that you claim you didn't know what he meant which was incriminating, which indicated to any person I think with common sense that

A When I read the *Evening Star* that evening.

Q What did you think when you read the *Evening Star* that evening?

A I thought a possibility might exist of involvement in this matter.

he had done something wrong, didn't that flash in your mind when he said: my boys got caught last night, I used somebody from here I shouldn't have done. Didn't that occur to you it was mighty strange you knew nothing about this matter that you didn't see anything wrong with that remark?

A Not at that point in time, no, sir.

Q When did it dawn on you there might be something wrong or improper about that remark, Mr. Sloan?

Defense Attorney: I further submit to the Court that what Your Honor has read constituted an extensive examination by the Court alone. It is not the ordinary course of events where a United States Attorney is asking questions like that and the defense would have the free opportunity to object. In this instance the Court was conducting what I believe to be an inquiry addressed to the witness to satisfy the Court as to certain facts.

I might point out to the Court that the press has characterized the testimony of Mr. Sloan as being particularly damaging to my client and I object to any further attention being called to Mr. Sloan's testimony, and I object to the jury hearing the portion of the transcript that Your Honor has referred to.

The defense in exercising its constitutional rights, and in exercising its judgment saw fit at the conclusion of the prosecutor's direct examination not to ask any questions. That should conclude the matter.

The Court: Let me tell you one thing: I exercise my judgment as a Federal Judge and Chief Judge of this Court and I done it on many occasions and in the presence of the jury examined witnesses where I thought all the facts were not brought out by counsel on either side. As long as I am a Federal Judge I will continue to do it.

As I said, the Court of Appeals might reverse me in this case, I am not concerned with that. I am concerned with doing what I think is the right thing at the moment and that is the reason I am going to read this testimony to the jury. I could care less what happens to this case on appeal, if there is an appeal. I am not interested in that. I am interested in doing what I think is right.

Now your client is smiling. He is probably not impressed with what I am saying. I don't care what he thinks either. Is that clear to you? You made your record.

Let me say this further for the benefit of you or anybody else that a federal judge can take the testimony of any witness in the presence of a jury and in his charge to the jury he might say to the jury—which I never do—members of the jury, take Mr. X's testimony, you heard his testimony. Whether he be a prosecution witness or a defense witness, you heard his testimony. Now, I personally wouldn't believe his testimony, I think he is a liar.

The Court: Now I believe that the Watergate affair, gentlemen, the subject of this trial, should not be forgotten. Some good can and should come from a revelation of sinister conduct whenever and wherever such conduct exists. I am convinced that the greatest benefit that can come from this prosecution will be its impact as a spur to corrective action so that the type of activities revealed by the evidence at trial will not be repeated in our nation.

For these reasons I recommend your full cooperation with the Grand Jury and the Senate Select Committee. You must understand that I hold out no promises or hopes of any kind to you in this matter but I do say that should you decide to speak freely I would have to weigh that factor in appraising what sentence will be finally imposed in this case. Other factors will of course be considered but I mention this one because it is one over which you have control and I mean each one of the five of you.

In conclusion, the Court's aim is to acquire a thorough acquaintance with the character and history of the Defendants so as to be able to impose that sentence which most fully comports with justice in each individual case.

Appendix III

Government Misconduct

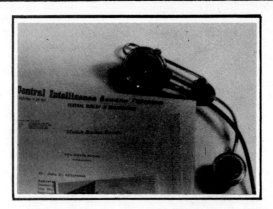

The following documents, arranged chronologically, were released publicly partly by the judge in the second trial of Daniel Ellsberg and Anthony Russo in the Pentagon Papers case. and partly by John Dean III. They include:

July 1970. Memos from Tom Charles Huston, White House aide, to H. R. Haldeman and others relating to the top secret White House plan for domestic intelligence.

July 3, 1972. A confidential FBI interview report showing that presidential counsel John Dean had substantial knowledge of the activities of E. Howard Hunt long before he conducted the alleged house investigation of the Watergate affair.

April 30, 1973. An FBI report of an interview with presidential counselor John Ehrlichman showing his knowledge of the establishment of the Plumbers.

May 8, 1973. An FBI report of an interview with former special counsel to the President Chuck Colson giving further details on the Plumbers.

May 9, 1973. A memo from L. Patrick Gray concerning wiretapping of Ellsberg and newsmen.

May 10, 1973. Memo from the Justice Department to Judge Byrne in reply to some stiff questions he put to officials; the answers claim that the material Judge Byrne wants cannot be located.

Undated. Copy of a secret Central Intelligence Agency memorandum concerning activities of Hunt and Liddy.

Recommendations
TOP SECRET
Handle via Comint Channels
only
Operational Restraints on Intelligence Collection
A. INTERPRETIVE RESTRAINTS ON COMMUNICATIONS INTELLIGENCE
RECOMMENDATION:
Present interpretation should be broadened to permit and program for coverage by N.S.A. of the communications of U.S. citizens using international facilties.
RATIONALE:
The F.B.I. does not have the capability to monitor international communications. N.S.A. is currently doing so on a re-

stricted basis, and the information is particularly useful to the White House and it would be to our disadvantage to allow the F.B.I. to determine what the N.S.A. should do in this area without regard to our own requirements. No appreciable risk is involved in this course of action.
B. ELECTRONIC SURVEILLANCE AND PENETRATIONS
RECOMMENDATION:
Present procedures should be changed to permit intensification of coverage of individuals and groups in the United States who pose a major threat to the internal security.

Also, present procedures should be changed to permit intensification of coverage of foreign nationals and diplomatic establishments in the United States of interest to the intelligence community.

At the present time less than [UNCLEAR] electronic penetrations are operative. This includes coverage of the C.P.U.S.A. (Communist Party, USA and organized crime targets), with only a few authorized against subject of pressing internal security interest.

Mr. Hoover's statement that the F.B.I. would not oppose other agencies seeking approval for the operating electronic surveillances is gratuitous since no other agencies have the capability.

Everyone knowledgeable in the field, with the exception of Mr. Hoover concurs that existing coverage is grossly inadequate. C.I.A. and N.S.A. note that this is particularly true of diplomatic establishments, and we have learned at the White House that it is also true of new Left groups.
C. MAIL COVERAGE
RECOMMENDATION:
Restrictions on legal coverage should be removed.

Also, present restrictions on covert coverage should be relaxed on selected targets of priority foreign intelligence and internal security interest.
RATIONALE:
There is no valid argument against use of legal mail covers except Mr. Hoover's concern that the civil liberties people may become upset. This risk is surely an acceptable one and hardly serious enough to justify denying ourselves a valuable and legal intelligence tool.

Covert coverage is illegal and there are serious risks involved. However, the advantages to be derived from its use outweigh the risks. This technique is particularly valuable in identifying espionage agents and other contacts of foreign intelligence services.

D. SURREPTITIOUS ENTRY

RECOMMENDATION:

Present restrictions should be modified to permit procurement of vitally needed foreign cryptographic material.

Also, present restrictions should be modified to permit selective use of this technique against other urgent security targets.

RATIONALE:

Use of this technique is clearly illegal; it amounts to burglary. It is also highly risky and could result in great embarrassment if exposed. However, it is also the most fruitful tool and can produce the type of intelligence which cannot be obtained in any other fashion.

The F.B.I. in Mr. Hoover's younger days, used to conduct such operations with great success and with no exposure. The information secured was invaluable.

N.S.A. has a particular interest since it is possible by this technique to secure material with which N.S.A. can break foreign cryptographic codes. We spend millions of dollars attempting to break these codes by machines. One successful entry can do the job successfully at no dollar cost.

Surreptitious entry of facilities occupied by subversive elements can turn up information about identities, methods of operations, and other invaluable investigative information which is not otherwise obtainable. This technique would be particularly helpful if used against the Weathermen and Black Panthers.

The deployment of the executive protector force has increased the risk of surreptitious entry of diplomatic establishments. However, it is the opinion of all except Mr. Hoover that the technique can still be successfully used on a selective basis.

E. DEVELOPMENTS OF CAMPUS SOURCES

RECOMMENDATION:

Present restrictions should be relaxed to permit expanded coverage of violence-prone campus and student-related groups.

Also C.I.A. coverage of American students (and others) travelling or living abroad should be increased.

RATIONALE:

The F.B.I. does not currently recruit any campus sources among individuals below 21 years of age. This dramatically reduces the pool from which sources may be drawn. Mr. Hoover is afraid of a young student surfacing in the press as an F.B.I. source, although the reaction in the past to such events has been minimal. After all, everyone assumes the F.B.I. has such sources.

The campus is the battleground of the revolutionary protest movement. It is impossible to gather effective intelligence about the movement unless we have campus sources. The risk of exposure is minimal and where exposure occurs the adverse publicity is moderate and short-lived. It is a price we must be willing to pay for effective coverage of the campus scene. The intelligence community, with the exception of Mr. Hoover, feels strongly that it is imperative that [UNCLEAR] increase the number of campus sources this fall in order to forestall widespread violence.

C.I.A. claims there are not existing restraints on its coverage of overseas activities of U.S. nationals. However, this coverage has been grossly inadequate since 1965 and an explicit directive to increase coverage is required.

F. USE OF MILITARY UNDERCOVER AGENTS

RECOMMENDATION:

Present restrictions should be retained.

RATIONALE:

The intelligence community is agreed that the risks of lifting these restraints are greater than the value of any possible intelligence which would be acquired by doing so.

BUDGET AND MANPOWER RESTRICTIONS

RECOMMENDATION:

Each agency should submit a detailed estimate as to projected manpower needs and other costs in the event the various investigative restraints herein are lifted.

RATIONALE:

In the event that the above recommendations are concurred in, it will be necessary to modify existing budgets to provide the money and manpower necessary for their implementation. The intelligence community has been badly hit in the budget squeeze. (I suspect the foreign intelligence operations are in the same shape) and it may be necessary to make some modifications. The projected figures should be reasonable, but will be subject to individual review if this recommendation is accepted.

MEASURES TO IMPROVE DOMESTIC INTELLIGENCE OPERATIONS

RECOMMENDATION:

A permanent committee consisting of the F.B.I., C.I.A., N.S.A., D.I.A. and the military counterintelligence agencies should be appointed to provide evaluations of domestic intelligence estimates, and carry out the other objectives specified in the report.

RATIONALE:

The need for increased coordination, joint estimates, and responsiveness to the White House is obvious to the intelligence community. There are a number of operational problems which need to be worked out since Mr. Hoover is fearful of any mechanism which might jeopardize his autonomy. C.I.A. would prefer an ad hoc committee to see how the system works, but other members believe that this would merely delay the establishment of effective coordination and joint operations. The value of lifting intelligence collection restraints is proportional to the availability of joint operations and evaluation, and the establishment of this interagency group is considered imperative.

TOP SECRET
ANALYSIS AND STRATEGY

Memorandum for: H.R. HALDEMAN
From: Tom Charles Huston
SUBJECT: Domestic intelligence review

1. Background

A working group consisting of the top domestic intelligence officials of the F.B.I., C.I.A., D.I.A., N.S.A., and each of the military services met regularly throughout June to discuss the problems outlined by the President and to draft the attached report. The discussions were frank and the quality of work first-rate. Cooperation was excellent and all were delighted that an opportunity was finally at hand to address themselves jointly to the serious internal security threat which exists.

I participated in all meetings, but restricted my involvement to keeping the committee on the target the President established. My impression that the report would be more accurate and the recommendations more helpful if the angencies were allowed wide latitude in expressing their opinions and working out arrangements which they felt met the President's requirements consistent with the resources and missions of the member agencies.

2. Mr. Hoover

I went into this exercise fearful that the C.I.A. would refuse to cooperate. In fact, Dick Helms was most cooperative and helpful and the only stumbling block was Mr. Hoover. He attempted at the first meeting to divert the committee from operational problems and redirect its mandate to the preparation of another analysis of existing intelligence. I declined to acquiesce in this approach, and succeeded in getting the committee back on target.

When the working group completed its report, Mr. Hoover refused to go along with a single conclusion drawn or support a single recommendation made. His position was twofold:

(1) Current operations are perfectly satisfactory and (2) No one has any business commenting on procedures he has established for the collection of intelligence by the F.B.I. He attempted to modify the body of the report, but I successfully opposed it on the grounds that the report was the conclusion of all the agencies, not merely the F.B.I. Mr. Hoover then entered his objections as footnotes to the report. Cumulatively, his footnotes suggest that he is perfectly satisfied with current procedures and is opposed to any change whatsoever. As you will note from the report, his objections are generally inconsistent and frivolous—most express concern with possible embarrassment to the intelligence community (i.e., Hoover) from public disclosure of clandestine activities.

Admiral Gayler and General Bennett were greatly displeased by Mr. Hoover's attitude and his insistence on footnoting objections. They wished to raise a formal protest and sign the report only with the understanding that they opposed the footnotes. I prevailed upon them not to do so since it would only aggravate Mr. Hoover and further complicate our efforts. They graciously agreed to go along with my suggestions in order to avoid a nasty scene and jeopardize the possibility of positive action resulting from the report. I assured them that their opinion would be brought to the attention of the President.

3. Threat Assessment

The first 23 pages of the report constitute an assessment of the existing internal security threat, our current intelligence coverage of this threat, and areas where our coverage is inadequate. All agencies concurred in this assessment, and it serves to explain the importance of expanded intelligence collection efforts.

4. Restraints on Intelligence Collection

Part Two of the report discusses specific operational restraints which currently restrict the capability of the intelligence community to collect the types of information necessary to deal effectively with the internal security threat. The report explains the nature of the restraints and sets out the arguments for and against modifying them. My concern was to afford the President the strongest arguments on both sides of the question so that he could make an informed decision as to the future course of action to be followed by the intelligence community.

I might point out that of all the individuals involved in the preparation and consideration of this report, only Mr. Hoover is satisfied with existing procedures.

Those individuals with the F.B.I. who have day-to-day responsibilities for domestic intelligence operations privately disagree with Mr. Hoover and believe that it is imperative that changes in operating procedures be initiated at once.

I am attaching to this memorandum my recommendations on the decision the President should make with regard to these operational restraints. Although the report sets forth the pros and cons on each issue, it may be helpful to add my specific recommendations and the reasons therefore in the event the President has some doubts on a specific course of action.

5. Improvement in Interagency Coordination

All members of the committee and its working group, with the exception of Mr. Hoover believe it is imperative that a continuing mechanism be established to effectuate the coordination of domestic intelligence efforts and the evaluation of domestic intelligence data. In the past there has been no systematic effort to mobilize the full resources of the intelligence community in the internal security area and there has been no mechanism for preparing community-wide domestic intelligence estimates such as is done in the foreign intelligence area by the United States Intelligence Board. Domestic intelligence information coming into the White House has been fragmentary and unevaluated. We have not had, for example, a community-wide estimate of what we might expect short or long term in the cities or on the campuses or within the military establishment.

Unlike most of the bureaucracy, the intelligence community welcomes direction and leadership from the White House. There appears to be agreement with the exception of Mr. Hoover, that effective coordination within the community is possible only if there is direction from the White House. Moreover, the community is pleased that the White House is finally showing interest in their activities and an awareness of the threat which they so acutely recognize.

I believe that we will be making a major contribution to the security of the country if we can work out an arrangement which provides for institutionalized coordination within the intelligence community and effective leadership from the White House.

6. Implementation of the President's decisions.

If the President should decide to lift some of the current restrictions and if he should decide to authorize a formalized domestic intelligence structure, I would recommend the following steps:

A) Mr. Hoover should be called in privately for a stroking session at which the President explains the decision he has made, thanks Mr. Hoover for his candid service and past cooperation, and indicates he is counting on Edgar's cooperation in implementing the new decisions.

B) Following this Hoover session, the same individuals who were present at the initial session in the Oval Office should be invited back to meet with the President. At that time, the President should thank them for the report, announce his decisions, indicate his desires for future activity, and present each with an autographed copy of the photo of the first meeting which Ollie took.

C) An official memorandum setting forth the precise decisions of the President should be prepared so that there can be no misunderstanding. We should also incorporate a review procedure which will enable us to ensure that the decisions are fully implemented.

I hate to suggest a further imposition on the President's time, but think these steps will be necessary to pave over some of the obvious problems which may arise if the President decides, as I hope he will, to overrule Mr. Hoover's objections to many of the proposals made in this report. Having seen the President in action with Mr. Hoover, I am confident that he can handle this situation in such a way that we can get what we want without putting Edgar's nose out of joint. At the same time, we can capitalize on the good will the President has built up with the other principals and minimize the risk that they may feel they are being forced to take a back seat to Mr. Hoover.

7. Conclusion

I am delighted with the substance of this report and believe it is a first-rate job. I have great respect for the integrity, loyalty, and competence of the men who are operationally responsible for internal security matters and believe that we are on the threshold of an unexcelled opportunity to cope with a very serious problem in its germinal stages when we can avoid the necessity for harsh measures by acting swift, discreetly and decisively to deflect the threat before it reaches alarming proportions. I might add, in conclusion, that it is my personal opinion that Mr. Hoover will not hesitate to accede to any decision which the President makes, and the President should not, therefore, be reluctant to overrule Mr. Hoover's objections. Mr. Hoover is set in his ways and can be bullheaded as hell, but he is a loyal trooper. Twenty years ago he would never have raised the type of objection he has here but he's getting old and worried about his legend. He makes life tough in this area, but not impossible—for he'll respond to direction by the President and that is all we need to set the domestic intelligence house in order.

TOP SECRET
Decision Memorandum
The White House
Washington

July 15, 1970

TOP SECRET
Handle via Comint Channels Only

Subject: Domestic Intelligence

The President has carefully studied the special report of the Interagency Committee on Intelligence (ad hoc) and made the following decisions:

1. Interpretive Restraint on Communications Intelligence

National Security Council Intelligence Directive Number 6 (NSCID-6) is to be interpreted to permit N.S.A. to program for coverage the communications of U.S. citizens using international facilities.

2. Electronic Surveillances and Penetrations

The intelligence community is directed to intensify coverage of individuals and groups in the United States who pose a major threat to the internal security. Also, coverage of foreign nationals and diplomatic establishments in the United States of interest to the intelligence community is to be intensified.

3. Mail Coverage

Restrictions on legal coverage are to be removed, restrictions on covert coverage are to be relaxed to permit use of this technique on selected targets of priority foreign intelligence and internal security interest.

4. Surreptitious Entry

Restraints on the use of surreptitious entry are to be removed. The technique is to be used to permit procurement of vitally needed foreign cryptographic material and against other urgent and high priority internal security targets.

5. Development of Campus Sources

Coverage of violence prone campus and student related groups is to be increased. All restraints which limit this coverage are to be removed. Also, C.I.A. coverage of American students (and others) travelling or living abroad is to be increased.

6. Use of Military Undercover Agents

Present restrictions are to be retained.

7. Budget and Manpower

Each agency is to submit a detailed estimate as to projected manpower needs and other costs required to implement the above decisions.

8. Domestic Intelligence Operations

A committee consisting of the directors or other appropriate representatives appointed by the directors of the F.B.I., C.I.A., N.S.A., D.I.A., and the military counterintelligence agencies is to be constituted effective August 1, 1970, to provide evaluations of domestic intelligence, prepared periodic domestic intelligence estimates, carry out the other objectives specified in the report, and perform such other duties as the President shall from time to time assign. The director of the F.B.I. shall serve as chairman of the committee. Further details on the organization and operations of this committee are set forth in an attached memorandum.

The President has directed that each addressee submit a detailed report, due on September 1, 1970, on the steps taken to implement these decisions. Further such periodic reports will be requested as circumstances merit.

The President is aware that procedural problems may arise in the course of implementing these decisions. However, he is anxious that such problems be resolved with maximum speed and minimum misunderstanding. Any difficulties which may arise should be brought to my attention in order that an appropriate solution may be found and the President's directives implemented in a manner consistent with his objectives.

Tom Charles Huston

TOP SECRET
Handle via Comint Channels Only
ORGANIZATION AND OPERATIONS
OF THE INTERAGENCY GROUP
ON DOMESTIC INTELLIGENCE
AND INTERNAL SECURITY (IAG)

1. Membership

The membership shall consist of representatives of the F.B.I., C.I.A., D.I.A., N.S.A., and the counterintelligence agencies of the Departments of the Army, Navy and Air Force. To insure the high level consideration of issues and problems which the President expects to be before the group, the directors of the respective agencies should serve personally. However, if necessary and appropriate, the director of a member agency may designate another individual to serve in his place.

2. Chairman

The director of the F.B.I. shall serve as chairman. He may designate another individual from his agency to serve as the F.B.I. representative on the group.

3. Observers

The purpose of the group is to effectuate community-wide coordination and secure the benefits of community-wide analysis and estimating. When problems arise which involve areas of interest to agencies or departments not members of the group, they shall be invited, at the discretion of the group, to join the group as observers and participants in those discussions of interest to them. Such agencies and departments include the Departments of State (I&R, Passports); Treasury (IRS, Customs); Justice (BNDD, Community Relations Service); and such other agencies which may have investigative or law enforcement responsibilities touching on domestic intelligence or internal security matters.

4. White House Liaison

The President has assigned to Tom Charles Huston staff responsibility for domestic intelligence and internal security affairs. He will participate in all activities of the group as the personal representative of the President.

5. Staffing

The group will establish such sub-committees or working groups as it deems appropriate. It will also determine and implement such staffing requirements as it may deem necessary to enable it to carry out its responsibilities, subject to the approval of the President.

6. Duties

The group will have the following duties:

A) Define the specific requirements of member agencies of the intelligence community.

B) Effect close, direct coordination between member agencies.

C) Provide regular evaluations of domestic intelligence.

D) Review policies governing operations in the field of domestic intelligence and develop recommendations.

E) Prepare periodic domestic intelligence estimates which incorporate the results of the combined efforts of the intelligence community.

F) Perform such other duties as the President may from time to time assign.

7. Meetings

The group shall meet at the call of the chairman, a member agency, or the White House representative.

8. Security

Knowledge of the existence and purposes of the group shall be limited on a strict "need to know" basis. Operations of, and papers originating with, the group shall be classified "top secret handle via Comint channels only."

9. Other Procedures

The group shall establish such other procedures as it believes appropriate to the implementation of the duties set forth above.

[TOP SECRET]

FEDERAL BUREAU OF INVESTIGATION

Date of Transcription 7/3/72

Mr. JOHN DEAN, Legal Counsel to RICHARD M. NIXON, President of the United States, Executive Office Building, 17th and Pennsylvania Ave., N.W., Washington, D.C. provided Special Agents DANIEL C. MAHAN and MICHAEL J. KING of the FBI, one cardboard box, which he stated was the effects of Mr. HOWARD HUNT taken from Room 338 of the Executive Office Building. The effects contained in this box provided by Mr. DEAN are listed as follows:

One small metal box;

One .25 caliber automatic Colt revolver, bearing Serial Number 321803;

One clip for this revolver, containing live ammunition;

One holster;

One Rolodex file;

One copy of the book "Pentagon Papers";

Numerous sheets of carbon copy papers;

Two White House pads;

Numerous sheets of White House stationery;

One desk calendar;

A quantity of office supplies, three stamp pads, scissors, pens and pencils, scotch tape, staples, staple gun, glue, and a clipboard;

Two folders (instructions of office operation);

One blanket;

One plastic carrying case.

Mr. FIELDING, Assistant to the Legal Counsel to RICHARD M. NIXON, President of the Untied States, Executive Office Building, 17th and Pennsylvania Avenue, N.W., Washington, D.C., furnished Special Agents DANIEL C. MAHAN and MICHAEL J. KING of the FBI with one large cardboard box sealed with tape marked with pen "TOP SECRET".

An inventory of the contents of that box is listed as follows:

1. One brown envelope marked "HOWARD HUNT, Eyes Only. Personal Unclassified".

2. Six brown envelopes containing classified material relating to the "Pentagon Papers".

3. One tan folder marked "ELLSBERG" containing numerous papers concerning one DANIEL ELLSBERG.

4. One tan folder marked "Pentagon Papers" containing newspaper articles.

5. One tan folder marked "Time and Pay Records" containing verification of hours worked at the White House.

6. One tan folder marked "Correspondence" containing copies of letters.

7. One tan folder marked "Press Contacts" containing press contacts and newspaper articles.

8. One tan folder marked "JOHN PAUL VANN" containing a newspaper article.

9. One empty gray folder.

10. One black attache case containing the following list of items:

Four Nel-Com Transceivers Technical Manual and Operating Instructions Bell and Howell 148-174 NCS

Two antenna—UG-447/U and numbered 74868;

RG-58a/U, Balden 8259 Antenna Lead Wire;

Four rechargeable model B1 nickel cadmium batteries—Bell and Howell;

One tear gas cannister/General HK VII, M/G. General Ordnance Equipment Corporation, Pittsburgh, Pa.;

Two microphones—simulated chapstick containers;

Three earphones, numbered 8813, 9042;

Four antenna, bendable wire;

Six jack wires;

One shoulder harness with white lead wire and phone jack;

Three shoulder harnesses;

Three belt harnesses;

Three operating instructions for Bell and Howell Portable Transmitter;

One Mobil Oil Company map of Delaware, Maryland, Virginia and West Virginia, with pencil circle around Warrenton, Virginia area and with pencil circle around Union Station area;

Two lead wires with black and pink end;

One Avis rental car map of the Baltimore, Maryland and WDC area, with circles around junction of Route 695 and 195, circle in the area of junction with George Washington Memorial Parkway and 195, circled area of junction with George Washington Memorial Parkway and Route 166, circled area of junction of

Capital Beltway and Maryland Route 190 (River Road), circled area of junction with 1270 and 1495, circled area of Campbell Corner, Maryland, circled area of 14th and M Streets, N.W., with a pencil route traced from the Rooms of Representatives Office Buildings to the 14th and M Street areas.

Interviewed on 6/28/72 at Washington, D.C. File # W50-139-166
by: DANIEL C. MAHAN and MICHAEL J. KING DCM:mc
Date dictated 6/29/72

FEDERAL BUREAU OF INVESTIGATION

Date of Verification: 4/30/73

John D. Ehrlichman, Advisor to the President, was contacted in his office at the Executive Office of the President.

It was explained to Mr. Ehrlichman that this interview was being conducted at the specific request of the Justice Department. He was told that information had been received alleging that on an unspecified date the offices of an unnamed psychiatrist retained by DANIEL ELLSBERG, had been burglarized apparently to secure information relating to ELLSBERG. Mr. EHRLICHMAN was advised the purpose of this interview was to learn what knowledge he might have concerning this alleged burglary.

Mr. EHRLICHMAN recalled that sometime in 1971, the President had expressed interest in the problem of unauthorized disclosures of classified government information and asked him to make inquiries independent of concurrent FBI investigation which had been made relating to the leak of the Pentagon Papers. Mr. EHRLICHMAN assumed this responsibility and was assisted in this endeavor by EGIL KROGH, a White House assistant, and DAVID YOUNG of the National Security agency. A decision was made by them to conduct some investigation in the Pentagon Papers leak matter "directly out of the White House." G. GORDON LIDDY and E. HOWARD HUNT were "designated to conduct this investigation".

Mr. EHRLICHMAN knew that LIDDY and HUNT conducted investigation in the Washington, D.C. area and during the inquiries were going on to the west coast to follow up on leads. There was information available that ELLSBERG had emotional and moral problems and LIDDY and HUNT sought to determine full facts relating to these conduct traits. HUNT endeavored to prepare a "psychiatric profile" relating to ELLSBERG. The efforts of LIDDY and HUNT were directed toward an "in depth investigation of ELLSBERG to determine his habits, mental attitudes, motives etc."

Although Mr. EHRLICHMAN knew that LIDDY and HUNT had gone to California in connection with the above inquiries being made by them, he was not told that these two individuals had broken into the premises of the psychiatrist for ELLSBERG until after this incident had taken place. Such activity was not authorized by him, he did not know about this burglary until after it had happened, he did "not agree with this method of investigation" and when he learned about the burglary he instructed them "not to do this again".

Mr. EHRLICHMAN does not recall who specifically reported to him about the above-mentioned burglary but it was verbally mentioned to him. He does not know the name of the psychiatrist involved nor the location of this individual. He does not know whose idea it was to commit this burglary. Mr. EHRLICHMAN has no knowledge whether anything was obtained as a result of this activity.

Interviewed on 4/27/73 at Washington, D.C. File # 65-11613
by: SA EDWARD L. GRAMPP and SA CHARLES A. REGAN
ELG:jrk Date dictated 4/30/73

FEDERAL BUREAU OF INVESTIGATION

Date of Transcription 5/8/73

CHARLES V. COLSON, former Special Counsel to the President, was interviewed in the presence of his attorneys DAVID SHAPIRO and JUDAS BEST, in their offices at 1735 New York Avenue, N.W., Washington, D.C. Mr. COLSON was advised he was being contacted at the request of the Department of Justice to Determine if he could furnish information about an investigation conducted on behalf of the White House into the public disclosures of the Pentagon Papers and specifically for information he may have about an alleged burglary of the office of DANIEL ELLSBERG's psychiatrist by E. EDWARD HUNT and G. GOR-

DON LIDDY during the course of that investigation.

Mr. COLSON voluntarily signed a waiver of rights, (FD 395) and advised as follows:

Mr. COLSON recalled attending meetings in early July, 1971, at the White House concerning the disclosures of the Pentagon Papers and described these meetings as "kind of panic sessions" to determine what was going on and trying to establish what was going to be published next by the newspapers and the accuracy of these publications. Mr. COLSON indicated he was not involved in the White House investigation into the Pentagon Papers disclosures, but was engaged in the Government's litigation to stop publication of the Papers. He was engaged on an almost full-time basis at this time with the preapration of the President's August 15 economics decision initiating Phase I of the Price Freeze.

When the Pentagon Papers were first published in the "New York Times" there was a need in the White House for someone to do research and co-ordinate assignments involving investigation into the leak. COLSON recalled he recommended HUNT, whom he had known for a period of years and several other individuals for this assignment. HUNT was subsequently interviewed by JOHN D. EHRLICHMAN, former Assistant to the President.

Later, Mr. COLSON received a telephone call from Mr. EHRLICHMAN who was then in California with the President, asking whether HUNT could be brought in and directing that he should be put to work on the investigation.

Mr. COLSON asked his staff secretary to process the necessary papers regarding the employment. HUNT was assigned to COLSON's staff for internal budget processing only.

Mr. COLSON knew that the "plumbers", (publicly identified as EGIL KROGH, DAVID YOUNG, HUNT and LIDDY) were conducting a check for a personality profile of DANIEL ELLSBERG to determine what motivated him, what kind of "wild things" he might do. Mr. COLSON said there was an enormous concern over leaks of sensitive information at that time.

Mr. COLSON had no discussions or advanced information of the alleged burglary. He knew the Plumbers were going to the West Coast but did not know which of them would actually make the trip. He first heard about the alleged burglary sometime later at a meeting and he could not recall the time of the meeting or who was present. He thought the meeting may have been a private one with Mr. EHRLICHMAN. He believes Mr. EHRLICHMAN told him he does not recall specifically, but he gained the impression from the conversation that "they" tried to get the records of ELLSBERG's psychiatrist and did not get them. EHRLICHMAN told him this was a national security matter and not to be discussed with anyone. Mr. COLSON never heard any discussion of a burglary attempt on the home of ELLSBERG's psychiatrist.

Mr. COLSON was asked if he had any other discussions with White House Staff members about the burglary. He recalled in connection with the Watergate investigation prior to the time when he was questioned by the Federal Bureau of Investigation (FBI) and gave a deposition to Mr. GILBERT of the United States Attorney's office, he asked JOHN DEAN, Counsel to the President, what to do if the "Pentagon Papers question came up."

DEAN told him that if asked, he was not to discuss the matter, inasmuch, as it was a national security matter of the highest classification and that he (DEAN) would interrupt such questions if present. He recalled receiving the same instructions from Mr. ERLICHMAN in late March or April, 1973. He never discussed the burglary with HUNT or LIDDY.

Concerning a current newspaper story that HUNT reportedly tried to talk to Mr. COLSON sometime later about the burglary, COLSON recalled a chance meeting with HUNT one morning in his outer office. HUNT was waiting for him but Mr. COLSON could not recall when the meeting took place. HUNT told him that he was on his way to give a briefing on what "they" had learned about ELLSBERG, and that he had about a half an hour before the briefing and he wanted to talk to COLSON about it. COLSON told HUNT he did not have time to talk to him then, that he was in a hurry. HUNT did not try to broach the subject matter again.

Concerning the memorandum from COLSON to JON HUNSTMAN dated September 13, 1971, referring in accordance with an earlier arrangement the reimbursement of HUNT for the following expenses: Air fares for two men from New York City to Washington, D.C. $53,00; Dinner check, Miami—$35.85; Motel bill for three men, Los Angeles—$156.90, COLSON advised as follows:

COLSON furnished a copy of this memorandum from his own office files to the Federal Brueau of Investigation in the summer

of 1972 when he was asked about HUNT's travel. This was the first occasion on which he had seen the memorandum and he did not know to what the entries on the Memorandum related or the identity of the three men referred to in the memo. COLSON never saw any of HUNT's vouchers or claims for reimbursement. These were initialed and submitted by COLSON's secretary.

Concerning a recent newspaper story according to which EGIL KROGH reportedly said he requested funds from COLSON for implementing the effort to acquire information about ELLS-BERG, COLSON could not recall giving KROGH money for the trip to California. He has a vague recollection that at about that time, Jr. EHRLICHMAN spoke to him about getting some funds, maybe for KROGH, but when he checked with Mr. EHRLICH-MAN later, ERHLICHMAN could not recall the request.

From time to time COLSON saw memorandums prepared for the White House group working on the Pentagon Papers investigation, but he saw no reports prepared by that group. The memorandums which were shown to him by HUNT because of COLSON's general interest in the issue of the Pentagon Papers, spoke of HUNT's frustrations trying to get things done in the Plumbers' unit and HUNT's analyses of the investigation. COLSON had no information about the whereabouts or results of investigation conducted by that group.

COLSON had no knowledge of other illegal activities engaged in by the group conducting the Pentagon Papers investigation on behalf of the White House.

UNITED STATES GOVERNMENT
MEMORANDUM

To: Assistant Attorney General   Date: May 9, 1973
         Criminal Division
From: Acting Director, FBI

Attached hereto is a brief memorandum concerning the ongoing investigation of alleged wire taps possibly relevant to the Ellsberg case. My recommendation is that this memorandum be immediately filed with the court.

Enclosure

PRELIMINARY REPORT CONCERNING ONGOING INVESTIGATION OF POSSIBLE WIRE TAPS OF NEWSMEN AND OTHERS

Shortly after assuming office as Acting Director of the FBI my attention was called to the newspaper allegation that FBI personnel had been wire tapping unidentified newsmen. I was also informed that a search of the FBI records had not disclosed the existence of any such wire taps. Nevertheless, on May 4, 1973 I initiated an investigation to interview present and retired FBI personnel for the purpose of determining, if possible, whether there had been any such taps. A preliminary report which I received last night indicates that an FBI employee recalls that in late 1969 and early 1970 Mr. Ellsberg had been overheard talking from an electronic surveillance of Dr. Morton Halperin's residence. It is this employee's recollection that the surveillance was of Dr. Halperin and that Mr. Ellsberg was then a guest of Dr. Halperin.

I have no information concerning the substance of the conversation nor has the investigation to date been able to find any record of such a conversation. The investigation, of course, is not complete and further facts bearing upon the wire taps may be uncovered. Nevertheless, in view of the Court's expressed desire for prompt information relating to this matter, I am at this time, giving you this preliminary report which may be relevant to the trial now in progress.

Appendix IV

Nixon's Statements

It is ironic that Richard Nixon's political career is spotted with famous speeches. He is not a brilliant orator. His delivery is sometimes awkward, sometimes monotonous, always arched and rigid. Empathy is not easily evoked by a Nixon address. If one is looking for catchy political phrases or lasting rhetoric, Nixon is not the man to search out.

Yet, starting with his "Checkers" speech, Nixon's public statements have been widely quoted and terribly revealing. It is possible to evaluate the political status of the man simply by using his public statements as a measure. "You won't have Nixon to kick around any more" can conjure nothing less than a man in the throes of defeat. "It will be a victory for America, in these next four years we, all of us, can work together to achieve our common great goals . . ." could come only from a Nixon on the eve of his second inauguration.

After his poor showing in the nationally televised debates with John F. Kennedy in 1960, Nixon set out to change his dispassionate, manipulative public image. That meant altering the style of his speeches, the tone of his addresses, the phrasing of his delivery. It also meant speaking less. Once in the White House, Nixon held fewer press conferences than any other modern President. He took to the airwaves only when it was unavoidable. Watergate forced him into the media limelight.

August 29, 1972
Excerpts of Press Conference

THE PRESIDENT: We will go right ahead with our questions, because I know you want to cover perhaps some international as well as domestic matters, including, I understand, for the first time, political matters.

Q: Mr. President, are you personally investigating the mishandling of some of your campaign funds, and do you agree with former Secretary Connally that these charges are harmful to your re-election?

THE PRESIDENT: Well, I commented upon this on other occasions, and I will repeat my position now.

With regard to the matter of the handling of campaign funds,

we have a new law here in which technical violations have occurred and are occurring, apparently, on both sides. As far as we are concerned, we have in charge, in Secretary Stans, a man who is an honest man and one who is very meticulous—as I have learned from having him as my treasurer and finance chairman in two previous campaigns—in the handling of matters of this sort.

Whatever technical violations have occurred, certainly he will correct them and will thoroughly comply with the law. He is conducting an investigation on this matter, and conducting it very, very thoroughly, because he doesn't want any evidence at all to be outstanding, indicating that we have not complied with the law.

Q: Mr. President, wouldn't it be a good idea for a special prosecutor, even from your standpoint, to be appointed to investigate the contribution situation and also the Watergate case?

THE PRESIDENT: With regard to who is investigating it now, I think it would be well to notice that the FBI is conducting a full field investigation. The Department of Justice, of course, is in charge of the prosecution and presenting the matter to the grand jury. The Senate Banking and Currency Committee is conducting an investigation. The Government Accounting Office, an independent agency, is conducting an investigation of those aspects which involve the campaign spending law.

Now, with all of these investigations that are being conducted, I don't believe that adding another special prosecutor would serve any useful purpose.

The other point that I should make is that these investigations—the investigation by the GAO, the investigation by the FBI, by the Department of Justice—have, at my direction, had the total cooperation of the—not only the White House but also of all agencies of Government.

In addition to that, within our own staff, under my direction, counsel to the President, Mr. Dean, has conducted a complete investigation of all leads which might involve any present members of the White House staff or anybody in the Government. I can say categorically that his investigation indicates that no one in the White House staff, no one in this Administration, presently employed, was involved in this very bizarre incident.

At the same time, the committee itself is conducting its own investigation, independent of the rest, because the committee desires to clear the air and to be sure that, as far as any people who have responsibility for this campaign are concerned, that there is nothing that hangs over them. Before Mr. Mitchell left as campaign chairman he had employed a very good law firm with investigatory experience to look into the matter. Mr. MacGregor has continued that investigation and is continuing it now.

I will say in that respect that anyone on the campaign committee, Mr. MacGregor has assured me, who does not cooperate with the investigation or anyone against whom charges are leveled where there is a prima facie case where those charges might indicate involvement, will be discharged immediately. That, also, is true of anybody in the Government. I think under these circumstances we are doing everything we can to take this incident and to investigate it and not to cover it up.

What really hurts in matters of this sort is not the fact that they occur, because overzealous people in campaigns do things that are wrong. What really hurts is if you try to cover it up. I would say that here we are, with control of the agencies of the Government and presumably with control of the investigatory agencies of the Government with the exception of GAO, which is independent. We have cooperated completely. We have indicated that we want all the facts brought out and as far as any people who are guilty are concerned, they should be prosecuted.

This kind of activity, as I have often indicated, has no place whatever in our political process. We want the air cleared. We want it cleared as soon as possible.

April 17, 1973
Statement to the Press

I have two announcements to make. Because of their technical nature, I shall read both of the announcements to the members of the press corps.

The first announcement relates to the appearance of White House people before the Senate select committee, better known as the Ervin committee.

For several weeks, Sen. Ervin and Sen. Baker and their counsel have been in contact with White House representatives John Ehrlichman and Leonard Garment. They have been talking about ground rules which would preserve the separation of powers without suppressing the facts.

I believe now an agreement has been reached which is satisfactory to both sides. The committee ground rules as adopted totally preserve the doctrine of separation of powers. They provide that the appearance by a witness may in the first instance, be in executive session, if appropriate.

Second, executive privilege is expressly reserved and may be asserted during the course of the questioning as to any questions.

Now much has been made of the issue as to whether the proceedings could be televised. To me, this has never been a control issue, especially if the separation of powers problem is otherwise solved, as I now think it is.

All members of the White House staff will appear voluntarily when requested by the committee. They will testify under oath and they will answer fully all proper questions.

I should point out that this arrangement is one that covers this hearing only in which wrongdoing has been charged. This kind of arrangement, of course, would not apply to other hearings. Each of them will be considered on its merits.

My second announcement concerns the Watergate case directly.

On March 21, as a result of serious charges which came to my attention, some of which were publicly reported, I began intensive new inquiries into this whole matter.

Last Sunday afternoon, the Attorney General, Assistant Attorney General Petersen and I met at length in the FOB Executive Office Building to review the facts which had come to me in my investigation and also to review the progress of the Department of Justice Investigation.

I can report today that there have been major developments in the case concerning which it would be improper to be more specific now except to say that real progress has been made in finding the truth.

If any person in the executive branch or in the government is indicted by the grand jury, my policy will be to immediately suspend him. If he is convicted, he will of course be automatically discharged.

I have expressed to the appropriate authorities my views that no individual holding in the past or at present a position of major importance in the administration should be given immunity from prosecution.

The judicial process is moving ahead as it should, and I shall aid it in all appropriate ways and have so informed the appropriate authorities.

As I have said before and I have said throughout this entire matter, all government employees and especially White House staff employees are expected fully to cooperate in this matter. I condemn any attempts to cover up in this case, no matter who is involved.

April 30, 1973
Television Address

Good evening.

I want to talk to you tonight from my heart on a subject of deep concern to every American.

In recent months members of my administration and officials of the Committee for the Re-election of The President, including some of my closest friends and most trusted aides, have been charged with involvement in what has become to be known as the Watergate Affair.

These include charges of illegal activity during the preceding 1972 Presidential election and changes that responsible officials participated in an effort to cover up that illegal activity.

The inevitable result of these charges has been to raise serious questions about the integrity of the White House itself. Tonight I wish to address those questions.

Last June 17 while I was in Florida trying to get a few days rest after my visit to Moscow, I first learned from news reports of the Watergate break-in. I was appalled at this senseless illegal action and I was shocked to learn that employees of the re-election committee were apparently among those guilty. I immediately ordered an investigation by appropriate government authorities.

On September 15, as you will recall, indictments were brought against seven defendants in this case. As the investigation went forward, I repeatedly asked those that conducted the investigation whether there was any reason to believe that members of my administration were in any way involved. I received repeated assurance there were not. Because of these continuing reassurances, because I believed the reports I was getting, because I had faith in the persons from whom I was getting them, I discounted the stories in the press that appeared to implicate members of my administration or other officials of the campaign committee. Until March of this year, I remained convinced that the denials were true and that the charges of involvement by members of the White House staff were false.

The comments I made during this period, the comments made by my press secretary in my behalf, were based on the information provided to us at the time we made those comments. However, new information then came to me, which persuaded me that there was a real possibility that some of these charges were true and suggesting further there had been an effort to conceal the facts, both from the public—from you—and from me. As a result, on March 21st, I personally assumed the responsibility for coordinating intensive new inquiries into the matter, and I personally ordered those conducting the investigations to get all the facts and to report them directly to me, right here in this office.

I again ordered that all persons in the government, or at the re-election committee, should cooperate fully with the FBI, the prosecutors and the grand jury.

I also ordered that any one who refused to cooperate in telling the truth would be asked to resign from government service. And with ground rules adopted that would preserve the basic Constitutional separation of powers between the Congress and the Presidency, I directed that members of the White House staff should appear and testify voluntarily under oath before the Senate committee which was investigating Watergate, I was determined that we should get to the bottom of the matter, and that the truth should be fully brought out no matter who was involved. At the same time, I was determined not to take precipitate action and to avoid if at all possible, any action that would appear to reflect on innocent people. I wanted to be fair. But I knew that in the final analysis, the integrity of this office, public faith in the integrity of this office, would have to take priority over all personal considerations.

Today, in one of the most difficult decisions of my Presidency, I accepted the resignation of two of my closest associates in the White House—Bob Haldeman, John Ehrlichman—two of the finest public servants it has been my privilege to know. I want to stress that in accepting these resignations, I mean to leave no implication whatever of personal wrongdoing on their part. And I leave no implication tonight of implication on the part of others who have been charged in this matter. But in matters as sensitive as guarding the integrity of our democratic process, it is essential not only that rigorous legal and technical standards be observed, but also that the public—you—have total confidence that they are both being observed and enforced by those in authority, and particularly by the President of the United States.

They agreed with me that this move was necessary in order to restore that confidence, because Attorney General Kleindienst, though a distinguished public servant, my personal friend for 20 years, with no personal involvement whatever in this matter, has been a close personal and professional associate of some of those who are involved in this case, he and I both felt it was also necessary to name a new attorney general. The counsel to the President, John Dean, has also resigned.

As new attorney general, I have today named Elliott Richardson, a man of unimpeachable integrity and rigorously high principles. I have directed him to do everything necessary to insure that the Department of Justice has the confidence and the trust of every law abiding person in this country. I have given him absolute authority to make all decisions bearing upon prosecution of the Watergate case, and related matters. I have instructed him that if he should consider it appropriate, he has the authority to name a special supervising prosecutor for matters arising out of the case.

Whatever may have appeared to have been the case before, whatever improper activities may yet be discovered in connection with this whole sordid affair, I want the American people, I want you, to know beyond the shadow of a doubt that during my term as President, justice will be pursued fairly, fully and impartially no matter who is involved. This office is a sacred trust, and I am determined to be worthy of that.

Looking back at the history of this case, two questions arise: How could it have happened? Who is to blame? Political commentators have correctly observed that during my 27 years in politics, I have always previously insisted on running my own campaigns for office. But 1972 presented a very different situation. In both domestic and foreign policy, 1972 was a year of crucially important decisions, of intense negotiations, of vital new directions, particularly in working toward the goal which has been my overriding concern throughout my political career—the goal of bringing peace to America, peace to the world.

That is why I decided as the 1972 campaign approached that the Presidency should come first and politics second. To the maximum extent possible, therefore, I sought to delegate campaign operations, to remove the day-to-day campaign decisions from the President's office and from the White House. . . .

Who then is to blame for what happened in this case? For specific criminal actions by specific individuals, those who committed those actions must, of course, bear the liability and pay the penalty. For the fact that alleged improper actions took place in the White House or within my campaign organization, the easiest course would be for me to blame those to whom I delegated the responsibility to run the campaign.

But that would be a cowardly thing to do. I will not place the blame on subordinates, on people whose zeal exceed their judgement, and who may have done wrong in a cause they deeply believed in to be right. In any organization, the man at the top must bear the responsibility. That responsibility therefore belongs here, in this office. I accept it. And I pledge to you tonight from this office that I will do everything in my power to insure that the guilty are brought to justice, and that such abuses are purged from our political processes in the years to come, long after I have left this office.

Some people, quite properly appalled at the abuses that occurred, will say that Watergate demonstrates the bankruptcy of the American political system. I believe precisely the opposite is true. Watergate represented a series of illegal acts and bad judgements by a number of individuals. It was the system that has brought the facts to light and that will bring those guilty to justice. A system that in this case has included a determined grand jury, honest prosecutors, a courageous judge, John Sirica, and a vigorous free press.

It is essential that we let the judicial process go forward, respecting those safeguards that are established to protect the innocent as well as to convict the guilty. It is essential that in reacting to the excesses of others, we not fall into excesses ourselves. It is also essential that we not be so distracted by events such as this that we neglect the vital work before us, before this nation, before America at a time of critical importance to America and the world.

Since March, when I first learned that the Watergate affair might in fact be far more serious than I had been led to believe, it has claimed far too much of my time and my attention. Whatever may now transpire in the case, whatever the actions of the grand jury, whatever the outcome of any eventual trials, I must now turn my full attention—and I shall do so once again—to the larger duties of this office. I owe it to this great office that I hold. And I owe it to you, my country.

I know that as Attorney General, Elliott Richardson will be There is also vital work to be done right here in America—to insure prosperity, and that means a good job for everyone who wants to work, to control inflation—that I know worries every housewife—everyone who tries to balance a family budget in America, to set in motion new and better ways of insuring progress toward a better life for all Americans.

On Christmas Eve, during my terrible personal ordeal of the renewed bombing of North Vietnam, which after 12 years of war, finally helped bring America peace with honor, I sat down just before midnight, I wrote out some of my goals for my second term as President.

Let me read them to you.

"To make it possible for our children, and for our children's children, to live in a world of peace.

"To make this country be more than ever a land of opportunity—of equal opportunity, full opportunity for every American.

"To provide jobs for all who can work, and generous help for all who cannot.

"To establish a climate of decency, and civility, in which each person respects the feelings and the dignity and the God-given rights of his neighbor.

"To make this a land in which each person can dare to dream, can live in his dream—not in fear, but in hope—proud of his community, proud of his country, proud of what America has meant to himself and to the world."

These are great goals. I believe we can, we must, work for them. We can achieve them. But we cannot achieve these goals unless we dedicate ourselves to another goal.

We must maintain the integrity of the White House, and that integrity must be real, not transparent. There can be no white-wash at the White House.

We must reform our political process—ridding it not only of the violations of the law, but also of the ugly mob violence and other inexcusable campaign tactics that have been too often practiced and too readily accepted in the past—including those that may have been a response by one side to the excesses or expected excesses of the other side. Two wrongs do not make a right.

I have been in public life for more than a quarter of a century. Like any other calling, politics has good people and bad people. And let me tell you, the great majority in politics in the Congress, in the Federal government, in the state government, are good people. I know that it can be very easy, under the intensive pressures of a campaign, for even well-intentioned people to fall into shady tactics—to rationalize this on the grounds that what is at stake is of such importance to the nation that the end justifies the means. And both of our great parties have been guilty of such tactics in the past.

In recent years, however, the campaign excesses that have occurred on all sides have provided a sobering demonstration of how far this false doctrine can take us. The lesson is clear: America, in its political campaigns, must not again fall into the trap of letting the end, however great that end is, justify the means.

I urge the leaders of both political parties, I urge citizens, all of you, everywhere, to join in working toward a new set of standards, new rules and procedures—to ensure that future elections will be as nearly free of such abuses as they possibly can be made. This is my goal. I ask you to join in making it America's goal.

When I was inaugurated for a second term this past January 20, I gave each member of my senior White House staff a special four-year calendar, with each day marked to show the number of days remaining to the Administration.

In the inscription on each calendar, I wrote those words: "The Presidential term which begins today consists of 1,461 days—no more, no less. Each can be a day of strengthening and renewal for America; each can add depth and dimension to the American experience. If we strive together, if we make the most of the challenge and the opportunity that these days offer us, they can stand out as great days for America, and great moments in the history of the world."

I looked at my own calendar this morning up at Camp David as I was working on this speech. It showed exactly 1,361 days remaining in my term. I want these to be the best days in America. I deeply believe that America is the hope of the world, and I know that in the quality and wisdom of the leadership America gives lies the only hope for millions of people all over the world, that they can live their lives in peace and freedom. We must be worthy of that hope, in every sense of the word.

Tonight I ask for your prayers to help me in everything that I do throughout the days of my Presidency to be worthy of their hopes and of yours.

God bless America and God bless each and everyone of you.

May 22, 1973
Statement to the Press

Allegations surrounding the Watergate affair have so escalated that I feel a further statement from the President is required at this time.

A climate of sensationalism has developed in which even second- or third-hand heresay charges are headlined as fact and repeated as fact.

Important national security operations which themselves had no connection with Watergate have become entangled in the case.

As a result, some national security information has already been made public through court orders, through the subpoenaing of documents and through testimony witnesses have given in judicial and congressional proceedings. Other sensitive documents are now threatened with disclosure. Continued silence about those operations would compromise rather than protect them, and would also serve to perpetuate a grossly distorted view—which recent partial disclosures have given—of the nature and purpose of those operations.

The purpose of this statement is threefold:

First, to set forth the facts about my own relationship to the Watergate matter.

Second, to place in some perspective some of the more sensational—and inaccurate—of the charges that have filled the headlines in recent days, and also some of the matters that are currently being discussed in Senate testimony and elsewhere.

Third, to draw the distinction between national security operations and the Watergate case. To put the other matters in perspective, it will be necessary to describe the national security operations first.

In citing these national security matters, it is not my intention to place a national security "cover" on Watergate, but rather to separate them out from Watergate—and at the same time to explain the context in which certain actions took place that were later misconstrued or misused.

Long before the Watergate break-in, three important national security operations took place which have subsequently become entangled in the Watergate case.

The first operation, begun in 1969, was a program of wiretaps. All were legal, under the authorities then existing. They were undertaken to find and stop serious national security leaks.

The second operation was a reassessment, which I ordered in 1970, of the adequacy of internal security measures. This resulted in a plan and a directive to strengthen our intelligence operations. They were protested by Mr. Hoover, and as a result of his protest they were not put into effect.

The third operation was the establishment, in 1971, of a Special Investigations Unit in the White House. Its primary mission was to plug leaks of vital security information. I also directed this group to prepare an accurate history of certain crucial national security matters which occurred under prior administrations, for which the government's records were incomplete.

Here is the background of these three security operations initiated in my administration.

By mid-1969, my administration had begun a number of highly sensitive foreign policy initiatives. They were aimed at ending the war in Vietnam, achieving a settlement in the Middle East, limiting nuclear arms and establishing new relationships among the great powers. These involved highly secret diplomacy. They were closely interrelated. Leaks of secret information about any one could endanger all.

Exactly that happened. News accounts appeared in 1969, which were obviously based on leaks—some of them extensive and detailed—by people having access to the most highly classified security materials.

There was no way to carry forward these diplomatic initiatives unless further leaks could be prevented. This required finding the source of the leaks.

In order to do this, a special program of wiretaps was instituted in mid-1969 and terminated in February, 1971. Fewer than 20 taps, of varying duration, were involved. They produced important leads that made it possible to tighten the security of highly sensitive materials. I authorized this entire program. Each individual tap was undertaken in accordance with procedures legal at the time and in accord with long-standing precedent.

The persons who were subject to these wiretaps were determined through coordination among the director of the FBI, my assistant for national security affairs, and the Attorney General. Those wiretapped were selected on the basis of access to the information leaked, material in security files, and evidence that developed as the inquiry proceeded.

Information thus obtained was made available to senior officials responsible for national security matters in order to curtail further leaks.

In the spring and summer of 1970, another security problem reached critical proportions. In March a wave of bombings and explosions struck college campuses and cities. There were 400 bomb threats in one 24-hour period in New York City. Rioting and violence on college campuses reached a new peak after the Cambodian operation and the tragedies at Kent State and Jackson State. The 1969-1970 school year brought nearly 1800 campus demonstrations, and nearly 250 cases of arson on campus. Many colleges closed. Gun battles between guerrilla-style groups and police were taking place. Some of the disruptive activities were receiving foreign support.

Complicating the task of maintaining security was the fact that in 1966, certain types of undercover FBI operations that had been conducted for many years had been suspended. This also had substantially impaired our ability to collect foreign intelligence information. At the same time, the relationships between the FBI and other intelligence agencies had been deteriorating. By May, 1970, FBI Director Hoover shut off his agency's liaison with the CIA altogether.

On June 5, 1970, I met with the Director of the FBI (Mr. Hoover), the Director of the Central Intelligency Agency (Mr. Richard Helms), the Director of the Defense Intelligence Agency (General Donald V. Bennett) and the Director of the National Security Agency (Admiral Noel Gayler). We discussed the urgent need for better intelligence operations. I appointed Director Hoover as chairman of an interagency committee to prepare recommendations.

On June 25, the committee submitted a report which included specific options for expanded intelligence operations, and on July 23 the agencies were notified by memorandum of the options approved. After reconsideration, however, prompted by the opposition of Director Hoover, the agencies were notified five days later, on July 28, that the approval had been rescinded. The options initially approved had included resumption of certain intelligence operations which had been suspended in 1966. These in turn had included authorization for surreptitious entry—breaking and entering, in effect—on specified categories of targets in specified situations related to national security.

Because the approval was withdrawn before it had been implemented, the net result was that the plan for expanded intelligence activities never went into effect.

The documents spelling out this 1970 plan are extremely sensitive. They include—and are based upon—assessments of certain foreign intelligence capabilities and procedures, which of course must remain secret. It was this unused plan and related documents that John Dean removed from the White House and placed in a safe deposit box, giving the keys to Judge Sirica. The same plan, still unused, is being headlined today.

Coordination among our intelligence agencies continued to fall short of our national security needs. In July, 1970, having earlier discontinued the FBI's liaison with the CIA, Director Hoover ended the FBI's normal liaison with all other agencies except the White House. To help remedy this, an Intelligence Evaluation Committee was created in December, 1970. Its members included representatives of the White House, CIA, FBI, NSA, the Department of Justice, Treasury and Defense, and the Secret Service.

The Intelligence Evaluation Committee and its staff were instructed to improve coordination among the intelligence community and to prepare evaluations and estimates of domestic intelligence. I understand that its activities are now under investigation. I did not authorize nor do I have any knowledge of any illegal activity by this Committee. If it went beyond its character and did engage in any illegal activities, it was totally without my knowledge or authority.

On Sunday, June 13, 1971, the *New York Times* published the first installment of what came to be known as "The Pentagon Papers." Not until a few hours before publication did any responsible government official know that they had been stolen. Most officials did not know they existed. No senior official of the government had read them or knew with certainty what they contained.

All the government knew, at first, was that the papers comprised 47 volumes and some 7,000 pages, which had been taken from the most sensitive files of the Departments of State and Defense and the CIA, covering military and diplomatic moves in a war that was still going on.

Moreover, a majority of the documents published with the first three installments in *The Times* had not been included in the 47-volume study—raising serious questions about what and how much else might have been taken.

There was every reason to believe this was a security leak of unprecedented proportions.

It created a situation in which the ability of the government to carry on foreign relations even in the best of circumstances could have been severely compromised. Other governments no longer knew whether they could deal with the United States in confidence. Against the background of the delicate negotiations the United States was then involved in on a number of fronts—with regard to Vietnam, China, the Middle East, nuclear arms limitations, U.S.-Soviet soviet relations and others—in which the utmost degree of confidentiality was vital, it posed a threat so grave as to require extraordinary actions.

Therefore during the week following the Pentagon Papers publication, I approved the creation of a Special Investigations Unit within the White House—which later came to be known as the "Plumbers." This was a small group at the White House whose principal purpose was to stop security leaks and to investigate other sensitive security matters. I looked to John Ehrlichman for the supervision of the group.

Egil Krogh, Mr. Ehrlichman's assistant, was put in charge. David Young was added to this unit, as were E. Edward Hunt and G. Gordon Liddy.

The unit operated under extremely tight security rules. Its existence and functions were known only to a very few persons at the White House. These included Messrs. Haldeman, Ehrlichman and Dean.

At about the time the unit was created, Daniel Ellsberg was identified as the person who had given the Pentagon Papers to the *New York Times*. I told Mr. Krogh that as a matter of first priority, the unit should find out all it could about Mr. Ellsberg's associates and his motives. Because of the extreme gravity of the situation, and not then knowing what additional national security . . . of his assignment, I did not authorize and had no knowledge of any illegal means to be used to achieve this goal.

However, because of the emphasis I put on the crucial importance of protecting the national security, I can understand how highly motivated individuals could have felt justified in engaging in specific activities that I would have disapproved had they been brought to my attention.

Consequently, as President, I must and do assume responsibility for such actions despite the fact that I at no time approved or had knowledge of them.

I also assigned the unit a number of other investigatory matters, dealing in part with compiling an accurate record of events related to the Vietnam war, on which the Government's records were inadequate (many previous records having been removed with the change of administrations) and which bore directly on the negotiations then in progress. Additional assignments included tracing down other national security leaks including one that seriously compromised the U.S. negotiating position in the SALT talks.

The work of the unit tapered off around the end of 1971. The nature of its work was such that it involved matters that, from a national security standpoint, were highly sensitive then and remain so today.

These intelligence activities had no connection with the break-in of the Democratic headquarters, or the aftermath.

I considered it my responsibility to see that the Watergate investigation did not impinge adversely upon the national security area. For example, on April 8, 1973, when I learned that Mr. Hunt, a former member of the Special Investigations Unit at the White House, was to be questioned by the U.S. Attorney, I directed Assistant Attorney General Petersen to pursue every issue involving Watergate but to confine his investigation to Watergate and related matters and to stay out of national security matters. Subsequently, on April 25, 1973, Attorney General Kleindienst informed me that because the government had clear evidence that Mr. Hunt was involved in the break-in of the office of the psychiatrist who

had treated Mr. Ellsberg, he, the Attorney General, believed that despite the fact that no evidence had been obtained from Hunt's acts, a report should nevertheless be made to the court trying the Ellsberg case. I concurred, and directed that the information be transmitted to Judge Byrne immediately.

The burglary and bugging of the Democratic National Committee headquarters came as a complete surprise to me. I had no inkling that any such illegal activities had been planned by persons associated with my campaign; if I had known, I would not have permitted it. My immediate reaction was that those guilty should be brought to justice and, with the five burglars themselves already in custody, I assumed that they would be.

Within a few days, however, I was advised that there was a possibility of CIA involvement in some way.

It did seem to me possible that, because of the involvement of former CIA personnel, and because of some of their apparent associations, the investigation could lead to the uncovering of covert CIA operations totally unrelated to the Watergate break-in.

In addition, by this time, the name of Mr. Hunt had surfaced in connection with Watergate, and I was alerted to the fact that he had previously been a member of the Special Investigations Unit in the White House. Therefore, I was also concerned that the Watergate investigation might well lead to an inquiry into the activities of the Special Investigations Unit itself.

In this area, I felt it was important to avoid disclosure of the details of the national security matters with which the group was concerned. I knew that once the existence of the group became known, it would lead inexorably to a discussion of these matters, some of which remain, even today, highly sensitive.

I wanted justice done with regard to Watergate; but in the scale of national priorities with which I had to deal—and not at that time having any idea of the extent of political abuse which Watergate reflected—I also had to be deeply concerned with ensuring that neither the covert operations of the CIA nor the operations of the Special Investigations Unit should be compromised. Therefore, I instructed Mr. Haldeman and Mr. Ehrlichman to ensure that the investigation of the break-in not expose either an unrelated covert operation of the CIA or the activities of the White House investigations unit—and to see that this was personally coordinated between General Walters, the Deputy Director of the CIA, and Mr. Gray of the FBI. It was certainly not my intent, nor my wish, that the investigation of the Watergate break-in or of related acts be impeded in any way.

On July 6, 1972, I telephoned the acting director of the FBI, L. Patrick Gray, to congratulate him on his successful handling of the hijacking of a Pacific Southwest Airlines plane the previous day. During the conversation Mr. Gray discussed with me the progress of the Watergate investigation, and I asked him whether he had talked with General Walters. Mr. Gray said that he had, and that General Walters had assured him that the CIA was not involved. In the discussion, Mr. Gray suggested that the matter of Watergate might lead higher. I told him to press ahead with his investigation.

It now seems that later, through whatever complex of individual motives and possible misunderstandings, there were apparently wide-ranging efforts to limit the investigation or to conceal the possible involvement of members of the administration and the campaign committee.

I was not aware of any such efforts at the time. Neither, until after I began my own investigation, was I aware of any fund raising for defendants convicted of the break-in at Democratic headquarters, much less authorize any such fund raising. Nor did I authorize any offer of executive clemency for any of the defendants.

In the weeks and months that followed Watergate, I asked for, and received, repeated assurances that Mr. Dean's own investigation (which included reviewing files and sitting in on FBI interviews with White House personnel) had cleared everyone then employed by the White House of involvement.

(1) I had no prior knowledge of the Watergate bugging operation, or of any illegal surveillance activities for political purposes.

(2) Long prior to the 1972 campaign, I did set in motion certain internal security measures, including legal wiretaps, which I felt were necessary from a national security standpoint and, in the climate then prevailing, also necessary from a domestic security standpoint.

(3) People who had been involved in the national security operations later, without my knowledge or approval, undertook illegal activities in the political campaign of 1972.

(4) Elements of the early post-Watergate reports led me to suspect, incorrectly, that the CIA had been in some way involved. They also led me to surmise, correctly, that since persons originally recruited for covert national security activities had participated in Watergate, an unrestricted investigation of Watergate might lead to and expose those covert national security operations.

(5) I sought to prevent the exposure of these covert national security activities, while encouraging those conducting the investigation to pursue their inquiry into the Watergate itself. I so instructed my staff, the Attorney General and the acting director of the FBI.

(6) I also specifically instructed Mr. Haldeman and Mr. Ehrlichman to ensure that the FBI would not carry its investigation into areas that might compromise these covert national security activities, or those of the CIA.

(7) At no time did I authorize or know about any offer of executive clemency for the Watergate defendants. Neither did I know until the time of my own investigation, of any efforts to provide them with funds.

With hindsight it is apparent that I should have given more heed to the warning signals I received along the way about a Watergate cover-up and less to the reassurances.

With hindsight, several other things also become clear:

With respect to campaign practices, and also with respect to campaign finances, it should now be obvious that no campaign in history has ever been subjected to the kind of intensive and searching inquiry that has been focused on the campaign waged in my behalf in 1972.

It is clear that unethical, as well as illegal, activities took place in the course of that campaign.

None of these took place with my specific approval or knowledge. To the extent that I may in any way have contributed to the climate in which they took place, I did not intend to; to the extent that I failed to prevent them, I should have been more vigilant.

It was to help ensure against any repetition of this in the future that last week I proposed the establishment of a top-level, bipartisan, independent commission to recommend a comprehensive reform of campaign laws and practices. Given the priority I believe it deserves, such reform should be possible before the next congressional elections in 1976.

It now appears that there were persons who may have gone beyond my directives, and sought to expand on my efforts to protect the national security operations in order to cover up any involvement they or certain others might have had in Watergate. The extent to which this is true, and who may have participated and to what degree, are questions that it would not be proper to address here. The proper forum for settling these matters is in the courts.

To the extent that I have been able to determine what probably happened in the tangled course of this affair, on the basis of my own recollections and of the conflicting accounts and evidence that I have seen, it would appear that one factor at work was that at critical points various people, each with his own perspective and his own responsibilities, saw the same situations with different eyes and heard the same words with different ears. What might have seemed insignificant to one seemed significant to another; what one saw in terms of public responsibility, another saw in terms of political opportunity; and mixed through it all, I am sure, was a concern on the part of many that the Watergate scandal should not be allowed to get in the way of what the administration sought to achieve.

The truth about Watergate should be brought out—in an orderly way, recognizing that the safeguards of judicial procedure are designed to find the truth, not to hide the truth.

With his selection of Archibald Cox—who served both President Kennedy and President Johnson as Solicitor General—as the special supervisory prosecutor for matters, related to the case, Attorney General designate Richardson has demonstrated his own determination to see the truth brought out. In this effort he has my full support.

Considering the number of persons involved in this case whose testimony might be subject to a claim of executive privilege, I recognize that a clear definition of that claim has become central to the effort to arrive at the truth.

Accordingly, executive privilege will not be invoked as to any testimony concerning possible criminal conduct or discussions of possible criminal conduct, in the matters presently under investigation, including the Watergate affair and the alleged cover-up.

I want to emphasize that this statement is limited to my own recollections of what I said and did relating to security and to the Watergate. I have specifically avoided any attempt to explain what other parties may have said and done. My own information on those other matters if fragmentary, and to some extent contradictory. Additional information may be forthcoming of which I am unaware. It is also my understanding that the information which has been conveyed to me has also become available to those prosecuting these matters. Under such circumstances, it would be prejudicial and unfair of me to render my opinions on the activities of others; those judgements must be left to the judicial process, our best hope for achieving the just result that we all seek.

As more information is developed, I have no doubt that more questions will be raised. To the extent that I am able, I seek to set forth the facts as known to me with respect to those questions.

August 15, 1973
The Written Statement

On May 17 the Senate Select Committee began its hearings on Watergate. Five days later, on May 22, I issued a detailed statement discussing my relationship to the matter. I stated categorically that I had no prior knowledge of the Watergate operation, and that I neither knew of nor took part in any subsequent efforts to cover it up. I also stated that I would not invoke executive privilege as to testimony by present and former members of my White House staff with respect to possible criminal acts then under investigation.

Thirty-five witnesses have testified so far. The record is more than 7,500 pages and some 2 million words along. The allegations are many, the facts are complicated, and the evidence is not only extensive but very much in conflict. It would be neither fair nor appropriate for me to assess the evidence or comment on specific witnesses or their credibility. That is the function of the Senate Committee and the courts. What I intend to do here is to cover the principal issues relating to my own conduct which have been raised since my statement of May 22, and thereby to place the testimony on those issues in perspective.

I said on May 22 that I had no prior knowledge of the Watergate operation. In all the testimony, there is not the slightest evidence to the contrary. Not a single witness has testified that I had any knowledge of the planning for the Watergate break-in.

It is also true, as I said on May 22, that I took no part in, and was not aware of, any subsequent efforts to cover up the illegal acts associated with the Watergate break-in.

In the summer of 1972, I had given orders for the Justice Department and the FBI to conduct a thorough and aggressive investigation of the Watergate break-in, and I relied on their investigation to disclose the facts. My only concern about the scope of the investigation was that it might lead into CIA or other national-security operations of a sensitive nature. Mr. Gray, the Acting Director of the FBI, told me by telephone on July 6 that he had met with General Walters, that General Walters had told him the CIA was not involved, and that CIA activities would not be compromised by the FBI investigation. As a result, any problems that Mr. Gray may have had in co-ordinating with the CIA were moot. I concluded by instructing him to press forward vigorously with his own investigation.

During the summer of 1972, I repeatedly asked for reports on the progress of the investigation. Every report I received was that no persons, other than the seven who were subsequently indicted, were involved in the Watergate operation.

On September 12, at a meeting attended by me and by the Cabinet, senior members of the White House staff and a number of legislative leaders, Attorney General Kleindienst reported on the investigation. He informed us that it had been the most intensive investigation since the assassination of President Kennedy, and that it had been established that no one at the White House, and no higher-ups in the campaign committee, were involved. His report seemed to be confirmed by the action of the grand jury on September 15, when it indicted only the five persons arrested at the Watergate, plus Messrs. Liddy and Hunt.

Those indictments also seemed to me to confirm the validity of the reports that Mr. Dean had been providing to me, through other members of the White House staff—and on which I had based my August 29 statement that no one then employed at the White House was involved. It was in that context that I met with Mr. Dean on September 15, and he gave me no reason at that meeting to believe any others were involved.

Not only was I unaware of any cover-up, but at that time, and until March 21, I was unaware that there was anything to cover up.

Then and later, I continued to have full faith in the investigations that had been conducted and in the reports I had received, based on those investigations. On February 16, I met with Mr. Gray prior to submitting his name to the Senate for confirmation as permanent Director of the FBI. I stressed to him that he would be questioned closely about the FBI's conduct of the Watergate investigation, and asked him if he still had full confidence in it. He replied that he did; that he was proud of its thoroughness, and that he could defend it with enthusiasm.

My interest in Watergate rose in February and March as the Senate Committee was organized and the hearings were held on the Gray nomination. I began meeting frequently with my counsel, Mr. Dean, in connection with those matters. At that time, on a number of occasions, I urged my staff to get all the facts out, because I was confident that full disclosure of the facts would show that persons in the White House and at the Committee for the Re-election of the President were the victims of unjustified innuendoes in the press. I was searching for a way to disclose all of the facts without disturbing the confidentiality of communications with and among my personal staff, since that confidentiality is essential to the functioning of any President.

It was on March 21 that I was given new information that indicated that the reports I had been getting were not true. I was told then for the first time that the planning of the Watergate break-in went beyond those who had been tried and convicted, and that at least one, and possibly more, persons at the Re-election Committee were involved. It was on that day also that I learned of some of the activities upon which charges of cover-up are now based. I was told then that funds had been raised for payments to the defendants, with the knowledge and approval of persons both on the White House staff and at the Re-election Committee. But I was only told that the money had been used for attorneys' fees and family support, not that it had been paid to procure silence from the recipients.

I was also told that a member of my staff had talked to one of the defendants about clemency, but not that offers of clemency had been made. I was told that one of the defendants was currently attempting to blackmail the White House by demanding payment of $120,000 as the price of not talking about other activities, unrelated to Watergate, in which he had engaged. These allegations were made in general terms. They were portrayed to me as being based in part on supposition, and they were largely unsupported by details or evidence.

These allegations were very troubling, and they gave a new dimension to the Watergate matter. They also reinforced my determination that the full facts must be made available to the grand jury or to the Senate Committee. If anything illegal had happened, I wanted it to be dealt with appropriately according to the law. If anyone at the White House or high up in my campaign had been involved in wrongdoing of any kind, I wanted the White House to take the lead in making that known.

When I received this disturbing information on March 21, I immediately began new inquiries into the case and an examination of the best means to give to the grand jury or Senate Committee what we then knew and what we might later learn.

On March 21, I arranged to meet the following day with Messrs. Haldeman, Ehrlichman, Dean and Mitchell to discuss the appropriate method to get the facts out. On March 23, I sent Mr. Dean to Camp David, where he was instructed to write a complete report on all that he knew of the entire Watergate matter. On March 28, I had Mr. Ehrlichman call the Attorney General to find out if he had additional information about Watergate generally or White House involvement. The Attorney General was told that I wanted to hear directly from him, and not through any staff people, if he had any information on White House involvement or if information of that kind should come to him. The Attorney General indicated to Mr. Ehrlichman that he had no such information.

When I learned on March 30 that Mr. Dean had been unable to complete his report, I instructed Mr. Ehrlichman to conduct an independent inquiry and bring all the facts to me. On April 14, Mr. Ehrlichman gave me his findings, and I directed that he report them to the Attorney General immediately. On April 15, Attorney General Kleindienst and Assistant Attorney General Petersen told me of new information that had been received by the prosecutors.

By that time the fragmentary information I had been given on March 21 had been supplemented in important ways, particularly by Mr. Ehrlichman's report to me on April 14, by the information Mr. Kleindienst and Mr. Petersen gave me on April 15, and by independent inquiries I had been making on my own. At that point, I realized that I would not be able personally to find out all of the facts and make them public, and I concluded that the matter was best handled by the Justice Department and the grand jury.

On April 17, I announced that new inquiries were under way, as a result of what I had learned on March 21 and in my own investigation since that time. I instructed all Government employes to co-operate with the judicial process as it moved ahead on this matter and expressed my personal view that no immunity should be given to any individual who had held a position of major importance in this Administration.

My consistent position from the beginning has been to get out the facts about Watergate, not to cover them up.

On May 22, I said that at no time did I authorize any offer of executive clemency for the Watergate defendants, nor did I know of any such offer. I reaffirm that statement. Indeed, I made my view clear to Mr. Ehrlichman in July, 1972, that under no circumstances could executive clemency be considered for those who participated in the Watergate break-in. I maintained that position throughout.

On May 22, I said that "it was not until the time of my own investigation that I learned of the break-in at the office of Mr. Ellsberg's psychiatrist, and I specifically authorized the furnishing of this information to Judge Byrne." After a very careful review, I have determined that this statement of mine is not precisely accurate. It was on March 17 that I first learned of the break-in at the office of Dr. Fielding, and that was four days before the beginning of my own investigation on March 21. I was told then that nothing by way of evidence had been obtained in the break-in.

On April 18, I learned that the Justice Department had interrogated or was going to interrogate Mr. Hunt about this break-in. I was gravely concerned that other activities of the special-investigations unit might be disclosed, because I knew this could seriously injure the national security. Consequently, I directed Mr. Petersen to stick to the Watergate investigation and stay out of national-security matters.

On April 25, Attorney General Kleindienst came to me and urged that the fact of the break-in should be disclosed to the court, despite the fact that, since no evidence had been obtained, the law did not clearly require it. I concurred, and authorized him to report the break-in to Judge Byrne.

In view of the incident of Dr. Fielding's office, let me emphasize two things:

First, it was and is important that many of the matters worked on by the special-investigations unit not be publicly disclosed because disclosure would unquestionably damage the national security. This is why I have exercised executive privilege on some of these matters in connection with the testimony of Mr. Ehrlichman and others. The Senate Committee has learned through its investigation the general facts of some of these security matters, and has to date wisely declined to make them public or to contest in these respects my claim of executive privilege.

Second, I at no time authorized the use of illegal means by the special-investigations unit, and I was not aware of the break-in of Dr. Fielding's office until March 17, 1973.

Many persons will ask why, when the facts are as I have stated them, I do not make public the tape recordings of my meetings and conversations with members of the White House staff during this period.

I am aware that such terms as "separation of powers" and "executive privilege" are lawyers' terms, and that those doctrines have been called "abstruse" and "esoteric." Let me state the common sense of the matter.

Every day, a President of the United States is required to make difficult decisions on grave issues. It is absolutely essential, if the President is to be able to do his job as the country expects, that he be able to talk openly and candidly with his advisers about issues and individuals, and that they be able to talk in the same fashion with him. Indeed, on occasion, they must be able to "blow off steam" about important public figures. This kind of frank discussion is only possible when those who take part in it can feel assured that what they say is in the strictest confidence.

The Presidency is not the only office that requires confidentiality if it is to function effectively. A member of Congress must be able to talk in confidence with his assistants. Judges must be able to confer in confidence with their law clerks and with each other. Throughout our entire history, the need for this kind of confidentiality has been recognized. No branch of Government has ever compelled disclosure of confidential conversations between officers of other branches of Government and their advisers about Government business.

The argument is often raised that these tapes are somehow different because the conversations may bear on illegal acts, and because the commission of illegal acts is not an official duty. This misses the point entirely. Even if others, from their own standpoint, may have been thinking about how to cover up an illegal act, from my standpoint I was concerned with how to uncover the illegal acts. It is my responsibility under the Constitution to see that the laws are faithfully executed, and in pursuing the facts about Watergate, I was doing precisely that. Therefore, the precedent would not be one concerning illegal actions only; it would be one that would risk exposing private presidential conversations involving the whole range of official duties.

The need for confidence is not something confined to the Government officials. The law has long recognized that there are many relations sufficiently important that things said in that relation are entitled to be kept confidential, even at the cost of doing without what might be critical evidence in a legal proceeding. Among these are, for example, the relations between a lawyer and his client, between a priest and a penitent, and between a husband and a wife. In each case it is thought to be so important that the parties be able to talk freely with each other, that they need not feel restrained in their conversation by fear that what they say may someday come out in court, that the law recognizes that these conversations are "privileged," and that their disclosure cannot be compelled.

If I were to make public these tapes, containing as they do blunt and candid remarks on many subjects that have nothing to do with Watergate, the confidentiality of the office of the President would always be suspect. Persons talking with a President would never again be sure that recordings or notes of what they said would not at some future time be made public, and they would guard their words against that possibility. No one would want to risk being known as the person who recommended a policy that ultimately did not work. No one would want to advance tentative ideas, not fully thought through, that might have possible merit but that might, on further examination, prove unsound. No one would want to speak bluntly about public figures here and abroad.

I shall therefore vigorously oppose any action which would set a precedent that would cripple all future Presidents by inhibiting conversations between them and the persons they look to for advice.

This principle of confidentiality in presidential communications is what is at stake in the question of the tapes. I shall continue to oppose any efforts to destroy that principle, which is indispensable to the conduct of the Presidency.

I recognize that this statement does not answer many of the questions and contentions raised during the Watergate hearings. It has not been my intention to attempt any such comprehensive and detailed response, nor has it been my intention to address myself to all matters covered in my May 22 statement. With the Senate hearings and the grand-jury investigations still proceeding, with much of the testimony in conflict, it would be neither possible to provide nor appropriate to attempt a definitive account of all that took place.

Neither do I believe I could enter upon an endless course of explaining and rebutting a complex of point-by-point claims and charges arising out of that conflicting testimony which may engage committees and courts for months or years to come, and still be able to carry out my duties as President.

While the judicial and legislative branches resolve these matters, I will continue to discharge to the best of my ability my constitutional responsibilities as President of the United States.

Appendix V

The Ervin Hearings

SENATE SELECT COMMITTEE ON PRESIDENTIAL CAMPAIGN ACTIVITIES

Sam J. Ervin Jr., Democrat of North Carolina, Chairman
Howard K. Baker Jr., Republican of Tennessee, Vice Chairman
Lowell P. Weicker Jr., Republican of Connecticut
Herman E. Talmadge, Democrat of Georgia
Daniel K. Inouye, Democrat of Hawaii
Joseph M. Montoya, Democrat of New Mexico
Edward J. Gurney, Republican of Florida
Samuel Dash, Chief Counsel and Staff Director
Fred D. Thompson, Chief Minority Counsel

Following are excerpts from the testimony of several important witnesses before the Ervin committee,

McCord

The following is a partial transcript of testimony given by convicted Watergate conspirator James W. McCord Jr. before the Ervin committee on Friday, May 18, 1973.

McCord: I will state as a preliminary that the dates of the telephone calls that I refer to in this statement are to the best of my recollection; they may be inaccurate by a day or two. . . .

Political pressure from the White House was conveyed to me in January 1973 by John Caulfield to remain silent, take executive clemency by going off to prison quietly, and I was told that while there, I would receive financial aid and later rehabilitation and a job. I was told in a January meeting in 1973 with Caulfield that the President of the United States was aware of our meeting, that the results of the meeting would be conveyed to the President, and that at a future meeting there would be a personal message from the President himself.

Sen. Ervin: I would like to state at this point that the testimony of Mr. McCord as to what was told to him by John Caulfield would not be accepted in a court of law to connect the President with what Mr. Caulfield was doing, but it is admissible to show whether or not Mr. Caulfield was a party to any agreement to connect the President for any information on what is known as the Watergate affair, but it is not received in connection to the President at this stage.

Sen. Gurney: I think it ought to be pointed out at that time that at this time, January, 1973, it is my understanding that Mr. Caulfield was not in the White House at all, but was employed, I think by the Treasury Department.

McCord: The second paragraph is on the afternoon of January 8, 1973, the first day of the Watergate trial, Gerald Alch, my attorney, told me that William O. Bittman, attorney for E. Howard Hunt, wanted to meet with me at Bittman's office that afternoon. When I asked why, Alch said that Bittman wanted to talk with me about "whose word I would trust regarding a White House offer of executive clemency". Alch added that Bittman wanted to talk with both Bernard Barker and me that afternoon.

I had no intention of accepting executive clemency, but I did want to find out what was going on, and by whom, and exactly what the White House was doing now. A few days before, the White House had tried to lay the Watergate operation off on CIA, and now it was clear that I was going to have to find out what was

up now. To do so involved some risks. To fail to do so was in my opinion to work in a vacuum regarding White House intentions and plans, which involved even greater risks, I felt.

Around 4:30 p.m. that afternoon, January 8th, while waiting for a taxi after the Court session, Bernard Barker asked my attorneys and me if he could ride in the cab with us to Bittman's office, which was agreed to. There he got out of the cab and went up towards Bittman's office. I had been under the impression during the cab ride that Bittman was going to talk to both Barker and me jointly, and became angered at what seemed to me to be the arrogance and audacity of another man's lawyer calling in two other lawyer's clients and pitching them for the White House. Alch saw my anger and took me aside for about a half hour after the cab arrived in front of Bittman's office, and let Barker go up alone. About 5:00 p.m. we went up to Bittman's office. There Alch disappeared with Bittman, and I sat alone in Bittman's office for a period of time, became irritated.

Mr. Alch finally came back, took me aside, and said that Mr. Bittman had told him that I would be called that same night by a friend I had known from the White House. I assumed this would be John Caulfield who had originally recruited me for the Committee for the Reelection of the President position.

About 12:30 p.m. that same evening, I received a call from an unidentified individual who said that Caulfield was out of town and asked me to go to a pay phone booth near the Blue Fountain Inn on Rte. 355 near my residence, where he had a message for me from Caulfield. There the same individual called and read the following message:

"Plead guilty.

"One year is a long time, You will get executive clemency. Your family will be taken care and when you get out you will be rehabilitated and a job will be found for you.

"Don't take immunity when called before the Grand Jury."

Dash: Now, Mr. McCord, did you recognize that voice at all? Do you know who was speaking to you on the telephone?

McCord: I do not know who the man was, the voice I heard over the telephone before in previous calls.

I heard the voice before, I do not know the identity of the man who called. . . .

Sometime in July, 1972, shortly after I got out of jail, which was in June 1972, about midday there was a note in my mailbox at my residence and when I opened the letter, which had not been stamped nor sent through the mails it was a note from Caulfield signed "Jack" which said, "Go to the phone booth on Rte. 355 near your home" and gave three alternate times at which I could appear at the phone booth for a telephone call from him. . . .

I went to the telephone, to that telephone booth on Rte. 355 that afternoon, the same afternoon, as I best recall, and I heard the voice that I have referred to in this memorandum of today. I do not know that individual's identity, he had an accent that I would refer to as a New York accent. He said that he had formerly worked for Jack Caulfield. He said, "I am a friend of Jack's, I formerly worked with him. Jack will want to talk with you shortly. He will be in touch with you soon."

I received a call subsequently from Mr. Caulfield. To the best of my recollection it came to my home first and it said, "Go to the same phone booth on Rts. 355", which I did, and there Mr. Caulfield told me that he was going overseas in a few days. He said "If you have any problem, call my home and leave word and I will call you back from overseas to your residence."

McCord: . . . On Wednesday evening, January 10, 1973, the same party (the unidentified voice), to the best of my recollection, called and told me by phone that Jack would want to talk with me by phone on Thursday night, the following night, January 11 when he got back into town and requested that I go to the same phone booth on Rte. 355 near the Blue Fountain Inn. He also conveyed instructions regarding a personal meeting with Mr. Caulfield on Friday night, January 12th. On Thursday evening, January 11, the same party called me at home, and told me that Caulfield's plane was late and that he–speaking of Caulfield–wanted to meet with me personally the same evening, that is Thursday evening, after arrival. I told him that I would not do so but would meet with him Friday night if he desired. Later that evening, Thursday evening, about 9:30 p.m. Caulfield called me on my home phone and insisted on talking with me but my family refused to let him do so, since I was asleep.

On Friday night, January 12 from about 7 p.m. to 7:30 p.m. I met Caulfield at the second overlook, that is . . . at the parking area for looking at the Potomac . . . on George Washington Park-way in Virginia.

Mr. Dash: Mr. McCord, how did you know to go there? How was it arranged?

McCord: I believe it was stated in the Thursday evening call at which this unidentified party said Caulfield would want to meet with me personally and on Friday night and to go to the second overlook on George Washington Parkway and he specified the time and that is what I followed through. I met with Caulfield at the second overlook on George Washington Parkway, that is the second one leaving Washington and going out to Virginia, and talked with him in his car, in his automobile. Caulfield advised that he had been attending a law enforcement meeting in San Clemente, California, and had just returned. I advised him that I had no objection to meeting with him to tell him my frame of mind but that I had no intention of talking executive clemency or pleading guilty; that I had come to the meeting at his request and not of my own, and was glad to tell him my views.

He said that the offer of executive clemency which he was passing along and of support while in prison and rehabilitation and help toward a job later "was a sincere offer." He explained that he had been asked to convey this message to me and he was only doing what he was told to do. He repeated this last statement several times during the course of the meeting we had then, and I might add during subsequent meetings which he and I had.

My response was that I would not even discuss executive clemency or pleading guilty and remaining silent, but I was glad to talk with him so that there was no misunderstanding on anyone's part about it.

I might explain that the trial was going on during this period, this was the first week of the trial, which began on January 8th.

Caulfield stated that he was carrying the message of executive clemency to me "from the very highest levels of the White House." He stated that the President of the United States was in Key Biscayne, Florida, that weekend, referring to the weekend following January 8, the following meeting that we were in then, and that the President "had been told of the results of the meeting".

Sen. Ervin: Now the same rule previously announced, this evidence is competent to show what, if anything, John Caulfield did to induce Mr. McCord to plead guilty and keep silent: It is not any evidence at the present state of the hearing that connects, that makes any indication whatever and has any relevancy as to the President. . . .

McCord: He further stated that "I may have a message to you at our next meeting, from the President himself."

I advised Caulfield that I had seen the list of witnesses for the trial and had seen Jeb Magruder's name, appearing as a government witness. I advised him that it was clear then that Magruder was going to perjure himself and that we were not going to get a fair trial, and others were going to be covered for (I was referring to John Mitchell, John Dean and Magruder) and I so named those individuals incidentally in the conversation, and I said that this was not my idea of American justice. I further advised Caulfield that I believed that the government had lied in denying electronic interception of my phone calls from my residence since June 17, 1972 and that I believed that the administration had also taped the phones of the other defendants during that time. I mentioned two specific calls of mine which I had made during September and early October, 1972, which I was certain had been intercepted by the government, and yet the government had blithely denied any such tapping. These were my words to Mr. Caulfield.

I did not hear from Caulfield on Saturday, but on Sunday afternoon he called and asked to meet me that afternoon about an hour later at the same location on George Washington Parkway. He stated that there was no objection to renewing the motion on discovery of government wiretapping, and that if that failed, that I would receive executive clemency after 10 to 11 months. I told him I had not asked anyone's permission to file the motion.

He went on to say that "the President's ability to govern is at stake. Another Teapot Dome scandal is possible and the government may fall. Everybody else is on track but you. You are not following the game plan. Get closer to your attorney. You seem to be pursuing your own course of action. Do not talk if called before the grand jury, keep silent, and do the same if called before a congressional committee".

My response was that I felt a massive injustice was being done, that I was different from the others, that I was going to fight the fixed case, and had no intention of either pleading guilty, taking executive clemency or agreeing to remain silent. He repeated the statement that the government would have difficulty to continuing to be able to stand. I responded that they do have a problem, but that I had a problem with the massive injustice of the whole trial being a sham, and that I would fight it every way I know.

I should make a correction in the sentence I just read in saying the whole trial being a sham, because I did not at that point in time make any reference at any time to Judge Sirica to the contrary of his being anything but an honest and dedicated judge, and I do not want the sentence to be misread.

He—talking about Caulfield—asked for a commitment that I would remain silent and I responded that I would make none. I gave him a memorandum on the dates of the two calls of mine in September, 1972, and October, 1972, that I was sure had been intercepted and said that I believed the government had lied about them. He said that he would check and see if in fact the government had done so.

On Monday night, January 19, 1973, Caulfield called me again at the phone booth at Rte 355 near my residence. I informed him that I had no desire to talk further, that if the White House had any intention of playing the game straight and giving us the semblance of a fair trial they would check into the perjury charge of mine against Magruder, and into the existence of the two intercepted calls previously referred to, and hung up.

On Tuesday morning, the next morning, about 7:30 a.m., Caulfield called and asked me again to meet him and I responded not until they had something to talk about on the perjured testimony and the interrupted calls. He said words to the effect "give us a week" and a meeting was subsequently arranged on January 25, when he said he would have something to talk about.

About 10 a.m. on Thursday, January 25, in a meeting lasting until about 12:30 a.m., correction, 12:30 p.m. we drove in his car toward Warrenton, Virginia and returned—that is, we drove there and returned—and a conversation ensued which repeated the offers of executive clemency and financial support while in prison, and rehabilitation later. I refused to discuss it.

He stated that I was "fouling up the game plan". I made a few comments about the "game plan". He said that "they" had found no record of the interception of the two calls I referred to, and said that perhaps it could wait until the appeals.

He asked what my plans were regarding talking publicly, and I said that I planned to do so when I was ready; that I had discussed it with my wife and she said that I should do what I felt—I must and not to worry about the family. I advised Jack that my children were now grown and could understand what I had to do, when the disclosures came out.

He responded by saying that "You know that if the administration gets its backs to the wall, it will have to take steps to defend itself" I took that as a personal threat and I told him in response, that I had had a good life, that my will was made out and that I had thought through the risks and would take them when I was ready.

He said that if I had to go off to jail that the administration would help with the bail premiums. I advised him that it was not a bail premium, but $100,000 straight cash and that that was a problem I would have to worry about, through family and friends. On the night before sentencing, Jack called me and said that the administration would provide the $100,000 in cash if I could tell him how to get it funded through as intermediary. I said that if we ever needed it I would let him know. I never contacted him thereafter; neither have I heard from him.

That completes the statement.

Magruder

The following is a partial transcript of testimony given by Jeb Stuart Magruder before the Ervin Committee on Thursday, June 14, 1973. Magruder was the deputy director of the Committee to Re-elect the President. In this excerpt, Magruder admits his complicity in almost every aspect of the Watergate break-in and cover-up, the first high Nixon official to commit such an act of contrition.

Mr. Dash: Could you give us some of the context of the earlier plans on the intelligence operations that now Mr. Liddy was going to fill?

Magruder: In September of 1971 we had a luncheon meeting, John Dean called and asked me to join him and Jack Caulfield for lunch. At that time they had envisioned a private investigating firm being formed by Mr. Caulfield, they called the project Sandwedge and the idea would be Mr. Caulfield would leave the White House for this private investigating firm and this firm would then be available for the committees to re-elect the President.

In November of 1971, it was indicated to me that the project was not going to get off the ground and subsequently G. Gordon Liddy came into the picture after that.

Q. When Mr. Liddy did come into the picture were you aware of his prior relationships in the White House with the so-called plumbers group?

A. No, I was not.

Q. Who, finally approved Mr. Liddy's position at the committee?

A. Mr. Mitchell.

Q. Did there come a time when Mr. Liddy did present his plan to the Attorney General, Mr. Mitchell?

A. The first meeting was February 27. I am sorry, January 27, 1971. And we had a meeting in Mr. Mitchell's office.

Q. Who attended that meeting in Mr. Mitchell's office on January 27?
A. Mr. Mitchell, Mr. Dean, Mr. Liddy and myself.
Q. Could you describe in detail what occurred on January 27 in Mr. Mitchell's office?
A. Mr. Liddy brought with him a series of charts, they were professionally done charts, and had color, some color, on each of the charts. As I recall, there were approximately six charts, each chart contained a subject matter and was headed by a code word. I cannot recall many of the code words, the one I do recall is Gemstone. I think one was called Target but I cannot specifically recall the other code words. Each chart had a listing of certain types of activities with a budget and as I recall there was one chart that totaled up the activities and the budget totaled to the million figure that he had mentioned previously.
Q. Liddy was presenting this in the form of a show and tell operation?
A. Yes, that is correct.
Q. Could you give us to your best recollection what some of these projects were?
A. They were, of course, the projects, including wiretapping, electronic surveillance, and photography. There were projects relating to the abduction of individuals, particularly members of radical groups that we were concerned about on the convention at San Diego. Mr. Liddy had a plan where the leaders would be abducted and detained in a place like Mexico and that they would then be returned to this country at the end of the convention.

He had another plan which would have used women as agents to work with members of the Democratic National Committee at their convention and here in Washington, and hopefully, through their efforts, they would obtain information from them.
Q. With regard to the use of these women as agents, did this involve the use of a yacht at Miami?
A. He envisioned renting a yacht in Miami and having it set up for sound and photographs.
Q. And what would the women be doing at that time?
A. Well, they would have been, I think you could consider them call girls.
Q. Now, what was the total budget that he presented at this meeting?
A. Approximately a million dollars.
Q. Mr. Magruder, what was Mr. Mitchell's reaction, Mr. Dean's reaction, your own reaction when you heard this presentation?
A. I think all three of us were appalled. The scope and size of the project was something that at least in my mind was not envisioned. I do not think it was in Mr. Mitchell's mind, or Mr. Dean's although I can't comment on their state of mind at that time.

Mr. Mitchell, in an understated way, which was his method of dealing with difficult problems like this, indicated that this was not an acceptable project.
Q. And did Mr. Mitchell give Mr. Liddy any instructions at the end of this meeting?
A. He indicated that he would go back to the drawing board and come up with a more realistic plan.
Q. So it would be true that Liddy, at least, left that meeting without being discouraged from continuing to plan an intelligence operation.
A. I would say he was encouraged, but he was given the right to come up with a more reasonable plan.
Q. Did you have any discussion with Mr. Liddy after the meeting?
A. Yes, he left with John Dean and I on our way back to the committee and indicated his being disturbed because he had assumed that everyone would have accepted this project at face value. We indicated that certain of these things were inappropriate and that he would have to redo them and come back at a later date.
Q. Did you make any report of the meeting to anyone after the meeting?
A. Yes, I made a report to Mr. Strachan at the White House.
Q. Was this telephone conversation with Mr. Strachan in which you did report the general nature of the discussion consistent with your general reporting to Mr. Strachan as you did from time to time, matters that should get to the White House staff?
A. Yes, everything that I did at the committee everything that we did was staffed to Mr. Strachan so that he could alert other officials at the White House as to our activities.
Q. Was there a second meeting on the Liddy Plan, Mr. Magruder?
A. Yes, the following week in February, February 4th, as I recall, we met at 11 A.M. in the morning.
Q. How did that meeting come about, who attended?
A. Mr. Liddy indicated that he was ready to discuss a reduced pro-

posal. I alerted Mr. Dean and he set up an appointment with Mr. Mitchell and we reviewed a reduced proposal.
Q. Where was this meeting?
A. At the Justice Department. . . .

We discussed the potential target of the Democratic National Committee headquarters, primarily because of information we had relating to Mr. O'Brien that we felt would be possibly damaging to the Democratic National Committee. We discussed the possibility of using electronic surveillance at the Fontainebleu Hotel, which was going to be the Democratic National Committee headquarters, and we discussed the potential of using the same method at the Presidential headquarters.

Also, at that meeting, Mr. Mitchell brought up that he had information—it was either Mr. Mitchell or Mr. Dean—that they had information relating to Senator Muskie that was in Mr. Greenspun's office in Las Vegas. He was a publisher of the newspaper in Las Vegas.

Mr. Liddy was asked to review the situation in Las Vegas to see if there would be potential for any entry into Mr. Greenspun's.
Q. What was the general kind of information that you would be looking for in these break-ins or electronic surveillance?
A. Well, I think at that time, we were particularly concerned about the ITT situation. Mr. O'Brien has been a very effective spokesman against our position on the ITT case and I think there was a general concern that is he was allowed to continue as Democratic National Chairman, because he was certainly their most professional political operator, that he could be very difficult in the coming campaign. So we had hoped that information might discredit him.
Q. What was Mr. Mitchell's reaction to this presentation at the second meeting?
A. We agreed that it would not be approved at that time, but we would take it up later; that he just didn't feel comfortable with it even at that level.
Q. But again, would it be true to say that at least Mr. Liddy was encouraged to continue in his planning?
A. Yes, I think that is correct.
Q. Now, after this meeting, Mr. Magruder, did you report to anyone about the meeting?
A. Yes, I sent the documents that Mr. Liddy had given us at the meeting to Mr. Strachan.
Q. And did those documents contain all of what Mr. Liddy had presented at that meeting?
A. They did not contain, as an example, the discussion on targets because that was a discussion and that was not in the documents.
Q. Did you have a telephone conversation with Mr. Strachan concerning that meeting?
A. Yes, I indicated the general context of that meeting.
Q. And did that include Mr. Mitchell's suggestions concerning the Las Vegas mission?
A. I cannot recall specifically that point, but I would assume that I probably discussed the key targets that we had discussed.
Q. And that would include the Democratic National Committee headquarters and Mr. O'Brien?
A. Yes.
Q. Did there come a time after the second meeting that you had some difficulty with Mr. Liddy and Mr. LaRue played some role in that?
A. I met him, ran into him on the third floor of our building, and asked him would he be more cooperative in producing the work that we needed quickly? He indicated some disturbance with me at that time.
Q. What was the difficulty that did occur?
A. Well, I simply put my hand on Mr. Liddy's shoulder and he asked me to remove it and indicated that if I did not, serious consequences could occur.
Q. Was he more specific than serious consequences?
A. Well, he indicated that he would kill me. But I want to make it clear that I did not, I do not regard that and I do not now regard that as a specific threat. It was simply Mr. Liddy's mannerism.
Q. Now, did there come a time when you had a third and final meeting with Mr. Mitchell on the Liddy plan on or about March 30, 1972?
A. Yes. We had, there had been a delay in the decision-making process at the committee because of the ITT hearings. Mr. Mitchell was on vacation at Key Biscayne. I went down to Key Biscayne, Mr. LaRue was there, and we met and went over approximately 30 some decision papers mainly relating to direct mail and advertising, the other parts of the campaign.

The last topic we discussed as the final proposal of Mr. Liddy's which was for approximately $259,000. We discussed it, brought up again the pros and cons, I think I can honestly say that no one was particularly overwhelmed with the project, but I think we felt that the information could be useful and Mr. Mitchell agreed to approve the project and I then notified the parties of Mr. Mitchell's approval.

Q. Now, prior to going down to Key Biscayne you would send over a copy to Mr. Strachan?

A. My formal position with Mr. Mitchell was we would send over key papers before we discussed it with Mr. Mitchell, so if there was any questions in those papers, Mr. Haldeman or Mr. Strachan could get back to us their opinion on a subject.

Q. Now, this quarter million dollar project you say Mr. Mitchell approved in Key Biscayne, what was that project specifically?

A. It was specifically approval for initial entry into the Democratic National Committee Headquarters in Washington, and that at a further date if the funds were available, we would consider entry into the Presidential contenders' headquarters and also potentially at the Fontainebleu Hotel in Miami.

Q. Now, when you say that project was approved included the entry of the Democratic National Committee headquarters and perhaps other entries, did that also include the use of electronic surveillance or bugging?

A. It included electronic surveillance and photography or documents, photographic of documents.

Q. Do you recall Mr. Sloan questioning an initial large sum of money, $83,000 which Mr. Liddy requested after the approval of the plan?

A. Yes.

Q. Could you tell us what happened and how that was resolved?

A. Well, he had called me and said that Mr. Liddy wanted a substantial sum. I indicated that Mr. Liddy did have that approval. Mr. Sloan evidently then went to Mr. Stans. Mr. Stans went to Mr. Mitchell, Mr. Mitchell came back to me and said why did Gordon need this much money and I explained to him this was in effect front end money that he needed for the equipment, and the early costs of getting his kind of an operation together. Mr. Mitchell understood, evidently told Mr. Stans it had been approved and the approval was complete.

Q. Well, do you recall a discussion that you had with Mr. Liddy concerning an effort to enter the McGovern headquarters?

A. Yes. After the first entry of the D.N.C. headquarters, Mr. Strachan and I were in my office and Mr. Liddy came in and indicated that he had had trouble the night before, that they tried to do a survey of the McGovern headquarters and Mr. Liddy came in and indicated that to assist this he had shot a light out. At that time both Mr. Strachan and I became very concerned because we understood from Mr. Liddy that he would not participate himself nor would anyone participate in his activities that could be in any way connected with our committee.

Q. Now, there was this entry into the Democratic National Committee headquarters, which occurred May 27, Memorial Day weekend of 1972, did Mr. Liddy report that to you?

A. Yes. He simply indicated that he had made a successful entry and had placed wiretapping equipment in the Democratic National Committee.

Q. Who participated with you without forcing you in the working up of the fabricated story?

A. Well, there were a series of meetings. They were mainly held in Mr. Mitchell's office. The main participants typically were Mr. Mitchell, Mr. LaRue, Mr. Mardian, Mr. Dean. Much of the meetings would be on subjects that were perfectly I think, acceptable to discuss.

You know it is very hard for me to pinpoint exactly when and how we came up with the cover-up story, but it became apparent when we found out the sums were in the $200,000 range that we had to come up with a very good story to justify why Mr. Liddy would have spent that amount of money on legal activities.

Q. Could you tell us why the story required that the break-in involvement be cut off at Mr. Liddy and not at you?

A. Well, there was some discussion about me and I volunteered at one point that maybe I was the guy who ought to take the heat, because it was going to get to me, and we knew that. And I think it was, there were some takers on that, but basically, the decision was that because I was in a position where they knew that I had no authority to either authorize funds or make policy in that committee, that if it got to me, it would go higher, whereas Mr. Liddy, because of his past background it was felt that would be believable that Mr. Liddy was truly the one who did originate it.

Q. When you testified to the grand jury that time, did you testify

to the false story?

A. Yes, I did.

Q. What role did Mr. Dean play in preparing you for your grand jury appearance?

A. I was briefed by our lawyers and Mr. Mardian. Also, I was interrogated for approximately two hours by Mr. Dean and approximately a half hour in a general way Mr. Mitchell.

A. They made assurances about income and being taken care of from the standpoint of my family and a job afterwards and also that there would be good opportunity for executive clemency. But having worked at the White House and being aware of our structure there, I did not take that as meaning that had a direct relationship to the President at all.

In fact, the use of his name was very common in many cases where it was inappropriate; in other words, where he had not had any dealings in the matter. So, I knew that this did not necessarily mean it came from the President or anyone else other than Mr. Dean or Mr. Mitchell.

Q. Did you have a meeting with Mr. Haldeman in January, 1973?

A. Yes, I did.

Q. Could you briefly tell us what the nature of that meeting was and what was discussed?

A. It was to discuss future employment regarding myself and Mr. Porter's employment. Also, I thought I had better see Mr. Haldeman and tell him what had actually happened. I thought probably that this maybe was becoming scapegoat time and maybe I was going to be the scapegoat, and so I went to Mr. Haldeman and I said I just want you to know that this whole Watergate situation and the other activities was a concerted effort by a number of people, and so I went through a literally monologue on what had occurred. That was my first discussion with Mr. Haldeman where I laid out the true facts.

Q. Do you know what day or date approximately in January this occurred?

A. It would have been before the Inaugural.

Sen. Baker: On January 27, February 4, and March 30, you met to discuss the Liddy plan?

A. Yes Sir.

Q. It is important for us to know, Mr. Magruder, what took place at that meeting. It is important for me to know exactly how the assent was given.

A. Well, as I recall, it was the last subject we brought up at our meeting. It had the figures and the amounts and it was quite obvious as to what they were for. There would be dollars next to equipment, as an example, and so on, and we discussed the pros and cons, Mr. LaRue and Mr. Mitchell and I, not any great feeling of acceptance to this plan, with the exception that supposedly these individuals were professional, the information could be valuable. Mr. Mitchell simply signed off on it in the sense of saying "Okay, let's give him a quarter of a million dollars and let's see what he can come up with."

Q. You say Mr. Mitchell signed off on it. Do you mean physically initialed it or signed it?

A. No sir, I mean he said, we will give Mr. Liddy the $250,000.

Q. And he identified the targets? Did that include the Democratic National Committee headquarters at the Watergate?

A. Yes, sir.

Q. Was there any question in your mind that the plan was agreed to by Mr. Mitchell?

A. No, sir, there was no doubt. But it was a reluctant decision. I think that it is important to note. It was not one that anyone was overwhelmed with at all. But it was made and he did make it.

Sen. Inouye: We have received testimony that Mr. Strachan was a very important conduit, that he was the liaison between the committee and the White House; that on the other end was Mr. Haldeman.

A. Yes, sir.

Q. Did you receive any indication that Mr. Strachan did in fact convey those memos and messages that you have been sending to him?

A. Well, Mr. Strachan had a method of working with Mr. Haldeman. And that was he would do a summary sheet capsulizing activities of the campaign. It was a straightforward memo that condensed much of the information that he would give Mr. Strachan. That was his typical method of dealing, I think, with Mr. Haldeman.

Q. Did you receive any feedback from Mr. Haldeman indicating that he had in fact received these memos?

A. No, sir, I did not know of any involvement by Mr. Kleindienst.

Q. Mr. Gray?

A. No sir.

Q. Now, when you discussed this matter in January, I presume that you told Mr. Haldeman everything you knew about the cover-up?

A. I think my main purpose Senator, was to just indicate that there were a number of people involved and that in case people's memory was growing short I hoped he realized it was not myself or any other single individual who was involved in this cover-up.

Q. This was in January?

A. Yes, sir.

Q. Were you surprised when the President announced that he had decided to begin an investigation on March 21?

A. Was I surprised?

Q. Yes.

A. Well, knowing full well of Mr. Dean's role I could well imagine that the President possibly had been informed incorrectly, since he was investigating his own problem. I could see where he could very easily have misled individuals at the White House to protect himself.

Q. But you had notified Mr. Haldeman in January of the correct activities.

A. Yes, sir.

Q. Mr. Magruder, in your testimony this morning, you have indicated that there were several who knew about the cover-up. I will list a few names. Mr. Dean knew about the cover-up?

A. Yes, yes sir.

Q. Mr. Mitchell knew about the cover-up?

A. Yes sir.

Q. Mr. Haldeman knew about the cover-up?

A. Directly from my knowledge only in January. I did not know directly before.

Q. Mr. Ehrlichman knew about the cover-up?

A. I did not ever know that Mr. Ehrlichman knew about the cover-up.

Q. Mr. Kalmbach?

A. I only knew in Mr. Kalmbach's case he was funding the cover-up.

Q. Mr. Mardian?

A. Yes, sir.

Q. Mr. Kleindienst?

A. No, sir, I had no direct knowledge of Mr. Gray's involvement.

Q. Mr. Strachan?

A. He was aware of the cover-up.

Q. Mr. LaRue?

A. Yes, he was aware.

Q. Mr. Egil Krogh?

A. I cannot specifically recall any direct knowledge that I would have known that he knew about the cover-up.

Q. Mr. Colson?

A. I have no direct knowledge that Mr. Colson knew about the cover-up.

Q. Mr. Stans?

A. Only the discussion I had in June with Mr. Stans which would indicate some knowledge after that point to some extent.

Q. Mr. Sloan?

A. Yes, I am sure he knew about the cover-up.

Q. Finally, the President?

A. To my knowledge no, no direct knowledge.

Dean

The following are excerpts from the testimony of John Dean III before the Ervin Committee. The statement was read by Dean on June 25 and 26, 1973.

John Dean:

To one who was in the White House and became somewhat familiar with its interworkings, the Watergate matter was an inevitable outgrowth of a climate of excessive concern over the political impact of demonstrators, excessive concern over leaks, an insatiable appetite for political intelligence, all coupled with a do-it-yourself White House staff, regardless of the law. However, the fact that many of the elements of this climate culminated with the creation of a covert intelligence operation as part of the President's re-election committee was not by conscious design, rather an accident of fate.

It was not until I joined the White House staff in July of 1970 that I fully realized the strong feelings that the President and his staff

had toward antiwar demonstrators—and demonstrators in general.

I also recall that the information regarding demonstrators—or rather lack of information showing connections between the demonstration leaders and foreign governments or major political figures—was often reported to a disbelieving and complaining White House staff that felt the entire system for gathering such intelligence was worthless. I was hearing complaints from the President personally as late as March 12th of this year.

I was made aware of the President's strong feelings about even the smallest of demonstrations during the late winter of 1971, when the President happened to look out the windows of the residence of the White House and saw a lone man with a large 10-foot sign stretched out in front of Lafayette Park.

I ran into Mr. Dwight Chapin who said that he was going to get some "thugs" to remove that man from Lafayette Park. He said it would take him a few hours to get them, but they could do the job. I told him I didn't believe that was necessary. I then called the Secret Service and within 30 minutes the man had been convinced that he should move to the back-side of Lafayette Park. There the sign was out of sight from the White House. I told Mr. Chapin he could call off the troops.

I also recall that the first time I ever traveled with the President was on his trip in 1971 to the Football Hall of Fame.

When the President arrived at the motel where he was spending the night in Akron, across the street were chanting, Vietcong-flag-waving demonstrators. The President told the Secret Service agent beside him, in some rather blunt synonyms, to get the demonstrators out of there. The word was passed, but the demonstrators couldn't be moved.

It was after observing that incident a major part of any Presidential trip advance operation was insuring that demonstrators were unseen and unheard by the President.

In early February of 1972, I learned that any means—legal or illegal—were authorized by Mr. Haldeman to deal with demonstrators when the President was traveling or appearing some place. I would like to add that when I learned of the illegal means that were being employed, I advised that such tactics not be employed in the future and if demonstrations occurred—they occurred.

There was a continuing dissatisfaction with the available intelligence reports. The President himself discussed this with me in early March of this year, as a part of the planned counter-offensive for dealing with the Senate Watergate investigation. The President wanted to show that his opponents had employed demonstrators against him during his re-election campaign.

We never found a scintilla of viable evidence indicating that these demonstrators were part of a master plan; nor that they were funded by the Democratic political funds; nor that they had any direct connection with the McGovern campaign. This was explained to Mr. Haldeman, but the President believed that the opposite was, in fact, true.

It was late June or early July that Jack Caulfield came to me to tell me that Colson had called him in, at Ehrlichman's direction, and instructed him to burglarize the Brookings Institute in an effort to determine if they had certain leaked documents. What prompted Mr. Caufield to come to me was that he thought the matter was most unwise and that his instructions from Colson were insane.

Colson had instructed him to plant a fire bomb in the building and retrieve the documents during the commotion that would ensure. Mr. Caulfield said Colson's entire argument for burglarizing the Brookings was based on a publication he had obtained indicating that the Brookings was planning for the fall (1971) a study of Vietnam based on documents of a current nature, and a former consultant to the N.S.C. worked there.

I arranged to see Ehrlichman and told him that the burglary of Brookings was insane and probably impossible. He said O.K. and he called Mr. Colson to call it off.

It was not until almost a year or more later that Mr. Mardian told me that he had gone to see the President to get instructions regarding the disposition of wiretap logs that related to newsmen and White House staffers who were suspected of leaking. These logs had been in possession of Mr. William Sullivan, an assistant director of the F.B.I.

About Feb. 22d or 23d of this year, *Time* magazine notified the White House it was going to print a story that the White House had undertaken wiretaps of newsmen and White House staff and requested a response.

The White House press office notified me of this inquiry.

I then called Mr. Ehrlichman and told him about the forthcoming story in *Time* magazine. I asked him how Mr. Ziegler should handle it. He said Mr. Ziegler should flatly deny it—period.

Turning now to the so-called "plumbers" unit that was created to deal with leaks.

Shortly after Krogh told me about his unit, he told me that they were operating out of a super secured location in the basement of the Executive Office Building. He invited me down to see the unit, which I did and he showed me the sensor security system and scrambler phone.

As I have indicated, the June, 1971, publication of the Pentagon papers caused general consternation at the White House over the leak problem. As a part of that effort, Mr. Haldeman instructed Mr. Fred Malek, Mr. Larry Higby, Mr. Gordon Strachan and myself to develop follow-up strategy for dealing with leaks. Malek was to take charge and Mr. Haldeman was to be brought in as the "lord high executioner" when a leak was uncovered. This project was to complement and not compete with the plumbers. To the best of my knowledge this project never uncovered the source of a single leak.

The pre re-election White House thrived on political gossip and political intelligence. I knew of the type of information they sought even before I joined the White House staff. During the summer of 1969, while I was working at the Justice Department, the then Deputy Attorney General, Richard Kleindienst, called me into his office and told me that the White House wanted some very important information. Mr. Kleindienst instructed me to call Mr. Deloach, then deputy director of the F.B.I., and obtain from him information regarding the foreign travels of Mary Jo Kopechne.

It was not until I joined the White House staff that Caulfield was assigned to develop political intelligence on Senator Edward Kennedy. Mr. Caulfield told me that within some six hours of the accident at Chappaquiddick on July 18, 1969, he had a friend on the scene conducting a private investigation. Caulfield also informed me that his instructions were to continue surveillance of Senator Kennedy.

In the fall of 1971 I received a call from Larry Higby, who told me that Haldeman wanted 24 hour surveillance of Senator Kennedy.

Caulfield told me that he thought that this was most unwise because it could uncover his activities in that Senator Kennedy was bound to realize he was under surveillance and it could easily be misinterpreted as someone who was planning an attack on his life, and the police or the F.B.I. might be called in to investigate. I agreed fully with Caulfield. After some initial resistance, I convinced Higby that it was a bad idea and the day-in, day-out, surveillance concept was called off. Instead, Caulfield was to keep a general overview of Senator Kennedy's activities and pursue specific investigations of activities that might be of interest.

Political intelligence often came from unexpected sources. For example, during the spring of 1972, a top man at the Secrete Service brought me information regarding Senator McGovern. I asked Mr. Colson if he were interested. He was very interested and had the information published.

The next time I recall meeting with Mr. Liddy was at a meeting in Mitchell's office on Jan. 27, 1972. Liddy was going to present his intelligence plan. I met Magruder and Liddy at Mitchell's office. Liddy had a series of charts or diagrams which he placed on an easel and the presentation by Liddy began.

I did not fully understand everything Mr. Liddy was recommending at the time because some of the concepts were mindboggling.

Plans called for mugging squads, kidnapping teams, prostitutes to compromise the opposition, and electronic surveillance. He explained that the mugging squad could, for example, rough up demonstrators that were causing problems. The kidnapping teams could remove demonstration leaders and take them below the Mexican border.

The prostitutes could be used at the Democratic convention to get information as well as compromise the person involved. I recall Liddy saying that the girls would be high class and the best in the business. When discussing the electronic surveillance he said that he had consulted with one of the best authorities in the country and his plan envisioned far more than bugging and tapping phones. He said that under his plan, communication between ground facilities and aircraft could also be intercepted.

I recall Mitchell's reaction to the "Mission Impossible" plan. When the presentation was completed, he took a few long puffs on his pipe and told Liddy that the plan he had developed was not quite what he had in mind and the cost was out of the question.

He suggested he go back and revise his plan, keeping in mind that he was not interested in the demonstration problem.

At that point I thought the plan was dead, because I doubted if Mitchell would reconsider the matter.

I returned from a four-day trip to the Far East on the morning of June 18th. I called my assistant, Fred Fielding, it was at this time that I first learned from Mr. Fielding of the break-in at the D.N.C. headquarters. Mr. Fielding told me that he thought I should return home immediately as there might be a problem.

Accordingly, I flew back to Washington and arrived on Sunday evening. I had a brief conversation with Mr. Fielding and he informed me that he had learned from Jack Caulfield that Mr. McCord from the re-election committee was among those arrested in the D.N.C. on Saturday and also that one of the Cubans arrested had a check that was made out by Howard Hunt to some country club. I recall that my immediate reaction was that Chuck Colson was probably involved.

On Monday morning, June 19th, I received a call from Jack Caulfield who repeated what Mr. Fielding had told me on Sunday evening. Mr. Caulfield informed me that he had received the information from Mr. Boggs of the Secret Service. I next received a call from Magruder and I told Magruder that I had just arrived back in the country and did not know any of the facts surrounding the incident, but I would look into it.

I next received a call from Ehrlichman, who instructed me to find out what I could and report back. I recall that Ehrlichman told me to find out what Colson's involvement was in the matter and he also suggested I speak with Mr. Kleindienst to see what the Justice Department knew about it.

I next received a call from Gordon Strachan who said he wanted to meet with me.

I next talked with Chuck Colson on the phone. I asked him what he knew about the incident and he vehemently proposed that he knew nothing and had no involvement in the matter whatsoever.

I recall asking Colson if Hunt still worked for him and again he became very defensive and stated that he was merely on his payroll because Ehrlichman had so requested.

Colson also expressed concern over the contents of Hunt's safe. Over the weekend of June 17-18th, Hunt had told Colson to get the materials out of his—Hunt's—office safe.

I next contacted Liddy and asked to meet with him.

Mr. Liddy told me that the men who had been arrested in the D.N.C. were his men and he expressed concern about them. I asked him why he had men in the D.N.C. and he told me that Magruder had pushed him into doing it.

Liddy was very apologetic for the fact that they had been caught and that Mr. McCord was involved. He told me that he had used Mr. McCord only because Magruder had cut his budget so badly.

He also told me that he was a soldier and would never talk. He said that if anyone wished to shoot him on the street, he was ready. As we parted I said I would be unable to discuss this with him further. He said he understood.

After returning to my office Gordon Strachan told me that he had been instructed by Haldeman to go through all of Mr. Haldeman's files over the week-end and remove and destroy damaging materials. He told me that this material included such matters as memoranda from the re-election committee, documents relating to wiretap information from the D.N.C., notes of meetings with Haldeman, and a document which reflected that Haldeman had instructed Magruder to transfer his intelligence gathering from Senator Muskie to Senator McGovern. Strachan told me his files were completely clean.

That afternoon, Ehrlichman instructed me to call Liddy to have him tell Hunt to get out of the country. I did this without even thinking. Shortly after I made the call, however, I realized that no one in the White House should give such an instruction and raised the matter. Colson chimed in that he also thought it unwise and Ehrlichman agreed. I immediately called Liddy again to retract the request and he informed me that he had already passed the message and it might be too late to retract.

Colson raised the matter of Hunt's safe. Colson, without getting specific, said it was imperative that someone get the contents of Hunt's safe. Colson suggested, and Ehrlichman concurred, that I take custody of the contents of the safe.

It was on June 20th or 21st that Strachan and Mr. Richard Howard came to my office. Strachan informed me that Haldeman had authorized an expenditure by Colson of some funds, but the entire amount had not been expended and he was turning over the remainder to me to hold. I placed the cash, $15,200, in my safe. I informed Mr. Fielding of my office of the fact that the cash was in my safe and where it had come from.

The cash remained in my safe untouched until Oct. 12th, 1972 when I removed a packet of bills amounting to $4,850 and placed my personal check for that amount with the remaining cash. I removed the $4,850 after I had failed to make arrangements to pay for the anticipated expenses of my wedding, and honeymoon.

At no time when I was making personal use of part of these funds did I plan—or believe—that I would not have to account for the entire amount at some point in time.

Returning now to the contents of Mr. Hunt's safe, it was mid-morning on Tuesday, June 20th, when the G.S.A. men brought several cartons to my office, which contained the contents of Hunt's safe.

During the afternoon, Fielding and I began going through the cartons of Hunt's materials, [including a] briefcase, which contained electronic equipment.

Among the papers were numerous memoranda to Chuck Colson regarding Hunt's assessment of the plumbers unit, a number of materials relating to Mr. Daniel Ellsberg, a bogus cable, that is other cables spliced together into one cable, regarding the involvement of persons in the Kennedy Administration in the fall of the Diem regime in Vietnam, a memorandum regarding some discussion about the bogus cable with Colson and William Lambert, some materials relating to an investigation Hunt had conducted for Colson at Chappaquiddick, some materials relating to the Pentagon papers.

He told me to shred the documents and "deep six" the briefcase. I asked him what he meant by "deep six." He leaned back in his chair and said: "You drive across the river on your way home at night—don't you? I said yes. He said, "Well, when you cross over the bridge on your way home just toss the briefcase into the river."

After leaving Ehrlichman's office I thought about what he had told me to do and was very troubled. I raised it with Fielding and he shared my feelings that this would be an incredible action—to destroy potential evidence. I think Mr. Fielding appreciated my quandry—when Ehrlichman said something, he expected it to be done.

In addition to the conversations that I was having with Gray regarding the status of the investigation, Mitchell, Ehrlichman and Haldeman thought that I should see the F.B.I. reports.

In early July I raised with him [Gray] my receiving some of the raw F.B.I. data regarding the investigation. Gray said that he would have to check but wanted an assurance from me that this information was being reported to the President and that was the principal purpose of the request. I assured him that it was being reported to the President. Even though I was not directly reporting to the President at that time, I was aware of the fact that Ehrlichman or Haldeman had daily discussions with the President, and I felt certain, because Haldeman often made notes, about the information I was bringing to their attention, that this information was being given to the President.

I believe it was after the 21st of July when I received a summary report that had been prepared on the investigation to that stage. Mardian insisted that he be permitted to see the F.B.I. reports.

Mr. Mardian became very excited because of the scope of the investigation that Gray was conducting and the tone of the cables he was sending out of headquarters. Mardian clearly thought that Gray was being too vigorous in his investigation of the case and was quite critical of Gray's handling of the entire matter. He demanded that I tell Gray to slow down, but I never did so.

It was during the meeting in Mitchell's office on June 23d or 24th that Mardian first raised the proposition that the C.I.A. could take care of this entire matter if they wished. Mitchell suggested I explore with Ehrlichman and Haldeman having the White House contact the C.I.A. for assistance.

Ehrlichman thought it was a good idea. He told me to call General Walters because he was a good friend of the White House and the White House had put him in the deputy director position so they could have some influence over the agency.

When General Walters came to my office I asked him if there was any possible way that C.I.A. could be of assistance in providing support for the individuals involved. General Walters told me that while it could, of course, be done, he told me that he knew the director's feelings about such a matter and the director would only do it on a direct order from the President. He then went on to say that to do anything to compound the situation would be most unwise and that to involve the C.I.A. would only compound the problem because it would require that the President become directly involved.

When I reported this to Ehrlichman, he very cynically said that General Walters seems to have forgotten how he got where he is today.

It was while I was in San Clemente, at the end of August, that the President announced at a press conference the so called "Dean Report" which cleared everybody presently employed at the White House or in the Administration from any complicity in the Watergate matter. This statement was made on Aug. 29th, 1972.

I had no advance knowledge that the President was going to indicate that I had investigated the matter and found no complicity on the part of anybody at the White House or anyone presently employed in the Administration. I first learned of the matter when I heard it on a television news broadcast.

Had I been consulted in advance by the President, I would have strongly opposed the issuing of such a statement. First, I was aware that Gordon Strachan had close, daily, liaison with Magruder and had carried information relating to wiretapped conversations into the White House and later destroyed incriminating documents at Haldeman's direction.

Secondly, I had never been able to determine whether Haldeman had advance knowledge or not, and in fact, had never asked him because I didn't feel I could.

Thirdly, I had always suspected, but never been able to completely substantiate my suspicion, that Colson was far more knowledgeable than he protested.

I don't know if the President's statement was meant to be a very literal play on carefully chosen words or whether he intended to give it the broad-brush interpretation that it later received.

The issuing of the so-called "Dean Report" was the first time I began to think about the fact that I might be being set-up in case the whole thing crumbled at a later time.

On or about Sept. 9th or 10th, I received a Presidential request from both Haldeman and Colson. The President felt that the best defense to the actions being pursued by the Democrats, and the charges and implications that were stemming from the lawsuits being filed by the Democrats, was our own counteroffensive with our own series of lawsuits against the Democrats. Colson called me and reported that he had just come from the President's office and that the President wanted action on this as quickly as humanly possible. I informed Mr. Colson that I was working on it but that I wasn't going to suggest filing any lawsuit or taking any action that was not well founded

It was also about this time, later July-early September, that I learned during a meeting in Mitchell's office that Mr. Roemer McPhee was having private discussions with Judge Richey regarding the civil suit filed by the Democrats. I was told by Parkinson, and later McPhee, that Judge Richey was going to be helpful whenever he could. I subsequently talked with Mr. McPhee about this, as late as March 2d of this year, when he told me he was going to visit the judge's rose garden over the weekend to discuss an aspect of the case.

On Sept. 15th the Justice Department announced the handing down of the seven indictments by the Federal grand jury. Late that afternoon I received a call requesting me to come to the President's Oval Office.

The President told me that Bob [Haldeman] had kept him posted on my handling of the Watergate case, told me I had done a good job and he appreciated how difficult a task it had been and the President was pleased that the case had stopped with Liddy. I told him that I thought that there was a long way to go before this matter would end and that I certainly could make no assurances that the day would not come when the matter would start to unravel.

Early in our conversation the President said to me that former F.B.I. director Hoover had told him shortly after he had assumed office in 1969 that his campaign had been bugged in 1968. The President said that at some point we should get the facts out on this and use this to counter the problems that we were encountering.

The President asked me when the criminal case would come to trial and would it start before the election. I told the President that I did not know. I said that the Justice Department had held off as long as possible the return of the indictments, but much would depend on which judge got the case. The President said that he certainly hoped that the case would not come to trial before the election.

The President then asked me about the civil cases that had been filed by the Democratic National Committee and Common Cause. I then told the President that the lawyers at the re-election committee were very hopeful of slowing down the civil suit filed by the Democratic National Committee because they had been making ex parte contacts with the judge handling the case and the judge was very understanding and trying to accommodate their problems. The President was pleased to hear this and responded to the effect that "well that's helpful."

The conversation then moved to the press coverage of the Watergate incident and how the press was really trying to make this into a major campaign issue. At one point in this conversation I recall the President telling me to keep a good list of the press people giving us trouble, because we will make life difficult for them after the election.

The conversation then turned to the use of the Internal Revenue Service to attack our enemies. I recall telling the President that we had not made much use of this because the White House didn't have the clout to have it done, that the Internal Revenue Service was a rather Democratically oriented bureaucracy and it would be very dangerous to try any such activities. The President seemed somewhat annoyed and said that the Democratic administrations had used this tool well and after the election we would get people in these agencies who would be responsive to the White House requirements.

While the Segretti matter was not directly related to the Water gate, the cover-up of the facts surrounding Mr. Segretti's activities was consistent with other parts of the general White House cover-up which followed the Watergate incident.

I first heard of Mr. Segretti when Gordon Strachan called me in late June and told me that the F.B.I. had called a friend of his, by the name of Donald Segretti, and requested to interview him. Strachan gave me a very general description of Segretti's activities and said that he was a "dirty tricks" type operator who was being paid by Mr. Kalmbach. He also informed me that Mr. Chapin had been involved in hiring Segretti.

Several days after Segretti's F.B.I. interview, he called me and said he told the f.B.I. everything he knew about Mr. Hunt and the fact that he had no knowledge of the Watergate incident and that the agents had not pressed him in a manner that required him to reveal the names of Strachan, Chapin, and Kalmbach.

I received a call from Mr. Chapin who indicated that Segretti was very concerned about the fact that he was being called before a Federal grand jury in Washington investigating the Watergate. And that he was concerned again that he might have to reveal the names of Strachan, Chapin, and Kalmbach.

After my conversation with Chapin, I called Mr. Petersen at the Department of Justice and explained the problem. I told Pe-

tersen that to the best of my knowledge Segretti had no involvement in the Watergate incident but he had had dealing with Hunt in connection with some campaign actitivies he had been performing for the White House. I also informed him that he was being paid by the President's personal attorney, Mr. Kalmbach and that he had been recruited by Chapin and Strachan. I said that these facts, if revealed, would be obviously quite embarrasing and could cause political problems during the waning weeks of the election. Mr. Petersen said that he understood the problem.

I later learned from Segretti that the names had come out during the grand jury appearance and I had a discussion later with Petersen also on the subject in which he told me that Mr. Silbert had tried to avoid getting into this area and in fact did not ask him the question which resulted in his giving the names, rather that a grand juror had asked the question despite the fact that the prosecutors had tried to gloss over it.

I had by this time learned the full story, that in fact Haldeman, in a meeting with Kalmbach, had approved Segretti's activities and authorized Kalmbach to make the payments to Segretti. In discussing this with Chapin and Strachan before their appearance, they both had great concern about revealing Haldeman's involvement. In fact, I recall that Strachan came into my office and said that he would, if necessary, perjure himself to prevent involving Haldeman in this matter.

As the press accounts of Segretti's activities lingered on after the election as well as the continuing Watergate stories, there was serious discussion about putting the facts out. In late November, I recall a conversation with Haldeman in his office. I told him that I thought the then pending trial would be put back into a grand jury and it was very likely that any reconvened grand jury would get into questions of obstruction of justice which would lead right to us.

Haldeman said that the President wished, now that the election was over, to get rid of the Watergate and related matters by laying them open but based on what I had just told him he said it doesn't seem to be a very viable option.

It was the first week of December that Mitchell called me and said that we would have to use some of the $350,000 fund to take care of the demands that were being made by Hunt and the others for money. He indicated that the money that was taken out would be returned in order that the fund could be made whole again. He asked me to get Haldeman's approval.

I called Haldeman and described the situation in full to him and that I had told Mitchell that I was very reluctant to see White House money used. I told Haldeman that I didn't think this was a good idea to further involve the White House in raising money for these men but I frankly had no answer. Haldeman said he did not like it either, but since we had the assurance that the money would be returned, I should inform Strachan that he could make the delivery of the money to the committee.

I do not recall how much money was delivered by Strachan but I believe it was either $40,000 or $70,000.

It was sometime shortly before the trial when the demands reached the crescendo point once again. O'Brien and LaRue came to my office and told me the seriousness of the problem. Subsequently, Mitchell called me and told me that once again I should ask Haldeman to make available the necessary funds. I told him I thought it was time to get the entire money out of the White House rather than continue as we were with, every few weeks, further bites being taken out of the apple.

After we discussed the matter Haldeman said send the entire damn bundle to them but make sure that we get a receipt for $350,000. After receiving my instructions from Haldeman I called Strachan and told him that he was to deliver the remainder of the money to LaRue but that he was to make certain that he got a receipt for $350,000. Strachan later told me that LaRue refused to give him a receipt.

I would now like to turn to my direct dealings with the President which began in late February of 1973 with regard to the Watergate and related matters. I feel I can best set forth what transpired at these meetings by discussing what occurred at each meeting. Meeting on Feb. 27th:

This was the first meeting I had had with the President since my Sept. 15, 1972 meeting which related to the Watergate. It was at this meeting that the President directed that I report directly to him regarding all Watergate matters. He told me that this matter was taking too much time from Haldeman's and Ehrlichman's normal duties and he also told me that they were principals in the matter, and I, therefore, could be more objective than they.

The President then told me of his meeting with Senator

Baker and the Attorney General. He told me that Senator Baker had requested that the Attorney General be his contact point and that I should keep in contact with the Attorney General to make sure that the Attorney General and Senator Baker were working together.

The President recounted that he had told Senator Baker that he would not permit White House staff to appear before the Select Committee, rather he would only permit the taking of written interrogatories. He told me he would never let Haldeman and Ehrlichman go to the Hill. He also told me that Senator Gurney would be very friendly to the White House and that it would not be necessary to contact him because the President said Senator Gurney would know what to do on his own.

I had received word before I arrived at my office that the President wanted to see me. He asked me if I had talked to the Attorney General regarding Senator Baker. I told him that the Attorney General was seeking to meet with both Senator Ervin and Senator Baker, but that a meeting date had not yet been firmed up.

He said that he had read in the morning paper about the Vesco case and asked me what part if any his brother Ed had had in the matter. I told him what I knew of his brother's involvement, which was that he was an innocent agent in the contribution transaction. We then discussed the leak to *Time* magazine of the fact that the White House had placed wiretaps on newsmen and White House staff people. The President asked me if I knew how this had leaked. I told him that I did not. He asked me who knew about it. I told him that Mr. Sullivan, Mr. Mark Felt, and Mr. Mardian were aware of it.

Before departing his office, he again raised the matter that I should report to him directly and not through Haldeman and Ehrlichman. I told him that I thought he should know that I was also involved in the post June 17th activities regarding Watergate. I briefly described to him why I thought I had legal problems, in that I had been a conduit for many of the decisions that were made and therefore could be involved in an obstruction of justice. He would not accept my analysis and did not want me to get into it in any detail other than what I had just related. He reassured me not to worry, that I had no legal problems. (I raised this on another occasion with the President, when Dick Moore was present.)

The first meeting on this date and the afternoon meeting which occurred on March 1st related to preparing the President for his forthcoming press conference. The President asked me a number of questions about the Gray nomination hearings and facts that had come out during these hearings.

In particular I can recall him stating that there should be no problem with the fact that I had received the F.B.I. reports. He said that I was conducting an investigation for him and that it would be perfectly proper for the Counsel to the President to have looked at these reports. I did not tell the President that I had not conducted an investigation for him because I assumed he was well aware of this fact and that the so-called Dean investigation was a public relations matter, and that frequently the President made reference in press conferences to things that never had, in fact occurred. I was also aware that often in answering Watergate questions that he had made reference to my report and I did not feel that I could tell the President that he could not use my name. There had been considerable adverse publicity stemming from the Gray hearings and the fact that Gray was turning over F.B.I. information to the Senate Judiciary Committee.

He also told me the F.B.I. Watergate materials should not be turned over by Gray. I informed him that I had a meeting several days prior with Mr. Sullivan who had been at the F.B.I. for many years and Sullivan had alluded to the fact that the F.B.I. had been used for political purposes by past Administrations. I cited a few examples that Mr. Sullivan had given me. The President told me to get this information from Sullivan. He also told me that I should gather any material I could gather regarding the uses and abuses of the F.B.I. by past Administrations so that we could show that we had not abused the F.B.I. for political purposes. The President told me that he was convinced that he had been wiretapped in 1968 and the fact that de Loach had not been forthcoming indicated to the President that de Loach was probably lying. He told me that I should call Don Kendall, de Loach's employer and tell him that de Loach had better start telling the truth because "the boys are coming out of the woodwork." He said this ploy may smoke de Loach out.

He also asked me who else might know about the bugging of his 1968 campaign, and I suggested that Mr. Tolson, Hoover's for-

mer assistant might have some knowledge of it. He told me that he probably ought to call Mr. Tolson and wish him happy birthday or good health and possibly get some information from him when he talked to him.

This was a rather lengthy meeting, the bulk of which was taken up by a discussion about the Gray hearings and the fact that the Senate Judiciary Committee had voted to invite me to appear in connection with Gray's nomination. It was at this time we discussed the potential of litigating the matter of executive privilege and thereby preventing anybody from going before any Senate committee until that matter was resolved. The President liked the idea very much, particularly when I mentioned to him that it might be possible that he could also claim attorney/client privilege on me so that the strongest potential case on executive privilege would probably rest on the Counsel to the President.

I told him that obviously, this idea would have to be researched. He told me that he did not want Haldeman and Ehrlichman to go before the Ervin hearings and that if we were litigating the matter on Dean, that no one would have to appear. Toward the end of the conversation, we got into a discussion of Watergate matters specifically. I told the President about the fact that there were money demands being made by the seven convicted defendants. And that the sentencing of these individuals was not far off. It was during this conversation that Haldeman came into the office. After this brief interruption by Haldeman's coming in, but while he was still there, I told the President about the fact that there was no money to pay these individuals to meet their demands. He asked me how much it would cost. I told him that I could only make an estimate that it might be as high as a million dollars or more. He told me that that was no problem, and he also looked over at Haldeman and repeated the same statement.

He then asked me who was demanding this money and I told him it was principally coming from Hunt through his attorney. The President than referred to the fact that Hunt had been promised executive clemency. He said that he had discussed this matter with Ehrlichman and contrary to instructions that Ehrlichman had given Colson not to talk to the President about it, that Colson had also discussed it with him later. He expressed some annoyance at the fact that Colson had also discussed this matter with him.

The conversation then turned back to a question from the President regarding the money that was paid to the defendants. He asked me how this was done. I told him I didn't know much about it other than the fact that the money was laundered so it could not be traced and then there were secret deliveries. I told him I was learning about things I had never known before, but the next time I would certainly be more knowledgeable. This comment got a laugh out of Haldeman. The meeting ended on this note and there was no further discussion of the matter and it was left hanging just as I have described it.

As I have indicated, my purpose in requesting this meeting particularly with the President was that I felt it necessary that I give him a full report of all the facts that I knew and explain to him what I believed to be the implication of those facts. It was my particular concern with the fact that the President did not seem to understand the implications of what was going on.

For example, when I had earlier told him that I thought I was involved in an obstruction of justice situation he had argued with me to the contrary after I had explained it to him. Also, when the matter of money demands had come up previously he had very nonchalantly told me that that was no problem and I did not know if he realized that he himself could be getting involved in an obstruction of justice situation by having promised clemency to Hunt. What I had hoped to do in this conversation was to have the President tell me that we had to end the matter now.

I began by telling the President that there was a cancer growing on the Presidency and that if the cancer was not removed that the President himself would be killed by it. I also told him that it was important that this cancer be removed immediately because it was growing more deadly every day. I then gave him what I told him would be a broad overview of the situation.

I told him I did not know if Mitchell had approved the plans but I had been told that Mitchell had been a recipient of the wiretap information and that Haldeman had also received such information through Strachan. I then proceeded to tell him some of the highlights that had occurred during the cover-up. I told him that Kalmbach had been used to raise funds to pay these seven individuals for their silence at the instructions of Ehrlichman, Haldeman, and Mitchell and I had been the conveyor of this instruction to Kalmbach. I told him that after the decision had been made that

Magruder was to remain at the re-election committee. I had assisted Magruder in preparing his false story for presentation to the grand jury. I told him that cash that had been at the White House had been funneled back to the re-election committee for the purpose of paying the seven individuals to remain silent.

I then proceeded to tell him that perjury had been committed, and for this cover-up to continue it would require more paying and more money. I told him that the demands of the convicted individuals were constantly increasing. I then told the President how this was just typical of the type of blackmail that the White House would continue to be subjected to and that I didn't know how to deal with it.

I also told the President that I thought that I would, as a result of my name coming out during the Gray hearings, be called before the grand jury and that if I was called to testify before the grand jury or the Senate committee, I would have to tell the facts the way I know them. I said I did not know if executive privilege would be applicable to any appearance I might have before the grand jury.

I concluded by saying that it was going to take continued perjury and continued support of these individuals to perpetuate the cover-up and that I did not believe it was possible to continue it; rather I thought it was time for surgery on the cancer itself and that all those involved must stand up and account for themselves and that the President himself get out in front of this matter. I told the President that I did not believe that all of the seven defendants would maintain their silence forever. In fact, I thought that one or more would very likely break rank.

After I finished, I realized that I had not really made the President understand because after he asked a few questions, he suggested that it would be an excellent idea if I gave some sort of briefing to the Cabinet and that he was very impressed with my knowledge of the circumstances but he did not seem particularly concerned with their implications.

It was after my presentation to the President and during our subsequent conversation the President called Haldeman into the office and the President suggested that we have a meeting with Mitchell, Haldeman and Ehrlichman to discuss how to deal with this situation. What emerged from that discussion after Haldeman came into the office was that John Mitchell should account for himself for the pre-June 17th activities and the President did not seem concerned about the activities which had occurred after June 17th.

After I departed the President's office I subsequently went to a meeting with Haldeman and Ehrlichman to discuss the matter further. The sum and substance of that discussion was that the way to handle this now was for Mitchell to step forward and if Mitchell were to step forward we might not be confronted with the activities of those involved in the White House in the cover-up. Accordingly, Haldeman, as I recall, called Mitchell and asked him to come down the next day for a meeting with the President on the Watergate matter.

In the later afternoon of March 21st Haldeman and Ehrlichman and I had a second meeting with the President.

[It] was a tremendous disappointment to me because it was quite clear that the cover-up as far as the White House was going to continue. I recall that while Haldeman, Ehrlichman and I were sitting at a small table in front of the President in his Executive Office Building that I for the first time said in front of the President that I thought that Haldeman, Ehrlichman and Dean were all indictable for obstruction of justice and that was the reason I disagreed with all that was being discussed at that point in time.

It had been my impression that Haldeman and Ehrlichman were going to try to get Mitchell to come forward and explain his involvement in the matter. This did not occur. Mitchell said that he thought that everything was going along very well with the exception of the posture of the President on executive privilege. He said that he felt that the President was going to have to come back down somewhat or it would appear he was preventing information from coming out of the White House.

On Friday, March 23d, Paul O'Brien called to tell me about Judge Sirica's reading McCord's letter in open court. I then called Ehrlichman to tell him about it. He said he had a copy of the letter.

After my conversation with Ehrlichman, the President called. Referring to our meeting on March 21st and McCord's letter, he said: "Well, John, you were right in your prediction." He then suggested I go up to Camp David and analyze the situation. He did not instruct me to write a report, rather he said to go to Camp David, take your wife and get some relaxation. He then alluded to the fact that I'd been under some rather intense pressure lately. But he had

been through this all his life and you can't let it get to you. He said that he was able to do his best thinking at Camp David, and I should get some rest and than assess where we are and where we go from here and report back to him. I told him I would go.

My wife and I arrived at Camp David in the midafternoon. As we entered the cabin in which we were staying the phone was ringing. The operator said it was the President calling but Haldeman came on the phone. Haldeman said that while I was there I should spend some time writing a report on everything I knew about the Watergate. I said I would do so. I asked him if it was for internal use or public use. He said that would be decided later.

I spent the rest of the day and the next day thinking about this entire matter. I reached the conclusion, based on earlier conversations I had with Ehrlichman, that he would never admit to his involvement in the cover-up. I didn't know about Haldeman, but I assumed that he would not because he would believe it a higher duty to protect the President. The more I thought about it the more I realized that I should step forward because there was no way the situation was going to get better—rather it would only get worse. My most difficult problem was how I could end this mess without mortally wounding the President.

On Sunday evening, March 25th, I was informed that the L. A. *Times* and The Washington *Post* were going to print a story that Magruder and I had prior knowledge of the June 17th bugging of the Democratic National Committee. I considered the story libelous then, as I do today.

On Monday morning, March 26th, I had a conversation with Haldeman about the story in The L. A. *Times*. I told him I was prepared to file a libel suit and had retained a lawyer. I told him that he knew that I had not known of the June 17th Watergate break-in in advance, that my knowledge of the entire matter ended with the second meeting in Mitchell's office. I told Haldeman that Magruder knew that I had no prior knowledge, but I didn't know if he would admit it publicly. Haldeman concurred in the fact that I had no prior knowledge and suggested I call Magruder and tape his conversation. I did call Magruder and by using a dictaphone held to the receiver, record the call. The long and short of this conversation was that Magruder acknowledged that the newspaper accounts were a "bum rap" for me because I had not had prior knowledge of the break-in.

March 28th, Haldeman called me at Camp David and requested that I return to Washington. He told me that he was meeting with Mitchell and Magruder and that they wished to meet with me about my knowledge of the meetings in Mitchell's office.

I went to meet with Mitchell and Magruder. They told me they wished to talk to me about how I would handle any testimonial appearance regarding the Jan. 27th and Feb. 4th meetings which had occurred in Mitchell's office.

Magruder said that it had been I who had suggested that the meetings be treated as dealing exclusively with the election law and that explained my presence. I told them that there was no certainty that I would be called before the grand jury or the Senate committee. That that if I were called, I might invoke Executive privilege, so the question of my testimony was still moot. They were obviously both disappointed that I was being reluctant in agreeing to continue to perpetuate their earlier testimony.

On either March 28th or 29th, Mr. Krogh came to my office. He said he h̶ ̶ come to express sympathy for me as a result of the adverse publicity I had received during the Gray hearings. He then began telling me that he had not himself had a good day since his own confirmation hearings and that he had been haunted by his experiences at the White House.

I told Krogh that I thought that there was a very likely possibility that the Senate Watergate committee could stumble into the Ellsberg burglary. I told him that there were documents in the possession of the Justice Department which had been provided by the C.I.A. in connection with the Watergate investigation which contained pictures of Liddy standing in front of Mr. Ellsberg's doctor's office in California. I told him that I had learned from the C.I.A. that these pictures had been left in a camera returned by Hunt to the C.I.A. and the C.I.A. had developed the pictures. I said I did not believe that the Justice Department knew what the pictures were all about but that any investigator worth his salt would probably track down the incident as a result of the pictures. I told him that Ehrlichman had requested that I retrieve the documents from the Justice Department and get them back to the C.I.A. where they might be withheld from the committee investigations but the C.I.A. had been unwilling to do it.

Krogh was very distressed to hear this news but said that maybe it was for the best in that he had personally been haunted by this incident for so long that he would like to get it out in the open. I asked him if he had received his authorization to proceed with the burglary from Ehrlichman. Krogh responded that no, he did not believe that Ehrlichman had been aware of the incident until shortly after it had occurred: Rather, he had received his orders right out of the "Oval Office." I was so surprised to hear this that I said, "You must be kidding." And he repeated again that he had received his instructions out of the Oval Office.

April 2d my attorneys went to the Government prosecutors and told them that I was willing to come forward with everything I knew about the case.

As I began explaining what I knew it was evident that the prosecutors had no conception of how extensive the cover-up was so I tried to provide them with all the details that I could remember. Also, as the conversations regarding the cover-up began to get into more and more specifics we moved into areas that came closer and closer to the President, but prior to April 15th I did not discuss any of the areas of Presidential involvement.

I felt that I should tell Haldeman that I was going to meet with the prosecutors so I called him. He said that I should not meet with the prosecutors because, as he said, "Once the toothpaste is out of the tube, it's going to be very hard to get it back in."

During the week of April 9th to April 14th, I had several conversations with Ehrlichman and Haldeman. I recall some discussions however, regarding getting Mitchell to step forward. The theory was—"if Mitchell takes the rap the public will have a high level person and be satisfied and the matter will end."

On Monday April 9th, Mitchell called me and told me he was coming to Washington and wanted to meet with me.

The sum and substance of the meeting was that if and when I were called to testify I would testify fully and honestly. Mitchell said that he understood and did not suggest that I do otherwise. He did, however, believe that my testimony would be very harmful to the President and said that he felt that I should not testify if at all possible.

There were other discussions that week in which Haldeman and Ehrlichman talked about pinning the entire matter on Mitchell.

The more I told the prosecutors about the cover-up the more interested they became in it. At this time, Haldeman and Ehrlichman were still unaware of my direct dealings with the prosecutors.

I did not tell them at that point that I had had private meetings with the prosecutors or that I had told the prosecutors of the extent of involvement of Haldeman and Ehrlichman [but] I was quite confident that I had gotten the message through to Ehrlichman and Haldeman that they had a serious problem themselves and I had put them on final notice that I wasn't playing the cover-up game any longer.

I realized that indeed my message had gotten through, about one o'clock on Saturday night or Sunday morning, I received a call from Mr. Shaffer. He said that the prosecutor had called him and that the Attorney General had called Mr. Petersen and them and wanted a full report on everything that was going on before the grand jury and where the grand jury was headed. The meeting with the Attorney General was to occur about 2 A.M. at the Attorney General's home. The Attorney General was being summoned to the President's office and the next morning to discuss the entire matter. I told Mr. Shaffer that I had hoped to tell the President personally that I had gone to the prosecutors several weeks ago.

I then wrote out a message for the President. In short, I told the President that I hoped he did not interpret my going to the prosecutors as an act of disloyalty, that I would meet with him if he wished to discuss the matter with me. Within forty-five minutes of sending this message I had a call from the White House operator informing me that the President wished to meet me at 9:00 P.M.

The President was very cordial when we met. I told the President that I had gone to the prosecutors. And, that I did not believe that this was an act of disloyalty but, rather in the end it would be an act of loyalty. I informed the President that I told the prosecutors of my own involvement and the involvement of others. The President almost from the outset began asking me a number of leading questions, which made me think that the conversation was being taped and that a record was being made to protect himself.

I also recall that the conversation turned to the matter of Liddy not talking. He said something about Liddy was waiting for a signal and I told him that possibly he was waiting for a signal from the President.

It was during this part of the conversation that the President picked up the telephone and called Henry Petersen and pretended with Petersen that I was not in the room but that the matter of Liddy's coming forward and talking had arisen during our conversation. The President relayed to Petersen that if Liddy's lawyer wanted to see him to get a signal that the President was willing to do this. The President also asked me about Petersen and I told him if anyone could give him good advice Henry Petersen could.

Erlichman

The following are excerpts of testimony by John D. Ehrlichman, formerly Nixon's chief adviser for domestic affairs, given on July 24.

Ehrlichman: Mr. Chairman, and members of the committee, at the time of my resignation (from the White House April 30, 1973) I assured the President that I intended to spend such time and personal resources as I had in the statement of the truth of these matters now before this committee....

Because I sincerely do not believe I am guilty of any wrongdoing, I have not invoked the Fifth Amendment, nor have I attempted to negotiate "immunity" for myself from anyone....

I am here to refute every charge of illegal conduct on my part which has been made during the course of these hearings, including material leaked to the news media. What I say here will not be new but it may be different from what you have been reading in the papers....

It has been repeatedly said that this is not a trial; that the committee will recommend legislation, not assess guilt or innocence. At the same time, the soundness and integrity of the President, his staff and many close associates have been impugned and directly put in issue here. Many important questions about the White House, the Presidency, and its staff system have also been asked here, but not answered. I hope and believe I can contribute a few of those answers and also perhaps some measure of perspective.

Mr. Dean began his statement with a somewhat superficial but gallery-pleasing repetition of the old story about fear and

paranoia in the Nixon White House. Why, Mr. Dean wondered, was there all that overplayed concern about hippies coming to Washington to march peacefully down Pennsylvania Avenue? Mr. Dean's explanation is simply that we were all suffering from some advanced forms of neurosis, and nothing else—some strange White House madness. He suggests he was the only sane one in the bunch....

I submit that on this general subject there are some realities of governmental life to be weighed in your deliberations.

From its first days the Nixon administration sought a stable peace abroad and a return of our POWs from Southeast Asia. To get these results required the President to undertake foreign policy moves and initiatives which were completely interrelated and extremely delicate. In pursuit of this result we necessarily gave earnest attention to the staffing of critical government positions with people loyal to the President's objectives. And the problems of leaks, demonstrations, bombings and terrorism, public opinion and congressional support were understandably on the President's mind.

Today the Presidency is the only place in the nation where all the conflicting considerations of domestic and international politics, economics and society merge; it is there that street violence and civil rights and relations with Russia and their effect on China and the Cambodian military situation and a thousand other factors and events are brought together on the surface of one desk and must be resolved.

Some of these events in 1969 and 1970 included hundreds of bombings of public buildings in this country, a highly organized attempt to shut down the federal government, which you will all remember....Taken as a part of an apparent campaign to force upon the President a foreign policy favorable to the North Vietnamese and their allies, these demonstrations were more than just a garden variety exercise of the First Amendment.

Just as, and because, they affected the President's ability to conduct foreign policy, they required the President's attention and concern. Had he and his staff been ignorant of the significance of such a campaign, or merely indifferent, they, that is the President and his staff, would have been subject to the proper criticism of all citizens interested in securing a stable peace in Southeast Asia and the return of our POWs.

But the President did understand these events to be important in the overall foreign policy picture and they received balanced attention along with other events and factors...From close observation I can testify that the President is not paranoid, weird, psychotic on the subject of demonstrators or hypersensitive to criticism.

It has been my experience that, in the trial of a long lawsuit with a great number of witnesses, it becomes hard for the lawyers, witnesses, judge and jury to remember that anything else ever happened in the community back at the time of the disputed event except that event itself....

Here is what appears to be this great big thing, a burglary, a "cover-up," "horrors" all going on, and witness after witness goes over the exquisite details of a few meetings, phone calls, memos, and conversations, day after day here. One begins to think, surely, all of this could not possibly have passed unseen by anyone of even average awareness. How, then, could people on the White House staff have failed to know all of these so obvious and often repeated and significant details, and failed to blow the whistle on the wrongdoers long before the ninth month?

John Dean said one thing in his testimony falser than all the other falsehoods there, when he said:

(The Watergate) "was probably the major thing that was occurring at this point in time," meaning, in the context of Senator Baker's question in the White House between June 17 and September 15, 1972.

As liaison to the domestic operating departments and agencies I frequently carried to them the President's expressions of criticism and suggestions for change. To the uninformed this undoubtedly would appear to create tensions between a Cabinet secretary and me. But, actually, I think I maintained a good and frequent contact and good relations with our domestic secretaries, including the several Attorneys General, over my three years in this position. I confess I did not always bring them good news, but then that was not my job. They and I shared a mutual objective, I think, and that was to do all we could to help the President accomplish his stated goals.

As many here know, not everyone in the Executive Branch in the first term shared these goals. There were a number of holdovers in the Executive Branch who actively opposed the President's policies, especially his foreign policy, but also in the area of domestic affairs, I can assure you.

These people conducted a kind of internal guerrilla warfare against the President during the first term, trying to frustrate his goals by unauthorized leaks of part of the facts of a story, or of military and other secrets, or by just plain falsehood. The object was to create hostility in the Congress and abroad and to affect public opinion. Henry Kissinger, Secretary Rogers, and others were seriously concerned that this kind of internal sabotage of administration policy could actually ruin our chances to negotiate a strategic arms limitation treaty and terminate the Vietnam situation on a stable basis, for example. A similar threat to a good result in Vietnam was posed by the combination of street demonstrations, terrorism, violence and their effect on public and Congressional support for the President's policy.

In his 1960 campaign Mr. Nixon was involved in every minute detail. In 1968 when he invited me to work in the 1968 campaign to manage the campaign I agreed to manage the campaign tour only after securing his promise that he would completely delegate detailed control of the advance work, logistics and schedule. And his participation in these details was minimal in 1968.

In 1972 with the foreign situation as it was, the President decided quite early that he simply could not and would not involve himself in the day-to-day details of the Presidential primaries, the convention and the campaign. He made a very deliberate effort to detach himself from the day-to-day strategic and tactical problems. And so the regular work of the White House relating to government and the nation's problems continued unabated. If anything, we on the domestic side were busier with the President on governmental business than in other years.

In 1972 the President had to delegate most of his political role and it went to people not otherwise burdened with governmental duties. As a result, I personally saw very little of the campaign activity during the spring and early summer of 1972....

I began to spend more time with Ron Ziegler, press secretary at the White House, in the late spring of 1972, helping him to understand the campaign issues, reviewing the research with him, etc. It became more important than ever for me to keep ahead of developments and in this connection I asked Mr. Dean to inform me as early as possible of significant changes, or new events in the Watergate case, so Ron Ziegler and I could deal with new issues which would be arising in the press. It was for this purpose that I talked to Dean about Watergate in most instances.

In addition, the President formed an advisory group which met twice a week to look at the campaign in overview, at long range, and to discuss any needed changes. Attending these Monday and Thursday morning meetings were Clark MacGregor, John Mitchell, Bob Haldeman, Bryce Harlow, Charles Colson and I. Presumably, I was the substantive issue man in the group. Since Watergate was a campaign issue it was discussed in these meetings; it was never a major subject of discussion, however, and if anyone in the group knew more than the others he didn't share his secrets there....

All of this was superimposed upon active involvement in legislative, budget and operational domestic problems, through the summer and early fall of 1972.

During the summer and fall of 1972 there were tough legislative issues which took the President's time and ours in great quantities. Busing, Water Quality, Phase II of the Economic Program, and Welfare Reform are, I know, subjects familiar to you all. They were critical issues to the Senate as they were to the President.

Federal government overspending was also a hot issue and we were engaged in documenting a catalogue of bad Federal spending programs to justify the Congressional repeal or reduction of a great many programs that spent great sums of federal money with little or no benefit to the public. During those months, along with a great many others, we were trying to understand Senator McGovern's $1,000 a year welfare plan and figure out its true cost, and we were researching and analyzing about 20 other major campaign issues ranging from tax reform to the death penalty....

From June to September, 1972, my staff and I put in long days, the (GOP) Convention Platform having imposed additional burdens on some of us. After the convention, the speeches, position papers and political statements and releases kept the pressure on us. It was a very busy time.

John Dean, on the other hand, never found things so quiet and he planned the most expensive honeymoon in the history of the White House staff right along this period.

The committee has had the log of how I spent my office time

over the years. As it shows, the vast percentage of my time was devoted to domestic policy issues....

And how much time did I actually spend wih Mr. Dean learning about the (Watergate) break-in or keeping abreast of developments to assist Ron Ziegler on the issues, or with Mr. Dean on any other subject for that matter in the weeks following Watergate?

We invariably met either in my office, or more rarely in Mr. Haldeman's (with the exception of just three or four meetings) most of which were held out of town.

The logs for these two offices, Mr. Haldeman and mine, demonstrate clearly the frequency of my meetings with Mr. Dean.

Remember: Dean testified that keeping Watergate covered up was a tremendous drain of my time and told of all the conferences and meetings I was having with him about it. Let's be clear: I did not cover up anything to do with Watergate. Nor were Mr. Dean and I keeping steady company during all these weeks.

I have compiled our meetings in two week periods from June 17 through the election, the "critical period," presumably, and here on page 27 of the statement, Mr. Chairman, you will see that compilation. In the first two weeks June 17 to July 1, which was the period when we were trying to learn about this new campaign issue, and whether the White House, the CIA or anyone else were connected with it, I had nine meetings with Mr. Dean.

In the second two weeks I had only one meeting. In the third two weeks, three. In the fourth two weeks, two. In the fifth two weeks, one. In the sixth two weeks, two. In the seventh two weeks, Sept. 13 to 26, none. In the eighth two weeks, none. In the ninth two weeks, again none, and finally, from Oct. 25 to election day three, for a total of 22.

It should be noted that this is the total number of our face-to-face contacts on all subjects, not just Watergate. These were all contacts, including group meetings.

Of the total 22 contacts, two related to Presidential papers and testamentary planning, one related to convention planning, one related to grain sales, two on general campaign planning, one regarding the President's financial statement to be released, one regarding settlement of the common cause lawsuit. Of the remainder not all were devoted to talk about aspects of Watergate, I am certain....

The vast percentage of my working time was spent on substantive issues and domestic policy. About one-half of 1 percent was spent on politics, the campaign and the events with which you have been concerning yourself as a Committee. That is the context in which I hope you will receive this testimony.

Similarly, you must measure the President's role in all of this in true perspective. The 1972 campaign, the Watergate and its investigation competed for his attention with the claims of hundreds of members of Congress, economists, diplomats, educators, scientists, labor leaders, businessmen and countless other citizens, and with the demands of the problems of the nation in their manifold and compound complexities, with the daily mail and the endless meetings, the speeches and other communication with the public, with the need for management, leadership, inspiration and the need and desire for time to study and think. I see redeeming aspects in this process.

I have faith that good can result from this Committee's efforts. In the future participants in political campaigns will surely be aware of the history of this time. And the standards which they will wish to impose upon themselves will be the product of the lessons of that history, whatever it may turn out to be. I have great optimism that the lessons of the history of this era will bring only good for this country.

Dash: Mr. Ehrlichman, I think you indicated in your statement an extreme loyalty to the President in the position you held, first as counsel to the President, then as Special Assistant to the President in domestic affairs. Would you tell the Committee, when did you first begin to work with President Nixon in any political campaign?

Ehrlichman: Late in 1959...I was an advance man in the 1960 campaign.

Dash: How did you obtain this assignment?

Ehrlichman: Through Bob Haldeman, who was the campaign tour manager in that campaign.

Dash: Could you tell the Committee how you knew Mr. Haldeman at that time?

Ehrlichman: Yes, we had been at the University (of Southern California) together.

Dash: I would take it, then, you were very close friends?

Ehrlichman: Not terribly close friends in college. We kept track of one another casually over the years and I was a guest at his home

in Connecticut during a trip East in 1959 and he asked me if I would be interested in taking a leave from my practice and working in a political campaign....

Dash: Now, in the '68 campaign, did you play any role in the political campaign?

Ehrlichman: I was the tour director.

Dash: And what function did the tour director have?

Ehrlichman: Well, that is largely dealing with problems of scheduling, advancing and logistics. And the care and feeding of the press. (Laughter.)

Dash: Care and feeding of the press...Now, when Mr. Nixon was elected President, you joined the White House staff first as counsel to the President?

Ehrlichman: That is correct.

Dash: When did you move from the position to the position of assistant to the President for domestic affairs?

Ehrlichman: It was near the beginning of 1970. I can't recall the exact date, but in the first couple of months of 1970, I believe....

Dash: ...did you consider Mr. Haldeman as senior to you in the White House staff?

Ehrlichman: Well, I don't think anybody on the White House ever considers anybody else senior to him.

Dash: I take it other than the President?

Ehrlichman: Right.

(Laughter.)

Ehrlichman: Well, it is a sort of a metaphysical concept among the assistants to the President as to who is senior to whom. My reporting relationship, so to speak, was direct to the President at that point and only on in a limited number of cases did I come under Mr. Haldeman's area of interest, so to speak....

Dash: ...Did there come a time when you were asked to develop a capability in the White House for intelligence-gathering?

Ehrlichman: Intelligence-gathering? The answer would be no.

Dash: ...were you ever asked to set up a special unit in the White House for the purpose of determining whether certain leaks had occurred in major national security areas?

Ehrlichman: In point of fact I was—and strictly in terms of your question. I was asked to set it up. Mr. Krogh was asked to set it up.

Dash: Who is Mr. Krogh?

Ehrlichman: Bud Krogh, Egil Krogh Jr., was a member of the Domestic Council staff, and he was asked by the President to form this special unit. I was designated as one to whom Mr. Krogh could come with problems in connection with it, and the President said also that he could come to him with problems.

Dash: Were you in at the beginning of the setting up of this plan?

Ehrlichman: Yes, I was.

Dash: And you knew what the unit was to do?

Ehrlichman: Yes.

Dash: What was the unit to do?

Ehrlichman: The unit as originally conceived was to stimulate the various departments and agencies to do a better job of controlling leaks and the theft or other exposure of national security secrets from within their departments. It was a group which was to bring to account, so to speak, the various security offices of the Departments of Defense and State and Justice and CIA, to get them to do a better job.

Dash: ...Was it ever called or was it ever referred to as an investigative unit?

Ehrlichman: Subsequently...it became an investigation unit....

Dash: Now, Mr. (David) Young (former White House appointments Secretary to Dr. Henry Kissinger) also worked in this unit, did he not?

Ehrlichman: Yes.

Dash: And he worked under Mr. Krogh?

Ehrlichman: He worked as a kind of a co-chairman.

Dash: Is this the special investigations unit that later became, began to be known popularly as the plumbers?

Ehrlichman: Yes.

Dash: ...Now, you did become aware at some point in time—at this point, I don't want to go into this specifically—of the activities of staff members of the special investigations unit (the "plumbers"), Mr. Hunt and Mr. Liddy, with regard to the office of Mr. Ellsberg's psychiatrist?

Ehrlichman: Yes, I did.

Dash: And that took place when, the so-called break-in of Ellsberg psychiatrist's?

Ehrlichman: I have heard two dates, but it was around Labor Day of 1971.

Dash: And I take it that was a fact-gathering project?

Ehrlichman: That was the fact-gathering project that I mentioned before in relation to the theft to the secrets and the turnover to the Russians and the dilemma we had of the (FBI) not moving on this.

Dash: Would it also be a, even more of a serious campaign issues (than the Watergate) if it developed or was revealed that Mr. Hunt and Mr. Liddy had broken into the office of Mr. Ellsberg's psychiatrist, the same two people?

Ehrlichman: No, I would not think so. They were certainly identified as former White House people in the media, and that was, that connection was, known....

Dash: Are you telling the committee that additional information, that these former White House staffers working under your direction had broken into Mr. Ellsberg's psychiatrist's office, would not have created an even more serious embarrassing situation for the campaign?

Ehrlichman: I would not think so, Mr. Dash, for several reasons. No, 1, that episode was a part of a very intensive national security investigation which had been impressed with a very high security classification. The likelihood of that being disclosed was very slight.

No. 2, those people were operating, at least I believe they were operating, under express authorization—

Dash: Express authorization to break in?

Ehrlichman: Yes, sir. Under a national security situation, under a situation of considerable moment to the nation in the theft of top secret documents, and their apparent delivery to the Soviet Embassy. It never was my view that Hunt and Liddy, as individuals, had done something that was completely irrational in that break-in. In other words, they were operating in a national security setting and pursuant to either instructions or authorization and, that being the case, that had never been a subject which I considered to be seriously embarrassing.

Dash: ...I am not trying to probe into any other secrets, but certainly at the time in June, 1972, right after the break-in you were aware of, and I take it, he (President Nixon) was aware of the break-in?

Ehrlichman: ...I cannot speak for the President on that. I can only say that I was aware of it.

Dash: ...Mr. Ehrlichman, prior to the luncheon recess you stated that in your opinion, the entry into the Ellsberg psychiatrist's office was legal because of national security reasons. I think that was your testimony.

Ehrlichman: Yes.

Dash: Have you always maintained that position?

Ehrlichman: Well, I do not know—

Dash: When I say always, I am not going back into eons of time.

Ehrlichman: I do not know that I have ever been asked to maintain it one way or the other. I have had a—I had an awareness of the President's constitutional powers and capacity.

Dash: Well, do you recall when we had our first interview in my office, and we discussed this issue you expressed shock that such a thing had occurred, and indicated that you had informed Mr. Young or Mr. Krogh to see that this thing should not happen again but you did not take any action such as ordering the firing of these people because of the general sensitive issues that were involved. Do you recall that?

Ehrlichman: Well, that is not on the ground of illegality, Mr. Dash. I do not think you asked me at that time whether—what my legal opinion was, for whatever it is worth. What you were asking me was what I did, and that is what I did.

Dash: Well, if it was legal you would ordinarily have approved it, would you not?

Ehrlichman: Well, no, the thing that troubled me about it was that it was totally unanticipated....

Dash: Who was it authorized by?

Ehrlichman: Well, I am under the impression that it was authorized by Mr. Krogh. I say under the impression, that has been my consistent impression, but it is not based on any personal knowledge.

Dash: Well, now, as a matter of fact, Mr. Ehrlichman, did you not personally approve in advance a covert entry into the Ellsberg psychiatrist office for the purpose of gaining access to the psychoanalyst's reports?

Ehrlichman: ...I approved a covert investigation. Now, if a covert entry means a breaking and entering the answer to your question is, no.

Dash: Well, let me read to you a memorandum...The memorandum is dated Aug. 11, 1971, and it is a memorandum to you from Bud Krogh and David Young, "Subject: Pentagon Papers

Project—status report as of August 11, 1971."

I think the relevant information is in paragraph (2) rather than the progress report of (1). Let me just read paragraph 2.

"We have received the CIA preliminary psychological study (copy attached at Tab A) which I must say I am disappointed in and consider very superficial. We will meet tomorrow with the head psychiatrist, Mr. Bernard Malloy, to impress upon him the detail and depth that we expect. We will also make available to him here some of the other information we have received from the FBI on Ellsberg."

Now, more significant, "In this connection we would recommend that a covert operation be undertaken to examine all the medical files still held by Ellsberg's psychoanalyst covering the two-year period in which he was undergoing analysis."

And there is a provision here for approve, disapprove. There is an "E", which I take it you would recognize as your "E"...and the handwriting is "If done under your assurance that it is not traceable."

Ehrlichman: That is correct.

Dash: Now, how would you interpret in this connection your assistance recommending to you in this connection, "We would recommend that a covert operation be undertaken to examine all medical files still held by Ellsberg's psychoanalyst covering the two-year period in which he was undergoing analysis", and their recommendation taking place sometime prior to the entry and approved by you?

Ehrlichman: Well, no interpretation necessary, Mr. Dash. This was in the setting of a previous conversation in which it was contemplated that these two men would go to the coast to do this investigation as the President's statement of May 22 says.

The effort here was to find out everything that could be found out about the people and the circumstances surrounding Ellsberg in all respects....

Dash: Now, would your understanding of covert operation be that by a, not a breaking and entering, but being let in by impersonating themselves to be somebody else into the building. Isn't that a covert operation?

Ehrlichman: I suppose that phrase could include that. It could include a lot of things....

Dash: Did Mr. Young and Mr. Krogh call you while you were in Cape Cod after Mr. Hunt and Mr. Liddy came back, and tell you that they had established that it was feasible that they could get access and that you said, "OK, go ahead and let them do it."

Do you recall that call that Mr. Krogh and Mr. Young made to you in Cape Cod?

Ehrlichman: No....

Dash: Would you be surprised if I told you that Mr. Young would so testify?

Ehrlichman: Yes, I would.

Ervin: ...Mr. Ehrlichman, do I understand that you are testifying that the Committee to Re-Elect the President and those associated with them constituted an institution that gave $450,000 to some burglars and their lawyers merely because they felt sorry for them?

(Applause and laughter.)

Ehrlichman: I am afraid I am not your best witness on that, Mr. Chairman. I do not know what their motives were. I think those will appear in the course of the proceeding.

Ervin: You stated this was a defense fund just like that given to Angela Davis and to Daniel Ellsberg, did you not?

Ehrlichman: I stated that was my understanding of it.

Ervin: Yes. Well, Daniel Ellsberg and the Angela Davis defense funds were raised in public meetings and the newspapers carried news items about it, did they not?

Ehrlichman: I am not sure that we know who the donors to those funds were. I dare say there are many people in this country who contributed to those funds who would not want it known.

Ervin: Yes. But do you not think most of the people contributed their funds because they believed in the causes they stood for?

Ehrlichman: I assume that.

Ervin: Well, certainly, the Committee to Re-Elect the President and the White House aides like yourself did not believe in the cause of burglars or wiretappers, did you?

Ehrlichman: No.

Ervin: Can you—

Ehrlichman: I didn't contribute a nickel. Mr. Chairman.

Ervin: Yes.

(Laughter.)

Ervin: You authorized somebody else to contribute?

Ehrlichman: No, I would like to set that straight, if I might, Mr. Chairman.

The only reason that anybody ever came to me about Mr. Kalmbach raising money was because of this arrangement that we had entered into that we would protect Mr. Kalmbach if he wished to be protected from requests to raise money. Now that is—it was a situation where obviously he didn't wish to be protected. He made the judgment, he made it independent of me, and whether I conceded to it or not obviously didn't make any difference.

Ervin: Did he ever talk to you about that?

Ehrlichman: Not until after the fact.

Ervin: I will ask you if he didn't come to you and not only talk about having known you a long time and you having known his family but didn't he⅜ask you whether it was a proper or legal operation?

Ehrlichman: Mr. Chairman, the testimony is that that meeting, according to Mr. Kalmbach was the 26th of July when he was long into this, and as I have already testified.

Ervin: He testified he had become dubious about the propriety of it and he went to you for reassurance?…And he also testified when he got to you you told him it was all right and to see that the money was delivered in secret because if he didn't deliver it in secret their heads would be in their laps. Didn't that occur?

Ehrlichman: No. As a matter of fact, Mr. Chairman, as I have just told Mr. Thompson (minority counsel) I would be terribly slow to reassure Herb Kalmbach, whom I consider a good and close friend, of the propriety of any such undertaking without checking it first, if he had asked me, and I am testifying to you, Mr. Chairman, that he did not ask me.

Ervin: Well, you recall his testimony was to the effect that I have given you?

Ehrlichman: You mean about the head in the lap business?

Ervin: Yes, that the heads would roll.

Ehrlichman: I suspect that what was said there was that certainly Mr. Kalmbach's involvement—

Ervin: I am not asking about that. My question is didn't he have a conversation in which you told him to do it in secret because otherwise "if it get's out, our heads will be in their laps."

Ehrlichman: …I had a conversation with Mr. Kalmbach, Mr. Chairman, and I have no doubt that we, if he says so, that we discussed the question of secrecy because I do recall his saying that Mr. (Anthony) Ulasewicz was carrying money back and forth.

Now, I had in my mind at that time the realization that this, what I considered to be a legitimate undertaking, could be terribly misconstrued if someone were to impute the efforts of the President's lawyer to this defense fund for Watergate burglars. I mean there is room for misunderstanding, I think you have stated the misunderstanding very eloquently in your opening question.…

Ervin: Well, let us go on to something else. You said something about the burglarizing of the office of the psychiatrist of Ellsberg was justified by the President's inherent power under the Constitution, did you not?

Ehrlichman: Yes, sir.

Ervin: And you referred to a certain statute.

Ehrlichman: I referred to a statute in which the Congress in 1968 made a recognition of that inherent power.

Ervin: Is that 18 U.S. Code 2511?

Ehrlichman: Yes, sir.

Ervin: Will you please tell me—now, this statute has nothing to do with burglary…This has to do with the interception or disclosure of wire or oral communications prohibited.

Ehrlichman: No, sir, it also has to do with the Congress' recognition of what the Constitution provides with relation to the powers of the President.

Ervin: Is there a single thing in there that says that the President can authorize burglaries?

Ehrlichman: Well, let us read it, Mr. Chairman.

Ervin: …It says here that this statute, which makes it unlawful to intercept and disclose wire or other communications, says that this shall not interfere with the constitutional power of the President to—

Ehrlichman: To do anything.

Ervin:—to do anything necessary to protect the country against five things…The first says actual or potential attacks or other hostile acts of a foreign power. You do not claim that burglarizing Dr. Ellsberg's psychiatrist's office to get his opinion, his recorded opinion, of intellectual or psychological state of his patient is an attack by a foreign power, do you?

Ehrlichman: Well, we could have a lot of fun with all four of these until we get to the operative one, Mr. Chairman.

Ervin: Well, Mr. Ehrlichman, the Constitution specifies the President's powers to me in the Fourth Amendment. It says: "The right of the people to be secure in their persons, houses, papers, and effects, against unreasonable searches and seizures, shall not be violated, and no warrant shall issue, but upon probable cause, supported by oath or affirmation, and particularly describing the place to be searched, and the person or things to be seized."

Nowhere in this does it say the President has the right to suspend the Fourth Amendment.

Ehrlichman: No, I think the Supreme Court has said the search or seizure or whatever it is has to be reasonable and they have said that a national security undertaking can be reasonable and can very nicely comply with the Fourth Amendment.

But, Mr. Chairman, the Congress in 1968 has said this: "Nothing contained in this Chapter or in Section 605 of the Communications Act," and so forth, "shall limit the constitutional power of the President to take such measures as he deems necessary to protect the nation against", and then it goes on, "to protect national security information against foreign intelligence activities."

Now, that is precisely what the President was undertaking. He was not undertaking it under this statute. He was undertaking it under that constitutional power which you gentlemen and other members of the Congress recognized in this section.

Ervin: Yes, I have studied that statute…And there is not a syllable in there that says the President can suspend the Fourth Amendment or authorize burglary. It has no reference to burglary. It has reference only for interception and disclosure of—interception of wire or oral communications.…

Haldeman

The following are excerpts of testimony by H.R. (Bob) Haldeman, the former White House chief of staff, given on August 1.

Talmadge: Mr. Haldeman, we have had evidence here before the Committee from witnesses…concerning White House requests for audits into individual's tax returns. Will you comment on that?

Haldeman: I can only comment to the extent, Senator, that there have been over the time that I was in the White House a number of inquiries made or pieces of information brought to the attention of various people within the White House from time to time that there were potential questions that should be investigated regarding business or financial activities of individuals, and there was a concern or a feeling that the IRS had been during the time of our administration being out of office and subsequently even during the time that this administration came into office, there had been considerably more zeal shown by the IRS in looking into potential questions of those who were supporters of this administration than zeal shown in looking into inquiries that were directed or raised regarding those who were known and vocal opponents of the administration, and these factors would be brought to the attention of various people at the White House from time to time with a query as to why there wasn't some kind of investigation into the dealings of some particular person with regard to some matter and those would be referred to the IRS. That would be the context in which I recall the question being raised.

Talmadge: Here, I believe, is a "talking paper" prepared for you to use with (IRS director Johnnie) Walters…and here is paragraph (c) "H.R. Haldeman" or "H.R.H." I assume that means you, "should tell the Secretary Walters must be more responsive in two key areas, personnel and political actions. First, Walters should make personnel changes to make IRS responsive to the President. Walters should work with Fred Malek immediately to accomplish this goal. (Note: there will be an opening for General Counsel IRS in the near future. This should be the first test of Walters cooperation.)"

Did you use this talking paper?

Haldeman:…This doesn't indicate to whom, by whom it was prepared or to whom, it was directed. I agree with you it does refer to "H.R.H. should tell the Secretary." I don't recall seeing it.…

Weicker: Mr. Haldeman, last night I took your opening statement

after the hearings were over and I read it and I re-read it and there was something about it that bothered me and I think I finally put my finger on what it was....

And what bothered me was the fact that...you listed various and sundry acts, violent in nature, illegal acts, and then left the intimation that these acts belonged to Sen. McGovern, the Democratic-Party, etc.

Now, I know that is not exactly the way it reads if you read it very carefully but that is the impression that is given, and this is what bothered me, was the impression that even now in your statement you are trying to give the same image to the opposite candidate and the opposite party, that it is my contention and which I intend to prove here this morning that you tried to give during the course of the campaign, specifically—specifically that the opposition party and the opposition candidate are soft on communism and soft on law and order.

You say in your opening statement, and let me read it.

"Moreover, the pranksterism that was envisioned would have specifically excluded such acts as the following: violent demonstrations and disruption, heckling or shouting down speakers, burning or bombing campaign headquarters, physical damage or trashing of headquarters and other buildings, harassment of candidates' wives and families by obscenities, disruption of the National Convention by splattering dinner guests with eggs and tomatoes, indecent exposure, rock throwing, assaults on delegates, slashing bus tires, smashing windows, setting trash fires under the gas tank of a bus, knocking policemen from their motorcycles."

"I know that this committee and most Americans would agree that such activities cannot be tolerated in a political campaign."

Mr. Haldeman, I would first of all point out it is not a question as to whether these activities could be tolerated. These activities which you listed are clearly illegal and they are not a question of whether we agree on it or not. In most cases there are specific laws that are meant to be enforced against such activities, which enforcement, of course, is in the hands of various judicial local states and federal officials.

"But unfortunately the activities I have described are all activities which took place in 1972 against the campaign of the President of the United States by his opponents."

Now, do you mean by that word "opponents" in your statement at that point of your statement the Democratic Party or Sen. McGovern?

Haldeman:...I immediately went on to say, and I quote from the next following sentence in my statement: "Some of them took place with the clear knowledge and consent of agents of the opposing candidates in the last election.

"Others were acts of people who were clearly unsympathetic to the President but may not have had direct order from the opposing camp."

In the following paragraph when I referred to the fact that there had been no investigation and little publicizing I again characterized the two different possibilities by saying:

"Either those which were directly attributable to our opponent or those which certainly served our opponent's interest but did not have his sanction," clearly recognizing, Senator, the precise point that you are making here, and I do recognize it.

Weicker: The precise point that I am making is I want you to clearly tell me exactly which of these acts, rather than comingling the two, and giving an impression, I want you to tell me which of these illegal acts you ascribe to Sen. McGovern and/or the Democratic Party.

Haldeman: I am not able to do that at this time, Senator. I have indicated to the committee yesterday that the documentation on these is available, it was my understanding that the committee had it. I find apparently it does not and I will make sure it gets it and that that verification can be made item by item and I would emphasize that this is a, such a list....

Weicker: Well, now, isn't it actually true, isn't it actually true, Mr. Haldeman—let's cite here the next paragraph, "So far there has been no investigation of these activities and very little publicizing of them either those which were directly attributable to our opponents or those which certainly served our opponents' interests but did not have his sanction."

Now, isn't it true that the acts which you list there didn't serve your opponents' interests, that they did on occasion serve your candidate's interests?

Haldeman: If they did, I can't conceive of how they did, sir.

Weicker: All right, I want to submit to you a document on White House stationery, memorandum for Mr. H.R. Haldeman from Ronald H. Walker....

"The White House, Washington, Oct. 14, 1971, 5:00 p.m.

"Memorandum for: Mr. H.R. Haldeman.

"From: Ronald H. Walker.

"1. The most recent intelligence that has been received from the advanceman, Bill Henkel, and the USSS (United States Secret Service) is that we will have demonstrators in Charlotte tomorrow. The number is running between 100 and 200; the advanceman's gut reaction is between 150 and 200. They will be violent," with a pencilled underlining of "violent," "they will have extremely obscene signs," underlining "obscene" and next to the word "obscene" pencilled in writing which to me, and you will have to confirm this, seems to be the same as the writing below your initialling appears to be yours, if not, I want you to say so, saying "good."

Is that your writing there where it says "good?"

Mr. Haldeman: I believe it is, yes, sir.

Weicker: "As has been indicated by their handbills. It will not only be directed toward the President, but also toward Billy Graham"...where you pencilled in "great."

(Laughter.)

I would also request along with the chairman the fact that order is kept in this room. This is an extremely serious matter, a document which is now being presented and the one to follow I think probably get to the very heart of this entire investigation.

Ervin: And Senator, I might state I can testify about that because I went down to Charlotte on that occasion with the President and I saw my constituent, Billy Graham, and I can testify there were about a handful of students or young people rather with some placards there that really didn't interfere with anybody.

Weicker (quoting the memo again): "According to Henkel and the USSS, and it is also indicated on the handbills being distributed by the demonstrators, the Charlotte police department is extremely tough and will probably use force to prevent any possible disruption of the motorcade or the President's movements."

And again the penciling "good" next to that.

Then No. 3, I had better, best read the whole exhibit:

"My instructions to Henkel are to control the demonstrators outside the Coliseum as much as he can with the help of the USSS and the police department, from the city of Charlotte. He is to set up as fine a screening system as possible. There are 8,000 seats in the Coliseum and we have printed up 25,000 tickets. It is a known fact that there are demonstrators who have tickets. Therefore it will be necessary for us to set up a screening system to eliminate anyone that has a false or fake ticket.

"We will set up our normal checkpoints, using 25 Veterans of foreign Wars and between 50 and 60 ushers that are being provided by the local Republican Party. There will also be a volunteer lawyer corps to handle any legal questions that migh arise, as far as us denying entrance on the grounds of a phony ticket.

"The thing that bothers me is that we are for the most part paralleling the system that we had designed for the Wright-Paterson Air Force Museum dedication in Dayton, Ohio. Realizing the attention that was drawn to the techniques used there, and the concern that has since been expressed by Ziegler, Warren, and most vehemently by Pat Buchanan, the feeling is that the press corps especially the liberals are very much aware of how the demonstrators are being handled, and although the White House has not been identified with these processes, we are very much suspect. Buchanan maintains that they will be the lookout for demonstrators and how they are being handled, and it is his feeling that this could be extremely damaging to the President's posture, even if the White House is only indirectly involved. The Billy Graham people have been of great help but they've got their own problems with citizens' organizations sponsoring the Billy Graham Day, and have pretty well backed off from any of the arrangements with the exception of crowd building.

"Therefore, we have got very little support in handling demonstrations in the hall.

"Question: should we continue with our plan to prevent demonstrators from entering the Coliseum?"

Under "Yes" the initial "H," and the pencil notation, "As long as it is local police and local volunteers doing it, not our people."

My question specifically relates to what mentality it is in the White House that goes ahead and indicates "good" when the word "violence" is mentioned, when "obscene" is mentioned, at which violence and which obscenity is to be directed against the President of the United States. How in any way can that be good?

Haldeman: Senator, I can explain that, I think, very easily.

The problem that we had during the campaign of violence, of demonstrations of obscene signs, of efforts to heckle and shout down the President when he was delivering a speech were very great. They were not recognized as being very great and there was an attempt made in the coverage of many of these events to present this as a totally off-the-cuff reaction of certain people in the audience who were just there and disagreed with what the President said and were expressing their disagreement in a proper exercise of their right to do so as contrasted to planned organizations that were put together for the purpose of creating violence and creating these things in the way that the intelligence indicated this one was going to be handled.

The reason for reacting to the indication that they would be violent, obscene and directed toward Billy Graham as good was that if, in fact, they were going to do this in this way it would be seen that they were doing so clearly. Sometimes they weren't that ineffective. They did a better job of disguising their true intents and their true method of operation, and the reaction of "good" to those indications was very much in that sense.

Let me point out that the whole point of the memo very strongly confirms my feeling that this sort of activity was not to our benefit in showing the extremes that, steps that were planned, in order to try to avoid these people having the opportunity to carry out their violence and their obscenity and directing it toward the President and Billy Graham, at least in the hall. We had no real practical means of doing much outside the hall and, in fact, as I recall that meeting there were some demonstrations outside but there was reasonably good control and the Charlotte police force, I think, was extremely tough, and I think they did do a good job, including, as I recall, at that occasion some local police forces did you have to use force in order to restrain the activities that were attempted. That happened in this case. But as you can see here there were strong efforts made by our advance men to try to avoid incidents and this kind of problem.

We had the intelligence that there were going to be this group there, that they would be violent and have obscene signs. That at least would show up with the public there and the press there and in a place like North Carolina where the people are wise enough not to feel that that is a very good thing to do, that it would put

this in its true perspective.

Montoya: Are you acquainted with the project which was launched in the White House to develop an "enemies" list?

Haldeman: I am aware of the existence of enemy lists or opponents lists, yes, sir.

Montoya: What do you know about it?

Haldeman: I know that from time to time we received from within the White House and from outside the White House, from supporters of the administration, both in the Congress and from the general public, complaints that people in and out of government were being treated by the White House in ways that people that were opposed to administration policies, and specifically who were vocally expressing public opposition to administration policies, and this would most frequently relate to the position on the war in Vietnam because that was the policy most thoroughly under discussion.

People who were expressing vocal opposition were at the same time being extended extraordinary courtesies by the White House in the form of invitations to social events and other functions at the White House, appointments to honorary boards and commissions, inclusion on delegations to events, and that sort of thing?

Montoya: I am talking about enemies, not friends.

Haldeman: No, sir, that is what I am talking about, people, I am talking about complaints by friends that people who were opponents and were vocally expressing their opposition were being, in the view of our friends, treated like friends in the sense of receiving these special courtesies from the White House.

Montoya: And you were compiling a list of these people?

Haldeman: And as a result of the concern by our friends that we were in their view unwisely extending these courtesies to the people who were opposing administration policies, and on some occasions people who, after receiving an invitation to the White House and being at the White House used that as a platform for getting extraordinary publicity for their expression of opposition, that as a result of these complaints there was a program of drawing up a list of those who in prominent public positions were believed to be expressing opposition to administration policies, and who, therefore, should not be receiving these courtesies. This was in the same context as a list of those who were supporting such policies and who should be extended such courtesies and who many times were not.

Montoya: Have you seen Exhibit 50, which has been introduced by Mr. Dean in evidence here?

Haldeman: I am not sure that I have. I would like to see it.

Montoya: Or Exhibit 10, and I will read you some names. What did these people have to do with the Vietnam War?

Haldeman: Excuse me, sir, but could I have copies of those?

Montoya: Yes, sir, let me just read them and then you can comment on them. Mr. Eugene Carson Blake, Mr. Leonard Bernstein, Arthur Fisher, Ed Guttman, Maxwell Cain, Charles Dison, Howard Stein, Al Lowenstein, Morton Halperin, Leonard Woodstock, Dan Schorr, Mary McGrory, Lloyd Cutler, Thomas Watson, Tom Weicker, Clark Clifford. That is the list? Do you want to see—

Haldeman: No, sir, I do not need to see it. I would think that the public record of the time would indicate that a number of those people were, in fact, quite vocally and publicly opposing administration positions on the war.

Montoya: Why did you label them as enemies, then? Do they not have a right to comment on the war?

Haldeman: Why, certainly, they did, but they did not have a right to be extended the courtesy of the President's hospitality in order to express their opposition.

Montoya: Well, are you in effect telling me that this enemies list was compiled so that it would serve as an exclusion list for the White House?

Haldeman: In effect, yes.

Montoya: Why was so much time wasted in the White House with memos and communications between staff members in trying to compile this list, then?

Haldeman: First of all, I don't believe a great deal of time was wasted in doing so. The time that was expended in doing it was for the purpose that I have indicated and was a part of carrying out the effort of the White House to extend our policies to carry out the policies of the administration—rather than to provide a forum for the expression of opposition.

Montoya: Well, if your objective was, as you have stated it, why was it an effort to involve IRS in auditing some of these people and why were there orders from the White House to the FBI to check on some of these people:

Haldeman: I would like to know what those orders were and perhaps I can respond to them.

Montoya: All right. Mr. Higby, who was your administrative assistant, has given information to this committee that while he was in the Grand Tetons with the President and you, he was asked by you to call Mr. Hoover and get a complete background on Daniel Schorr, and Mr. Higby did this, and he has submitted testimony to this committee in secret to that effect.

Now, would you deny that?

Haldeman: No, sir.

Montoya: Did you do that?

Haldeman: I requested a background report on Mr. Schorr, or asked Mr. Higby to request one, not in connection with the enemies list and I am not sure in what connection it was, but I am sure there was something that arose at the time that this request was made and I don't know in what context, but there had been, as has been indicated here in earlier testimony, concern from time to time about statements that were made and the reasons for them in terms of national security questions and I don't know that this was in such a context because I simply don't recall what the reason was for it.

Montoya: Why would you order a check in that context? Was Mr. Schorr being considered for an appointment?

Haldeman: No, sir he was not.

Montoya: Why would you check on him, then?

Haldeman: The check was made—I don't know why but the check was made.

Montoya: You ordered it?

Haldeman: The request for the check was in connection with something apparently—I assume that arose at that time—that generated a request for the background report on Mr. Schorr. The request I would like to emphasize, Senator, was not a request for an investigation of Mr. Schorr and at the time that the request was made it was for the background file which the FBI has on individuals, that is, a summary report on their activities and background.

Montoya: Wouldn't you call that "investigate" when the FBI goes out to try to get the background on an individual?

Haldeman: When they go out to do it I would, but the request was not that they go out to do it. The request was for the file, what happened.

Montoya: What file? Do you have a file in the White House on Mr. Schorr?

Haldeman: No, sir. The FBI did, or may have.

Montoya: How did you know they have?

Haldeman: They have a file on most people who are known publicly and the request was for whatever file they have.

Montoya: You mean the FBI has a file on every American that is known publicly?

Haldeman: I think they probably do. I have not been through their files so I can't verify that.

Montoya: Well, you just stated that—

Haldeman: I said I think they did.

Montoya: Now, assuming that Mr. Schorr is one case, now I will give you an instance where you ordered FBI checks on eight other individuals. Did you do that?

Haldeman: I don't know. I would like to hear what they are.

Montoya: Well, Mr. Butterfield has so testified that you did.

Haldeman: Could I hear them, please?

Montoya: Yes. The testimony of Butterfield is as follows. It is on page 10 of his interview before the Committee, and this is his testimony. Haldeman and occasionally Ehrlichman had requested an FBI check on non-appointees. To Butterfield's recollection—this is a memorandum of his testimony—to Butterfield's recollection there may have been eight such requests. Among them were Frank Sinatra, Daniel Schorr, Helen Hayes. Now, what do you have to say to that?

Haldeman: In the case—

Montoya: Was Helen Hayes being considered for an appointment?

(Laughter)

Haldeman: Quite possibly so. Helen Hayes had helped presidential appointments and commissions at a number of times and that is quite possible.

Montoya: Was Frank Sinatra being considered for an appointment?

Haldeman: No, sir. Frank Sinatra was being considered as an entertainer at the White House and was an entertainer at the White House.

Montoya: And was Daniel Schorr being considered for entertainments at the White House?

(Laughter)

Haldeman: No, sir. I have already covered the Daniel Schorr appointment....

Weicker: Let me read (another memo) dated Feb. 10, 1973. Memorandum for John Dean from H. R. Haldeman.

"We need to get our people to put out the story on the foreign or Communist money that was used in support of demonstrations against the President in 1972. We should tie all 1972 demonstrations to McGovern and thus to the Democrats as part of the peace movement.

"The investigation should be brought to include the leads directly to McGovern and Teddy Kennedy. This is a good counteroffensive to be developed. In this connection we need to itemize all the disruptions such as the Century Plaza, San Francisco, Statue of Liberty, and so on.

"You should definitely order Gray to go ahead on the FBI investigation against those who tapped Nixon and Agnew in 1968.

"We need to develop the plan on to what extent the Democrats were responsible for the demonstrations that led to violences or disruption.

"There's also the question of where we should let out the Fort Wayne story now—that we ran a clean campaign compared to theirs, libel and slander such as against Rebozo, et cetera."

And lastly—I beg pardon, reading directly—"We could let Evans and Novak put it out and then be asked about it to make the point that we knew and the President said it was not to be used under any circumstances.

"In any event, we have to play a very hard game on this whole thing and get our investigations going as a countermove."

Is that what the document states?

Haldeman: That is what this document states.

Weicker: And this document states it is a memorandum from you to John Dean. Is that a memorandum that you prepared?

Haldeman: I will accept responsibility for the memorandum, although because of some bad English and other problems in it, I would point out that it is not initialed by me, which it would have been had I written the memorandum and sent it. I believe that this was a memorandum prepared from notes or from telephonic instructions to a staff member who then wrote it up and sent it out over my name. Having said that, I am disclaiming responsibility for the English and typos, and accepting overall responsibility for the memorandum.

Weicker: In other words, accepting responsibility for the thrust of the memorandum, if not the actual words used?

Haldeman: Yes sir.

Weicker: Well, I guess the first thing to ask here is I would like to get your version as to what this first paragraph means, "We need to get our people to put out the story on the foreign or communist money that was used in support of demonstrations against the President in '72. We should tie all 1972 demonstrations to McGovern and thus to the Democrats as part of the peace movement."

Haldeman: I think there was, or I know that there was, some information, I don't know how good it was that there was foreign money used to support the financing of demonstrations. The point here was to develop the story that that had been the case, develop the facts on it.

Skipping down to the fourth paragraph it does say, "We need to develop the plan on to what extent" this is the bad English again, but, "To what extent the Democrats were responsible for the demonstrations that lead to violence or disruption."

In other words, this was to determine the facts and get out the story with the objective to tying, where the facts did so, tying those demonstrations to those who were responsible for them....

I am asking to develop a plan on to what extent the Democrats were responsible for demonstrations that led to violence or disruption.

Weicker: You say "We need to get our people to put out the story on the foreign or Communist money that was used in support of demonstrations against the President in '72. We should tie all 1972 demonstrations to McGovern and thus to the Democrats as part of the peace movement." This is one paragraph here, the head of this memorandum.

Haldeman: That is right, I am reading....

Weicker: Are you trying to tie the Democratic Party to Communist money or foreign money?

Haldeman: I am trying to tie the demonstrations that were instigated by McGovern or McGovern campaign people to those people. I am trying to get out the story of what the facts were in regard to the instigation of and financing of demonstrations.

Weicker: Well, now, this is dated Feb. 10, 1973. And interestingly enough I have made my own notes and I go back to your opening statement before this Committee and I expressed myself as to imagine that you were trying to portray here being rather clever with words, as to these matters being linked to the Democratic candidate, to the Democratic Party.

And I didn't receive or I didn't get this particular memorandum until after I had made my own impression as to what thought you were trying to convey in your opening statement, so, in other words, I had my impression of your opening statement in trying to tie the Democratic Party and George McGovern to the image of being soft on communism and being soft on law and order and all of a sudden this memorandum appears and here you are suggesting as a counteroffensive that these entities, this individual, and this party be tied in with foreign and Communist money and that it be tied into the demonstrations. Is this what you—let me ask you, is this what you—believed during the course of the campaign of 1972? Was this to be the thrust of the attack?

Haldeman: Let me—I don't understand your references to soft on communism and soft on law and order. Is there something that I have said that leads to that?

Weicker: Well, I think that you're definitely trying to make a link-up here. I just have your own memorandum before me on that point.

Haldeman: My own memorandum makes no reference to McGovern being soft on communism.

Weicker: No, it just tries to go ahead to link Mr. McGovern to demonstrations and to communism, is that right?

Haldeman: Tries to link Mr. McGovern or the McGovern campaign to—

Weicker: And the Democrats.

Haldeman: And the Democrats and the peace movement to the demonstrations and to the point that I understood there was backing on or information on that there was foreign or communist money used in support of demonstrations. If, in fact, those were facts it was my feeling that they should be known.

Weicker: No, you say, you don't want to develop the fact, "We need to get our people to put out the story on the foreign or Communist money that was used" in the last election.

Haldeman: He says that was the case.

Weicker: Do you mean to tell me that as a man closest to the President of the United States, you issued a directive linking the Democratic Party, and the Democratic candidate, to communist money, to demonstrations because you thought that was the case, that you are willing to go ahead and do that as the man closest to the President of the United States, you were willing to throw that party and that name around in that fashion?

Haldeman: Only if it is the case, Senator, and only—

Weicker: Isn't it your job before you issue a memorandum to make sure that it either is or is not the case?

Haldeman: Isn't that—

Weicker: Isn't that what this country is about?

Haldeman: That is why the memorandum was directed to the counsel to the President who had the facts, as I understood it, on this case.

Weicker: "We need to get our people to put out the story," this is not a request for an investigation. If it were a request for an investigation wouldn't this be the type of thing which certainly we should put into the hands of our law enforcement branches here in the United States, either the FBI, CIA, the National Security group or any valid law enforcement branch. This isn't a request for an investigation of these facts. This is to put out the story.

Haldeman: It was my understanding that there were facts that led to these points.

Weicker: What are the facts?

Haldeman: I don't know. I have stated what my understanding was. Mr. Dean was the one I understood had the facts.

Weicker: I think I have come close to my time now, Mr. Chairman. I am going to be candid with you, and I am going to be candid with you, and I am going to continue on this subject every 10 minutes until we go and get this right out on the table. But I want you to know this, that if I am emotionally wraught up at this point in time it is because these things have been imputed or an attempt has been made, and I think we have stopped here, to impute these matters and other matters here to your party and to your candidate.

I am going to tell you, my job is to go ahead and beat Democrats and I have done a pretty good job, quite frankly....

But this type of business here when it emanates from the highest councils in the land, I think is a disgrace, and I think, quite frankly, the tactics, this is Feb. 10, 1973, I don't think there has been any change in tactics from the election campaign of '72 as to when you sit before this committee right now, Mr. Haldeman.

Gray

The following are excerpts from testimony of L. Patrick Gray III, former acting director of the FBI, given on August 6th:

Weicker:...in light of the President's statement of April 30, where he states that on March 21 he personally assumed the responsibility for new inquiries and personally ordered those conducting the investigations to "get all the facts and report them directly to me right here in this office," my first question to you is did you ever receive after March 21 or from March 21 on a directive from the President of the United States relative to these Watergate matters, which directive inquired of you as to what your investigations were producing, sir?

Gray: No sir. The President did telephone me on March 23 and this was the typical buck-up type of call.

Weicker: And you received from March 21 on—we will get to the phone conversation in a minute—no order from the President as one who was conducting the investigation "to get all the facts and to report them directly to me"—the President—"right here in this office?"

Gray: I did not, sir, and I received no such order from anybody.

Weicker: All right now, would you please tell the Committee as to what happened in the phone call of March 23?

Gray: The March 23 phone call from the President, once again, it was a surprise to me. I did not really expect to see it.

That followed the testimony I had given on March 22 and which in response to a question from Senator (Robert) Byrd (D-W. Va.) I had said that Mr. Dean had probably lied when he was talking with our agents and the way the questions were phrased by Senator Byrd there was no other answer I could give. But the President called me on March 23 and it was in the nature of a buck-up call to say, and I cannot remember his precise words, but to say I know the beating that you are taking up there and it is very unfair and there will be another day to get back at our enemies and there will always be a place for you in the Nixon Administration, and I thanked the President and then I remembered distinctly him saying, "You will recall, Pat, that I told you to conduct a thorough and aggressive investigation," and I remembered that so distinctly because I had the eerie feeling that this was being said to me but why, and I related it immediately to the July 6 telephone conversation I had had with the President in the previous year.

Weicker: You do recall the nature of the conversation. It was, Number 1, to buck you up in relation to your confirmation hearings, and having done that, the President turned to you and said, "You will remember, Pat—our previous conversation?"

Gray: No, he just said, "You will remember, Pat, I told you to conduct a thorough and aggressive investigation."

Weicker: Now, Mr. Gray, I would like to move along, if we can, to the events of April, more specifically those events which commenced with your telling me of the burning of the files in your office on April 25...but I would like to move from April 25 to the afternoon of the 26th of April and have you recount to the Committee in your own words what transpired in the late afternoon of April 26.

Gray: Well, Senator Weicker, it was after 6 o'clock in the evening when I was leaving and I believe it to be somewhere between 6:15 and 6:30 and I was driving out the gate and the police officer there, of the GSA security force, Officer Cousin, whom I used to say hello to every night as we drove out, exchanging a few pleasantries, said to me that Mr. Petersen had called and it is urgent and you are to call him right away, and I got out of my car and I walked into the guard booth there and I telephoned Mr. Petersen and Mr. Petersen said that he had had a call from the Attorney General, Attorney General Kleindienst, and Attorney General Kleindienst wanted to meet with us in his office at 7 p.m....

And I said, fine, I will go back up to my office and wait a while, and I asked my driver...to park the car and wait for me....I walked over to the Attorney General's office and I walked right in, walked through the conference room, walked into the secretary's area and picked up the phone, called Mr. Petersen and told him that I was here in the Attorney General's office and just then the Attorney General walked in—I could hear his footsteps—and I told Mr. Petersen the Attorney General walked in, come on up, and I went back immediately and the Attorney General said to me the President had called him and is concerned about the reports that these files were burned and that we had to meet and make some recommendation to the President.

By then, Mr. Petersen had come up. We both sat in chairs in front of the Attorney General's desk and I told them that I had spoken with you. I did not say to them that you had talked to the press, even though you had told me that you did. You said to me you are probably going to be the angriest man in the world at me for talking to the press and I told you, no you ought to be the angriest man in the world at me. I did not say that you had given this information to the press but I said I believe that Senator Weicker knows all about this because I have spoken to him.

Then Mr. Kleindienst said let's have a drink.

(Laughter)

And Mr. Petersen and Mr. Kleindienst and I all went into a little private office off of his main office and Mr. Kleindienst fixed a drink for himself and for Mr. Petersen and I do not drink. Mr. Kleindienst was sitting right in front of me facing me and he said to me, "It doesn't seem to me that you can continue as acting Director of the FBI," and I said, "Well, Dick, it does seem to me that I can continue as Acting Director of the FBI because these files had absolutely nothing to do with Watergate and the men and women of the FBI know this investigation, but that I will accede to whatever the President wishes. If he wishes me to continue to serve, I will serve. If he wishes me to resign, I will resign."

Mr. Kleindienst then went into his other office and said he was going to talk to the President and during his absence Mr. Petersen was pacing up and down in the office, walking back and forth, and I remember him distinctly saying "Pat, I am scared." And I said, "Henry, why?" And I am still sitting there in that chair. And he said, "I am scared because it appears that you and I are expendable and Haldeman and Ehrlichman are not." And I said, "Henry, do you think I should get a lawyer?" And this is the first time I had entertained the idea—and he said, "Yes." And I did. Later.

But then Mr. Kleindienst came back into the office and sat down in the chair again, facing me, and said, "The President wants you to continue to serve as Acting Director" and I said, "Fine, Dick, I will do it." And then, all three of us left the office. We walked out of the office together.

Weicker: Now, would you move to the morning of the 27th.

Gray: Well, when I got home that evening I got—it was after 8 o'clock and I did quite a bit of thinking about this and I thought that I had better really resign, that this was not the thing to have done and that there was no way in the world that I would be able to explain it to the FBI. It would take too long. So coming into the office that next morning, I asked two members of my personal staff, the oldest two members, to come in and sit down with me. I told them all the facts and I said, I just feel that I can no longer command the FBI. They agreed with me and I told them, I said, all right....

I had Mr. (Mark) Felt (acting associate FBI director) set up the meeting with the Assistant Directors at 11:30 in my conference room so I could appear before them and tell them. And I did. I met with them and I told them exactly what had happened and I said, Mr. Felt will tell you all the details but I feel that I can no longer command the FBI.

I shook hands and I said goodbye.

I think it was then, at about noon, that I called presidential aide Mr. (Larry) Higbee.

I told him at that time that my resignation had been written and was on its way over, and he said let me talk to them, the (presidential) party down there in Mississippi, before you send this over.

And then there was another call at 1:59. Mr. Higbee spoke to me and said, "Please send your resignation over. They are expected back at 3:00 o'clock. And I believe it was in this call that I told him I also wanted to issue a statement along with this resignation of mine and this—my recollection is that took him aback a little bit and he said "Nobody at the White House is going to want to issue this statement," and I said, "No, my statement is harmless. I am going to issue it," and I read it to him. And then he called me back at 2:09 p.m. and told me to go ahead and send the resignation over and send the statements over to him, which I did.

Weicker: Now, after your resignation was announced, did you receive any information...or any indication that according to White

House officials, those associates with the White House, the fact that yours was not a resignation but rather you had been kicked out?

Gray: Yes, sir, I left the Department that afternoon about 2:45 p.m. and drove as I recall to Connecticut and I think it was the next day that I talked with my executive assistant, who told me that there had been stories that had been carried on the wires to the effect that I had been thrown out and that he had taken it upon himself to—because he had participated in this whole thing with me—he had taken it upon himself to issue a correcting statement attributed to FBI sources.

Weicker: Then, at any point, I repeat, between March 21 and April 27, which marked the date of your resignation at any time during that period did you or were you requested by the President of the United States to give to him information facts, etc. relative to the Watergate situation?

Gray: I was not given any orders by the President of the United States or anyone to give them any facts about the Watergate situation until Mr. Petersen came to me on April 16, and I have already testified to that in my statement. This is when they asked me whether John Dean had given me two of Howard Hunt's files.

Weicker: After March 30, it has been testified to before this committee, that Mr. Ehrlichman was placed in charge of the Watergate investigation as of March 30, so my question to you is, aside from the phone call of April 15, which phone call again has been testified to before this committee, and also I believe has been testified to by you, did Mr. Ehrlichman make any inquiry of you as to the matters attendant to Watergate?

Gray: No sir, he did not.

Talmadge: These Hunt papers that were turned over to you on June 28, I believe it was, 1972 is that right?

Gray: Yes, sir, in the evening.

Talmadge: And they told you never to let them see the light of day?

Gray: Yes, sir, these, as I best remember it, Senator Talmadge, this was in the concluding remarks of Mr. Dean when he said to me that these have national security implications, they are political dynamite and clearly they should not see the light of day.

Talmadge: Was it your thinking when you received that order that Tennyson must have had in mind when he wrote the charge of the Light Brigade, "Their's was not to reason why, but do or die."

Gray: I do not know that I thought in those terms, Senator Talmadge...I took this as an order....

Talmadge: You accepted it as an order and you executed it as order and you carried it out as an order, is that correct?

Gray: That is correct.

Talmadge: What did you think the source of this authority was?

Gray: Well as I have testified, I cannot really say it came from the President but I can say to you, Senator Talmadge, that one thing I neglected to say in the course of the conversation in the Attorney General's little private office when he was sitting there after having talked with the President, Mr. Kleindienst said to me there must be no implication that in burning these files there was any attempt of a cover-up at the White House, and I told him, I said, Dick, I clearly got instructions, I thought, to burn those files and I burned them and that is going to be my testimony.

Talmadge: You assumed that Dean's authority came from the President, did you not?

Gray: He was standing right there in the presence of the top assistant to the President.

Talmadge: You assumed that Ehrlichman's order came from the President?

Gray: I had to believe they were acting for the President, yes.

Talmadge: You assumed that it came from the Chief Executive of the United States of America...?

Gray: I made that assumption but, Senator Talmadge, in fairness and decency and honesty I have to say I just cannot testify under oath that the President ordered them to do this.

Talmadge: You were in the navy. When you got an order from the Fleet Commander you assumed it came from the Chief of Naval Operations did you not? And, in turn, that he was appointed by the President of the United States, correct?

Gray: That is correct.

Talmadge: I believe you in some statement stated you wrote the President, I believe...in 1968, to beware of his subordinates, they were attempting to wear his stripes as Commander-in-Chief, is that correct?

Gray: Yes, sir, I wrote that to him.

Talmadge: What made you think then that his subordinates were trying to take advantage of the positions that they were being placed in?

Gray: That was very early in the game and I did not know any of these subordinates but I knew sometimes this would occur in the area of the White House politics and I was merely telling him that. I had nothing specific in mind, Senator Talmadge, because I did not even know who were going to be the subordinates.

Talmadge: That was foreboding on your part on behalf of a friend?

Gray: Yes, sir.

Talmadge: You had that suspicion in 1968. What made you abandon that suspicion in 1972?

Gray: The thought never occurred to me at all again; you know that letter had to be dredged up out of memory.

Talmadge: You assumed, then, when they gave those instructions it came from the Chief Executive of the United States of America?

Gray: No question about it, because I had had prior experience in the administration and I knew that those men did give orders. I knew that they used to come over and do that sort of thing, they used to do that at HEW.

Talmadge: The only evidence that this Committee has had to date implicating the President of the United States is that of John Dean and you and General Walters.

Did you think that your conversation with the President on July 6, 1972, was sufficient to adequately put him on notice, that the White House staff was engaged in obstructing justice?

Gray: I don't know that I thought in terms of obstruction of justice but I certainly think there was, it was adequate to put him on the notice that the members of the White House staff were using the FBI and the CIA.

Talmadge: Do you think an adequate, do you think a reasonable and prudent man on the basis of the warning that you gave him at that time, would have been alerted to the fact that his staff was engaged in something improper, unlawful, and illegal?

Gray: I do because I frankly...I expected the President to ask me some questions.

Talmadge: I believe you made a denial to someone that you burned papers last Christmas during the Christmas celebration, during that period in Connecticut. Who did you make that denial to?

Gray: Assistant Attorney General Henry Petersen on April 16 of this year in my office.

Talmadge: Did you make any other denial that was a fabrication or falsehood?

Gray: I didn't tell the whole story, the correct story to Senator Weicker....

Talmadge: You failed to volunteer at that time or did you tell him an outright falsehood?

Gray: I told him an outright falsehood, I said I burned those papers in the FBI and it was not true, I did not tell him the truth.

Talmadge: That is twice you yourself, Captain, have admitted you told a falsehood. Why do you think this committee should believe you now rather than maybe believing you were still telling a falsehood.

Gray: I am sitting up here testifying to you under oath and knowing full well that the substance of my testimony is critically important to this nation.

Talmadge: You are a lawyer, you are well aware of the penalty of perjury?

Gray: Yes, sir.

Cover & Book design / Spencer Zahn
James Joern / Photographer
Drawings / Timothy Claxton
Keeper of the File / C.S.

Composition by Walter T. Armstrong, Inc. The text type is Century Expanded set on a *Fototronic 1200* system with a *Digital pdp8/e* Computer.
The cover was printed by Neo Litho. The book was printed by Cam Glo.